Documenta Q

Reconstructions of Q
Through Two Centuries of Gospel Research
Excerpted, Sorted, and Evaluated

General Editors
James M. Robinson
The Claremont Graduate School

Paul Hoffmann
University of Bamberg

John S. Kloppenborg
University of St. Michael's College

Managing Editors
Stanley D. Anderson
Sterling G. Bjorndahl
Shawn Carruth
Christoph Heil

The Database

of the

International Q Project

Q 11:2b-4

Shawn Carruth and Albrecht Garsky

Volume Editor
Stanley D. Anderson

PEETERS
Leuven
1996

The Greek text of the *Novum Testamentum Graece*, 27th edition 1993 is used with permission of the Deutsche Bibelgesellschaft, Stuttgart.

CIP Royal Library Albert I, Brussels

ISBN 90-6831-788-1 (Peeters Leuven)
ISBN 2-87723-295-6 (Peeters France)
D. 1996/0602/14

© PEETERS, Bondgenotenlaan 153, B-3000 Leuven, Belgium

Introduction

The existence of Q was first included in a hypothesis to account for the Synoptic data in 1838, by Christian Hermann Weisse in *Die evangelische Geschichte kritisch und philosophisch bearbeitet*. This has been the predominant view since 1863, when Heinrich Julius Holtzmann published *Die synoptischen Evangelien: Ihr Ursprung und geschichtlicher Charakter*. Since then scholars have debated the exact wording of individual sayings in Q in a vast body of literature published in several languages and scattered among journals, commentaries and monographs for over a century. The literature has in effect become overwhelming and hence inaccessible.

Many scholars have made no effort to move behind Matthew's and Luke's divergences to establish the wording of Q itself, but have merely designated verses as those "behind" which the Q text lurked. This is perhaps the most disconcerting effect of the absence of any manuscript evidence for Q itself. For such a procedure leaves Q nowhere really accessible to serious detailed discussion.

While fraught with various uncertainties, the reconstruction of Q is not in fact as hopeless or hypothetical a project as is sometimes imagined. Comparison of Matthew and Luke in the double tradition indicates that there is verbatim or near-verbatim agreement in approximately fifty percent of the words. Additionally, in a significant number of instances, it is reasonably clear that one Evangelist has intervened in Q, for example, transporting a saying to a new location where it can function in a Markan pericope, or furnishing it with a framework that belongs to the conceptual interests of that Evangelist. In such cases, the history of scholarship reflects a near-unanimous verdict in favor of the other Evangelist.

Of course there are cases where no certainty is possible as to a given Q wording. But any actual papyrus has lacunae that can be filled only with a certain degree of probability or not at all, and yet the more nearly certain parts of the text fully deserve publication. Just so the text of Q, though not extant on papyrus, is eminently worthy of being critically reconstructed and published, to the extent this can be done with a reasonable degree of probability.

Often only a passing observation as to which Evangelist altered the Q wording at a single divergence in a given saying has led to the inference that the whole saying was to be reconstructed according to the other Evangelist. But in textual criticism we have learned that one scribal error does not necessarily mean that the same scribe is in error at the next divergent reading. Hence each text must be divided into variation units delimiting precisely the extent to which a divergence at one point, e.g. in the choice of a preposition, brings with it of necessity other divergences, e.g. the case of the preposition's object, and on the other hand the extent to which the surrounding context is not of necessity drawn into that error, i.e. is not part of that same variation unit. Hence the sayings of Q have here been analyzed into their respective variation units, each of which involved a discrete decision on the part of the diverging Evangelist and hence a discrete decision on our part in the effort to reconstruct the original wording of Q.

When one Evangelist can be seen to have altered the text of Q, this does not imply necessarily that the other Evangelist has preserved the Q reading. Both may in fact have altered Q (just as at times both altered Mark). Hence at each variation unit one must to a degree analyze each Evangelist separately, deciding largely in terms of that Gospel alone whether that Evangelist has preserved or altered the Q text, leaving it a relatively open question, to be analyzed in a logically distinct operation, whether the other Evangelist has or has not retained the Q wording.

The discussion of a given variation unit can best be understood in the chronological sequence of the history of scholarship. For it is not only relevant to establish who first represented a given point of view that then came to be widely cited. It is also important to be able to place a given opinion within the context of the conscious or unconscious assumptions of a given generation or school of thought. Divergences in wording between Matthew and Luke have been explained on the assumption that Jesus on different occasions presented the same saying but with the normal fluctuations of each "performance"; or that Matthew and Luke used different translations of an original Aramaic saying; or that the transmitting communities shaped sayings to fit their varying situations; or that the redactors introduced their own stylistic and theological preferences. Such factors may always deserve consideration, but in a given epoch may have been weighed very differently. This subjectivity of a given generation or school of thought becomes more apparent as one studies the history of the problem in chronological order.

Such considerations have been constitutive in the way the material has here been organized. The texts of Matthew, Q and Luke are presented in parallel columns, with sigla delimiting each variation unit, which in turn is numbered, so that each can be investigated seriatim in the database of scholarly literature that follows. Each variation unit is presented in four sequences, each in chronological order: Those who have presented reasons to the effect that Luke has preserved the text of Q; then those who have argued that Luke has not preserved the text of Q; then those who have advocated Matthew as preserving the text of Q; and then those who have contested that Matthew equals Q. The presentation is basically conservative, in that it is primarily designed to make accessible what the scholarly tradition has produced thus far. But it is also itself critically creative, in that the analysis of the scholarly literature is followed by Evaluations in which members of the project have brought to expression their own conclusions. The user is then free to move forward into one's own creative use of the scholarly tradition.

This undertaking grew out of the Q Seminar of the Society of Biblical Literature (1985-1989), which then was reconstituted by the Research and Publications Committee of the Society of Biblical Literature as the International Q Project. The team of over forty members has met just before the Annual Meeting of SBL at the convention site, and then in second and third annual meetings at the project's centers, Claremont, CA, USA; Bamberg, Germany; and Toronto, Canada. The procedure has been that for each pericope one member collected and sorted the scholarly literature and wrote a first Evaluation. Then one or more other members responded with their own Evaluations. All this was distributed in advance of a project meeting so that the resultant divergences could be discussed and resolved at such a session. The fall issue of the *Journal of Biblical Literature* contained each year (1990-1995) the preceding year's results. Thus the critical text of Q became promptly accessible.

From the beginning it was assumed that the project would be open-ended, to stay abreast of ongoing scholarship, much as Bible translations and critical texts of the Greek New Testament are never "final," but are no sooner published than the next revision is already underway. An Editorial Board of the International Q Project is in charge of this continuing revision, of which *Documenta Q* is itself a major result: The refinement of the formatting of variation units, the supplementing of the scholarly literature, the reformulations of the Evaluations, the General Editors' establishment of a revised critical text (to be published also in a single volume), and the Managing Editors' publication of this massive database in individual volumes of *Documenta Q*, is the fruit of this continuing research.

The future volumes are to appear preferably in their Q sequence, from the discussion of the problem of an *Incipit* and the sayings of John in Q 3, to the conclusion of Q with the prophecy of the judging of the twelve tribes of Israel by Jesus' followers (Q 22:18,20). (Lucan chapter and verse numeration is used as a convenience and a mere convention.)

The present preliminary volume, out of that sequence, presents as a sample the Lord's Prayer (Q 11:2b-4). Those who receive this preliminary volume are encouraged to send to the Editorial Board whatever suggestions for the improvement of the series may seem appropriate. It is hoped that *Documenta Q*, to be supplemented in due time with a machine-readable updating, will become a standard tool to facilitate all Q research of the future.

The work of the International Q Project has been aided by grants from the Claremont Graduate School, the Deutsche Forschungsgemeinschaft, the Deutscher Akademischer Austauschdienst, the Institute for Antiquity and Christianity, the Social Sciences and Humanities Research Council of Canada, and the Society of Biblical Literature Research and Publications Committee, for all of which support we are very grateful.

The critical text of Q used here is that adopted by the General Editors, presupposing the work of the International Q Project. If the critical text were to depart from that published in *JBL*, the *JBL* reading would be recorded in a critical apparatus. Minority views among the General Editors are also recorded in a critical apparatus, identified by initials: JMR, PH, or JSK.

The Greek text is that of the *Novum Testamentum Graece*, 27th edition 1993, edited by Barbara Aland et al., Deutsche Bibelgesellschaft, Stuttgart. We thank Prof. Dr. Barbara Aland and Dr. Joachim Lange for their cooperation in this undertaking.

Sigla Used in the Greek Text

[αβγ] Square brackets in the text of Luke and Q enclose words or letters found in Luke but not in Matthew.

(αβγ) Parentheses in the text of Matthew and Q enclose words or letters found in Matthew but not in Luke.

⌐ ¬ The sigla ⌐ and ¬ surround transpositions in the order of Matthew's and Luke's shared material. The relative position where the other evangelist has placed the indicated material is shown in that Gospel by the siglum ⌐¬, enclosing no text. The sigla are retained at both locations in the reconstructed Q text so as to indicate what the other alternative was. No space between ⌐ and ¬ means that this position was rejected with a certainty of {A} or {B}. Space between ⌐ and ¬ means that this position has been rejected with a certainty only of {C} or {D} or is undecided (in which case default to Luke's position). For example,

⌐αβγ¬ χψω ⌐¬ means that "αβγ" is at Q's position with an A or B grade;

⌐αβγ¬ χψω ⌐ ¬ means that "αβγ" is at Q's position with a C or D grade, or the problem is undecided. (See below for an explanation of the letter grades.)

1 2 3 ... Small raised numerals following the closing siglum are used to number the variation units within a verse. The numbers are normally included only after the closing siglum. However when another variation unit falls within the position markers ⌐ and ¬, the number precedes the first position marker as well as following the last position marker, so that the numeration of the variation unit marked by ⌐ and ¬ may use a smaller number than the numeration of the other variation unit inside the position markers.

⁰/ ... \⁰ Variation unit number zero is reserved for the discussion about whether or not a verse (or a unit of more than a verse) is to be included in the Q text. Slashes are used to indicate the extent of the material being discussed.

⇒ When a closing ¬ or \ is in a different verse (or larger unit treated as a single unit) from its opening ⌐ or /, an arrow at the end of the first unit of the text of Q refers the reader to the verse where the respective closing ¬ or \ is found. E.g.: ¬¹ ⇒ Q 11:4 on a line by itself at the end of the verse Q 11:2 means that the discussion of order (contained in the Database of 11:2) has to do with the position in Q of the whole of 11:2-4. At the end of Q 11:4 there would be a corresponding reference on a line by itself, ⌜Q 11:2⌝, indicating where this variation unit began and hence where the relevant discussion is to be found.

1.2   When two numbers refer to distinct variants (since distinct decisions are involved), but yet the two numbers are adjacent, they are separated by a raised dot: 1.2.

( ) [ ]   When square brackets or parentheses enclose text that has no parallel in the other Gospel, empty brackets and parentheses (with space between them) are used at the equivalent position in the other Gospel to indicate the location of the difference between the texts.

() []   When it has been decided with a grade of {A} or {B} that the words in question do not belong in Q, the brackets or the parentheses are retained in the reconstructed Q text, but the space between them is removed, thus marking the place in Q where the relevant note occurs, while indicating that no text is assumed to occur here. If it is still undecided ({U}) whether the text is in Q, or decided pro *or* con with a grade no higher than {D}, the space is retained, since no strong opinion for eliminating a reading has been established: [ ] or ( ). (See below for an explanation of the letter grades.)

[()]   If it is decided that neither the text of Matthew nor of Luke was in
⟦[()]⟧   Q, the space is removed: [()] for a grade of {A} or {B}, ⟦[()]⟧ for
[( )]   a grade of {C}. But when it is decided with a grade of {D} or it is left undecided, {U}, that neither the text of Matthew nor of Luke was in Q, the space is retained, since no strong opinion for eliminating a reading has been established: [( )]. (See below for an explanation of the letter grades.)

⟦ ⟧   Double brackets are used in the reconstructed Q text to enclose reconstructions that are uncertain (i.e., {C} grades).
⟦()⟧ and ⟦[]⟧ indicate a {C} probability for excluding Matthean or Lukan text, in distinction from () and [] for {A} and {B} probabilities for excluding the text and ( ) and [ ] for {D} probabilities either for including or excluding the text, or for {U} grades. Double brackets enclose chapter and verse references when the whole verse or unit is graded {C}.
Issues of order are excepted from using double brackets, i.e., ⟦⌐⟧ or ⟦⌐⟧ or ⟦⌐⌐⟧ does not occur. (See below for an explanation of the letter grades.)

Q 11:~~1-~~ ~~2a,~~2b-4   If it has been decided that a verse or unit is not in Q, the numeration is marked through (i.e., Q 11:~~1-2a,~~2b-4 means that Luke 11:1-2a par. is not in Q, but Luke 11:2b-4 par. is).

Grades Used by the International Q Project

The International Q Project uses a letter grade {A}, {B}, {C}, {D}, or {U} to indicate the relative degree of certainty for each decision. {A} and {B} grades are considered convincing enough to be printed without qualification as part of the reconstructed Q text. {A} represents "virtual certainty": all of the good arguments are on one side of the decision. {B} represents "a convincing probability": there may be good arguments on both sides of the question, but the arguments on one side clearly outweigh the arguments on the other side. {C} represents "a hesitant possibility," with significant enough doubt that in the reconstructed text the reading is placed in double brackets (see above). The {D} grade is a way of indicating the decision towards which one is inclined, but without enough certainty to include the reading in the text. The {U} or Undecided grade indicates that there is not enough data to make an informed decision.

Sigla and Abbreviations Used in the Scholarly Literature

Special sigla and abbreviations used by various authors cited in the scholarly literature are listed here if they occur in four or more different places. When special sigla and abbreviations occur three or fewer times, an editorial gloss is added at each location.

Several Authors:
UV or U.V. = Unser Vater
VU or V.U. = Vater Unser
V. = Vater Unser
PN = Pater Noster

Weiß 1892
LQ = Q^{Luke}

Hirsch 1941
Lu I = the slightly enlarged form of Q that Luke worked from.

Gundry 1982, 1994
(x,y) where x and y are numbers, x represents the number of times the word is inserted in common tradition, and y represents the number of times the word is included in material peculiar to Matthew.

Schenk 1987

+ x where x is a number means that Matthew added the word in question x
    times to the source.

- y where y is a number means that Matthew eliminated the word in question
    y times from the source.

A-Mt = Matthean material that has no parallel in the other gospels.

Example:

=(Mk 5 - 2 + 15) + (Q 2 + 6) + (A-Mt 7)

This means that Matthew took the word over from Mark 5 times, omitted it
from Markan material 2 times, and added it to Markan material 15 times;
Matthew took the word over from Q twice, and added it to Q material 6
times; Matthew also has the word 7 other places.

Q 11:~~1-2a,~~2b-4

Database Authors
Shawn Carruth
Albrecht Garsky

Evaluators
Shawn Carruth
James M. Robinson
John S. Kloppenborg

Q 11:~~1-2a,~~2b

Matt 6:7-10	Q 11:~~1-2a,~~2b	Luke 11:1-2a,2b
^{0}/	^{0}/	^{0}/
^{1}⌐	^{1}⌐	^{1}⌐
(Προσευχόμενοι δὲ μὴ βατταλογήσητε ὥσπερ οἱ ἐθνικοί, δοκοῦσιν γὰρ ὅτι ἐν τῇ πολυλογίᾳ αὐτῶν εἰσακουσθήσονται. **6:8** μὴ οὖν ὁμοιωθῆτε αὐτοῖς· οἶδεν γὰρ ὁ πατὴρ ὑμῶν ὧν χρείαν ἔχετε πρὸ τοῦ ὑμᾶς αἰτῆσαι αὐτόν.)^2	$[()]^2$	[Καὶ ἐγένετο ἐν τῷ εἶναι αὐτὸν ἐν τόπῳ τινὶ προσευχόμενον, ὡς ἐπαύσατο, εἶπέν τις τῶν μαθητῶν αὐτοῦ πρὸς αὐτόν· κύριε, δίδαξον ἡμᾶς προσεύχεσθαι, καθὼς καὶ Ἰωάννης ἐδίδαξεν τοὺς μαθητὰς αὐτοῦ. **11:2** εἶπεν δὲ αὐτοῖς·]^2
6:9 (Οὕτως οὖν)^3 προσεύχ(ε)^{3}σθε (ὑμεῖς)^3 [ ]^3. Πάτερ (ἡμῶν)^4 (ὁ ἐν τοῖς οὐρανοῖς)^5· ἁγιασθήτω τὸ ὄνομά σου· **6:10** ἐλθέτω ἡ βασιλεία σου· (γενηθήτω τὸ θέλημά σου, ὡς ἐν οὐρανῷ καὶ ἐπὶ γῆς·)^6	$[\![[ὅταν]^3]\!]$ προσεύχ$[\![[η]^3]\!]$σθε $[\![()^3]\!]$ $[\![[λέγετε]^3]\!]$·. πάτερ ()^4 ()^5, ἁγιασθήτω τὸ ὄνομά σου· ἐλθέτω ἡ βασιλεία σου· ()^6	[ὅταν]^3 προσεύχ[η]^{3}σθε ( )^3 [λέγετε]^3·. Πάτερ ( )^4 ( )^5, ἁγιασθήτω τὸ ὄνομά σου· ἐλθέτω ἡ βασιλεία σου· ( )^6
ℓ^1 ⇒ Matt 6:10	ℓ^1 ⇒ Q 11:4	ℓ^1 ⇒ Luke 11:4
$\backslash^0$ ⇒ Matt 6:10	$\backslash^0$ ⇒ Q 11:4	$\backslash^0$ ⇒ Luke 11:4

JBL: <...> προσεύχεσθε· πάτερ.

^{0} Was the Prayer in Q?
^{1} Position of the Prayer in Q.
^{2} Did Q have an introduction (like Luke 11:1-2a or like Matthew 6:7-8)?
^{3} Luke's ὅταν προσεύχησθε λέγετε, or Matthew's οὕτως οὖν προσεύχεσθε ὑμεῖς.
^{4} Matthew's address with ἡμῶν.
^{5} Matthew's ὁ ἐν τοῖς οὐρανοῖς.
^{6} Matthew's γενηθήτω τὸ θέλημά σου, ὡς ἐν οὐρανῷ καὶ ἐπὶ γῆς.

Text Critical Issue: Is the variant reading of (162). 700; (Mcion according to Tertullian); GrNy "ἐλθέτω τὸ πνεῦμά σου τὸ ἅγιον ἐφ᾽ ἡμᾶς καὶ καθαρισάτω ἡμᾶς" original in Luke 11:2?

Pro

Resch 1895, 234: "Die von *Gregorius Nyssenus* und *Maximus*, sowie dem durch *Hoskier* herausgegebenen Evangeliencodex bezeugte Lesart zum Lucas-evangelium kommt wahrscheinlich auf Rechnung des dritten Evangelisten, dessen Vorliebe für die Erwähnung des πνεῦμα ἅγιον bekannt ist (vgl. nachstehend die Erläuterungen zu Lc. 11,13, wo der Evangelist ebenfalls zu Gunsten des πνεῦμα ἅγιον den Urtext geändert hat). Sehr frühzeitig wird dann aus der kirchlichen Praxis der ursprüngliche Wortlaut dieser Bitte wieder in die Lucas-Handschriften eingedrungen sein, vielleicht schon durch den Redaktor des ältesten Evangeliencanons, der ja auch den vollständigen Text des Herrengebetes Lc. 11,2-4 restituierte."

Blass 1897, XLIII: "Vincunt [Contra Marcionis lectionem] autem alteri testes [700; GrNy] et numero et auctoritate maximeque eo, quod maior est secundum eos cum vulgata lectione congruentia. Lucas igitur ... ea scripsit quae testatur Gregorius, neque modo in R (cuius non est Gregorius testis, neque saepe codex 700), sed utraque forma euangelii; vulgaris autem lectio e Matthaeo invecta est, idque iam ante tempora Marcionis, in cuius exemplo Lucae utraque infuit."

von Harnack 1904, 199-200: "woher sollte ein Späterer, wenn er das Vater-Unser bei Lucas in derselben Form las wie bei Matthäus, den Muth genommen haben, diese Form zu corrigiren und etwas ganz Neues einzusetzen? Und welches Motiv soll ihn geleitet haben? Die Bitte um das Kommen des Reiches konnte nicht einmal einem radicalen Spiritualisten anstössig sein. Denn wie leicht war sie umzudeuten! Umgekehrt aber—wie nahe lag es, den Lucastext auch hier mit Matthäus zu conformiren, zumal, nachdem sich die von Matthäus gebotene Form in den Gottesdiensten durchgesetzt hatte!

"Endlich, wenige Zeilen nach dem Vater-Unser (s. c. 11,13) steht bei Lucas der Satz. ... Man erkennt also, dass Lucas das ΠΝΕΥΜΑ ΑΓΙΟΝ in Sprüche Jesu eingefügt hat, wo die Überlieferung etwas Anderes bot, dass er die Bitte um den heiligen Geist als die erste und wichtigste voraussetzt, und dass er sie unmittelbar nach dem Vater-Unser erwähnt. Welche Bedeutung aber überhaupt das ΠΝΕΥΜΑ ΑΓΙΟΝ bei Lucas hat (eine Verwandtschaft mit Johannes!), braucht hier nicht ausgeführt zu werden. Es ist ein Centralbegriff in den Erzählungen der Apostelgeschichte, und besonders kommen c. 1,8; 11,15; 19,6 unserer Stelle sehr nahe. Was aber das 'ΚΑΘΑΡΙΣΑΤΩ' betrifft, so steht in der Apostelgeschichte c. 15,8f. die schlagende Parallele. ..."

"Aus diesen Gründen darf man meines Erachtens nicht zweifeln, dass Lucas die Bitte um den heiligen Geist im Text des Vater-Unsers geboten hat. Dass sie sich heute bei nur wenigen Zeugen des Textes noch findet, ist kein Gegengrund; denn 1. sind die Zeugen, wenn man sie nicht nur zählt, sondern auch wägt, sehr erheblich, 2. sind die Minuskelcodices auf diese Lesart bisher noch nicht untersucht worden; ganz *zufällig* ist man auf zwei Zeugen gestossen: es können zehn oder zwanzig oder noch mehr sein, welche die Lesart bieten, [200] 3. grade beim Vater-Unser musste sich der Matthäus-Text schnell durchsetzen und Entgegenstehendes verdrängen; dazu: es giebt im Neuen Testament nicht wenige alte, ja ursprüngliche Lesarten, die trotz der Menge der Handschriften und Versionen nur durch einen oder ein paar Zeugen überliefert sind."

Wellhausen 1904b, 57: "Wenn Lc. aber in 11,13 den heiligen Geist statt des Reiches Gottes gesetzt hat, so kann er es auch in der zweiten Bitte getan haben. Es ist wenigstens nicht vollkommen ausgeschlossen."

Wellhausen 1905, 72 (=1911, 63): "das Maranatha im Vaterunser [ist] vielleicht schon von Lukas verändert in 'dein heiliger Geist komme über uns' (11,2)."

von Harnack 1907, 47: "Die drei ersten Bitten [of the Our Father] fehlen wahrscheinlich, dafür ἐλθέτω τὸ πνεῦμά σου τὸ ἅγιον ἐφ᾽ ἡμᾶς καὶ καθαρισάτω ἡμᾶς."

von Harnack 1907, ET 1908, 63-64: "The first three petitions [of the Our Father] are probably wanting; read [64] in their place ἐλθέτω τὸ πνεῦμά σου τὸ ἅγιον ἐφ᾽ ἡμᾶς καὶ καθαρισάτω ἡμᾶς."

von Harnack 1923, 27: "Wir kennen Marcion hinreichend, um zu wissen, daß er sich einen solchen Zusatz nicht erlaubt hätte. War sie aber Marcion bereits überliefert, so spricht alles dafür, … daß sie ursprünglich ist, d.h. daß *Lukas* so geschrieben hat."

Loisy 1924, 315-316: "'Soit sanctifié ton nom'.—Au lieu de cette demande on lisait, semble-t-il, dans l'évangile de Marcion: 'Que ton Esprit saint vienne sur nous et qu'il nous purifie' (Grégoire de Nysse, Maxime le Confesseur et les mss. 162, 700 ont ce texte comme deuxième demande. Il n'est pas sûr que Marcion ait lu: 'et qu'il nous purifie'. Voici le texte de Tertullien, *Marc.* IV, 26, d'après lequel on peut reconstituer la forme de la prière dans Marcion, et il est à noter que Tertullien n'y apporte aucune rectification de forme: 'Cui dicam "Pater"?… A quo spiritum sanctum postulem? Ejus regnum optabo venire, quem numquam regem gloriæ audivi, in cujus manu etiam corda sunt regum? Quis mihi dabit panem cottidianum?… Quis mihi delicta dimittet? Quis non sinet nos deduci in temptationem?' On dirait que le texte de Marcion est aussi bien celui de Tertullien). On a là une variante plus ancienne que Marcion, et qui pourrait bien être le texte authentique de notre évangéliste, puisque la suite du discours (11,13) y fait une référence volontaire et direct (il n'est guère possible d'en douter si l'on compare Mt. 8,11): 'Combien plutôt le [316] Père du ciel donnera-t-il Esprit saint à ceux qui le lui demandent?' Il paraît arbitraire de renverser le rapport en supposant qu'une variante aurait été introduite dans la prière par l'influence de cette conclusion. Comme Marcion lisait ensuite: 'qu'arrive ton règne', on ne peut pas supposer non plus que la demande d'Esprit saint a été introduite pour éliminer la considération eschatologique. Mais il est de toute invraisemblance que Marcion ait lu les deux premières demandes en cette forme: 'Arrive sur nous ton Esprit saint, arrive ton règne'. Les allusions de Tertullien suggéreraient plutôt: 'Soit ton esprit saint sur nous', etc. La leçon de Grégoire de Nysse proviendrait de la confusion intervenue entre la demande de l'Esprit et la seconde demande: 'arrive ton règne'. Et si la leçon de Marcion est la leçon authentique de notre évangile, il en faudra conclure que celui-ci a emprunté l'oraison dominical à la pratique rituelle d'une communauté qui avait adapté la prière à ses réunions cultuelles et spécialement peut-être à la liturgie de l'initiation baptismale (cf. Seeberg dans *Neut. Studien Heinrici gewidmet*, 119)."

Streeter 1924, 277: "this reading was in the text of Luke used by Gregory of Nyssa in Cappadocia in 395; he says so plainly twice, and moreover gives no hint that he had even heard of any other reading. It is also quoted by Maximus of Turin, *c.* 450. So the reading was current both in the East and in the West to quite a late period. But it also stood in the text of Marcion (A.D. 140), and from Tertullian's comment on this it is not at all clear that his own text was in this respect different from Marcion's. Now in view of the immense pressure of the tendency to assimilate the two versions of this specially familiar prayer, and of the improbability that various orthodox Fathers should have adopted (without knowing it) the text of Marcion, the probability is high that the reading of *700, 162*, which makes the Gospels differ most, is what Luke wrote."

Klostermann 1929, 124: "Die Lesart, mit der auch D ἐφ' ἡμᾶς ἐλθάτω ἡ βασιλεία σου *zu uns komme dein Reich* zusammenhängen mag, erscheint zwar hier als sinngemäße Umsetzung des eschatologischen 'dein Reich komme' in eine auf die Gegenwart bezogene Bitte, ist aber sicher schon vor Marcion vorhanden gewesen und wohl authentischer Text des Lc (vgl. v. 13, der nicht erst im Verlauf als Textgeschichte auf v. 2 umgestaltend eingewirkt hat)."

Greeven 1931, 73-74: "Daß die Geistbitte bei Lukas ursprünglich ist, wird schon dadurch sehr wahrscheinlich gemacht, daß die Matthäusform des Vaterunsers alsbald die im Kult gebräuchliche wurde[5] und schwerlich eine so stark abweichende Variante hätte neben sich aufkommen lassen, wenn diese ihren Anspruch nicht auf zuverlässige Überlieferung gründen konnte. Außerdem ist noch der Umstand von Bedeutung, daß Lukas am Ende des zusammenhängenden Abschnittes über das Beten (11,1-13) einmal πνεῦμα ἅγιον einsetzt, wo Matthäus δόματα ἀγαθά hat (L. 11,13; Mt. 7,11). Damit erhält das Bildwort eine überraschende Pointe: es erscheint nicht mehr allgemein gemünzt auf beharrliches Bitten, sondern auf beharrliches Bitten um den Heiligen Geist. Das ist im Text, wie er uns vorliegt, eine Härte, würde sich aber sofort erklären, wenn wir im Vaterunser bei Lukas die Geistbitte voraussetzen dürfen. Schließlich spricht auch die Einleitung L. 11,1 für die Echtheit der Geistbitte, wenn man sie mit [74] Act. 19,2f vergleicht: Die mit der Johannestaufe Getauften wissen nichts vom Heiligen Geiste; das Vaterunser soll aber nach L. 11,1 ein Spezifikum der Jesusjünger sein, wie es entsprechend auch die Johannesjünger hatten."

73[5]: "Vgl. Did. 8,2 und die Tatsache, daß sowohl Tertullian (de oratione) als auch Gregor und Maximus (an den angef[ührten] Orten) jeweils vom Matthäustext des Vaterunsers ausgehen."

Lampe 1955, 170: "Although Marcion is the earliest witness to this reading, the clause occurs in a different position in his version of the prayer from that in which it was known to Gregory of Nyssa, and the absence of any obvious doctrinal reason which might account for Marcion having altered the Lord's Prayer in this fashion strongly suggests, when taken in conjunction with the conformity of the petition to Lucan teaching, that the clause must be authentic."

Leaney 1956, 104-105 (=1958, 60-61): "In the first place, the words are Lucan: in verse 13 Luke writes 'he will give (the) Holy Spirit' where Matthew (vii. 11) has 'he will give good things': in view of Matthew's notorious 'spiritualizing' tendency it is unlikely that the alteration is on his side here (cf. e.g. Matt. v. 3). For καθαρίζω of a spiritual or metaphorical purification cf. Acts x. 15, xi. 9, and especially xv. 9 where the gift of the Holy spirit is associated with a purification of the hearts of those who receive it. Here, indeed, there may be an echo of the Lucan version of the Lord's Prayer, in the words, 'the Holy Spirit', 'having cleansed', and 'tempt'. (See the whole passage Acts xv. 8-10.)

"Secondly, the support from tradition for the reading is far from negligible: for example, Gregory makes clear from the passage in *De Or. Dom.* iii[3] that the text of Luke as he knew it read this variant, in contrast, as he says, to Matthew's 'May thy kingdom [105] come'. …

"The text of Gregory may then be what Luke wrote. More general considerations will support this view. Luke's eschatological framework includes a Christ who reigns in heaven, and on earth through his vicegerents the Apostles, sending to them the Holy Spirit who empowers them to reign with the same effectiveness which he would have if actually present. Thus Pentecost fulfills John the Baptist's prophecy of the coming baptism by one who would baptize with (holy) spirit and fire (Luke iii. 16), an event thus probably answering at any rate for Luke the ancient question, 'Why were the Apostles not baptized?' Although Luke does not equate Pentecost with the Parousia (as is well shown by Acts i. 11), the coming of the spirit to the Apostles is an essential stage for the coming of the kingdom, its importance being summed up neatly and clearly in Acts i. 8."

104[3]: "Migne, *P.G.*, 44, 1157 C."

Gräßer 1957, 110-111: "Die Frage, ob *Lukas* diese Korrektur zugetraut werden darf, läßt sich nicht mit letzter Sicherheit entscheiden; es spricht aber doch [111] einiges dafür. Einmal Lc 11,13, wo Lukas das ἀγαθά von Mt 7,11 in πνεῦμα ἅγιον umändert, weil für ihn die Bitte um den heiligen Geist der eigentliche Inhalt des christlichen Gebetes ist. Warum? Damit stehen wir beim zweiten Punkt: weil *Lukas dem Phänomen des Geistes eine ausgezeichnete Stellung im Ablauf der Heilsgeschichte zugewiesen hat.* Und zwar besonders auch in seinem eschatologischen Entwurf, der gekennzeichnet ist durch die Umstellung von der Naherwartung auf die Dauer. Auf diese eschatologische Thematik hat der Geist einen ganz besonderen Bezug, wie einmal der Anfang der Apostelgeschichte durch die einfache Schilderung der Vorgänge (Pfingsten!) darlegt, zum anderen aber besonders Act 1,6ff., wo die Frage nach dem eschatologischen Wissen abgewiesen wird mit dem Hinweis auf den Empfang des heiligen Geistes, der in Aussicht gestellt wird. Hier wird deutlich, daß sich Lukas des Geistphänomens zur Bewältigung des Parusieproblemes bedient, und zwar im Sinne des *Ersatzes!*...

"Jetzt verstehen wir die Korrektur an der 2. Bitte: Es geht Lukas um das *Parusieproblem*, um das Durchhalten in einer heillosen Welt! Daher die Bitte um den heiligen Geist als des ausgezeichneten Garanten der christlichen Existenz in der Welt!"

Ott 1965, 117-118: "Gegen die Ursprünglichkeit der Geistbitte im lukanischen Vaterunser spricht nun freilich auf den ersten Blick die äußerlich recht schwache Bezeugung für die Geistbitte. Doch kann dies wohl bei näherem Betrachten nicht als entscheidender Gegengrund angeführt werden. Gerade bei einer weit verbreiteten, allgemein bekannten festen liturgischen Formel, wie sie das Vaterunser in der frühen Christenheit darstellte (vgl. Mt 6,9-13 mit Did 8,2f), muß man mit [118] früh einsetzenden Harmonisierungstendenzen rechnen."

Freudenberger 1968-69, 429-430: "Schließlich stellt eine Stelle wie Lk. xi. 20 ein m. E. unüberwindliches Hindernis dar, dem Evangelisten [430] selbst den Ersatz der Reichsbitte durch die Geistbitte zuzuschreiben; denn hier hat Matthäus in der Parallele xii. 28 die ursprüngliche, auch für Lukas singuläre Wendung ἐν δακτύλῳ θεοῦ zum geläufigeren und verständlicheren ἐν πνεύματι θεοῦ umgewandelt, während sie bei Lukas beibehalten ist. Bereits Harnack hat darauf hingewiesen,[2] daß man nach altchristlicher Vorstellung 'den Geist hat oder nicht hat—als tägliche Bitte erscheine die Bitte um den Heiligen Geist daher auffallend'. Er wollte deshalb diese Bitte als Eingang eines christlichen Initiationsgebetes ansehen; das ist aber nur möglich unter Absehung vom jüdischen Hintergrund gerade dieser Bitte und besonders vom Charakter des Vaterunsers, das auch in der lukanischen Form wiederholbares Gemeindegebet war. Wenn es aber unwahrscheinlich ist, daß Lukas eine vorhandene Reichsbitte gestrichen, bzw. daß er umgekehrt die Geistbitte neu geformt hat, bleibt demnach nur die Möglichkeit, daß Lukas die Bitte um das Kommen des Geistes und die Reinigung bereits in der Quelle gefunden hat, der er das Vaterunser entnahm."

430[2]: "In: *SAB* (1904), S. 205, ihm folgt z.B. Grässer a.a.O. S. 109."

Shelton 1982, 384: "Luke is not above changing the wording of sayings found in Mark or even expanding them;[52] one should not expect him to treat the Q material any differently. So Luke may be consciously responsible for the variant in 11:2 which fits in so well with the references to the Holy Spirit in 10:21 and 11:13."

384[52]: "For example, compare Luke 5:20, 32, 39; 8:45, 50; 18:42 with parallels."

Evans 1990, 480-481: "In place of this [481] petition [Thy kingdom come] there is a remarkable variant reading in Luke, 'Let thy holy Spirit come upon us and cleanse us'. ... [These words] more likely represent a liturgical adaptation of the Prayer, perhaps for use at baptism. As such, however, and despite the weak textual attestation, they might have stood already in Luke's version of the Prayer, or have been inserted by him (cf. his reference to the holy Spirit in v.13)."

O'Neill 1993, 8-10: O'Neill's thesis is that the Lord's Prayer derives from a collection of the brief prayers of Jesus. "I suggest for your consideration the hypothesis that Luke's version had at the beginning the answer to the request from a disciple to teach them to pray as John had taught his disciples. This answer ran as follows: 'When you pray say, Father let thy Spirit come and cleanse us'. This would be a good prayer to teach those who asked for a prayer as John's disciples used to ask him. John, we remember, baptized with water, but looked for one who would also baptize with the Spirit. This prayer, with various minor variations in wording, is given by Marcion (according to Tertullian), by the minuscules 700 and 162 from the eleventh and twelfth century, and by two Greek Fathers, Gregory of Nyssa and Maximus the Confessor. Marcion has this prayer in place of 'Hallowed be thy name' and the two minuscules, Gregory of Nyssa and Maximus the Confessor read 'Hallowed be thy name' and have it in place of 'Thy kingdom come'. I conjecture that Marcion's form of Luke was indeed the earliest version of Luke's collection. This collection began, [9] 'Father, let thy Spirit come and cleanse us'." O'Neill then conjectures that the Lukan text reflected in most of the manuscripts is a result of various scribal interventions. "They left us with a text of Luke that gave Jesus a prayer, 'Father, hallowed be thy name' in place of his actual prayer as preserved in Matthew, 'Our Father in heaven, hallowed be thy name'. They also left us with a text of Luke which does not allow us to see Luke's original opening: 'Father, let thy Spirit come and cleanse us'. [10] This prayer, too, was probably the prayer Jesus taught one of his disciples who said, 'Lord, teach us to pray as John also taught his disciples'. The clever scribes did not have the boldness to give us this prayer, and they only succeeded in maiming the other."

Philonenko 1995, 61: "L'usage liturgique du 'Notre Père' dans sa rédaction matthéenne a eu une forte tendance unificatrice, si bien que la rédaction lucanienne a été alignée sur le texte de *Matthieu*."

62: "Que cette demande de l'Esprit soit attestée par Marcion n'est pas nécessairement le signe de son origine marcionite, mais indique, plus vraisemblablement, que cette variante figurait dans le texte de *Luc* que Marcion a connu. De surcroît, l'adoption par Marcion de la leçon contestée pourrait avoir favorisé son élimination."

63: "Si l'on retient l'information donnée en Marc 1,7 selon laquelle le baptême de Jean aurait été un baptême d'eau, alors que le baptême de Jésus était un baptême d'Esprit, la demande de l'Esprit Saint, en *Luc* 11,2 pourrait avoir un caractère polémique à l'endroit des disciples de Jean."

65: Philonenko traces the traditions regarding the coming of God's Spirit in early Jewish literature, including that of the Essenes, and then says, "Cette attente de l'Esprit avait gagné des milieux piétistes ouverts à l'essénisme. Certains de leurs traditions ont été reprises dans les deux premiers chapitres de *Luc*."

66: "La demande de l'Esprit Saint a un arrière-plan qoumrânien précis qui est la marque de sa haute antiquité. La variante pourrait avoir appartenu au texte primitif de *Luc*. Sans doute n'est-il pas nécessaire de choisir entre la formule matthéenne, 'Que Ton Règne vienne' et la formule lucanienne, 'Que Ton Esprit vienne sur nous et qu'il nous purifie'. La Prière, proposée en exemple par Jésus à ses disciples, n'avait peut-être pas, dans sa formation initiale, le hiératisme que l'on prête aujourd'hui à l'Oraison dominicale. Le 'Notre Père' aura ainsi fait l'objet, dès l'origine, d'adaptations et de modifications qui, sans avoir été retenues par la liturgie, peuvent, comme la demande de l'Esprit Saint, prétendre à l'authenticité."

Con

Plummer 1896, 295[1]: "This addition may have been made when the Prayer was used at laying on of hands, and thus have got into some texts of Lk."

Dibelius 1911, 44: "der Matthäustext des Gebets ist in der Form gefeilt; insbesondere bilden Mt. 6,9.10 eine einheitliche Größe; es ist nicht anzunehmen, daß bei einer Konformation nur 1. und 2. Bitte, nicht aber Anrede, 3. (und 7.) Bitte in den Lukastext gekommen wären. Der Lukastext etwa von B, mit 1. und 2. Bitte, ohne 3. und 7. Bitte, darf danach auf Originalität Anspruch erheben."

Zahn 1920, 769: "*Am unwahrscheinlichsten ist die erste dieser Annahmen* [that Marcion has preserved the original text of Luke here]. Denn wie wäre die frühzeitige und bald beinah überall siegreiche Verdrängung des angeblich ursprünglichen Textes zu erklären? Religiös anstößig konnte für niemand die Bitte um den hl. Geist sein und sie an der Spitze eines von Jesus den Jüngern gegebenen Gebetes zu lesen, konnte um so weniger befremden, als die bei Lc folgende Nutzanwendung auf ein vertrauensvolles Bitten gerade um den hl. Geist hinausläuft (11,13).

"Auch die Neigung, die beiden ev Berichte über das VU einander gleichzumachen, welche die Textüberlieferung von Lc 11,2-4 sonst so mächtig beeinflußt hat, würde nicht dazu taugen, die allgemeine Einführung der 1. Bitte des Mt anstatt der angeblich von Mn [Marcion] bewahrten ursprünglichen 1. Bitte des Lc zu erklären; denn die ältesten und besten Zeugen für die wesentliche Identität der 1. Bitte bei beiden Evv: Orig., א B L Ss, Vulg haben den Text des Lc vom ersten bis zum letzten Wort von allen oder so gut wie allen Beimischungen aus Mt reingehalten. Zumal Orig., der de orat. 18,2ff., 22,1ff. das Verhältnis der beiden Berichte ausführlich erörtert, aber bei all seinem Interesse für die Textüberlieferung der Evv nichts von Varianten im Text des Lc oder des Mt zu sagen weiß, ist ein klassischer Zeuge für die Echtheit dieser Überlieferung. Dazu kommt, daß die gegenteilige Annahme die Tatsache unerklärt läßt, daß die kirchlichen Zeugen für Mn's [Marcion's] 1. Bitte (Min 700, Gregor Nyss.) diesen Text nicht wie Mn [Marcion] anstatt der 1. Bitte des katholischen Textes, sondern *neben* dieser als Ersatz der 2. Bitte bieten."

Lagrange 1921, 323: "Ce changement vient probablement de Marcion, qui aurait remplacé l'idée biblique du règne par celle de l'Esprit. Cependant, d'après Tertullien (*adv. Marc.* IV, 26), dans le Luc de Marcion l'Esprit aurait plutôt remplacé la sanctification du nom."

Easton 1926, 175: "Apparently it [the different reading] goes back to Marcion."

Creed 1930, 156: "for such a text there is no positive evidence. It is further to be noted that the textual evidence is less homogenous than Streeter states. ... On the whole the text of the best MSS. may be accepted as original with considerable confidence. Perhaps the variant originated ... in the liturgical usage of the Marcionites."

Hauck 1934, 149: "Sie [the petition for the Spirit] scheint ursprünglich eine Taufbitte zu sein, die irrig ins VU (durch Marcion?) hereingenommen wurde."

Rengstorf 1936, 145: "Manche Ausleger möchten in dieser Fassung den authentischen Text des Lukas finden, der mit Rücksicht auf Matthäus verdrängt worden sei. Doch wird man in ihr richtiger ein Ergebnis der Verknüpfung von Vaterunser und Taufe im Blick auf den mit dieser verbundenen Empfang des Geistes, also eine Art Initiationsgebet über dem Täufling, sehen."

Lohmeyer 1952, 191: "Aber hier widerspricht schon die sprachliche und stilistische Form der Bitte solchem [jesuanischen] Ursprung, denn sie lehnt sich an den Text der griechischen Bibel an. Sie wäre zudem innerhalb des Vaterunsers kaum begreiflich; weder fügt sie sich der sonst festgehaltenen Form der Bitten, in welchen nirgends zwei durch 'und' koordinierte Verben begegnen, noch dem sonst ausgesprochenen Inhalt ein. Was bedarf es noch der Bitte: 'Vergib uns unsere Sünden', wenn schon in der zweiten Bitte gebeten ist: 'Dein heiliger Geist reinige uns'? Und selbst wenn man diesem 'Reiniger' eine besondere Färbung geben wollte, sei es die der Heiligkeit oder auch nur die der 'reinen Lippen', von der Jesaja sagt, so ist die Tautologie nur verdeckt, aber nicht behoben; man vergißt zudem, daß noch der erste Johannesbrief beide Begriffe als gleichwertig behandelt: Gott 'ist getreu und gerecht, daß er uns die Sünden vergibt und reinigt uns von aller Ungerechtigkeit'. So gehört die Bitte also dem Vaterunser nicht an, sie bleibt eine spätere Bildung, und gebildet hat sie eine urchristliche Gemeinde und Tradition, welche auf alttestamentliche und jüdische Hoffnungen (Test. Jud. 24,2f.) gegründet in dem Werk des Täufers und Jesu Zeichen und Weg zur nahen eschatologischen Vollendung sehen und des Geistes harren, der kommen und sie reinigen wird."

Manson 1956, 105-106: "With the help of other evidence [the variant reading] can be traced back to very early times. It seems that it was known to, and perhaps used by, the heretic Marcion in the early part of the second century. What the full meaning of these various bits of evidence may be [106] I do not feel qualified or able to say dogmatically, but I strongly suspect that they reflect the use of the Lord's Prayer in connection with the rites of initiation into membership of the Christian community. ... But whatever may be the truth about details, there is no doubt about the main fact that baptism and the gift of the Holy Spirit were closely connected in the Apostolic Age."

106-107: Manson observes that in the accounts of baptism administered by John the Baptist, the rite is one of purification. "It seems to me not impossible that the cleansing work of water and fire has been transferred to the Holy Spirit; and that the reception of the Holy Spirit may have been thought of as the perfect cleansing of the human soul. If that was so, then this variant petition may perhaps be construed as a request for baptism with the Holy Spirit as the supreme cleansing of the spirit of man. This would suggest, in its turn, that it came into use in connection with the baptismal rite; and the distribution of the witnesses to this reading leads one to think that the change of reading took place in the Eastern Church rather than the Western. And, finally, the fact that this petition appears to have been known to Marcion and adopted into his version of the Lord's Prayer would suggest that it came into use very early. I do not think [107] it is at all likely that it is an original part of the Lord's Prayer as given by the Lord, but I can well imagine that it is a very early example of the way in which the Prayer was modified by liturgical use, as prayers constantly are unless you stick very rigidly to a written text."

Schmid 1956, 197: "Die bei Marcion statt der ersten, bei Gregor von Nyssa, Maximus Confessor und in einigen griechischen Handschriften an der Stelle der zweiten stehende Geistbitte ... muß schon auf Grund der Textbezeugung als späterer Einschub gelten."

Grundmann 1961, 232: "Die dem Vater-Unser widersprechende Parallelität des zweimaligen 'es komme' bei Marcion verbietet, diesen Text als ursprünglich anzusehen."

Perrin 1963, 91: "Manson examines all the sayings concerning the Kingdom of God in the Synoptic Gospels and comes to the conclusion that, in the earlier part of his ministry, Jesus spoke of the Kingdom as something that was coming (Mark 1.15, etc.), and, in the later part of his ministry, as something into which men enter (Mark 9.47, etc.).[2]"

91[2]: "The major exception to this is the petition 'Thy Kingdom come' in the Lord's Prayer. But at the time he wrote *Teaching* Manson was inclined to argue that the inclusion of this petition at Luke 11.2 was the result of textual assimilation to the Matthaean version, and to doubt the authenticity of this particular petition in the Matthaean version (*Teaching*, pp. 128 f.). This is a bold and altogether improbable assumption and Manson did not repeat it in his later *Sayings*, pp. 169, 266."

Ellis 1966, 163: "In any case the manuscript evidence is too scanty to regard this reading as original."

Jeremias 1967, 9: "Während die Matthäus-Fassung mit der uns geläufigen 7-Bitten-Fassung übereinstimmt ..., hat die Lukas-Fassung nach den ältesten Handschriften nur 5 Bitten: Sie lautet:

'Vater,
Geheiligt werde dein Name. ...'"

Jeremias 1967, ET 1964, 3: "It is quite improbable that the petition for the Holy Spirit should be the original text; its attestation is much too weak. From where, then does this petition originate? We know that it was an old baptismal prayer, and we may conclude that it was added to the Lord's Prayer when this was used at the baptismal ceremony. One may compare the fact that the Marcionite version of the Prayer ... has, in the petition for bread, 'Thy bread.' This is probably an allusion to the Lord's Supper; thus Marcion has both sacraments in view, baptism in this first petition and the Lord's Supper, which followed baptism, in his phrase 'Thy bread.'" This observation is found in the 1964 English translation, but is not included in any of the German versions.

7: "While the Matthean version agrees with that form which is familiar to us, a form of the Prayer with seven petitions ... the Lucan version has only five petitions according to the oldest manuscripts. It runs:
Father,
Hallowed be thy name. ..."

Jeremias 1971, 188[77]: "Diese Geistbitte ist keinesfalls ursprünglich ...; die ganz schwache Bezeugung, die schwankende Stellung und vor allem die Form, die von der Struktur der übrigen Bitten abweicht, schließen das aus. Sie dürfte vielmehr aus der Taufliturgie stammen, in der das Vaterunser und die Bitte um den Geist verbunden waren."

Jeremias 1971, ET 1971, 194[5]: "This petition for the spirit is certainly not original ...; the weak attestation, the difference in the position in which it appears, and above all its form, which varies from the structure of the other petitions, exclude this. It may, rather, derive from the baptismal liturgy in which the Lord's Prayer and the petition for the spirit were connected."

Metzger 1971, 155-156: "How shall this testimony [of the different readings] be evaluated? First, it is by no means certain that ἐφ' ἡμᾶς in codex Bezae should be taken as evidence of an earlier petition for the Holy Spirit; to pray that God's name may be hallowed upon us is entirely congruent with Old Testament references to causing the divine 'name to dwell there' (e.g. Dt 12.11; 14.23; 16.6, 11, where the Septuagint renders 'for my name to be invoked there'). Furthermore the evidence from Tertullian comes from a treatise written during his Montanist period, when he had a special fondness for texts pertaining to the Holy Spirit; in his earlier exposition of the Lord's Prayer he betrays no knowledge of the existence of such a petition. [156] Apparently, therefore, the variant reading is a liturgical adaptation of the original form of the Lord's Prayer, used perhaps when celebrating the rite of baptism or the laying on of hands. The cleansing descent of the Holy Spirit is so definitely a Christian, ecclesiastical concept that one cannot understand why, if it were original in the prayer, it should have been supplanted in the overwhelming majority of the witnesses by a concept originally much more Jewish in its piety." The same text in the 1994 ed. p. 131.

Danker 1972, 135: "The thought [of the variant reading] is in harmony with Luke's subsequent stress on the donation of the Spirit, but the change may well represent post-Lukan clarification that subsequently gained liturgical status and displaced the petition for the Kingdom."

Ernst 1977, 362: "Die Annahme, hier liege der ursprüngliche, später am Mt angeglichene Text vor, ist unbegründet. Die Emendation ist allerdings ein interessantes Zeugnis für die liturgische Verwertung des Herrengebetes."

Marshall 1978, 458: "A reading which is attested in only two late Greek MSS is highly unlikely to be original. Moreover, the witnesses to the variant show considerable differences among themselves; the oldest version in Marcion occupies a different place in the prayer as a whole. The apparent trace of the variant in D can be explained otherwise. ... It is more probable that the variant represents an early liturgical usage which has contaminated the text of Lk."

Fitzmyer 1985, 904: "'May your holy Spirit come upon us and purify us' (a modification probably derived from the use of the prayer in a baptismal liturgy; it is hardly ... an original part of the prayer or even of the Lucan form of it)."

Schneider 1986, 359: "In methodischer Hinsicht ist zunächst festzuhalten, daß die 'äußeren' Kriterien für die Echtheit der Geist-Bitte im Lk-Text schwach sind. Zwar können für eine Geist-Bitte außerhalb des Herrengebets verschiedene Zeugnisse angeführt werden. Doch gibt es für die Verankerung dieser Bitte im Vaterunser nur vier Textzeugen, von denen wiederum nur zwei Evangelienhandschriften sind. Die vier Zeugen ... sind außerdem vermutlich von einander nicht unabhängig. Der rekonstruierbare Vaterunsertext Marcions zeigt zwar, daß man die Geist-Bitte schon früh mit dem Gebet des Herrn verband. Jedoch lag ihre Stellung im Gesamtgefüge der Einzelbitten offensichtlich noch nicht fest. Die Hypothese einer ursprünglich am Rande notierten Glosse, die schließlich als Textkorrektur (und nicht als Kommentierung) verstanden und in den Text selbst aufgenommen wurde, kann den Befund der Textzeugen erklären."

Magne 1988a, 85: In a table comparing the variants represented by 700, 162, Gregory of Nyssa, and Maximus in one column; Marcion in a second column; Luke in a third column; Matthew in a fourth column and Tertullian in a fifth column, Magne writes "vienne ton règne" in the Lukan column.

Magne 1988b, 373-374: "Le début de la péricope de Lc 'Apprends-nous à prier comme Jean l'a appris à ses disciples' (Lc 11,1) avoue l'intention de remplacer par une prière attribuée à Jésus une prière attribuée à Jean. Celle-ci, d'après la variante de Lc 11,2, ne pouvait être que la transposition en prière adressée au Père de l'épiclèse baptismale citée dans les Actes de Thomas 27 et attestée par 1 Co 6,11, soit:

Père, que soit sanctifié ton Nom,
que vienne ton Esprit saint sur nous,
et qu'il nous purifie.

...

[374] Le 'Pater' selon Jean a été transformé en prière selon Jésus:
— la première demande 'Que soit sanctifié ton Nom' a été conservée;
— la seconde demande 'Que vienne ton E.-S. sur nous' a été dédoublée;
elle est devenue, d'une part, 'Que vienne ton règne'—puisque Jésus a prêché
le royaume comme Jean avait prêché le baptême—et, d'autre part, 'Donne-
nous chaque jour notre pain ἐπιούσιος'—puisque l'eucharistie est le sacrement
instituée par Jésus comme le baptême est le sacrement institué par Jean. ..."
In a table showing the development of the prayer from Pre-Q through Q to
Q^{Luke} and Q^{Matt}, Magne shows "vienne ton règne" as derived from Q.

Wiefel 1988, 214: "Der Text lehnt sich an alttestamentliche Wendungen
an: Ps. 50,13 LXX; 142,10 LXX. Eine marcionitische Herkunft ist von daher
kaum wahrscheinlich. Eher ist an urchristliche Kreise zu denken, die von einer
alttestamentlich-jüdischen Geisterwartung bestimmt waren. Die Anfügung an
die zweite Bitte lag sachlich nahe."

Delobel 1989, 300: "The demand for the Spirit does not correspond with
the New Testament concept of the coming of the Spirit. It pleads against the
hypothesis of a Lukan redaction that in Luke's view the promise of the Spirit
has been fulfilled (cf. Acts 2,14; 8,14-17; 10,44-48), and that the Lukan writings never attribute 'cleansing' to the Spirit. A later copyist may have been
inspired by Ez 36,22-32 LXX where the sanctification of God's name (v. 23),
the announcement of the cleansing (v. 25) and the reception of the Spirit
(v. 27) are mentioned."

Metzger 1991, 520: "Perhaps the most interesting variant reading in the text
of the Lucan form of the Lord's Prayer is in the second petition (Luke 11:2).
'Thy Holy Spirit come upon us and cleanse us' or something very similar is
found in two minuscule Greek MSS (162, 700) and was quoted by Gregory of
Nyssa (A.D. 395) and Maximus of Turin (c. 450). According to Tertullian, in
the middle of the 2d century Marcion apparently replaced the first petition by
this one. It is likely that the variant form is a liturgical adaptation of the original form of the Lord's Prayer, perhaps used when celebrating the rite of baptism
or the laying on of hands. Furthermore, the cleansing descent of the Holy Spirit
is so definitely a Christian ecclesiastical concept that, if it were original in the
prayer, it should have been supplanted in the overwhelming majority of texts
by a concept originally much more Jewish in its piety ('thy kingdom come')."

Meier 1994, 356: "A few manuscripts of Luke have alternate readings at
this point, but the scattered evidence is hardly sufficient to overturn the vast
majority of Lucan manuscripts. [Meier refers to Metzger 1971] The reading

'Your Holy Spirit come upon us and cleanse us' is found in place of the Lucan petition for the kingdom (with slight variation in the wording) in the 11th-century MS 700 and the 12th-century MS 162. The same basic reading is referred to in quotations by Gregory of Nyssa (4th century) and Maximus of Turin (5th century, perhaps in dependence on Gregory). Earlier, Tertullian seems to know of a petition for the Holy Spirit right after the invocation 'Father'; it is followed by the petition for the kingdom. Whether Tertullian is referring to the Lucan form of the Lord's Prayer known to him or to the 2nd-century heretic Marcion is not clear. At any rate, it is possible that at some time in the 2nd or 3rd century some manuscript(s) had the petition for the Spirit in place of the petition for the hallowing of the name (not the petition for the coming of the kingdom!). Codex Bezae (D) may have weak echo of this when it has 'Hallowed be your name' followed by 'Upon us may your kingdom come'; but, as Metzger points out, Bezae's reading is not necessarily a remnant of the petition for the Spirit. Moreover, the reference from Tertullian comes from a work he wrote during his Montanist period, 'when he had special fondness for texts pertaining to the Holy Spirit; in his earlier exposition of the Lord's Prayer he betrays no knowledge of the existence of such a petition' ([Metzger 1971] p.155). Most likely, the petition for the Spirit comes from the use of the Lord's Prayer in the liturgy, especially at baptism or the laying on of hands. Beyond the very weak attestation in the manuscripts, there is another reason for rejecting the petition for the Spirit as original in Luke. There would be no reason for Christians to replace such a perfectly Christian idea with what would have struck them as a vaguer one about the kingdom."

Schürmann 1994, 189-190: "Die sehr schwach bezeugte Geist-Bitte ... verdrängt eine andere Bitte, mal diese, mal jene; sie hat keinen festen Platz in der Überlieferung und ist schon von daher verdächtig: Sie bezeugt sich (vielleicht zunächst) bei Tert (Mcion?) anstelle der [190] Eröffnungsbitte, (später dann) bei GrNy MaxConf 700 anstelle der Basileia-Bitte (bei MaxConf wie 162 umgestellt und ohne ἐφ' ἡμᾶς). Johannes-Jünger hätten eventuell so auf Grund von Lk 3,16.17 (und Ez 36,25-27) beten können, nicht aber getaufte Jünger Jesu, schon gar nicht auf Anregung von Lukas; es würde trotz der betonten Geisttheologie des Lukas und des luk Einschubs V 13 ... Mut dazu gehören, die Bitte diesem zuzuschreiben[117]."

190[117]: "Zwar nennt Lukas die Christen einigemal (Apg 4mal) ἅγιοι, dazu Apg 20,32; 26,18 ἡγιασμένοι. Bitten um den Hl. Geist kennt Lukas außer Lk 11,13b ... diff Mt nirgends. Das Verbum καθαρίζω (durch den Glauben) findet sich nur in Apg 15,9 ähnlich gebraucht; nirgendwo 'reinigt' bei Lukas der Hl. Geist. Apg 1,8 ... ist formelhaft und darum kaum als Nachklang unserer Bitte zu sichern."

Evaluations

Carruth 1995: {A}, Luke = ἐλθέτω ἡ βασιλεία σου·

The paucity of textual evidence for the variant text in Luke as well as the variety in such manuscript evidence that does exist does not offer convincing support to claim that the variant derives from Luke. Even though Luke has an interest in the Holy Spirit, the cleansing activity of the Spirit is not found elsewhere in Luke or Acts (Delobel, Schürmann). It is much more likely, as numerous scholars have suggested, that the variant arises from ecclesiastical usage of the Prayer among some groups.

Robinson 1995: {A}, Luke = ἐλθέτω ἡ βασιλεία σου·

The variant text has been adequately explained as a secondary liturgical intrusion.

Q 11:~~1-2a,~~2b-4⁰: Was the Prayer in Q?

Luke and Matthew = Q

Pro

B. Weiß 1876, 181: See Q 11:~~1-2a,~~2b¹ Luke = Q, Pro.

B. Weiß 1878, 421: "Aus diesem hier vollständig erhaltenen Stück [Luke 11: 1-13] der älteren Quelle hat der erste Evangelist das Gebet des Herrn (Matth. 6,9-13) und die Verheissung der Gebetserhörung (Matth. 7,7-11) in die Bergrede verflochten. ... Dass beide Redactionen aus derselben griechischen Quelle stammen, zeigt schon das eigenthümliche ἐπιούσιον."

Resch 1895, 229: "Bezüglich der Quellenkritik ist *dreierlei* festzustellen: *erstlich*, was wohl ganz allgemein zugestanden ist, dass der erste und dritte Evangelist jeder selbstständig das Herrengebet aus der vorcanonischen Quelle geschöpft habe."

Plummer 1896, 293-294: "Note the marks of Luke's style: ἐγένετο, ἐν τῷ εἶναι, εἶναι προσευχόμενον, εἶπεν πρός, εἶπεν δέ, τὸ καθ' ἡμέραν, αὐτοί, παντί. The last three, which are in the Prayer itself, point to the conclusion that at least some of the differences in wording between this form and that in Mt. are due to Lk., and that the form in Mt. better represents the original, which would be in Aramaic. The differences cannot be accounted for by independent translation. The Greek of the two forms is too similar for that, especially in the use of the [294] perplexing word ἐπιούσιος. Both Evangelists must have had the Prayer in Greek."

B. Weiß 1898, 131: "Der erste Evangelist hat auch hier [6:9-13] den Text der gemeinsamen Quelle, aus der wohl auch die Einleitung V. 7 stammt, treuer reproduzirt (vgl. zu Lk 11,1)."

Wernle 1899, 68: "Das bei Lc vorangehende Stück vom zudringlichen Freund (11,5-8) stammt, da Mt es nicht kennt, aus anderer Quelle. Dagegen geht das Vaterunser wegen großer wörtlicher Übereinstimmung (ἐπιούσιος) trotz der Differenzen wohl auf die gemeinsame Quelle zurück, und da es in Mt 6 den Zusammenhang stört, wird es Lc am rechten Ort gegeben haben."

Holtzmann 1901, 14: "Selbst wenn Mt und Lc 2 verschiedene Redactionen der Spruchsammlung benutzt haben sollten, würde daher in unserem Fall [Luke 12:13-31; Matt 6:25-33] die Quelle des Lc den Zusammenhang der beiden Stücke, deren eines Mt weglässt, schon geboten haben. Ganz der gleiche Fall hat statt Lc 11,1-13 = Mt 6,9-13; 7,7-11, sofern Lc 5-8 bei Mt fehlt."

B. Weiß 1901, 458-459: "So gewiss die Einleitung formell und materiell (vgl. das Beten Jesu) von der Hand des Lk herrührt, so gewiss muss der Anlass des UV., das Mt 6,9-13 offenbar aus schriftstellerischen Motiven in die

Bergrede verflicht …, mit demselben aus einer Quelle geschöpft sein, da Lk sich in der Bitte des Jüngers denselben nicht auf eine Thatsache beziehen lassen konnte, die er nicht erwähnt hat, und die der von ihm benutzten evang. [459] Ueberlieferung völlig fremd ist. Dagegen zeigt [Luke] 5,33, wie durchaus wahrscheinlich dieselbe ist. Dass jene Quelle aber keine andere ist als die von Mt benutzte, also Q, zeigen die wörtlichen Uebereinstimmungen mit ihm im UV. (vgl. das ἐπιούσ. V. 3), während alle Abweichungen sich aufs Einfachste als schriftstellerische Modifikationen des Lk erklären."

B. Weiß 1907, 71: "Es [the Our Father] muß also [since Matthew has moved it into the Sermon on the Mount secondarily] in Q, woher es beide Evangelisten entlehnen (bem. das in der ganzen Grazität nicht mehr vorkommende ἐπιούσιος), einen anderen Anlaß gehabt haben, und einen solchen bietet Lk. 11,1."

Müller 1908, 51: In a chart he assigns Luke 11:2-4 to Q.

B. Weiß 1908, 31: Reconstruction.

Stanton 1909: In Table II, (found at the end of the volume without page number) "THE MATTER COMMON TO ST MATTHEW AND ST LUKE WHICH IS NOT DERIVED FROM ST MARK," Stanton lists The Lord's Prayer in bold type followed by an asterisk. This marking designates his opinion thus, "When the corresponding pieces in St Matthew and St Luke appear to have been derived from the same written Greek record, the descriptive heading is printed in thick type. … But there are also cases where it is probable that the same Greek document has been used to a large extent, though there are differences which may seem at first sight to render it doubtful. Here, too, the headings are given in thick type, but an asterisk has been affixed."

Wellhausen 1911, 58: "Die hier aufgeführten Stücke [a list containing also Matt 6:9-13/Luke 11:2-4] sind öfters Reden und Erzählungen zugleich, und zuweilen überwiegt die Erzählung. … Sie stammen offenbar aus einer zusammenhängenden Quelle, die man mit Q bezeichnet."

Castor 1912, 53: "The use by both evangelists of the unintelligible word ἐπιούσιον can also be best explained as coming from a common source."

230: Reconstruction.

Haupt 1913, 85: "Die Notiz über die Johannesjünger, mit der die Quelle den Abschnitt einleitete, mußte bei Mt, der das Vaterunser in die Bergpredigt aufnahm, wegfallen."

von Dobschütz 1914, 299-300: "The Lord's Prayer need not have been drawn by either of the two evangelists from a written source, such as Q; one or both might have taken it from oral tradition. We have, however, one piece of evidence for a common Greek source in the unusual Greek word used to render the adjective qualifying 'bread.' *Epiousios* is not found elsewhere in extant Greek literature, and our limited knowledge is supplemented by the statement of an ancient scholar of the highest rank, Origen, who expressly says that *epiousios* here seemed to be a new word coined [300] on the analogy of *periousios*. In view of the variation in other words (such as 'debts' and 'sins') the agreement in this unique term is only to be explained, so far as I can see, by the use of a common Greek source, and hence we may infer that the Lord's Prayer stood in Q, or in some other Greek source used both by Matthew and Luke."

McNeile 1915, 100: In a note on the material in Matthew's Sermon on the Mount, McNeile comments on the material it has in common with material in Luke but which is not in the context of the Sermon on the Plain in Luke. Of these "scattered passages" he says, "This discourse [here McNeile means the material shared by Matthew's Sermon on the Mount and Luke's Sermon on the Plain] doubtless stood in Q, as also the scattered passages in §2." Matt 6:9-13 // Luke 11:2-4 is included in §2.

Patton 1915, 136: "This is one of the sections that points most clearly to different recensions of Q in the hands of Matthew and Luke."

Lagrange 1921, 321: "En tout cas il y a eu à l'origine un texte commun et en grec."

Easton 1926, 176: "As the position of this section [in Luke] is not determined by the preceding context, it doubtless owes its place here to the order of Q."

Montefiore 1927, 99: "The Lord's Prayer did not, we may presume, form part of the original Sermon. And vi. 6 was originally followed by vi. 16. But Matthew uses this opportunity to introduce the Prayer which he found in his source (Q)."

Bacon 1930, 182-183: "Part of the Q discourse on Prayer (Lk 11:1-13) had been incorporated by Mt in 6:9-15, omitting the [183] narrative introduction and the accompanying parable."

Hauck 1934, 4: "Bestand von Q ... Lk 11,1-13 Jüngergebet Mt 6,7-15; 7,7-11."

Hirsch 1941, 101: "Woher stammt aber Luk 11,1-4? Ich halte es für das Natürlichste, auch diese Verse Q (Lu I) zuzuweisen. Die Entsprechungen zu Luk 11,1-4. 9-11 bei Matth stehn beide in der Bergpredigt (Matth 6,9ff; 7,7ff); das Verfahren des Matth wird weniger verwickelt, wenn beide Stücke in seiner Vorlage miteinander zusammenhingen. Man braucht nur anzunehmen, daß Matth 6,7-15 eine Komposition des Matth sind, in der er das Vaterunser aus Q in leicht erweiterter Gestalt mit zwei Sprüchen aus MaS [Matthean Sondergut] verband."

Kilpatrick 1946, 20: "Of Matt 6.1-18, vv. 9-13 are from Q and 14f. from Mark."

Leaney 1956, 103 (=1958, 59): "it [the Lord's Prayer] could be safely assigned to Q, if we assume this common written source."

Grundmann 1961, 228: "Die Worte [Luke 11:1-13] entstammen z.T. SLk, z.T. Q."

Freudenberger 1968-69, 431: "Für die Logienquelle als gemeinsame griechische Quelle des Vaterunsers bei Matthäus und Lukas spricht in erster Linie das rätselhafte ἐπιούσιος der vierten Bitte, doch kommt dieses Wort immerhin auch in Did. viii. 2 vor. Eine Abhängigkeit der Didache aber von der Logienquelle oder gar von Matthäus ist durchaus fragwürdig. Dieser gewichtige Einwand langt m. E. nicht aus, das Vaterunser der Logienquelle abzusprechen, wie es z.B. Streeter tut."

Hoffmann 1972, 39-40: "Die Bitten des Vater-unsers (Lk 11,2-4/Mt 6,9-13) entsprechen—trotz zahlreicher Probleme in der Einzelinterpretation—mit [40] der Bitte um das Kommen des Reiches der Naherwartung, die wir für Q voraussetzen."

Talbert 1974, 54: "Luke 11:1-13 is comprised of two Q traditions (Luke 11:2-4 = Matt 6:9-13 and Luke 11:9-13 = Matt 7:7-11) which are in different positions in the two gospels, between which is placed an L pericope (11:5-8)."

Edwards 1975, 130-131: Edwards includes the Prayer in his concordance.

Edwards 1976, xii: The Lord's Prayer is included in the Guide to the Contents of Q.

107: Edwards discusses the Prayer as reflective of Q's eschatological themes on pages 107-108 "Whether the sentence 'Thy kingdom come' is an authentic statement of Jesus or not, it certainly reflects the hope of the Q community for God's action in the future."

108: "The background for the petition in verse 3 ('Give us each day our daily bread') appears to be a wisdom-like assumption that God does assist his people by means of the regularity of his creation. The request is possibly for God to continue to uphold the created order which has supplied food up to this point. However, in relation to the previous statement, it may be a request for aid in these last days until the Kingdom finally arrives.

"Verse 4a is more prophetic than wisdom-like: the act-consequence relationship is based on an understanding of God which is not founded on the ways of the world. The concept of forgiveness appears twice in Q, here and the statement about forgiveness being available for those who sin against the Holy Spirit (#25 [Matt 12:31-32 // Luke 12:10]). The context for both these sayings is eschatological, the last days which are upon the community."

Schneider 1977, 256: "Beide Evangelisten denken nicht an eine von Jesus eingeschärfte Verpflichtung zum Gebet, sondern (mit Q) an die besondere *Weise* des Betens, die sich freilich in den Gegenständen der Gebetsbitten ausdrückt (vgl. Mt 6,9: *So* sollt ihr beten; Lk V 1: *Wenn* ihr betet, so sprecht…).”

Zeller 1977, 191: “Man kann … daran gehen, Q *vorgegebene Logienkomplexe* zu erschließen, die möglicherweise ihren eigenen 'Sitz im Leben' hatten. Darunter sind 6 größere Spruchgruppen, die um einen Kern von Mahnungen herumgewachsen sein dürften; sie richten sich offenbar nicht an Außenstehende, sondern an Bekenner Jesu. …

“III Gebet: (Lk 11,2-4?) Mt 7,7-11.”

Feldkämper 1978, 182: “Das Material dieses Abschnittes findet sich zu einem Teil auch bei Mattäus (11,2b-4 par Mt 6,9-13; 11,9-13 par Mt 7,7-11), dürfte also der Logienquelle entstammen.”

Marshall 1978, 455: “we do not have here simply two editorial modifications of the Q version of the prayer. More probably, Matthew has substituted the form of the prayer familiar to him for that which he found in Q. But did Luke's form come from Q, (with editorial modification)? Other variations from Q in the context (such as the inclusion of 11:5-8, peculiar to Lk., and the marked differences in wording between 11:11-13 and Mt. 7:9-11) have suggested that Luke is not here dependent on Q …, but on the whole it is probable that Luke has drawn this section, including the prayer, from Q, or rather from a recension of Q which may have differed in wording from that used by Mt. (It may be that Matthew's form of the prayer had already been incorporated in the recension of Q used in his church and available to him.)”

Schmithals 1980, 130: “Die uns geläufigere Form des 'Vater-Unser' findet sich Mat. 6,9-13; sie wurde gegenüber der Vorlage in der Spruchquelle Q, die Lukas in V. 2-4 im wesentlichen festgehalten hat, erst von Matthäus in die vorliegende Form gebracht. Q enthielt ein ursprünglich stark eschatologisch ausgerichtetes Gebetsformular, dessen einzelne Bitten auch in jüdischen Gebeten aus der Zeit Jesu begegnen.”

Schenk 1981, 61: Reconstruction.

Schweizer 1982, 125: “Der Q-Stoff [Luke 11] V.2-4 und das etwas veränderte Gleichnis V.9-13 sind in V.5-8 vorlukanisch mit einem weiteren Gleichnis aufgefüllt worden, das V.9f. gut illustriert.”

Schweizer 1982, ET 1984, 190: “The Q material in vss. 2-4 and the somewhat modified parable in vss. 9-13 were supplemented before Luke by the addition of vss. 5-8, a further parable providing a good illustration for vss. 9-10.”

Zeller 1984, 56: Reconstruction.

Fitzmyer 1985, 897: “Matthew and Luke have both derived their prayer from 'Q.'”

Lambrecht 1985, 133: “The text [of the Lord's Prayer] that emerges from this discussion is both pre-Matthean and pre-Lucan and may presumably be considered the source text for both Matthew and Luke. Some authors, however, point out that one must take into account a long liturgical tradition with a text such as the Lord's Prayer, and that the two versions in Mt and Lk would be the written offshoots of that tradition. This is why, they say, it is risky to consider both the expansions of Matthew and the wording changes of Luke as interventions to be ascribed to the evangelists themselves. Nevertheless, I think that these scholars too easily underestimate the redactional work that has taken place, and particularly how much was done by Luke."

Gnilka 1986, 214: "Um eine sichere Ausgangsbasis zu gewinnen, gehen wir von der Feststellung aus, daß Mt und Lk eine gemeinsame Vaterunser-Überlieferung zugrundeliegt (vermutlich in Q), die ihnen bereits in griechischer Sprache vorlag."

Kloppenborg 1987, 203: "Q 11:2-4, 9-13 comprises a short instruction on prayer."

205: "This instruction coheres with other parts of Q. Formally, it employs the typical sapiential admonition with a motive clause (cf. 6:27-28, 32-33; 6:37-38; 6:42, 43-44). Like 6:27-35, it portrays God as a generous patron, and as in 12:4-7, 22-31 it counsels the members of the community to rely completely upon God for provision of their daily needs. In both the prayer and 6:27-35 there is an assumed correspondence between the actions of God and those of Jesus' followers: generosity and forgiveness are marks both of God and of the children of God. The invocation of God as πάτερ in the prayer finds a counterpart in 6:27-35 which represents discipleship as *imitatio Dei* leading to divine sonship. It may be added as well that an ecclesial rather than a missionary Sitz of 11:2-4, 9-13 is the more probable. Thus it belongs to the same sphere of interests and applications as the inaugural sermon (6:20b-49) and to the expanded version of the discipleship 'speech' (9:57-62 + 10:2-11, 16).

"For our purposes it is sufficient to observe that 11:2-4, 9-13 is a composition from smaller units with a preponderance of sapiential logic and idiom, and functioning as an instruction on prayer. In its form, motif and style it coheres with other sapiential portions of Q."

Davies and Allison 1988, 591: Reconstruction.

591: "Both Mt 6.9-13 and Lk 11.2-4 are from Q. On this supposition, the differences between the two texts are to be ascribed to the redactional tendencies of the two evangelists. The advantage of this hypothesis is that, as we shall see, no objection can be raised on the basis of word statistics or stylistic considerations. Indeed, such phrases as 'Our Father who art in heaven' and 'on earth as it is in heaven', phrases which appear in Matthew but not in Luke, contain distinctively Matthean vocabulary. Furthermore, where the Matthean version is deemed by most scholars to be original, as in having the aorist tense in vv. 11 (δός) and 12 (ἄφες), the secondary character of the Lukan version can without difficulty be attributed to the third evangelist's editorial activity."

Sato 1988, 39: "Daß diese Spruchgruppe [Q 11:2-4, 9-13] in Q tatsächlich hier stand, ist wegen der übereinstimmenden Reihenfolge Lk 11,2-4.9-13; 11,14-23/Mt 6,9-13; 7,7-11; 12,22-30 wahrscheinlich."

Sato 1988, ET 1994, 171: "That this sayings cluster [Q 11:2-4, 9-13] in fact stood at this position in Q is made probable by the agreement in order between Luke 11:2-4, 9-13, 14-23 and Matt 6:9-13; 7:7-11; 12:22-30."

Taussig 1988, 25: "The so-called Lord's Prayer texts in Matt 6:9-13 and Luke 11:2-4 have indicators of very early origins. The two major indicators are its existence in Q (along with a subsidiary witness in the Didache) and the likely use of the Aramaic word 'abba.'"

25: Reconstruction.

Wiefel 1988, 215: "Die Kurzfassung des Lukas beruht nicht auf Kürzung, kann vielmehr nach Struktur und Aufbau als die ältere Gestalt gelten. Lukas dürfte sie in Q vorgefunden haben."

International Q Project 1990, 500: Reconstruction.

Kloppenborg 1990, 49: Reconstruction.

Koester 1990, 144: "there are a number of wisdom sayings which, in themselves, have no polemical intent (Q 11:27-28, 33, 34-36 = *Gos. Thom.* 79, 33b, 24). They may have been part of the original version of Q. The same can be assumed for the Lord's Prayer and for the community rule about asking and praying (Q 11:2-4, 9-13)."

Patterson 1993, 95: In a chart he assigns Lk 11:1-4 to Q.

Catchpole 1993, 28: "The Lord's Prayer. Matt 6:9-13/Q 11:2-4."

Mack 1993, 76: Mack includes the Prayer in his reconstruction of the original book of Q, the first layer of the tradition.

Nolland 1993, 611: "The degree of exact agreement in the Greek, especially with the shared use of the difficult term ἐπιούσιος ... counts in favor of a single translation into Greek as ultimately behind the two forms of the prayer." However, Nolland does not think Matthew and Luke drew on a common source for the Prayer. See Q 11:~~1-2a,~~2b-4⁰ Luke and Matthew = Q, Con.

Betz 1995, 349: "SM/Matt 6:7-15 clearly points to an original author different from the one who first conceived [Matt] 6:1-6, 16-18. ... While this author is responsible for the didactic part (6:7-8), the authoritative example of the Lord's Prayer is attributed to Jesus himself (6:9b-13). The addition of the eschatological-legal rule of 6:14-15 shows how the petition of 6:12 is to be implemented in the life of the community. This author was a member of the Jesus-movement who contributed the piece and thereby showed what he had learned from his master." Betz himself does not attribute the Prayer to the member of the Jesus-movement who is mentioned in the citation. His comment is included here to record Betz's view that Matt 6:7-15 is at least attributable to a source other than that of what he calls a Cult *Didache*. See Q 11:~~1-2a,~~2b-4⁰ Luke and Matthew = Q, Con.

Meadors 1995, 180-181: "The Lord's prayer advances our argument that Q contains fragments of tradition which describe Jesus' intent to gather the people of God for the eschatological day of salvation. In coherence with other Q passages,[156] the Lord's Prayer confirms [181] that Jesus in Q is more than a prophet."

180-181[156]: "The hypothesis of a Q original behind Mt. 6:9-13 and Lk. 11:2-4 is by no means problemless despite the vast number of scholars who judge the parallels between the two versions to be evidence of a Q *Vorlage* (See Kloppenborg, *Q-Parallels*, 84). Differences in wording and length prohibit certain proclamation of original form. Caution is appropriate despite attempts to see the differences in length as Matthew's expansion and the differences in tense and vocabulary as alternations typical of Luke's style. Jeremias originally resisted the redactional approach by citing the unlikelihood that the Gospel writers would have altered a sacred liturgical prayer well known to the intended audiences. To this warning, E. Lohmeyer adds that both versions of the prayer contain poetic structures—a fact that 'serves as a warning against any assumption that one form arose from the other as a result of abbreviation of expansion', (*The Lord's Prayer*, London: [181] Collins [1965] 30). Furthermore, word counts which often form the basis for ascribing a word or phrase to secondary redaction could be misleading in the case of the Lord's Prayer as the Evangelists could have adopted a form of speech from a known dominical teaching like the Lord's Prayer and subsequently repeated the usage elsewhere as characteristic of Jesus. Yet, despite the significant differences, a common Greek source seems probable in light of the parallels especially in regard to ἐπιούσιος—a word extremely rare in Greek literature but exactly parallel in the two versions of Jesus' prayer. If we seek a common source, Matthean priority falters on the fact that there are no Mattheanisms in Luke's prayer. In fact the petitions most characteristic of Matthew are absent from Luke. The expansion of the Lord's Prayer seems more likely than its reduction in light of known tendencies in later transmissions of Greek texts. Do we concede the prayer's background to Q? We hesitate. U. Luz has detected reminiscences of Matthew's version in Mk. 11:25 and 2 Ti. 4:18 and with less certainty Mk. 14:36, 38; Jn. 12:28; 17:15 (*Matthäus* I, 335). This evidence suggests that Matthew's greater length does not require redaction on the on the part of the first Evangelist, but rather the language may attest to the prayer as it existed at a very early stage." Square brackets around [1965] are Meadors' own.

Con

Wellhausen 1905, 67: "Nach inneren Merkmalen erscheint die Feldpredigt bei Lukas im Ganzen originaler als die Bergpredigt bei Matthäus; seine Disposition liegt auch bei jenem zu Grunde, sein Ton und seine Sprache ist durchweg frischer, gedrungener und volkstümlicher, weniger geistlich und biblisch. Beim Vaterunser ist das Verhältnis ähnlich; jedoch kann man zweifeln, ob es zu Q gehört."

Meyer 1921, 220: "Die Fassung des Gebets weicht von der bei Matthaeus in der Bergpredigt 6,9 ff. gegebenen so stark ab, daß sie unmöglich aus der gleichen Quelle stammen kann; auch ist sie bei Lukas von dem Anlaß und der Zurückführung auf den Vorgang des Johannes, die unmöglich in Q gestanden haben können, nicht zu trennen."

Streeter 1924, 277: "Now, even if we accept the reading of B, the difference between the two versions of the Lord's Prayer, Lk xi. 1-4 and Mt. vi. 9-13, is so great as to put a considerable strain on the theory that they were both derived from the same written source. But if we accept the reading of 700 (i.e. Lk xi.2d ἐλθέτω τὸ πνεῦμα ... ἐφ' ἡμᾶς) and its supporters, that theory becomes quite impossible.[1] We next notice that in neither Matthew nor Luke are the sayings in the immediate context derived from Q; the Lord's Prayer in Matthew is in the middle of a block of M, in Luke in the middle of a section of L material. The natural inference is that the respective versions belong to these two sources."

277[1]: "The rare word ἐπιούσιος remains as a remarkable point of contact between the two versions. I think it not impossible that its presence in Luke is due to an assimilation to Matthew which has infected all our authorities."

Crum 1927, 114: "The Unworldliness Passages begin at [Luke] chapter xi.
"But the prelude to the passage is x. 38-42, the story of Mary and Martha, the examples of unworldliness and anxious-mindedness.
"A kindred subject connects itself with the group, the subject of Prayer (xi. 1-13). There is an editorial introduction and the Lord's Prayer is introduced, whether from Q or elsewhere." Although this comment suggests that Crum admits of the possibility of the presence of the Prayer in Q, the comment is included in the arguments against its presence in Q because in his "conjectural reconstruction of Q" Crum does not include the prayer either in connection with Matt 6:1-6, 16-18 which he considers to be from Q (pp. 134-135) nor in connection with Luke 11:9-13 which he includes in Q with another collection of Q material he groups under the heading "Sayings, Of Unworldliness" (pp. 149-153).

Manson 1937, 167: "Another version of this prayer [Matt 6:9-13] appears in Lk. 11:2-4, which is probably to be assigned to L."

265: "The Lucan version [of the Lord's Prayer], which we assign to L, is shorter and differs from Mt. in several particulars."

Hunter 1950, 185, 209: Hunter assigns the Matthean and Lucan versions of the prayer to M and L respectively.

Knox 1957, 25: "Again Matthew has expanded his source, adding at vi. 7 a saying from his anti-Gentile collection, and following it with the Lord's prayer, derived from current liturgical tradition and practice."

26¹: "The position in which it [the Lord's Prayer] appears in Luke seems to show that it is one of a miscellaneous collection of sayings and incidents …; the introduction of Luke xi.1 looks quite artificial. Hence there is no necessary reason to suppose that Matthew and Luke derive it from the same source since the manuscript evidence for the omission of 'Thy will be done, as in heaven, so on earth' and 'But deliver us from evil' in Luke is strong; while the tendency to assimilation would be overwhelming, we have every reason to suppose that Matthew and Luke are here independent."

Evans 1963, 9-10: "if both versions are shown to be poems in their own right, each with its own distinctive structure and rhythm, it becomes more difficult to account for them in this way, and to account for the differences between them as variations of a common version in a written source. For it is [10] unlikely that alterations here and there to a poem will produce another poem. Hence the form critic will be inclined to suppose that the two versions came to Matthew and Luke independently of any written source, that each came along its own line of spoken tradition, perhaps through its use in the particular church each will have developed its own rhythmic pattern."

Schwarz 1968-69, 233: "Der verschiedene Inhalt dieser beiden Gebetslehren ist darin begründet, daß sie je für verschiedene Gemeinden bestimmt waren: die matthäische für judenchristliche, die lukanische für heidenchristliche Gemeinden; wobei der unterschiedliche Wortlaut der beiden Vater-Unser-Fassungen sich daraus erklärt, daß jeder der beiden Evangelisten den Text des Vater-Unsers *so* überliefert, wie er zu seiner Zeit in seinen Gemeinden gebetet wurde.

"Dieser Befund macht dreierlei deutlich; erstens: daß jene urchristlichen Gemeinden das Vater-Unser nicht geschaffen, sondern empfangen haben; zweitens: daß keine der beiden Fassungen durch Verkürzung oder Erweiterung aus der anderen entstanden ist; drittens: daß beide Fassungen Ausprägungen (hier verkürzt, dort erweitert) ein und derselben aramäischen Urfassung sind, die dann—der Schluß ist zwingend—direkt auf Jesus selbst zurückgehen muß."

Jeremias 1971, 189: "Was die Abweichungen der bei Matthäus und bei Lukas erhaltenen Fassungen angeht, so ist unser Ergebnis, daß sie nicht auf Eingriffe der Evangelisten (und überhaupt nicht auf individuelle Abänderung) zurückgehen, sondern daß wir die Fassungen zweier verschiedener Kirchen vor uns haben."

Jeremias 1971, ET 1971, 195: "The result that follows from this is that the deviations in the versions preserved in Matthew and Luke are not the result of the interference of the evangelists (and not at all the result of individual alterations). Rather, we have here the versions used in two different churches."

Shelton 1982, 379-381: "Given the Semitic character of the structure and [380] vocabulary of both versions, the variation in Luke from the word, ἁμαρτίας, to ὀφείλοντι in v. 4 while Matthew has ὀφείλημα twice is probably due to two different versions arising from two different translations from Aramaic; and therefore Luke probably is not responsible for the variation here unless he is translating it himself. It is unlikely that Luke is the translator since 'we appear [381] to have variant forms of a Greek prayer in the Gospels, since the parallelism in wording is so close.'[43] Thus it would seem that two separate traditions would be the best solution."

381[43]: "Marshall [1978; see 11:1-2a,2b-4⁰ Pro], Luke, p. 455."

Schnackenburg 1984, 95: "Beide Evangelisten haben nämlich das Vaterunser schon vorgefunden und in ihren jeweiligen Zusammenhang nur eingefügt. Wo fanden sie es vor? Sicherlich im liturgischen Leben und in der Gebetspraxis ihrer Gemeinden."

Schnackenburg 1984, ET 1995, 62: "Both evangelists came upon the Lord's Prayer and only inserted it into their respective contexts. Where did they come upon it? Surely in the liturgical and prayer life of their communities. That also explains their different wording of the text."

Davies and Allison 1988, 591: "There is, however, a drawback to thinking that both Mt 6.9-13 and Lk 11.2-4 come from Q: many scholars find it reasonable to assume that when the evangelists came to the Lord's Prayer, a known liturgical piece, they would have reproduced the version known and used in their own church services."

Evans 1990, 476: "The evangelists might have derived it [the Prayer] from Q, Matthew's version being an expanded form of the shorter form in Luke. But this is not necessary. Each could be giving the version with which he was familiar in his church."

Hagner 1993, 145: "Because this prayer is such an important piece of liturgical tradition, it is unnecessary to argue for common dependence upon Q to explain the common material. Quite probably the prayer was handed down in slightly differing versions in churches of different geographical regions. Thus Matthew and Luke may well have received it independently from different sources, despite both the agreements and disagreements."

Nolland 1993, 610: "it is unlikely that Luke and Matthew drew on a common literary source for the Lord's Prayer or its setting."

O'Neill 1993, 5: "I wish to argue, then, that the 'prayer' in Mt. 6.9-13 and *Did.* 8.2, and the 'prayer' in Lk. 11.2-4 are both collections of prayers of Jesus. Each collection is too varied ever to have been spoken in prayer by Jesus on any one occasion when he had concluded the set daily prayers. Most of these prayers were collected by the disciples as they heard their master conclude his prayers."

Meier 1994, 357-358: "One could question in what sense the Lord's Prayer should be said to belong to the Q material. If Q is defined broadly as whatever Matthew and Luke have in common that is not derived from Mark, obviously the Lord's Prayer is Q material. If, however, [358] one is thinking more specifically of one written document, one must allow for a number of possibilities. (1) The Lord's Prayer was in the copies of Q known to both Matthew and Luke, and each evangelist faithfully copied the form contained in his copy of the Q document, with at most a few redactional changes. [Meier refers to Polag 1977, Hoffmann 1972, and Schulz 1972] Perhaps some Q-critics pass over the Our Father in relative silence because they feel unsure about its presence in Q. All this leads us to a consideration of two other possibilities. (2) Some form of the Lord's Prayer was contained in each evangelist's copy of Q; but each evangelist, when he came to write down the Lord's Prayer in his own Gospel, naturally wrote the form of the prayer he regularly recited, however much it may have diverged from the form written in Q. (3) The Lord's Prayer was not contained at all in the Q documents; rather, it was known to both Matthew and Luke through independent oral traditions, communicated especially by the liturgical praxis of their local churches. Naturally, some of these possibilities could be combined or nuanced further: e.g., a written version in Q, modified at points by the evangelist because the liturgical praxis of his church, Q material already conflated with the special M or L material, etc."

Betz 1995, 335: "In the New Testament itself, the cultic instruction of [Matt] 6:1-18 has no parallels and is simply unique. While Q has no parallel even to any of its main sections, 6:7-13 at least has a parallel in Luke 11:1-4, while for the rule in Matt 6:14-15 parallel references exist in Mark 11:25-26; Matt 16:19; 18:18; and John 20:23. I should underscore that the entire cultic instruction of Matt 6:1-18, being Jewish, has no counterpart in the SP [Sermon on the Plain]."

349: "The Lord's Prayer ([Matt] 6:9b-13) comes from the historical Jesus himself. I can say this with confidence because of the multiple attestation of the prayer in Matt 6:9b-13; Luke 11:1-4; *Did.* 8.2, sources independently attributing the Lord's Prayer to Jesus."

370: "One can say, therefore, that the doctrinal frame of the SM [Sermon on the Mount], in which the Lord's Prayer is set [Matt 6:7-8], is secondary with regard to the prayer and its performance in the community. The doctrine is set forth only now, while the prayer was performed earlier. This leads me to conclude that the Lord's Prayer must have preceded the formulation of the SM; it preceded as an oral text."

370: "Liturgical material such as this type of prayer derives, when it is written down, from oral tradition. It is characteristic of liturgical material in general that textual fixation occurs at a later stage in the transmission of these texts, while in the oral stage variability within limits is the rule. These characteristics also apply to the Lord's Prayer. The three recensions, therefore, represent variations of the prayer in the oral tradition. When they were written down, these variant forms of the prayer became textually fixed. As a result I can state that there was never only *one original written* Lord's Prayer. The somewhat fluid state of the textual tradition, which one can observe in the critical apparatus of the editions of the New Testament as well as the church fathers, means that the oral tradition continued to exert an influence on the written text of the New Testament well into later times." Betz goes on to comment that even attempts to standardize the prayer in present day churches have not succeeded. He concludes that this present situation is indicative of the nature and function of oral texts.

371: "If the Lord's Prayer was part of Q, it must have become a part of it after the two versions of Q developed: Q/Matt received its prayer together with the SM, while Q/Luke received its version of the Lord's Prayer not as part of the SP but together with another instruction on prayer (Luke 11:2-13). ... The differences among the three recensions [Matt 6:9b-13; Luke 11:2b-4; *Did.* 8.2] point to an independent transmission prior to the fixations in writing, so that I do not assume that any one of them is *textually* dependent on another."

Evaluations

Carruth 1995: Luke and Matthew = Q {A}.

A number of scholars simply presume the presence of the Prayer in Q as can be seen from the data below on the position variant. Those who give reasons for its presence in Q most frequently offer as reasons the shared vocabulary and structure, the shared single-occurrence word ἐπιούσιος, and the fact that the Prayer is closely associated with Q's other material on Prayer, Q 10:21-22 and Q 11:9-13. In addition to this thematic association with prayer material, Koester also associates it with Q's sapiential character and notes its lack of polemic. Kloppenborg's demonstration of the coherence of the Prayer with other Q material is confirming evidence for the presence of the Prayer in Q.

Claims that the respective formulations of the Prayer derive from liturgical usage or from a prayer given by the historical Jesus rather than from a common written source do not of themselves preclude the possibility that Q included a written version of the Prayer. The close similarity of wording and structure of the prayer in Matthew and Luke allows the variations to be easily explained on the basis of the redactional activity of the evangelists

Robinson 1995: Luke and Matthew = Q {A}.

The shared structure and wording, as becomes clear in the subsequent analysis, indicate that one has to do with the same prayer in both Matthew and Luke.

The uncritical assumption has long since been abandoned that fluctuations in the wording and/or occasion of sayings in different Gospels indicate different occasions in the life of Jesus and hence different sources.

It is to be conceded that the Lord's Prayer seems to have been used in communal worship, and in this sense could have come to Matthew and Luke through oral tradition apart from Q. Jesus' own prayer life, emphasized especially by Luke (3:21; 5:16; 6:12; 9:18; 9:28-29, all redactional), provides here the redactional occasion (Luke 11:1a). But already the redactional request of his disciples to teach them to pray as John taught his disciples (similar to the Lucan redaction in Luke 5:33) envisages not a private prayer life but a prayer to be shared by a given community. The answer to the disciples' request is not in terms of technique, such as the Cult Didache offers (Matt 6:1, 2-4 [On Almsgiving], 5-6 [On Prayer], 16-18 [On Fasting]). Nor is it like the negative response to *Gos. Thom.* 6a ("In what way shall we pray?"), answered in *Gos. Thom.* 14a ("If you pray, you will be condemned."). Rather the answer, in terms of the prescribed wording of a prayer, indicates that the Lord's Prayer was understood as something to be recited, presumably in a shared way within the group. Given the prominence in it of bread, it could even have functioned as a Jewish mealtime prayer. Or it could be part of the evolution of the Kaddish (in whatever early form it may have existed at the time).

The preceding injunction in the Cult Didache not to pray in synagogues and the corners of the plaza, but rather in the privacy of a closet with the door shut, does not appear to have been originally composed in relation to the Lord's Prayer. Indeed a reason for ascribing the Prayer to Q rather than to M is that it does not fit into the context of the Cult Didache with which it has been secondarily merged. Matt 6:7 introduces the Lord's Prayer not as private prayer, but, by contrasting it to the babbling garrulousness ascribed to Gentile prayer, as something public enough that others might overhear.

The secondary doxology to the Matthean text appended in late manuscripts and also attested in *Did.* 8,2 indicates a continuing use in communal worship.

The communal usage continuing even today makes the Lord's Prayer one of the most obvious instances of sayings of Jesus having been remembered by means of their *Sitz im Leben*. But form criticism has shown that this was quite typical of the way sayings of Jesus were transmitted, without thereby eliminating the assumption of a written Greek Q. Thus the questioning as to whether the Prayer was in Q at all by Streeter (see Q 11:1,2a,2b-4⁰, Con), who did not think in terms of form criticism, was heeded only by a relatively few scholars, especially those who were more directly under his influence.

Even Streeter thought the Prayer's inclusion in Q would be "quite impossible" only on the basis of textual criticism. But his appeal to a relatively weak textual variant that would separate the Lukan wording still further from that of Matthew and thus weaken the probability of a shared source has not been followed by textual critics. His further suggestion that the unique term ἐπιού-σιος, present in both Gospels, indicating a shared written Greek source, could be removed from Luke on the grounds that it was a textual corruption derived from Matthew, is a conjectural emendation that has also not found support.

The Lord's Prayer (Q 11:2b-4) and its Interpretation (Q 11:9-13) are in Matthew in the same sequence as in Luke, though in Matthew they are held still further apart (Matt 6:9b-13 and Matt 7:7-11), largely as the result of other intervening interpolations into the Sermon on the Mount. Although the Cult Didache is not from Q, most of these other interpolations are. Thus the Prayer is in a (secondary) Q context in Matthew as well as in Luke.

The assumption that the Matthean and Lucan communities have influenced the wording has often taken the form of assuming that glosses derived from each community's usage had already worked their way into the copies the Evangelists used (Q^Matt and Q^Luke). Thus the very probable use of the Prayer by the Evangelists' respective communities can be well coordinated with the assumption that the Prayer was in Q.

Q 11:~~1-2a,~~2b-4[1]: Position of the Prayer in Q.

Luke = Q: After Q 10:24, before Q 11:9.

Pro

Holtzmann 1863, 148: "Zunächst liefert er [Luke] 10,25-37 eine Perikope, die er offenbar aus zwei ursprünglich ohne inneren Zusammenhang in Λ [Q] neben einander stehenden Abschnitten combinirt hat. Es folgt nämlich nun Lc. 25-28 die Erzählung von νομικός, die schon um ihrer Berücksichtigung bei Mt. 22,35 willen in Λ gestanden hat. Auch das folgende Gleichniss vom Samariter Lc. 30-35 ist ganz im Charakter der übrigen Parabeln aus Λ gehalten und fügt sich in dieser Quelle nur vermöge einer äusseren Ideenassociation—gleichsam ad vocem πλησίον—an. Obwohl es an sich nichts weniger, als eine illustrirte Definition des Begriffes πλησίον ist, hat doch Lucas durch die Verse 29.36.37 eine solche daraus machen wollen. ...—Noch einmal anknüpfend an den Täufer erscheint hierauf 11,1 eine kurze Überschrift, die Veranlassung zur Mittheilung des Mustergebets 2-4 = Mt. 6,9-13 wird, woran sich einige andere Reden Jesu über das Gebet Lc. 11,5-8.9-13 = Mt 7,7-11 anreihen. Lucas hat dieselben 5 mit καὶ εἶπεν πρὸς αὐτούς arrangirt."

B. Weiß 1876, 181: "Da es ganz undenkbar ist, daß Jesus dasselbe Mustergebet einmal bei besondrer Veranlassung (Luc. 11,1-4) und einmal ohne eine solche in der Bergrede gegeben haben sollte (vgl. noch Thol. Myr.) und da wir bereits sahen, daß die hier gegebene Einleitung v. 7.8 den geschlossenen Zusammenhang der letzteren zerreißt, so kann nur Luc. den richtigen Anlaß aus der apostol. Quelle, der er auch sonst nachweislich Cp. 11 folgt, erhalten haben."

Plummer 1896, 293: "But if the Prayer was delivered only once, then it is Lk. rather than Mt. who gives the historic occasion. ... Lk. would not invent this special incident."

B. Weiß 1901, 459: "Lk folgt also dem Faden von Q [11:1-4 follows upon 10:25-28], der ganz verschiedene Redestücke, die zeitlich in gar keiner Verbindung stehen und ganz verschiedene Situationen voraussetzen, zusammenreihte."

Loisy 1907, 598: "Rien ne s'oppose à ce que l'Oraison dominicale, la parabole de l'Ami importun [Luke 11:5-8] et celle de la Veuve [Luke 18:2-8], l'exhortation à une prière confiante aient été réunies ensemble dans la première rédaction du discours du Seigneur, de façon à former un recueil d'enseignements sur la prière."

B. Weiß 1907, 71: "Es [the Our Father] muß also in Q, woher es beide Evangelisten entlehnen, ... einen anderen Anlaß [than the Sermon on the Mount] gehabt haben, und einen solchen bietet Lk.11,1."

288: Regarding the Mission speech B. Weiß says, "zu ihnen [to the conversations with the returning disciples in Lk 10:17-24] werden auch die Verhandlungen über das Beten (11,1-13) gehört haben, die Matthäus in die Bergrede verflocht und die also in Q sich ebenfalls an die Aussendungsrede anschlossen. ...."

Müller 1908, 28: "Die Vorannahme war: Lk hat die formelle Treue der Textordnung von Q gewahrt. Bis jetzt konnte dafür geltend gemacht werden, daß er es an der Mk-Vorlage tut, ferner daß er nicht nur in 6,20-7,35 eine geschlossene Folge von Q hat, sondern sich ebenfalls in 9,57-13,30 alle Einschübe als solche in Q erweisen."

30: Müller's synopsis of Q shows Q 11:2-4 after Q 10:24.

B. Weiß 1908, 31: Reconstruction.

Castor 1912, 230: Reconstruction.

Lagrange 1921, 320: "Luc a une introduction qui lui est propre. C'est un des disciples qui demande à Jésus de leur apprendre à prier, comme Jean a fait pour ses disciples. Ce trait est respecté par la critique comme authentique. Et cela dispose bien en faveur du temps marqué par Lc."

Abrahams 1924, 101: "Though there are phrases in Matthew which make one inclined to prefer his version of the Lord's Prayer, it is generally felt Luke places it in a more natural setting."

Marriott 1925, 66: "the Lucan context is supported by (a) the fact that in Luke the Prayer is represented as having been given in response to a request by one of Christ's disciples on a particular occasion. It seems probable that in Q the Prayer stood with an introduction as in Lk. 11,1-4."

Easton 1926, 176: "As the position of this section [in Luke] is not determined by the preceding context, it doubtless owes its place here to the order of Q."

Jacobson 1978, 215: "The location of Lk 11:2-4/Mt 6:9-13 and Lk 11:9-13/Mt 7:7-11 within Q is difficult to establish because Luke and Matthew disagree on the location of both pericopes. However, there are a number of catchwords which not only link the two pericopes internally but provide links to the material which, in Luke, stands before and after the two pericopes. ... there is an abundance of catchwords, especially linking Lk 10:21f par; Lk 11:2-4 par and Lk 11:9-13par. There are a few catchword connections to Lk 11:14ff par but the catchwords are fewer and limited largely to 'every' and 'kingdom.'"

216: Jacobson's chart lists the following catchwords: πατήρ, υἱός, δίδωμι, πᾶς, βασιλεία, ἄρτος, οὐρανός.

Vassiliadis 1978, 71: "The sequence in which the Q sections of the Double Tradition occurred in the original Q-document is the one found in Luke."

Polag 1979, 48: Reconstruction.

Schenk 1981, 61: Reconstruction.

Crossan 1983, 97: "Q enshrined the two prayers of Q/Matt. 11:25-26 = Luke 10:21 and Q/Matt. 6:9-13 = Luke 11:2-4 within a series of Aphorisms 62-68. Aphorisms 67-68 are both a commentary on the Lord's Prayer and an appropriate conclusion for this later Q Wisdom theology."

343: In Appendix 2 Crossan lists these Aphorisms in the order he presumes for Q: Aphorism 62: Matt. 11:27 = Luke 10:22, Aphorism 63: Matt. 13:16-17 = Luke 10:23-24, Aphorism 64: Matt. 11:28-30, [Aphorism 65:] The Lord's Prayer: Matt. 6:9-13 = Luke 11:2-4, Aphorism 66: Matt. 7:6, Aphorism 67: Matt. 7:7-8 = Luke 11:9-10, Aphorism 68: Matt. 7:9-11 = Luke 11:11-13.

Zeller 1984, 56: Reconstruction.

Schmithals 1985, 220: "Folgt man im übrigen [where the sequence of Matthew and Luke do not agree] der Reihenfolge des Q-Stoffes im LkEv, sofern nicht Gründe eine Umstellung nahelegen, so erhält man folgende Reihenfolge in Q, die im einzelnen eine mehr oder weniger große Sicherheit bzw. Wahrscheinlichkeit für sich hat." In the list which Schmithals then gives, 11:1-4 follows 10:24 and is followed by 11:9.

Kloppenborg 1987, 203: "As the Lucan context shows, the prayer has been connected with a cluster of sayings on prayer."

205: "Although a reconstruction of the stages of growth of Q 11:9-13 must remain subjective, it is clear that the association of 11:2-4 with the following cluster of sayings presupposes that 11:9-10 (which contains no obvious reference to prayer) was already attached to 11:11-13. The connection of the prayer (11:2-4) with 11:9-13 is perhaps not simply a matter of common theme, but dependent also upon the catchwords (ἐπι)δίδωμι and ἄρτος and upon the common motif of God's provision of material needs."

206: See Q 11:~~1-2a~~,2b-4[0] Luke and Matthew = Q, Pro.

Crossan 1988, 127: "One can be relatively certain that the Q context extends to Q/Luke 11:2-4, 9-13 = Q/Matt 6:9-13; 7:7-11."

Tannehill 1988, 141-142: "Crossan [1988; see above] believes that the context of the aphorism [Q 11:9-10] in Q is preserved in Luke 11:2-4, 9-13. ... If this is so, the aphorism *Ask, Seek, Knock* immediately followed the Lord's Prayer in Q. This is not the only indication of a connection between this aphorism and the Lord's Prayer. Crossan asserts that Mark 11:24 is another version of the aphorism, to which the evangelist has added references to faith and prayer. We should [142] note that Mark 11:24 is immediately followed by an indication of the kind of petition to which a favorable answer is promised: 'Whenever you stand praying, forgive if you have anything against someone, in order that your Father in the heavens might also forgive you your trespasses.' This is a hortatory version of the prayer for forgiveness in the Lord's Prayer, and its relation to 11:24 suggests that forgiveness is one of the most important things one should ask for. The connection of 11:25 with the Lord's Prayer is indicated not only by the tie between forgiving others and being forgiven but also by the reference to God as the disciples' father, which is rare in Mark (this is the only clear instance). Matt 6:14-15, an instruction that comes directly after the Lord's Prayer and resembles Mark 11:25, also supports the connection of the Markan verse with this prayer."

International Q Project 1990, 500: Reconstruction.

Kloppenborg 1990, 49: Reconstruction.

Koester 1990, 168-169: In a chart demonstrating "how sayings in the Sermon on the Mount from other contexts of Q are interwoven with those which come from the inaugural sermon of Q 6:20-49," Koester lists Q 11:2-4 as one of the sayings from another context in Q. See p. 327 for a similar chart.

Jacobson 1992, 153: "The location of Q 11:2-4 and Q 11:9-13 is difficult to establish because Luke and Matthew disagree on the location of both pericopes. However, there are a number of catchwords, which not only link the two pericopes internally but also provide links to material which, in Luke, stands before and after the two pericopes. These catchwords are: 'father' (πατήρ): 10:21 (twice), 22 (twice); 11:2, (11), 13; 'son' (υἱός): Q 10:22 (twice); 11:11, 19; cf. 'babe' (νήπιος) in Q 10:21 and 'children' (τέκνα) in Q 11:13; 'to give' (διδόναι): Q 10:22; 11:3, 9, 11, 13; 'all/everything' (πᾶς): Q 10:22; 11:4, 10, 17; 'kingdom' (βασιλεία): Q 11:2, 17, 18, 20; 'bread' (ἄρτος): Q 11:3,11 (Matthew); 'heaven' (οὐρανός): Q 10:21; 11:2 (Matthew), 13 (16). ... Thus there seems to be a particularly strong linkage among Q 10:21-22; 11:2-4 and 11:9-13."

Mack 1993, 89: Reconstruction.

Schürmann 1994, 204: "Das [a shared 'Q-Vorlage'] legt ferner nicht nur die gemeinsame Abfolge Mt 6,9-13 ... 7,7-11 = Lk 11,2-4 ... 11,9-13 nahe, sondern auch der weitere Kontext, der zeigt, wie Matthäus—trotz aller Neuordnung—in Q wohl die Lk-Akoluthie gelesen hat. [230]"

204[230]: "Vgl. die weitgehend gleiche Akoluthie (abgesehen von zwei matth Vorwegnahmen in Mt 5 und einer in Mt 7): *Mt 6,9-13*/Lk 11,2-4; *Mt 7,7-11*/Lk 11,9-13; *Mt 5,15*/Lk 11,33; *Mt 6,22-23*/Lk 11,34-35; *Mt 6,25-33*/Lk 12,22-31; *Mt 6,19-21*/Lk 12,33-34; *Mt 5,25-26*/Lk 12,57-59; *Mt 7,13-14*/Lk 13,22-24; *Mt 7,22-23*/Lk 13,26-27; *Mt 8,11-12*/Lk 13,28-29. Vgl. außerdem die evtl. Reminiszenz in *Mt 6,8* an Lk 11,8."

Betz 1995, 371: "If the Lord's Prayer was part of Q, it must have become a part of it after the two versions of Q developed: Q/Matt received its prayer together with the SM [Sermon on the Mount], while Q/Luke received its version of the Lord's Prayer not as part of the SP [Sermon on the Plain] but together with another instruction on prayer (Luke 11:2-13)."

Vassiliadis 1995, 16: "It is indeed striking that Jesus' Thanksgiving (*eucharistia*) to the Father (Lk 10.21f. par) not only resembles the liturgical *anaphora* of the later Christian Eucharistic rite, but it is also structured—in regard to the *Lord's Prayer*—in exactly the same way with the post-anaphora rites. Both in the Q-Document and in the Eucharistic Liturgy the Lord's Prayer follows the *Anaphora*."

Con

Holtzmann 1901, 22-23: "Die meisten dieser [Herren-] Worte haben sich in ganz abgerissener Gestalt enthalten, indem die Veranlassungen und Gelegenheiten, welchen sie ihr Dasein erstmalig verdankten, verloren gingen. Sie haben darum, wie z.B. Mt 15,14 = Lc 6,39, als erratische Blöcke ganz verschiedene Ruhepunkte gefunden. ... In anderen Fällen ist es die Gleichartigkeit des Inhaltes, was die Verbindung bedingt, z.B. bei den Sabbatsprüchen Mc 2,23-3,6 = Mt 12,1-14 = Lc 6,1-11. Oft aber auch verknüpft nur der Gleichklang der Wörter oder eine ungefähre Verwandtschaft der Vorstellung im Gedächtniss den einen Spruch mit dem anderen und bestimmt so die Aufeinanderfolge der Elemente. Nur ad vocem lux schliesst sich an die Mahnung Lc 11,33, von der eigenen Begabung den richtigen Gebrauch für Andere zu machen, 11,34-36 der Hinweis an, wie viel für das ganze Leben des Menschen davon abhängt, dass es in seinem, die Lebensführung beherrschenden, Mittelpunkte licht geworden ist. ... [23] ... Nach solchen Gesichtspunkten und äusserlichen Motiven pflegt die mündliche Ueberlieferung zu gruppiren, und so hat auch die Hand des Lc 11,1-13; 12,1-12; 13,24-27 vereinigt, was in den Parallelen des Mt getrennt und isolirt auftritt."

von Harnack 1907, 127 [ET 1908, 180]: See Q 11:1-2a,2b¹ Matt = Q, Pro.

127¹: "Man erkennt jetzt, daß die großen Redekompositionen des Matth. ihre Grundlage schon in Q haben."

von Harnack 1907, ET 1908, 180²: "We now recognise that the great composite discourses of St. Matthew had their outline already given in Q."

Loisy 1924, 314: "Après l'anecdote des deux sœurs, l'évangéliste [Luke] amène l'instruction sur la prière, que peut-être il a placée en cet endroit parce qu'elle lui a semblé s'adresser à l'Église."

Bultmann 1931, 350: "Lukas hat ... einen Abschnitt über das Thema des Gebets gebildet: 11,1-4 das Unser-Vater, 11,5-8 die Parabel vom bittenden Freund, 11,9-13 Mahnung zum Bittgebet."

Bultmann 1931, ET 1968, 324: "Luke for example has composed a section on the theme of prayer: 11,1-4 the Lord's Prayer, 11,5-8 the parable of the importunate friend, 11,9-13 exhortation to intercession."

Evans 1963, 10: "Luke, who by special touches in his gospel goes out of his way to depict Jesus as a man of prayer, and who had already shown his interest in the prayers of the Baptist's disciples, will have introduced it into his story by a picture of Jesus praying alone, and the request of a disciple to be taught to pray as John's disciples had been taught by their master. In this way Luke wishes to trace the prayer which had already been in use in the Church back to its origin in Jesus, the man of prayer." See also Q 11:~~1-2a,~~2b¹ Matt = Q, Con.

Schnackenburg 1984, 92-93: "Der große Sammler Lukas hat hier [in the Travel Narrative] in eigener Regie vieles zusammengetragen, was er an Überlieferungen vorfand und für seine Leser für wertvoll hielt. Überschaut man das reiche Material, so fallen bestimmte Erzählkomplexe und Sprucheinheiten auf, die der Evangelist offenbar thematisch ordnen wollte. Nach der Jüngeraussendung (10,1-24) folgen drei Abschnitte, die der christlichen Lebensführung eine grundsätzliche Orientierung geben sollen: das Liebesgebot mit der Beispielerzählung vom barmherzigen Samariter (10,25-37), die zum Tun der Liebe ruft, die Szene mit Maria und Marta, die das Hören und Bedenken der Worte Jesu ans Herz legt (10,38-42), und schließlich ein längerer Abschnitt über das Gebet (11,1-13). Mir erscheint das wie ein urchristlicher Gemeindekatechismus, der unmittelbar zum christlichen Lebensvollzug anleitet. Liebestaten vollbringen, über das Wort Gottes, wie Jesus es verkündigt hat, nachsinnen und beten im Geiste Jesu sind wesentliche Elemente christlicher Lebensführung.

"Der Gebetsabschnitt Lk 11,1-13 enthält drei Stücke der Gebetsunterweisung Jesu, die Lukas festgehalten hat: an erster Stelle das Vaterunser (11,2-4), dann das Gleichnis vom bittenden Freund (11,5-8), das vielleicht zutreffender das Gleichnis vom erhörenden Freund genannt werden sollte, schließlich die Sprüche über vertrauensvolles Beten (11,9-13), die auch Matthäus in der Bergpredigt überliefert (7,7-11). Für diese aus der Jesusüberlieferung zusammengestellte Gebetsunterweisung hat Lukas, der mit Recht auch als [93] 'Evangelist des Gebetes' bezeichnet wird, eine besondere Einführung geschaffen. Häufig sagt er, daß Jesus im Gebet verweilte (3,21; 5,16; 6,12; 9,18.28f), und so beginnt er auch hier." See also Q 11:~~1-2a,~~2b¹ Matt = Q, Con.

Schnackenburg 1984, ET 1995, 61: "Luke, the great collector, has brought together here [in the Travel Narrative] under his direction much that he found in traditions and considered important for his readers. If one surveys this rich material, certain narrative complexes and aphoristic units are noticeable that the evangelist obviously wanted to arrange thematically. After the sending out of the disciples (Luke 10:1-24), three segments follow that are to provide a fundamental orientation for living the Christian life: the love command with the example of the parable of the Good Samaritan (Luke 10:25-37) which calls love to action; the scene with Mary and Martha, who ardently listen to and consider Jesus' words (Luke 10:38-42); and finally a longer section on prayer (Luke 11:1-13). This appears to be something of a catechism of the primitive Christian church that immediately introduces one to the fulfilled Christian life. Engaging in acts of love, based on the word of God as Jesus proclaimed it, and meditating and praying in the spirit of Jesus are essential elements of the Christian life.

"The section on prayer in Luke 11:1-13 contains three parts of Jesus' instruction on prayer: in the first position is the Lord's Prayer (Luke 11:2-4), then the parable of the importunate friend (Luke 11:5-8) which perhaps should more appropriately be called the parable of the listening friend, and finally the sayings on confident prayer (Luke 11:9-13), which Matthew also includes in the Sermon on the Mount (Matt. 7:7-11). For this instruction on prayer which was collected from the Jesus tradition, Luke, who is also justifiable characterized as the 'evangelist of prayer,' created a special introduction. Frequently he says that Jesus lingered in prayer (Luke 3:21; 5:16; 6:12; 9:18, 28f.), and he begins that way also here."

Stritzky 1989, 9: "Auch Lukas ordnet den Gebetsabschnitt (Lk 11,1-13) in eine Anleitung zu christlicher Lebensführung ein, zu deren Elementen das Vollbringen von Taten der Nächstenliebe (Lk 10,25-37), das Hören und Nachdenken über das Wort Gottes in der Verkündigung Jesu (Lk 10,38-42) und das Gebet gehören. Indem Lukas das Gebet an den Schluß stellt, erreicht er eine Klimax und zeigt dadurch an, welche große Bedeutung auch er dem Gebet innerhalb des christlichen Lebensvollzuges einräumt."

Heininger 1991, 99-100: "Einige übergreifende Begriffe garantieren die Kohärenz des Textes [Luke 11:1-13]: πατήρ (V.2.11.13), ἄρτος (V.3.5) und vor allem (ἐπι)δίδωμι (V.3.7.8[bis].9.11.12.13[bis]). In stilistischer Hinsicht sorgt dafür die Korrespondenz zwischen Bitte der Jünger und Antwort Jesu: dem τις τῶν μαθητῶν (V.1) entspricht das τίς bzw. τίνα δὲ ἐξ ὑμῶν der beiden Fragegleichnisse (V.5.11). In der Sache verschiebt sich mit zunehmender Textlänge ein wenig der Akzent: Geht es zunächst ganz allein um die Weise des Betens, so liegt am Ende der Ton stärker auf der Erhörungsgewißheit. Innerhalb dieses Prozesses hat Lk 11,5-8 so etwas wie eine Gelenkfunktion: VV.5-7 heben—die Auslegung wird das noch deutlich machen—auf die Erfüllung der Bitte ab und verweisen damit auf die VV.9-13, während V.8 noch einmal auf das Wie des Bittens (ἀναίδεια) rekurriert und somit die Verbindung nach vorne (V.2-4) sicherstellt. Die Gebetsunterweisung Lk 11,1-13 erweist sich also als durchdachte Komposition. ... Es liegt nahe, dafür eine redigierende Hand verantwortlich zu machen. ... In Frage kommt m.E. nur Lukas. Zum einen hat er ein geradezu systematisches [100] Interesse am Gebet. Damit trifft sich, daß die Einleitung (V.1) deutlich lk Spracheigentümlichkeiten verrät.

Das gilt auch für die Gleichniseinführung V.5 (καὶ εἶπεν πρὸς αὐτούς), die verschiedentlich als Indiz für vorlk Redaktion in Anspruch genommen wird, und für den Anschluß in V.9 mit κἀγὼ ὑμῖν λέγω. Schließlich liefert das Fragegleichnis Mt 7,9-11 par Lk 11,11-13 ein gewichtiges Argument. Die lk Version unterscheidet sich insofern von der mt, als sie statt der Bitte um Brot in V.12 die Bitte um ein Ei bringt. Nach allgemeiner Einschätzung bietet Matthäus den ursprünglichen Text, die Änderung des Lukas sei durch den Bezug zu Lk 10,19 (Schlangen und Skorpione) motiviert. Doch dürfte das Nächstliegende darin bestehen, daß Lukas die Brotbitte des Fragegleichnisses gestrichen hat, um eine Wiederholung zu vermeiden, weil er anders als Matthäus über einen zusätzlichen Text verfügt, der ebenfalls die Bitte um Brot zum Thema macht." Square brackets around "bis" are Heininger's.

Matt = Q: After Q 6:36 (Matt 5:48) before Q 12:33 (Matt 6:19).

Pro

von Harnack 1907, 127: "Es ergibt sich aus der Rede an die Jünger (dem Stoff in Matth. c. 10) und aus der richtigen Zusammenordnung von Nr. 33 und 43 [Q 11:46-52 und Q 13:34-35], sowie von Nr. 56 und 37 [Q 17:23-35 and Q 12:39-46], daß Matth. die Akoluthie der Quelle treuer bewahrt hat als Lukas. Hieraus folgt mit einer nicht geringen Wahrscheinlichkeit, daß auch die Teile der Bergpredigt, die dem Matth. und Luk. gemeinsam sind, die aber bei beiden nicht in der gleichen Reihenfolge stehen (Nr. 27 [Matt 6:9-13; Luke 11:2-4] .28 [Matt 7:7-11; Luke 11:9-13] ...), in Q in der Anordnung des Matth. gestanden haben und Luk. sie aus nicht mehr nachweisbaren Gründen (im Glauben, eine bessere τάξις noch aufspüren zu können) zerrissen und verteilt hat."

von Harnack 1907, ET 1908, 180: "From the discourse to the disciples and from the fact that in the first gospel the sections 33 and 43 [Matt 6:9-13; Luke 11:2-4], as well as the sections 56 and 37 [Matt 7:7-11; Luke 11:9-13], are correctly given in juxtaposition, we conclude that St. Matthew has preserved the order of the source more faithfully than St. Luke. It therefore follows with no slight probability that those parts of the Sermon on the Mount which are common to St. Matthew and St. Luke, and yet do not stand in the same order in the two gospels occurred in Q in the order of St. Matthew, and that St. Luke has separated and distributed them throughout his work for reasons which can no longer be discovered."

Carruth 1987: One might argue, that there is some connection between the Prayer and the Q material preceding it in Matthew with regard to content. If we remove the Matthean material from consideration, the Prayer follows the Q material Matthew has used in his last antithesis, Mt. 5:43-48. It includes sayings about loving one's enemies, praying for those who persecute one, becoming children of one's heavenly Father and becoming like the heavenly Father. The mention of prayer would then occur in both units and the content coheres with the petition about forgiveness and the parallelism between the forgiveness of God and the forgiving activity of the one who prays.

Con

Holtzmann 1863, 131: "Bekanntlich gibt es Fälle, wo Lucas zu einer Rede, die Mattäus nur im Zusammenhang einer grössern Predigt gibt, eine specielle Veranlassung hat. Das Gebet des Herrn z. B., bei Mattäus der Bergrede einverleibt, wird Lc. 11.1 besonders motivirt."

B. Weiß 1878, 421: See Q 11:~~1-2a,~~2b-4[0] Luke and Matthew = Q, Pro.

J. Weiß 1892, 464: "Die beiden Stücke [Luke 11] V. 1-4 und 9-13 hat Mt an zwei verschiedenen Stellen der Bergpredigt untergebracht (6,9-13. 7,7-11). Lk hat vielleicht den ursprünglichen Zusammenhang, den sie in Q hatten erhalten**."

464**: "Lk wird aber nicht direct aus Q, sondern aus der ihm zugänglichen Form von Q (LQ) geschöpft haben, wo die kleine Einleitung (V. 1) und die Parabel vom ungestüm bittenden Freund … hinzugekommen ist."

Resch 1895, 229: "Bezüglich der Quellenkritik ist *dreierlei* festzustellen: … dass—gegenüber der von dem ersten Evangelisten vorgenommenen Umschaltung Mt. 6,9-13—in Lc. 11,2-4 der ursprüngliche Standort des Gebetes erhalten ist."

Plummer 1896, 292: "Mt. might insert it to exemplify Christ's teaching on prayer."

B. Weiß 1898, 131: "Nach Lk 11,1-4 ist das nämliche Gebet, wenn auch kürzer, bei einer anderen Veranlassung gegeben. Aber an beiden Stellen, also zweimal, kann … das Gebet nicht gegeben sein; denn hat es Jesus seine Jünger schon in der Bergrede gelehrt, so ist die Bitte des Jüngers Lk 11,1 ungeschichtlich; ist diese aber geschichtlich, so kann das V. U. nicht schon vom Berg her im Jüngerkreis bekannt gewesen sein. Es kommt hinzu, dass der geschichtliche Anlass, welchen Lk. angiebt, durchaus keinen Verdacht eigener Kombination erweckt, während es sehr begreiflich ist, dass bei der Redaktion unseres Matth. da, wo die Bergpredigt von der rechten Art des Betens redet, dem Herrn auch schon jenes Mustergebet in den Mund gelegt ward."

Wernle 1899, 68: See Q 11:~~1-2a,~~2b-4[0] Luke and Matthew = Q, Pro.

von der Goltz 1901, 38: "Welches war die *Veranlassung* zur Mitteilung des Gebets des Herrn? Dass dasselbe erst von dem ersten Evangelisten in den

Zusammenhang der von ihm komponierten Bergrede gestellt wurde, ist wohl allgemein zugegeben.[2]"

38[2]: "Es zerreisst dort den Zusammenhang, der augenscheinlich den engen Anschluss von V. 16ff. an V. 5 und 6 verlangt (ὅταν προσεύχησθε, οὐκ ἔσεσθε ὡς οἱ ὑποκριταί ... ἀπέχουσι τὸν μισθὸν αὐτῶν · σὺ δὲ ὅταν προσεύχῃ. ... ὁ πατήρ σου ὁ βλέπων ἐν τῷ κρυπτῷ ἀποδώσει σοι, und ganz parallel V. 16 ὅταν δὲ νηστεύητε, μὴ γίνεσθε ὡς οἱ ὑποκριταί ... ἀπέχουσι κ. τ. λ. · σὺ δὲ νηστεύων ... καὶ ὁ πατήρ σου κ. τ. λ.""

B. Weiß 1901, See Q 11:~~1-2a,~~2b-4[0] Luke and Matthew = Q, Pro.

Wellhausen 1904a, 26: "Im Eingang [Matt 6:7] steht ein Participium, nicht ein Satz mit ὅταν, wie sonst; auch fehlt in 6,8 der Übergang von der pluralischen in die singularische Anrede. Also beginnt hier wohl ein Nachtrag (6,7-15), der die Einschiebung des Herrengebets zum Zweck hat, welches bei Lc an anderer Stelle und in anderer Weise eingeführt wird."

Loisy 1907, 597-598: "Toute cette introduction [to Matthew's Lord's Prayer] paraît artificielle. Le début imite celui des trois conseils sur les bonnes œuvres; la réflexion sur la connaissance que Dieu a de nos besoins est empruntée au discours sur la confiance en Dieu, que l'on trouvera un peu plus loin. Quant [598] à l'idée principale, à savoir qu'il ne faut pas répéter toujours les mêmes formules, au lieu de prouver que Matthieu a trouvé l'Oraison dominicale dans un contexte qui n'était pas celui de Luc, elle prouverait plutôt le contraire. ... Rien ne s'oppose à ce que l'Oraison dominicale, la parabole de l'Ami importun [Luke 11:5-8] et celle de la Veuve [Luke 18:2-8], l'exhortation à une prière confiante [Luke 11:9-13] aient été réunies ensemble dans la première rédaction des discours du Seigneur, de façon à former un recueil d'enseignements sur la prière. Matthieu aura laissé tomber les deux paraboles, et transposé la prière avec l'exhortation."

B. Weiß 1907, 70-71: "Daß das Vaterunser Mt. 6,9-13 ... [71] ... ein Einschub des Matthäus ist, folgt schon daraus, daß seine Einleitung, wonach es im Gegensatz zu heidnischer Vielrederei das Muster eines kurzen und doch vollständigen Gebets geben wollte (6,7f.) mit der Polemik gegen das ostentative Beten der Pharisäer (6,5f.) und darum mit dem Grundgedanken der Bergrede schlechterdings nichts zu tun hat. Es muß also in Q, woher es beide Evangelisten entlehnen, ... einen anderen Anlaß gehabt haben, und einen solchen bietet Lk.11,1."

von Dobschütz 1914, 301-302: "The verses [Matt 6:] 7-8, 9-13, 14-15, are insertions by the evangelist which destroy the harmonious structure of the passage with its three examples of good works,—almsgiving, praying, fasting,—as given in 6:1, 2-4, 5-6, 16-18. That these verses form an original unity, only partly obscured by the insertions, is obvious to anyone who has a feeling for symmetry. It is the catechetical method of Matthew which makes him gather at the same point everything [302] belonging to one topic. So we conclude that Matthew did not find the Lord's Prayer in its present surroundings, but himself gave it its position in the Sermon on the Mount."

McNeile 1915, 75-76: "The sequel of [Matt 6] v.6 is [Matt 6] v. 16; Mt. here groups sayings on Prayer [76] from other contexts."

Soiron 1916, 28: "Die nächste Spruchgruppe der Bergpredigt reicht von [Matt] 6,1-18 und erörtert die neue Frömmigkeit gegenüber der alten, pharisäischen. Auch dieser Abschnitt verrät deutlich die Spuren seiner Komposition. So lassen sich vor allem die Verse 7-15 als Einlage in diesen Abschnitt nachweisen. Zunächst fällt auf, wie die Verse 7 und 8 den vorhergehenden Sprüchen vom heuchlerischen und verborgenen Beten parallel gehen und etwas gezwungen durch die Worte angeschlossen sind: Προσευχόμενοι δὲ μὴ βαττολογήσητε, ähnlich wie v. 6: σὺ δὲ ὅταν προσεύχῃ, εἴσελθε κτλ. Darauf folgt das Vaterunser, das sich dadurch deutlich als Einlage nachweisen läßt, daß Lukas es 11,1-13 bringt und die Veranlassung berichtet, die die Jünger dem Herrn boten, es ihnen mitzuteilen."

Lagrange 1921, 320: "Car Mt. a sûrement inséré le *Pater* dans le discours sur la montagne, comme d'autres morceaux, pour compléter son enseignement sur la prière."

Marriott 1925, 65: "Matthew's Discourse has every appearance of being a compilation. It is the first of his great compendia of topically ordered matter, and, with the exception of the last (if we include in it Mt. 23), the longest. We know that he has rearranged matter drawn from Mark in cc. 8-9, and there is no reason to suppose that he has acted differently in regard to the matter which he has drawn from Q in cc. 5-7."

Bacon 1930, 347: Bacon writes of Matthew's supplements from Q to the tradition found in Matt 6:1-6 and 6:16-18, one of which is Q's discourse on Prayer found in Matt 6:9-13 and 7:7-11. "The former of these is interjected by Mt after the phrase 'The Father that seeth in secret will *reward* thee,' as giving further assurance of heavenly *reward*."

Schmid 1930, 231-232: "So stört das Vaterunser (Mt 6,9-15) den Zusammenhang zwischen den drei genau ebenmäßig gebauten Abschnitten vom Almosengeben, Beten und Fasten. Daß das Vaterunser als Muster eines knappen und inhaltsreichen Gebetes der in V7f verworfenen heidnischen βαττολογία gegenübergestellt wird, ist deutlich zu erkennen. Aber die Verse 7f stehen selbst in keinen rechten Zusammenhang mit V5f und dem eigentlichen Grundgedanken des Abschnitts 6,1-18, der die falsche Scheinfrömmigkeit der Pharisäer verwirft. Nicht die religiöse Heuchelei und äußerliche Ostentation wird in V7f verurteilt, sondern das falsche Beten der Heiden, die durch viele Worte Erhörung zu finden hoffen. Mt. 6,7-15 ist zweifellos ein Einschub des Evangelisten, der unter dem Thema 'Vom Beten' auch das klassische Gebet [232] der Christen unterbringen wollte."

Bultmann 1931, 350: "Mt hat in die Antithesen zur Gesetzesfrömmigkeit Kap. 5 nach dem Prinzip der Sachordnung V. 23f. die Mahnung zur Versöhnlichkeit eingefügt im Anschluß an das Thema des Tötens; ebenso V. 29f. die Worte über die Verführung im Anschluß an das Thema des Ehebruchs. Das Unser-Vater ist 6,9-13 den Worten über das Gebet angereiht und jenem wieder das Wort vom Vergeben (6,14f.) usw."

Bultmann 1931, ET 1968, 324: "In the antitheses on legal piety in Chap. 5, Matthew, following the principle of subject arrangement, has put the exhortation to forgiveness (vv. 23f.) immediately after the theme of killing; similarly the sayings about temptation in vv. 29f. are joined to the theme of adultery. The Lord's Prayer is made to follow the sayings about prayer in 6,9-13 and those in turn follow the saying about forgiveness (6,14f.), etc."

Schmid 1951, 197: "Im Unterschied zu Matthäus, der das Vaterunser systematisierend in die Bergpredigt einfügt und in Gegensatz zum falschen Beten der Pharisäer und der Heiden stellt, nennt Lukas auch den Anlaß, bei dem Jesus seine Jünger das Vaterunser gelehrt hat."

Schmid 1956, 73: "Daß diese Rede [the Sermon on the Mount] in der Gestalt, wie sie Matthäus bietet, erst vom Evangelisten zusammengestellt wurde, beweist sowohl ihre geringe logische Geschlossenheit als auch die Beobachtung, daß umfangreiche Teile von ihr, wie z.B. das Vaterunser ... bei Lukas in anderen Zusammenhängen stehen."

117-118: "Diese genaue Gleichheit der drei Stücke [Matt 6:2-4,5-6,16-18] in der Form beweist nicht bloß ihre Zusammengehörigkeit, sondern auch daß die [118] Verurteilung des wortreichen Geplappers (V. 7f) und das Vaterunser (V. 9-15) erst von Matthäus in diesen Zusammenhang gestellt worden sind."

Dupont 1958, 67: "L'explication s'impose d'elle-même: Matthieu a saisi l'occasion de la recommandation sur la manière de prier pour insérer des enseignements du même genre sans prendre garde qu'il bousculait ainsi l'ordonnance littéraire du passage, écartelant une péricope très homogène et fortement structurée."

Bonnard 1963, 81: "l'Oraison dominicale ne faisait probablement pas partie de ce contexte [Matt 6:1-18] dans la source orale ou écrite que Mat. a utilisée. En effet, elle interrompt la succession des trois instructions classiques sur l'aumône, la prière et le jeûne; d'autre part, Luc en a placé sa version, d'ailleurs fort différente, dans un autre contexte ([Luke] 11.2-4)."

Evans 1963, 91[4]: "This context is clearly artificial, since the Prayer can hardly have been given primarily as an example of brevity in prayer, without regard to its content. In practice the Church, in defiance of this context, has been most repetitious in its use of the Lord's Prayer."

10: "Matthew will ... have placed his version [of the Lord's Prayer] where it seemed to him most fitting—in that section of his gospel where he has gathered together Jesus' comments on the Jewish duties of religion, almsgiving, prayer, and fasting, as part of that collection of the teachings of Jesus, the Sermon on the Mount, which Matthew has constructed as he new Christian law given on a new holy mount." See also Q 11:~~1-2a,~~2b[1] Luke = Q, Con.

Katz 1973, 259: "Bei Matthäus ist das Vaterunser (Mt 6,9 bis 14) in einen größeren, sehr wahrscheinlich vorgegebenen Komplex eingefügt. ... Ob die Verse Mt 6,7f schon vor Matthäus mit dem Text des Vaterunsers verbunden waren oder auf Matthäus zurückgehen, ist nicht deutlich auszumachen. In jedem Fall ist das Vaterunser sekundär in eine Spruchreihe eingebaut worden, die nicht zur Logienquelle zu rechnen ist."

Zeller 1977, 187: "Eine redaktionelle Komposition, die überkommene Weisheitsworte auf die Ebene der Gemeinde transponiert (Pluralformen!), ist Mt 6,1-18, wo V. 9-13 ein Gemeindegebet, das Unser-Vater, eingearbeitet wurde."

Schürmann 1981, 129-130: "Matthäus hat uns die Situation der Gebets-unterweisung nicht überliefert; er stellt das Gebet des Herrn in einen systema-tischen Zusammenhang. Wenn er es zunächst dem Beten der Juden (Mt 6,5f) und dem der Heiden (Mt 6,7f) mit der Einleitung: 'Ihr aber, ihr sollt beten...' gegenüberstellt, dann will auch er nicht nur eine Anweisung über den rechten Geist des Betens geben (nicht den Menschen zu Gefallen wie die Juden, nicht plappernd und Gott magisch zwingen wollend wie die Heiden): Matthäus will im Zusammenhang die Frömmigkeitsübungen der [130] Gemeinde geordnet wissen, das Almosengeben (6,2-4), das Beten (6,5-15) und das Fasten (6,16-18), die Stellung zum Eigentum (6,19-34), das Zusammenleben (7,1-6). Er denkt hier also 'institutionell' und ist gewiß auch an dem von den Christen zu gebrauchenden Gebetsformular interessiert."

Gundry 1982, 104: "[Matthew] removes the prayer from its original context, and inserts it here to teach that Jesus' disciples ought to pray with an economy of words."

109: "Matthew has imported the Lord's Prayer from another context."

Gerhardsson 1984, 207-208: "The place which the Lord's Prayer (Matt 6:9b-13) occupies in its context is not without significance for the exposition of the prayer in Matthew. To begin with, the section 6:7-15 has been inserted into an older context structured in a remarkably strict fashion, though it is difficult to decide at precisely which stage of a presumably drawn out redac-tional process the insertion received its present place. ... [208] ...

"That we are dealing with an interpolation is evident. Four observations lead to this conclusion: (1) With regard to form, this section (vv 7-15) departs from the rigid pattern of the base composition (vv 1-6,16-21); the first two of the symmetrical examples are here separated from the third in an insensible, disturbing manner; (2) Whereas the base composition warns against hypocrisy and exhorts that righteousness be practised in secret, the interpolation (vv 7-15) warns against verbosity (vv 7-9) and a failure to forgive (vv 14-15); nor does the prayer itself (vv 9b-13) seem to be primarily conceived as an individual's prayer in his private room; (3) 'The hypocrites', i.e. the Pharisees and scribes, are mentioned as a contrasting background in the base composition, 'the heathen' in the interpolation; (4) In the base composition, prayer is classed as a 'righteous deed' (v 1), i.e. a *geistiger Opferdienst*, which will receive its 'recompense' and 'reward' from God (ἀποδιδόναι, vv 4,6,18, corresponding with μισθός, vv 1,2,5,16). In the interpolation, on the other hand, prayer is petition—prayer for 'what we need' (v 8)—which is 'heard' by God (εἰσακοῦσθαι, v 7)."

Schnackenburg 1984, 91: "im Unterschied zur Bergpredigt, die bei beiden Evangelisten etwa an der gleichen Stelle der Darstellung des Wirkens Jesu steht, ist das Gebet des Herrn in jeweils andere Zusammenhänge eingeordnet, bei Matthäus in die Bergpredigt, bei Lukas in die große, von ihm gestaltete Einschaltung, die man nach dem äußeren Rahmen auch 'Reisebericht' nennt (9,51-18,14 oder 19,27). Diese verschiedene Anordnung ist für die Intention der Evangelisten und den Hintergrund der Überlieferung beachtlich und aufschlußreich." See also Q 11:~~1-2a,~~2b[1] Luke = Q, Con.

Schnackenburg 1984, ET 1995, 60: "in contrast to the Sermon on the Mount, which for both evangelists takes approximately the same place in portraying the work of Jesus, the prayer of the Lord is placed in different contexts. In Matthew it is in the Sermon on the Mount; in Luke it is in the great interpolation he shaped which, according to its external framework, is also called the 'travel report' (Luke 9:51-18:14 or 19:27). These different arrangements are noteworthy and instructive in terms of the intention of the evangelists and the background of the tradition."

Luz 1985, 334: "Mt wird man die Plazierung im Anschluß an V7f zuschreiben."

Luz 1985, ET 1989, 370: "Probably the placing of the prayer following vv. 7-8 should be ascribed to Matthew."

Schneider 1985, 79: "Die drei gleichartig aufgebauten Weisungen der Bergpredigt über Almosen (Matt 6,2-4), Gebet (6,5f.) und Fasten (6,16-18) können als zusammenhängende Didache verstanden werden, die mit 6,7-8.9-13.14-15 einen sekundären Einschub erhielt: Sub voce *proseuchomai* ist das Vaterunser (6,9-13) samt einer Einleitung und einem Anhang in diese Didache eingefügt worden. Matthäus hat 6,7-8 wohl schon in wesentlichen Bestandteilen vorgefunden, jedoch die Form an die der drei Didache-Stücke angeglichen, die zunächst ein negativ bewertetes Verhalten vor Augen stellen (6,7f.) [Matt 6.2.5.16] und dann die positive Weisung folgen lassen [Matt 6,3f.6. 17f.]: hier das Vaterunser (6,9-13.14f.)." Square brackets are Schneider's.

Kloppenborg 1987, 80[133]: "The placement of the Lord's Prayer (#42) in Matthew may be due to the presence of the theme of prayer in special Matthaean material. H.-D. Betz ('A Jewish-Christian Cult *Didache* in Matt. 6:1-8,' *Essays on the Sermon on the Mount*, 55-69) argues that Matt 6:1-18 is a pre-Matthaean composition, consisting of a Jewish-Christian cult didache on almsgiving (6:2-4), prayer (6:5-6) and fasting (6:16-18) which was later supplemented by vv. 7-15."

202: "As indicated in chapter two, Matthew's placement of the prayer is influenced by the presence of the theme of prayer in a block of his special material which he interpolates in 6:1-18. Not only is his placement secondary, the wording of the prayer in Matthew is usually taken to be a development of the original."

Stritzky 1989, 8-9: "Bei dem von judenchristlicher Tradition geprägten Matthäus nimmt das Vaterunser einen zentralen Platz innerhalb der Bergpredigt (Mt 5-7) ein, und zwar im Kontext einer kritischen Auseinandersetzung [9] mit pharisäischer Frömmigkeitspraxis, der es im Hinblick auf Almosen, Gebet und Fasten (Mt 6,1-18) nicht auf die innere Einstellung, sondern allein auf die äußere Zurschaustellung ankommt, die zur Befriedigung der Eitelkeit und des Geltungsbedürfnisses dient. ...

"Geht man davon aus, daß in Mt 6,1-18 ein Gemeindekatechismus vorliegt, der Orientierungshilfe für das rechte Handeln des einzelnen ebenso wie für das Verhältnis der Gemeindemitglieder zueinander sein will, so ist anzunehmen, daß die Gemeinde des Matthäus zwar in einem von jüdischer Tradition geprägten Umfeld lebt, aber auch mit heidnischem religiösen Brauchtum vertraut ist; sonst hätte der Evangelist den Zusatz (Mt 6,7), der das heidnische Gebet kritisiert, nicht in die Gebetsunterweisung aufgenommen. Gleichzeitig hebt er damit die Stellung des Vaterunsers als Gebet der christlichen Gemeinde noch deutlicher hervor und läßt das Gebet überhaupt in den Mittelpunkt der Frömmigkeitspraxis treten."

Catchpole 1993, 223: "In Luke's use of Q material the pair of parables with which we have been concerned [Luke 11:5-8, 9-13] occurred immediately after the Lord's Prayer (11:2-4). Matthew confirms that in this respect Luke preserves Q, since (i) his 7:7-11/Luke 11:9-13 occurs very shortly after his version of the Lord's Prayer in 6:9-13, and (ii) he has adjacent to the Lord's Prayer in 6:7-8 a πολυλογία reference which matches the content of Luke 11:8."

Betz 1995, 350: "As already discussed, it is generally recognized that [Matt] 6:7-15 represents a secondary insertion into 6:1-6, 16-18. Most scholars attribute this insertion, not the material itself, to the evangelist Matthew. This is possible, but equally possible is that the pre-Matthean author/redactor of the SM [Sermon on the Mount] made the insertion; it is this latter option that I prefer. ...

"Why was the teaching on prayer ([Matt] 6:7-15) interpolated into 6:1-18? The reason seems to have been that the author/redactor of the SM found himself in the possession of two sources (*Vorlagen*) (6:1-6, 16-18 and 6:7-15) that he wanted to keep and to integrate in his work. He did so by combining the two instructions on prayer. A second reason seems to have been that 6:1-6, 16-18 alone appeared theologically insufficient because it did not show any connection with Jesus; indeed, it may not have had any. The interpolation of 6:7-15, therefore, made the section 6:1-6, 16-18 'Jesuanic.'"

Evaluations

Carruth 1995: Luke = Q {A}, after 10:24, before 11:9.

Scholarly opinion is heavily in favor of the Lukan position of this section as the original position in Q. As many note, it is quite clear that the Prayer disrupts the tightly structured composition of the parallel units on almsgiving, prayer and fasting in the Matthean position. While there is some thematic connection with Q material preceding the prayer in Matthew's context, such a connection with Q material which follows is difficult. Jacobson's, Crossan's and Kloppenborg's observations about the coherence of Q material in Luke's order are convincing.

The best explanation for the placement of the Prayer in Matthew is that it is the result of the first evangelist's redactional practice of gathering sayings material into units which serve his own purposes. The thematic and verbal coherence with other Q material in the context in Luke's order argues for Lukan order as representing Q with a high degree of probability, although, admittedly, this conclusion assumes that Q contained blocks of related material.

Robinson 1995: Luke = Q {B}, after Q 10:24, before Q 11:9.

It is probably the Q position that is here retained by Luke, for it seems to reflect a liturgical sequence. A prayer of Thanksgiving (Q 10:21) is followed, after some intervening material (Q 10:22-24; perhaps also Q 10:25-28), by a Prayer of Petition (Q 11:2-4) and a secondarily appended Doxology. As I suggested in 1964, this is a sequence that one might expect in early Jewish and Christian liturgical prayer. In fact such a structure (somewhat embellished) does occur in the mealtime prayers of *Did.* 9-10: Thanksgiving (9,2-3; 10,2-4); Petition (9,4a; 10,5a); Doxology (9,4b; 10,5b) (though the Lord's Prayer, to be recited three times a day, is distinct — 8,2 — from the mealtime/ eucharistic prayers). Vassiliadis has recently noted that this sequence continues into the later liturgy.

The Prayer (Q 11:2b-4) is followed by its Interpretation (Q 11:9-13), whose key words "ask, seek, knock" follow appropriately upon a Prayer of

Petition. The continuity of key terms through the three sections Q 10:21; 11:2b-4, 9-13 is even more striking, serving to indicate their original closer association.

The secondary nature of the Matthean position of the Lord's Prayer is apparent. The Cult Didache has its own rigorously formal structure, which is interrupted by the Prayer. The Prayer, with its own commentary (Matt 6:7-8, 14-15), does not actually fit the section On Prayer in the Cult Didache (Matt 6:5-6). Yet the location of the Prayer here is usually explained by appeal to prayer as the connecting link, leading to its interpolation into the Cult Didache. But a motivation for the location of the Cult Didache here in the Sermon is itself lacking, whereas there could be a catch-word connection for putting here the Prayer: In the immediately preceding context (Matt 5:44 = Q 6:28) prayer (for one's enemies) is mentioned. Although the Lord's Prayer does not include a petition for one's enemies, the allusion to praying may have provided the occasion for moving the Prayer forward from its position in Q 11 to the Sermon on the Mount, i.e. to Q 6. Q 6:35 had spoken of lending, expecting nothing in return (not included in Matt 5:44), and Q 11:4 to forgiving debts (interpreted by Matt 6:14-15 in the light of Mark 11:25 as forgiving trespasses). Once put in the Sermon, the Prayer could then have attracted secondarily the Cult Didache. Though this indicates an appropriateness of the Prayer in the Sermon at this place, the connection in the Lucan position is stronger.

In any case the Prayer finds its fitting context in other elements of Q that were also moved forward into the Sermon on the Mount, indicating that its original Q position was in association with them: The original Q Commentary on the Prayer (Q 11:9-13) was also brought into the Sermon on the Mount (Matt 7:7-11), but put after the section On Anxiety (Q 12:22-31, at Matt 6:25-33). Matthew considered On Anxiety an appropriate commentary, as the repetition of Q 12:30 (Matt 6:32) at Matt 6:7-8 indicates. The resultant Matthean positioning of the original Commentary, not adjoining the Prayer but at the conclusion of the body of the Sermon on the Mount (Matt 7:7-11), seems isolated from its appropriate context and hence secondary. It occurs just before the Golden Rule (Matt 7:12), also moved from its earlier position in the Q Sermon to become the *inclusio* (see Matt 5:20) of the body of the Sermon on the Mount.

Q 11:~~1-2a,~~2b²: Did Q have an introduction (like Luke 11:1-2a or like Matthew 6:7-8)?

Luke = Q: [Καὶ ἐγένετο ἐν τῷ εἶναι αὐτὸν ἐν τόπῳ τινὶ προσευχόμενον, ὡς ἐπαύσατο, εἶπέν τις τῶν μαθητῶν αὐτοῦ πρὸς αὐτόν· κύριε, δίδαξον ἡμᾶς προσεύχεσθαι, καθὼς καὶ Ἰωάννης ἐδίδαξεν τοὺς μαθητὰς αὐτοῦ. 11:2 εἶπεν δὲ αὐτοῖς·]²

Pro

B. Weiß 1876, 181: "Zwar die ganz allgemeine Einleitung, wonach Jesus sich an einem Orte aufhielt und betete, rührt formell und materiell zweifellos von seiner Hand her,¹ aber die Bitte eines Jüngers, sie beten zu lehren, wie auch Johannes seine Jünger gelehrt habe, stammt um so gewisser aus der Quelle her, als Luc. eine Angabe hierüber in seinem Bericht über den Täufer gar nicht hat, sondern unsre Stelle nur in seiner Weise 5,33 vorbereitet."
181¹: "Vgl. zu καὶ ἐγένετο ἐν τῷ εἶναι αὐτόν: 2,6. 9,18 und dieselbe noch 17mal im Ev. mit andern Verb. wiederkehrende Formel; zu ἐν τόπῳ τινί: Act. 27,8 und das 20mal im Ev., 18mal in den Act. wiederkehrende τόπος; zu dem Beten Jesu 3,21. 5,16. 6,12. 9,18. 28; zu ὡς ἐπαύσατο 5,4. 8,24 und das noch 6mal in den Act., nie in den andern Evv. vorkommende παύεσθαι."
B. Weiß 1878, 421: "Die Erwähnung des Betens Jesu rührt formell und materiell von der Hand des Luk. her und soll die Bitte des Jüngers motiviren, die gewiß aus der ältern Quelle herrührt; denn der Thatbestand, worauf sich καθὼς καὶ Ἰωάννης etc. bezieht, ist uns völlig unbekannt. Wahrscheinlich aber hatten die Johannesjünger ein bestimmt formulirtes Gebet von ihrem Lehrer überkommen."
von der Goltz 1901, 39: "Nach Lc. 11,1 dagegen haben ihn die Jünger selbst darum gebeten mit ausdrücklichem Hinweis darauf, dass auch Johannes seine Jünger beten lehrte. Diese Frage mit ihrer Begründung durch das Beispiel des Johannes darf um so eher als geschichtlich gelten, als sie sich deutlich unterscheidet von dem, was Lc. selbst im ersten Vers als Veranlassung der Bitte in einer merkwürdigen Unbestimmtheit angiebt. Jesus betet an einem Ort und als er aufhörte, bat einer der Jünger, er möchte auch sie beten lehren. Dadurch wäre eigentlich die Bitte 'Herr lehre uns beten' schon genügend motiviert gewesen. Aber dem Evangelisten war augenscheinlich aus älterer Tradition die Bitte der Jünger mit dem *Hinweis auf das Beispiel des Johannes* überliefert, ohne dass dort die Gelegenheit für solche Frage und Antwort angegeben war. Eine solche suchte er anzugeben durch die Einleitung V. 1a, die ganz deutlich seinen Stil verrät. Geschichtlich ist daher jedenfalls die

Begründung der Jüngerbitte durch das Beispiel des Johannes, ungeschichtlich die von Lc. selbst hinzugefügte Motivierung durch das Beispiel des Herrn selbst."

Holtzmann 1901, 363: "Die Umständlichkeit der Einleitung [Luke 11:] 1 gehört so gut wie 9,18 der Redaction an, während die motivirende Anrede mit ihrem Hinweis auf den Täufer (vorbereitet 5,33) der Quelle entnommen sein kann."

B. Weiß 1901, 458: "So gewiss die Einleitung formell und materiell (vgl. das Beten Jesu) von der Hand des Lk herrührt, so gewiss muss der Anlass des UV, das Mt 6,9-13 offenbar aus schriftstellerischen Motiven in die Bergrede verflicht …, mit demselben aus einer Quelle geschöpft sein."

Loisy 1907, 598: "Quant à l'introduction historique de Luc, Matthieu a pu en connaître l'essentiel, et la négliger, parce qu'il voulait mettre l'Oraison dominicale dans le discours sur la montagne."

599: "Il est probable que la source primitive ne contenait que la demande avec la réponse, sans indication de temps, ni de lieu, ni de personne."

B. Weiß 1907, 71: "Es [the Our Father] muß also [since Matthew has moved it into the Sermon on the Mount secondarily] in Q, woher es beide Evangelisten entlehnen (bem. das in der ganzen Gräzität nicht mehr vorkommende ἐπιούσιος), einen anderen Anlaß gehabt haben, und einen solchen bietet Lk. 11,1. Denn obwohl das καὶ ἐγένετο — ἐπαύσατο nach Form und Inhalt (bem. die Hervorhebung des Betens Jesu) nur die Vorstellung des Lukas ausdrückt, in welcher Situation einer seiner Jünger (wie der Gegensatz zeigt, im engsten Sinne) darauf kommen konnte, Jesum zu bitten, er möge sie beten lehren, wie Johannes seine Jünger beten gelehrt habe, so kann doch Lukas diese Bitte selbst nur in einer Quelle vorgefunden haben, da er selbst nie (auch nicht 5,33, wo ein unmittelbarer Anlaß dazu vorlag) die Tatsache, auf die sich der Jünger beruft, erwähnt hat."

B. Weiß 1908, 31: Reconstruction: καὶ εἶπέν τις τῶν μαθητῶν αὐτοῦ πρὸς αὐτόν· κύριε, δίδαξον ἡμᾶς προσεύχεσθαι, καθὼς καὶ Ἰωάννης ἐδίδαξεν τοὺς μαθητὰς αὐτοῦ. (καὶ εἶπεν ὁ Ἰησοῦς·). Jesus' speech starts with Matt 6:7, then follows immediately the Lord's Prayer.

Dibelius 1911, 43-44: "Zunächst sei das literarische Problem der Einleitung Lk. 11,1 untersucht. Von den beiden Motivierungen ist die erste sprachlich und sachlich mit aller Bestimmtheit auf das Konto des Evangelisten zu setzen.³ Die andere aber, d.h. die [44] Angabe, daß Johannes seine Jünger beten gelehrt habe, scheint aus dem Grunde nicht auf Lukas, sondern auf die Tradition zurückzugehen, weil Lukas die Gebetslehre des Täufers in der Erzählung nirgends—auch 5,33 nicht!—erwähnt. So werden wir als die ursprüngliche, von Lukas in seinem Stil bearbeitete Einleitung des Stückes die zweite Angabe ansehen."

43-44³: "Beweis: 1) Die Wendung ἐγένετο ἐν τῷ mit Inf. ist eine von Lukas bevorzugte Einleitungsformel: er hat nicht nur seine Sonderperikopen häufig so eingeführt (5,1 9,51 10,38 11,27 14,1 17,11), sondern auch anders eingeleitete Markusstücke mit dieser Anfangsformel versehen (3,21 5,12 8,40 9,18). 2) Lukas liebt es, Situationsangaben vor die überlieferten Perikopen zu setzen, und zwar bisweilen recht [44] unwahrscheinliche Angaben vgl. 14,1. ... 3) Lukas erwähnt das Beten Jesu mit Vorliebe, auch wo die anderen Referenten nichts davon wissen (3,21 5,16 6,12 9,18. 28f.)."

Castor 1912, 230: Reconstruction.

Haupt 1913, 85: See Q 11:~~1-2a,~~2b-4⁰ Luke and Matthew = Q, Pro.

Patton 1915, 136: "Luke's introduction to the prayer is certainly not his own invention, and is so appropriate that it is hard to believe that Matthew found it in connection with the prayer in his source and deliberately omitted it. Luke's form seems decidedly more primary."

Loisy 1924, 314: "Transition lourde et artificielle, dont la majeure partie porte la marque de l'évangéliste. Celui-ci aime à montrer Jésus priant; il le fait prier pour amener la question de la prière, et il ajoute le 'certain lieu.' On doit supposer que Jésus priait à l'écart (cf. IX, 18); et d'ailleurs c'est aux disciples seuls que la prière est enseignée. La source ne contenait probablement que la demande du disciple, avec la réponse, sans indication de temps ni de lieu."

Marriott 1925, 66: "It seems probable that in Q the Prayer stood with an introduction as in Lk. 11,1-4."

Easton 1926, 176: "This verse (in part?) is presumably from Q. For Q could not have given the Prayer without a preface of some sort, and Lk would not have introduced the reference to the Baptist. Lk evidently has conformed the first few words to the beginning of his last section (10:38), and may have modified elsewhere. W [B. Weiß], Wl [Wellhausen 1904b], Ls [Loisy, 1907] regard the introductory words (through 'ceased') as editorial, and the use of ὡς is certainly 'Lukan.' This preface would have been impossible in Mt's position of the prayer but W thinks that Mt 6:7f stood at this point in Q; the connection is excellent, while the verses would have been too Jewish for Lk. (2a) ὅταν and the subjunctive are of course from Lk; they presuppose Christian liturgical practice."

Montefiore 1927, 99: "In Luke the prayer has a different place and a different introduction, which may be older than that of Matthew."

Bussmann 1929, 67: "So wie wir oben gesehen haben, daß die Aussendungsrede in vier Quellen stand, so konnte auch das Herrengebet in zwei gestanden haben. Mt hat es ohne Einleitung, vielleicht stand es ohne solche in seiner Sonderquelle, woher er auch die vorhergehenden Worte über das Beten und die nachfolgenden über das Fasten (nach einem kleinen Einschub aus G [Geschichtsquelle]) genommen hat. Dann läßt sich aber schließen, daß die in

L 11,1 stehenden Worte über die Veranlassung, den Jüngern das Gebet zu geben, auch in R [Redenquelle] gestanden haben. Natürlich ist das nicht ganz sicher, da keine bestätigende Parallele vorhanden ist."

Klostermann 1929, 123: "**1a** καὶ ἐγένετο ἐν τῷ εἶναι αὐτὸν ἐν τόπῳ τινὶ (luk.) προσευχόμενον (wie 9,18) ὡς ἐπαύσατο κτλ.: die künstliche, auch im Stil ganz lukanische Einleitung gibt weder eine zeitliche Verknüpfung, noch eine genauere Angabe über den Ort oder die Person des fragenden Jüngers. **1b** κύριε, δίδαξον ἡμᾶς προσεύχεσθαι, καθὼς καὶ Ἰωάννης ἐδίδαξεν τοὺς μαθητὰς αὐτοῦ: die Bitte des Jüngers mit ihrer Bezugnahme auf ein Gebet der rivalisierenden Täufergemeinde (vgl. 5,33) stand wohl schon in Q."

Bacon 1930, 182-183: See Q 11:1̶-̶2̶a̶,2b-4⁰ Luke and Matthew = Q.

Creed 1930, 155: "The introductory sentence is peculiar to Luke. As it stands the verse bears characteristic marks of Lucan style, but it seems unlikely that it does not reproduce some earlier source—probably Q."

Hauck 1934, 149: "Die Rahmennotiz des Lk (v 1a) gibt, wie so oft, eine geschichtliche Situation zu dem überlieferten Wort. Sie enthält zwei Motive: Jesu eigenes Beten und die im Johanneskreis bestehende Gebetsregel. Das erste, stark durch Lk-Stil ausgezeichnet, dürfte auf Lk zurückgehen."

Hirsch 1941, 101: See Q 11:1̶-̶2̶a̶,2b-4⁰ Luke and Matthew = Q.

Knox 1957, 61: "It is of course likely enough that the narrative introduction xi. 1 owes something to Lucan editing. … Although it is exaggerated to call the Semitic καὶ ἐγένετο a 'characteristic' Lucan construction, since Luke never uses it in Acts, and it is frequent in Mark, appearing five times also in Matthew, yet it seems that Luke uses it as having a hieratic ring, and he may have introduced it here, though it is possible that in the cases where he introduces it into his revision of Mark without any excuse, he is following Mark's source rather than Mark himself. Nevertheless, it is quite likely that he himself has rewritten the introduction; incidentally it may be observed that xi. 1 might be the question which usually comes near the end of a collection, and that the whole of the original opening has been omitted."

Dupont 1958, 63-64: "Voyons d'abord le contexte de Luc. Le v. 1 indique l'occasion des enseignements qui vont suivre; plus exactement, non pas une occasion, mais deux: 1a, Jésus se trouve quelque part en prière, ce qui suggère à un disciple la pensée de lui demander une formule de prière; 1b, le disciple formule sa demande en se réclamant de Jean-Baptiste qui a enseigné une prière à ses disciples. La première indication, Jésus en prière, est un trait si caractéristique du troisième évangile qu'il est bien difficile de l'attribuer à un document antérieur; tout [64] porte à y voir la marque des préoccupations de Luc. Il n'en va pas de même pour la deuxième: Luc n'a pas inventé cette donnée concrète, que la première partie du verset rendait d'ailleurs inutile. Elle a toute chance de provenir de sa documentation."

Davies 1966, 5: "The difference in setting of this material in the two Gospels makes it clear that a prayer taught by Jesus to the disciples has become a prayer for use by the Church in Matthew."

Katz 1973, 269-271: "Die Einleitungswendung in Lk 11,1a καὶ ἐγένετο ἐν τῷ εἶναι αὐτὸν ἐν τόπῳ τινὶ προσευχόμενον, ὡς ἐπαύσατο geht, dies ist allgemein anerkannt, auf die lukanische Redaktion zurück. Denn dieser Vers fügt sich den anderen Belegen ein, an denen Jesus—betonter als bei Matthäus und Markus—als Beter dargestellt wird. Hier ist dieser Ort zwar nicht als 'Berg gekennzeichnet, aber die Szene ist dadurch, daß dieser τόπος τις erwähnt wird, ausdrücklich an Jesu Gebetsort verlegt'⁵. [270] Die zweite Einleitung, die Bitte der Jünger, 'Herr, lehre uns beten, wie Johannes seine Jünger lehrte', wird man nicht so schnell der Redaktion des Lukas zuschreiben, wenn zwischen dieser Bitte und der Geistbitte im Vaterunser ein redaktioneller Zusammenhang bestehen sollte. Da nach dem Ergebnis der äußeren Textkritik die Geistbitte für den Text des Lukas nicht nachgewiesen werden kann, muß auch bezweifelt werden, daß die zweite Einleitung in Lk 11,1b.c auf die Redaktion des Lukas zurückgeht. …

"Die Anrede Jesu mit κύριε kann auf eine vorlukanische Tradition hinweisen. Die Erwägungen zum Gebrauch des Kyrios-Titels im Lukasevangelium machten deutlich, daß grundsätzlich die Möglichkeit der Verwendung des Kyrios-Titels durch die lukanische Redaktion nicht auszuschließen ist, von Fall zu Fall aber genau zu prüfen ist, ob der Titel nicht bereits der Vorlage des Lukas angehörte, da Lukas selbst die Hoheitstitel nicht differenziert verwendet.

"Die zweite Einleitung zum lukanischen Vaterunser ist nun aber nicht nur durch den Kyrios-Titel gekennzeichnet, sondern auch durch die Gegenüberstellung der Jesus- und Johannesjünger. Man wird der Formulierung in Lk 11,1 eine gewisse Rivalität zwischen den beiden Gruppen entnehmen dürfen. Es scheint so, als ob die Jesusjünger betont ihre Eigenständigkeit gegenüber den Johannesjüngern in den Vordergrund stellen. Der 'Vorbildcharakter, den das Beten Jesu an dieser Stelle hat'¹, ist an dieser Stelle ganz dem Bestreben untergeordnet, [271] den Unterschied zwischen Jesus- und Johannesjüngern, der sich im Gebet manifestiert, zu verdeutlichen. Im Zusammenhang der Aussendungsrede wurde bereits gezeigt, daß die hellenistisch-judenchristliche Redaktion der Logienquelle eine gewisse 'Animosität' gegenüber Johannes dem Täufer erkennen läßt. Die Verbindung mit dem Kyrios-Titel bestärkt die Richtigkeit der Annahme, daß die zweite Einleitung, die Bitte der Jünger um ein besonderes Gebet, auf hellenistisch-judenchristliche Redaktion der Logienquelle zurückgeht."

269⁵: "Ott, Gebet S. 93 Anm. 8." See Q 11:1-2a,2b¹ Luke = Q, Con.
270¹: "Ott, Gebet S. 97."

Marshall 1978, 456: "The introductory verse to the section gives the setting. The style shows several Lucan features: καὶ ἐγένετο ἐν τῷ ... (1:8); ὡς (1:23); παύομαι (5:4); καθώς (1:2). These, however, are insufficient to prove Lucan creation of the setting ..., and the reference to John's disciples, which adds nothing to the scene, is hardly due to Luke. Interest in John is shown by both Q and Luke's special source material (3:10-14), but also by Luke himself (5:33). The reference to Jesus being at prayer could be due to Luke (cf. 3:21; 9:18), but there is no reason why such a situation could not have been the historical setting for the question of the disciples."

Polag 1979, 88: Reconstruction: Καὶ εἶπέν τις τῶν μαθητῶν αὐτοῦ· κύριε, δίδαξον ἡμᾶς προσεύχεσθαι, ὡς καὶ Ἰωάννης ἐδίδαξεν τοὺς μαθητὰς αὐτοῦ. εἶπεν δὲ αὐτοῖς·

89: As Lukan additions he lists: ἐγένετο ἐν τῷ εἶναι αὐτὸν ἐν τόπῳ τινὶ προσευχόμενον, ὡς ἐπαύσατο, πρὸς αὐτόν and καθώς.

Gundry 1982, 104: "Jesus taught the Lord's Prayer in response to a request that he teach his disciples to pray as John the Baptist had taught his disciples to pray (Luke 11:1-4). Matthew drops the narrative introduction, removes the prayer from its original context, and inserts it here to teach that Jesus' disciples ought to pray with an economy of words."

Zeller 1984, 56: "Mit einiger Sicherheit können wir annehmen, daß auf das Gebet Jesu zwei mit Imperativen eingeleitete Einheiten folgten, die die Jünger im Beten unterweisen. In der ersten überliefert er ihnen ein Gebetsformular, wohl mit folgenden Worten:

"Wenn ihr betet, so sprecht:

"Dazu ist eine Redeeinleitung in der Art von Lk 11,1b zu postulieren. Demnach wäre schon in Q die Konkurrenz der Johannesjünger, die Mt 11,2-6 ebenfalls durchschimmerte, der Anlaß zur Gebetsanweisung Jesu gewesen. Lk bereitet 5,33 durch einen Zusatz zu Mk darauf vor."

Patterson 1993, 95: In a chart he assigns Lk 11:1-4 to Q.

Schürmann 1994, 176-177: "Der Hinweis auf Johannes soll wohl nicht nur den Erzählungsfaden fortspinnen; er ist von Lukas Mk 2,18 par Lk 5,33 nachgebildet, wo er mit δεήσεις ποιοῦνται bereits 11,1b vorbereitet hatte. Lukas denkt sich—mit Q—den Kreis der Johannesjünger institutionalisiert (vgl. zu 3,15) und als eine zu seiner Zeit offenbar nicht unwichtige Gruppe. ... [177] ...

"V 1a wird luk Bildung sein. ... Den Grundbestand von V 1b kann die Q-Tradition Lukas zugetragen haben, weil dieser 5,33 diff Mk davon abhängig ist, wenn er dort den Gebetsbrauch der Johannesjünger—eigentlich kontextwidrig—einträgt. Auch kennt die Redenquelle Johannesjünger, sie versteht Johannes auch als 'Lehrer' (3,12 ...)."

Con

Holtzmann 1863, 131-132: "Bekanntlich gibt es Fälle, wo Lucas zu einer Rede, die Matthäus nur im Zusammenhang einer grössern Predigt gibt, eine specielle Veranlassung hat. Das Gebet des Herrn z.B., bei Matthäus der Bergrede einverleibt, wird Lc. 11,1 besonders motivirt. ... An sich liesse es sich leicht vorstellen, dass die Redefragmente in Λ [Q] öfters so völlig abgerissen aufeinander folgten, dass bereits Lucas sich veranlasst sah, dieselben einiger-massen zu arrangiren und zu [132] motiviren. Wir werden sehen, dass Lucas auch in der Bearbeitung von A [Urmarcus] zuweilen selbständige Scenerien liefert, wie 6,17. 21,5; warum sollte er sich diese Freiheit, die bei der Ein-reihung bloser Redefragmente aus Λ viel besser angebracht war, gerade hier versagt haben?"

Plummer 1896, 293: "Note the marks of Luke's style: ἐγένετο, ἐν τῷ εἶναι, εἶναι προσευχόμενον, εἶπεν πρός, εἶπεν δέ. ..."

Hawkins 1899, 20: In a chart listing "Words and Phrases characteristic of St. Luke's Gospel," Hawkins shows that ὁ κύριος is used of Jesus in narrative 13 times. It does not appear in Chaps. i, ii; 7 times in other peculiar parts; 6 times in common parts. The word is marked with an asterisk to show that Hawkins considers it among the most distinctive and important instances of Lukan vocabulary.

Wernle 1899, 68: "Die Einleitung 11,1 mag von Lc stammen, der gern solche Situationen sich ausdenkt."

Stanton 1909, 89: "After a request by the disciples to be taught to pray, which may possibly have been imagined by the evangelist [Luke] as an intro-duction, we have the Lord's Prayer, an Example of successful importunity, and an Exhortation to earnestness in prayer."

Cadbury 1920, 105-106: "In the introductions to new sections Luke shows the greatest independence. ... during the Galilean ministry, when more or less detached scenes are presented, Luke takes the liberty of rewriting the introduc-tions in his own way. Specific indications of time and place are frequently replaced by more general references, and details are added to supply [106] the invisible mental environment of the scene rather than its graphic physical scenery.

"A favorite form of preface is the use of καὶ ἐγένετο, ἐγένετο δέ." Cadbury lists Luke 11:1 as an example.

113: "Luke's interest in the prayer-life of Jesus has often been noticed, and this is a feature which he several times introduces into his setting for a scene. ... Luke is the only one of the Gospels to mention that Jesus prayed. In three other pericopes, Luke mentions that Jesus was praying, while the parallels say nothing of it: Luke 5,16 ... (cf. Mark 1,45); Luke 9,18 ... (cf. Mark 8,27); Luke 11,1 ... (cf. Matt. 6,9)."

115: "The verb διδάσκω occurs in Matt. 14 times, in Mark 17 times, in Luke 17 times."

169: "εἶπεν is by far the commonest word for introducing sayings or speeches in dialogue and the combination εἶπεν δέ is specifically Lucan."

Lagrange 1921, 321: "Style de Lc. καὶ ἐγένετο — ἐν τῷ εἶναι — προσευχό-μενον (i,10; iii,21; v,16; ix,18; Act. x,30; xi,5; xii,12); ὡς ἐπαύσατο (v,4)."

Creed 1930, 156: "Note the characteristic Lucan constr. ἐγένετο ἐν τῷ ... εἶπεν ... Lk. loves to picture Christ at prayer, cf. iii. 21 n. [p 57]"

57: "Luke emphasises the place of prayer in the life of Jesus, v. 16, vi. 12, ix. 18, 28, 29, xi. 1, and (with Mk. and Mt.) xxii. 41."

Schmid 1930, 232[1]: "Καὶ ἐγένετο ... προσευχόμενον κτλ. Diese Situations-angabe ist von der für den dritten Evangelisten charakteristischen Unbe-stimmtheit."

Bultmann 1931, 359: "Lk folgt z.T. der alten Methode, Redestücke an *überlieferte Apophthegmen anzuhängen.* ...

"Meist aber hat Lk *selbständig Einleitungen gebildet,* deren Motive er oft einfach den Worten, die er bringen wollte, entnahm. ... Für das Unser-Vater muß 11,1 die Situation des betenden Jesus und daran anschließend die Bitte der Jünger als Hintergrund dienen."

Bultmann 1931, ET 1968, 334: "In part Luke follows the old method of attaching speech sections to *Traditional Apophthegms.* ...

"But for the most part Luke has fashioned *his own introductions* independently, whose motifs he often simply borrows from the sayings he wants to reproduce. ... As a background of the Lord's Prayer in 11,1 we have the situation in which Jesus prayed and the request of the disciples which it prompted."

Leaney 1958, 184: "This first verse [Luke 11:1] is one of the most inter-esting of the short Lucan introductions to a section from his sources."

Ott 1965, 93[8]: "Hier [Luke 11:1] ist dieser Ort zwar nicht als Berg gekennzeichnet, aber die Szene ist dadurch, daß dieser τόπος τις erwähnt wird, ausdrücklich an Jesu *Gebetsort* verlegt. In Lk 22,40 steht ebenfalls τόπος für den Gebetsort, der in v. 39 durch τὸ ὄρος τῶν ἐλαιῶν bezeichnet ist: γενόμενος δὲ ἐπὶ τοῦ τόπου εἶπεν αὐτοῖς. Der Vorbildcharakter des Gebets Jesu wird dadurch—wie in der Szene auf dem Ölberg durch die dortige Rahmen-bemerkung 22,39—deutlich betont."

Schulz 1972, 84[185]: "Bei Lk ist dem V 2a eine weitere Einleitung in V 1 vorangestellt. Schon diese Doppelung der Einleitungen läßt vermuten, daß die 1. Einleitung, die bei Mt keine Parallele hat, red ist. ... Dieser Vermutung wird durch eine Untersuchung des Vokabelmaterials, das weithin lk Züge trägt, bestätigt: ἐγένετο + Verbum finitum 12mal bei Lk; 1mal bei Mt; τόπος Ev ca 4mal red; Apg 18mal; τίς + Substantiv Ev 38 mal; Apg 63mal; προσ-εύχεσθαι Ev 9mal red; Apg 16mal; παύεσθαι Ev 1mal red; Apg 6mal; τίς +

Gen Ev ca 9mal red; Apg ca 7mal; red Einfügung von μαθητής Ev ca 17mal;
εἶπεν πρός + Akk Ev ca 43mal red; Apg 26mal; κύριε als Anrede an Jesus Ev
ca 7mal; Apg 15mal; διδάσκειν Ev ca 10mal red; Apg 16mal.”

Feldkämper 1978, 179-181: “Klammern wir das inhaltliche Motiv des
betenden Jesu zunächst von unseren Überlegungen aus, so spricht ausser der
ἐγένετο-Konstruktion noch die Vorliebe des Lukas, Situationsangaben zu schaf-
fen, für die lukanische Redaktion der Gebetsnotiz 11,1f. Den Hinweis auf
Johannes und seine Jünger wird Lukas jedoch aus der Tradition übernommen
haben, weil er die 'Gebetslehre des Täufers in der Erzählung nirgends —auch
5,33 nicht!—erwähnt' (M. Dibelius [1911; see Q11:1-2a,2b-4², Luke = Q Pro],
Die urchristliche Überlieferung von Johannes dem Täufer, 43f.) und sonst am
Täufer kein selbständiges Interesse hat. Andererseits sind ihm die Johannesjünger als religiöse Gruppe bekannt (Lk 5,33 par Mk/Mt; Apg 19,1-6), [180]
denen gegenüber er die Jünger Jesu als eigentliche und einzige 'christliche'
Gemeinde herausstellen will, wie er auch das Verhältnis Johannes—Jesus
(Lk Kap. 1-2 und 3) in 'überbietender' Parallelisierung dargestellt hat.

“Die Notiz über das Beten Jesu ist der von 9,18 sehr ähnlich, sowohl in der
Formulierung … als auch in der Erwähnung der Jünger … sowie schliesslich
in der Frage bzw. der Bitte, die im ersten Fall Jesus an die Jünger richtet
(9,18b.20a), im zweiten einer der Jünger an Jesus (11,1). Aus der Tatsache,
dass in 9,18 die Gegenwart der Jünger … beim allein betenden Jesus … so sehr
betont wird, ergibt sich für 11,1, dass nach Lukas die Jüngerbitte um Gebetsbelehrung nicht bei einem erstmaligen Erleben des Betens Jesu gestellt wurde.
Wir dürfen deshalb die Frage stellen: Woher nimmt Lukas das Motiv der
Jüngerbitte um Gebetsbelehrung?

“Vergleichbar ist dieser Bitte bei Lukas nur noch die Bitte der Apostel um
Glaubensmehrung (17,5). Beide Bitten sind ohne Parallelen bei Mk/Mt. Sie
werden von den engsten Anhängern Jesu, den Jüngern und den Aposteln,
dem Kyrios vorgetragen, von dem sie etwas für sich selbst erbitten. Sowohl
die Bitten des Jüngers und der Apostel als auch die Antworten Jesu werden
jeweils durch einfaches εἶπεν/εἶπαν eingeleitet, und die Struktur der Bitten ist
in beiden Fällen die gleiche. Stellt man die beiden Texte einander gegenüber,
ist ihre Parallelität offensichtlich. …

“Damit hört die Parallele zwischen beiden Texten jedoch noch nicht auf.
In beiden Fällen wird in der Antwort Jesu das Hauptwort der Bitte wieder
aufgenommen (11,1.2 προσεύχεσθαι/προσεύχεσθε; 17,5.6 πίστιν). Den ersten
Teil der Unterweisung hat Lk jeweils mit Mt gemeinsam [181] (Lk 11,2b-4
par Mt 6,9-13 sowie Lk 17,6 par Mt 17,20); daran schliesst er beide Male ein
Gleichnis an, für das bei Mk/Mt jegliche Parallele fehlt (11,5-8; 17,7-10). Es
handelt sich um Gleichnisse, die nach Form und Inhalt einander sehr ähnlich
sind (vgl. die Struktur des Gleichnisses vom Typ 'Wer unter euch?...'; das

Verhältnis und die Verhaltensweisen zwischen Freund und Freund, Herr und Knecht). Auf weitere Einzelheiten können wir hier verzichten. Es genügt uns die Feststellung, dass Lukas die Themen des Gebetes und des Glaubens —kompositionell—in auffallend ähnlicher Weise behandelt hat."

182: "Wir fassen unsere Überlegungen dahingehend zusammen, dass wir meinen, Lukas habe sich für den Inhalt und die Formulierung der Gebetsnotiz 11,1.2a von Lk 9,18 und Mk 9,28f inspirieren lassen."

Jeremias 1980, 113: "Es gehört zu den Eigentümlichkeiten des 3. Evangelisten, daß er häufiger von einem Beten Jesu spricht, abgesehen von der Gethsemaneperikope 7mal. Da es sich in 5 dieser 7 Fälle um Zusätze des Lukas zum Markusstoff handelt (Lk 5,16; 6,12; 9,18; 9,18.28f.), also um Redaktion, könnten auch die beiden restlichen Belege (3,21; 11,1) analog einzuordnen sein. In der Tat ist zum mindesten 11,1 ganz von lukanischer Diktion geprägt."

195: "**11,1 Red** καὶ ἐγένετο ἐν τῷ ... ὡς ... εἶπέν τις: Das periphrastische καὶ ἐγένετο ist eines der markantesten lukanischen Charakteristika im dritten Evangelium. ... — ἐν τῷ εἶναι: im NT nur im Doppelwerk (Lk 2,6; 5,12; 9,18; 11,1; Apg 19,1). ... — ἐν τόπῳ τινί: Zum adjektivischen τις → 1,5 Red [p. 15]. —ὡς: als temporale Konjunktion ist lukanische Vorzugswendung → 1,23 Red [p. 45].-ἐπαύσατο: ist lk Vorzugswort → 5,4 Red [p. 131]. Nur Lk 8,24 (diff. Mk 4,39); 11,1; Apg 20,1; 1Kor 13,8 findet sich der absolute Gebrauch des Mediums. — εἶπεν ... πρός c.acc.: lukanisch → 1,13 Red [p. 33]. ...

"**11,2 Red** εἶπεν δέ: → 1,13 Red [p. 33]."

15: "Adjektivisches τις findet sich im NT gehäuft im lukanischen Doppelwerk (102mal: Ev 39/Apg 63), in den übrigen Evangelien nur ganz vereinzelt (Mt 1, Mk 3, Joh 7 bzw. 8). Die große Zahl von 63 Belegen in der Apg sowie 6 Einführungen eines adjektivischen τις in den lukanischen Markusstoff (Lk 8,27; 9,8.19; 18,18.35; 21,2) zeigen übereinstimmend, daß die Vorliebe für das adjektivische τις auf das Konto der Redaktion gehört."

45: "ὡς: Das als temporale Konjunktion gebrauchte ὡς ist eine von Lukas bevorzugte Wendung: Mk 1, Lk 18/Apg 29, Joh 18, Pls 4. Kennzeichnend für den lukanischen Gebrauch des ὡς temp. ist neben dieser beachtlichen Statistik: erstens die Beobachtung, daß von den 29 Belegen für ὡς temp., die die Apg aufweist, nicht weniger als 28 stereotyp auf ὡς ein δέ folgen lassen, während nur eine einzige Stelle καὶ ὡς bietet (1,10). Wendet man sich mit dieser Feststellung dem dritten Evangelium zu, so hat man die beiden ὡς δέ (5,4; 7,12) der Redaktion zuzuweisen ..., dagegen die 6 καὶ ὡς als vorlukanisch anzusprechen. Sie lassen einheitlich auf ὡς den Aorist folgen und stehen sämtlich im Nicht-Markusstoff des LkEv: 2,39; 15,25; 19,5.41; 22,66; 23,26. Zweitens ist zu beachten die Verbindung von ὡς temp. mit dem periphrastischen καὶ ἐγένετο, von der wir am Anfang des Abschnitts sprachen (5 Belege, lukanisch)."

131: "ἐπαύσατο: ist ein von Lukas gern benutztes Wort (Lk 3/Apg 6, sNT 6), das er 8,24 diff. Mk 4,39 in den Markusstoff einfügt. Im Nicht-Markusstoff steht dafür ἐκλείπω (Lk 16,9; 22,32; 23,45)."

33: "πρός c.acc. nach Verba dicendi zur Bezeichnung des (der) Angeredeten (ἀποκρίνεσθαι, γογγύζειν, δημηγορεῖν, εἰπεῖν, λαλεῖν, λέγειν, συζητεῖν) ist ausgesprochen lukanisch. Es findet sich nie bei Mt und Mk, dagegen 149mal (Ev 100/Apg 49) im lukanischen Doppelwerk, sonst im NT nur noch im JohEv 14mal und Hebr 6mal. Von den 100 Belegen im LkEv sind 29 Änderungen am bzw. Hinzufügungen zum Markusstoff. Zusammen mit den 49 Apg-Belegen erweisen sie πρός c.acc. nach Verba dic. zur Bezeichnung des (der) Angeredeten als markante lukanische Stileigentümlichkeit."

33: "εἶπεν (-ον, -αν) δέ findet sich am Satzbeginn außer Joh 12,6 im NT ausschließlich im lukanischen Doppelwerk und zwar 59mal im Ev, 15mal in der Apg. Von den 59 Belegen im LkEv sind 13 redaktionelle Änderungen am Markusstoff. Wir haben es also mit einem profilierten Lukanismus zu tun."

Beare 1981, 170: "The Lukan setting is plausible enough—it was not uncommon for Jewish teachers to compose forms of prayer for their disciples—but it is none the less a framework devised by Luke, not a fragment of the tradition as transmitted."

Fitzmyer 1981, 119: "*kai egeneto (egeneto de)* + a finite verb (indic.) without an intervening conjunction: … (in all, twenty-two times). Luke never seems to use this form in Acts (10:25 is problematic because of the initial *hōs*). Though it is found twice in Mark (1:9; 4:4), this is scarcely the source of Luke's use of it, since in those instances he changes what he borrows from the Marcan source (3:21) or omits it (8:5). Rather, it is to be recognized as a Septuagintism, since the asyndetic form is used in that translation of the MT for Hebrew *wayyehî … we-*, … especially when accompanied by the temporal clause, *en to* + infinitive (=Hebrew *be-* + infinitive). …

"The reader should note the frequency of this *kai egeneto/egeneto de* construction in Lucan Greek. It occurs so often as to be monotonous. … That is the way Luke has written his story of Jesus."

Schenk 1981, 61: Reconstruction: no introduction.

Schweizer 1982, 125: "Die Einleitung V.1 stammt von Lukas, dem Jesu eigenes Beten als Quelle alles Betens seiner Jünger wichtig ist. … Daß 'irgend einer' inner- oder außerhalb des Jüngerkreises (auch 9,57; 11,15; 21,5.7 immer gegen Mk oder Mt; vgl. 10,25; 20,27) direkt oder durch sein Verhalten eine Frage stellt und dadurch Jesu Belehrung auslöst, ist typisch lukanisch (11,27.45; 12,13.41; 13,1.23.31; 14,15; 15,2; 16,14; 17,5.20; 18,9; 19,11.39; 22,24.49; 23,27)."

Schweizer 1982, ET 1984, 190-191: "The introduction in vs. 1 comes from Luke, for whom Jesus' own prayer is important as the source of all prayer on the part of his [191] disciples. ... For 'someone' from within or without the circle of disciples (9:57; 11:15; 21:5, 7, always contra Mark or Matthew; cf. 10:25; 20:27) to pose a question directly or indirectly through his conduct, and thus initiate Jesus' instruction, is typically Lukan (11:27, 45; 12:13, 41; 13:1, 23, 31; 14:15; 15:2; 16:14; 17:5, 20; 18:9; 19:11, 39; 22:24, 49; 23:27)."

Schnackenburg 1984, 92-93: "Für diese aus der Jesusüberlieferung zusammengestellte Gebetsunterweisung hat Lukas, der mit Recht auch als [93] 'Evangelist des Gebetes' bezeichnet wird, eine besondere Einführung geschaffen. Häufig sagt er, daß Jesus im Gebet verweilte (3,21; 5,16; 6,12; 9,18.28f), und so beginnt er auch hier."

Schnackenburg 1984, ET 1995, 61: "For this instruction on prayer which was collected from the Jesus tradition, Luke, who is also justifiable characterized as the 'evangelist of prayer,' created a special introduction. Frequently he says that Jesus lingered in prayer (Luke 3:21; 5:16; 6:12; 9:18, 28f.), and he begins that way also here."

Fitzmyer 1985, 897-898: "Given the typically Lucan opening, *kai egeneto*, and his emphasis on Jesus at prayer and on counsels to pray ..., the introduction seems rather to have been [898] fashioned by Luke's redactional pen."

Kloppenborg 1987, 203: "Redaction by the evangelists has obscured the original Q Introduction."

Evans 1990, 475: "[Luke] supplies a context of Jesus at prayer (vv. 1-2) for introducing the Lord's Prayer."

International Q Project 1990, 500: Reconstruction: no introduction.

Ernst 1993, 269: "Lk hat mit der Situationsangabe einen feierlichen Vorbau für ein wichtiges Thema seiner Belehrung geschaffen."

Mack 1993, 89: Reconstruction: no introduction.

Nolland 1993, 612: "Except for ἐν τόπῳ τινί, 'in a certain place,' the first ten words are identical to the Lukan introduction in 9:18, while 'certain place' is itself almost certainly a piece of Lukan diction (he has a disproportionate fondness for both terms). The phrase ὡς ... ἐπαύσατο, 'when he stopped,' is found at 5:4. The εἶπεν πρός, 'said to,' idiom, the use of τις, 'a certain,' with 'disciples' (cf. 7:19 contrasted with Matt 11:2), and the address of Jesus as κύριε, 'Lord/Master/Sir,' may also be marks of Lukan style. We cannot be certain whether the comparison with John is traditional, or whether Luke is simply reiterating the parallelism between John and Jesus, which structures the Infancy Gospel and is important in chap. 7.

"It is likely that, different from its role on other occasions [here, Nolland points to Luke 9:18], the motif of Jesus at prayer is introduced here to suggest that the disciples desire to pray as Jesus himself prays."

Mell 1994, 158: Reconstruction: no introduction.

Carruth 1995: The address of Jesus as κύριος occurs 14 times in Luke. It occurs in material peculiar to Luke in 5:8; 9:54; 10:40;19:8; 22:38, 49. At Luke 5:12 he adds it to Mark 1:40 and at Luke 22:22 adds it to Mark 14:29. At Luke 18:41 κύριε replaces Mark's ῥαββουνί in Mark 10:51. It occurs in Lukan material in Q contexts in Luke 9:61 and 10:17. The most important occurrences for this variant are in Luke 12:41 where Peter addresses Jesus as κύριε and then asks a question to which the following Q parable appears to be a response; Luke 13:23 where the address is preceded by εἶπεν δέ τις πρὸς αὐτῷ, a question is asked and a Q saying follows; and Luke 17:37, καὶ ἀποκριθέντες λέγουσιν αὐτῷ· ποῦ κύριε; ὁ δὲ εἶπεν αὐτοῖς, which introduces a Q saying. These last three show Luke formulating introductions to Q material by having someone in the audience ask Jesus a question and pose the question with the address κύριε. The request of the disciples for instruction in prayer in Luke 11:1 appears to share this construction.

Matt = Q: (Προσευχόμενοι δὲ μὴ βατταλογήσητε ὥσπερ οἱ ἐθνικοί, δοκοῦσιν γὰρ ὅτι ἐν τῇ πολυλογίᾳ αὐτῶν εἰσακουσθήσονται. 6:8 μὴ οὖν ὁμοιωθῆτε αὐτοῖς· οἶδεν γὰρ ὁ πατὴρ ὑμῶν ὧν χρείαν ἔχετε πρὸ τοῦ ὑμᾶς αἰτῆσαι αὐτόν.)²

Pro

B. Weiß 1876, 181: "Dieser Bitte [of the disciples in Lk 11:1] wird Jesus in der Quelle bereits zunächst durch die (formell, wie materiell ganz den Charakter der Quelle tragende) allgemeine Anweisung Mtth. 6,7 entsprochen haben und dann mit der Formel v. 9 zu dem Mustergebet selbst übergangen sein. Offenbar ist nemlich v. 8 nur eine Reminiscenz an Mtth. 6,32 (=Luc. 12,30), die sich schon durch das der Quelle ganz fremde ὁ θεὸς ὁ πατὴρ ὑμῶν, sowie durch die Unterbrechung des Zusammenhangs als eine Einschaltung des Evangelisten verräth; denn v. 9 geht doch nur auf v. 7 zurück, und die v. 8 eingeflochtene Begründung der Warnung vor jenem heidnischen Miß-brauch ist immer nicht ganz passend, sofern sie das allerdings einzig vernünf-tige Motiv des wortreichen Betens voraussetzt, während doch v. 7 zeigt, daß die Heiden auf Grund ihrer πολυλογία als solcher Erhörung hoffen und auf jenen Zweck desselben gar nicht reflectiren. Luc. hat die allgemeine Warnung vor dem battologischen Gebete weggelassen, weil er eben das Gebet des Herrn nicht bloß als Muster eines rechten Gebetes geben, sondern es seinen Lesern als Gebetsformular einschärfen wollte, wie sein ὅταν προσεύχησθε λέγετε unzweideutig zeigt."

Resch 1895, 227-228: "Weiterhin jedoch ist *Weiss* auf dem richtigen Wege, wenn er Mt. 6,7, die Warnung Jesu vor dem battologischen Gebete, als unmittelbare—von Lc. weggelassene—Einleitung des Herrengebetes, aus dem

Urevangelium geschöpft sein lässt, dagegen Mt. 6,8 von diesem Zusammenhang ausschliesst. Wie wichtig ist hierbei die von *Weiss* nicht gewürdigte Thatsache, dass der *Codex Cantabrigiensis* einen selbstständigen aussercanonischen
Paralleltext von Mt. 6,7—nicht aber von v. 8!—als unmittelbare Einleitung
des Herrengebetes Lc. 11,2 einfügt, [228] also den von *Weiss* vermutheten
quellenmässigen Context wirklich herstellt."

B. Weiß 1898, 131: "Der erste Evangelist hat auch hier [6:9-13] den Text
der gemeinsamen Quelle, aus der wohl auch die Einleitung V. 7 stammt,
treuer reproduzirt (vgl. zu Lk 11,1)."

B. Weiß 1908, 31[14]: "Mt. 6,7 ist offenbar die Einleitung der Antwort Jesu,
die Luk. fortlassen mußte, weil er das Gebet eben nicht als Mustergebet faßt,
sondern als Gebetsformular."

Edwards 1975, 19-20: The concordance shows that Q has the expression
εἶπεν αὐτοῖς with Jesus as subject only in Q 11:17. Elsewhere Q uses εἶπεν
with Jesus as the unexpressed subject at 10:21 and 14:16.

Catchpole 1983, 422-424: "The warning in [Matt 6] vv. 7-8 against the
Gentile practice of prayer marked by βατταλογεῖν and πολυλογία stands out,
not only because its breaks into formal parallelism, but also because content-
wise (i) different persons are singled out for contrast, i.e. not the hypocrites
associated with the synagogues (vv. 2, 5) but the ἐθνικοί; (ii) the ground for
criticism is not ostentation or hypocrisy in the presence of men but the expec-
tation of gaining an answer to prayer by excessive verbosity; (iii) there is no
concern about reward but simply the assurance that the Father knows about
the need in question. So vv. 7-8 did not originally belong to the paranetic
collection which presently surrounds it.

"Where did vv. 7-8 originate? MattR is possible, but since Matthew is pre-
occupied with anti-Pharisaic polemic in this context it is somewhat unlikely.
If v. 1 is attributed to the evangelist, if Matt. v. 20 (which within the structure
of Matt. v-vii prepares for vi. 1) [423] is given due weight, if xxiii. 5 con-
tributes clear evidence of whom Matthew is attacking, then his preoccupa-
tions are not only clear but distinct from those of vi. 7-8. An alternative possibility would be some kind of M tradition, but we would then be faced with
a most extraordinary set of coincidences, which might better be regarded as
pointing in the direction of Q. (i) Verses 7-8 overlap with vi. 32, which is Q
material. Even more importantly, the combination of an adverse reference to
Gentiles and an affirmation that the Father knows about needs is specifically
a Q editorial combination: v. 32b is pre-Q and follows on from v. 31 to provide the final summary within the total unit, while v. 32a is a secondary inter-
ruption. Not only so, it also counts against MattR and for the link with v. 32
that the Q original will have referred to ὁ πατὴρ ὑμῶν without addition, as
does v. 8. (ii) It is typical of Q redaction to ask for a standard of behaviour

which surpasses that of the Gentiles, and, moreover, to do so by attributing to Gentiles behaviour which may equally characterize Jews. Thus first, concern about food and clothing (v. 32) can hardly be exclusively a Gentile concern. Secondly βατταλογεῖν/πολυλογία could just as well be predicated of Jews in view of Dan. iii. 26-45, 52-90; 2 Macc. i. 23-9; the Eighteen Benedictions and Kaddish material. ... Precisely such warnings had already been directed at Jewish personnel: Prov. x. 19 LXX; Eccles. v. 2; Sir. vii. 14. ... (iii) The links with Luke xi. 5-8 are notable. First, χρεία in Matt vi. 8 matches δώσει αὐτῷ ὅσων χρῄζει in Luke xi. 8. Secondly, Josephus B.J. 1.224 alerted us to the πολυλογία/ἀναίδεια link. If ἀναίδεια belongs to Luke xi. 8 by virtue of LukeR, πολυλογία cannot belong to Matt. vi. 7 by virtue of MattR, and so must stem from Q. Therefore, Luke responded editorially to pressure from both Luke xviii. 1-18 and Matt. vi. 7-8, since the inconsistency between it and the point he was making in xi. 8 was clear for all to see.

"The conclusion is that there existed in Q a collection of Material consisting of (a) Matt. vi. 7-8, which functioned as an editorial [424] introduction; (b) Matt. vi. 9-13/Luke xi. 2-4." Almost verbatim agreement in Catchpole 1993, 225-226.

Catchpole 1989, 381-382: "As it stands Matt. 6:7-8 overlaps with the sense of the QR addition in [Matt] 6:32a [πάντα γὰρ ταῦτα τὰ ἔθνη ἐπιζητοῦσιν] and, in the declaration οἶδεν γὰρ ὁ πατὴρ ὑμῶν ὧν χρείαν ἔχετε, almost exactly with the wording of the pre-Q conclusion in 6:32b. Its distinctiveness consists of its application to prayer, with the pointed rejection of verbosity, and in the concluding phrase πρὸ τοῦ ὑμᾶς αἰτῆσαι αὐτόν. The addition of this latter phrase to the received tradition about the Father's knowledge shows that in the mind of the Q editor there was no tension between praying and recalling the Father's knowledge, and also no tension between praying and depending upon the Father's provision to such an extent that ordinary work can be set aside and activist anxiety abandoned. Since on the QR level ((ἐπι)ζητεῖν was used as a synonym for μεριμνᾶν), and since on that same level 'seeking' the kingdom does not in any way preclude praying for [382] the coming of that kingdom (cf. Matt. 6:10/Luke 11:2) it is altogether natural to incorporate the outlook of the 'Cares' tradition and its characteristic terminology within a setting of prayer."

Tuckett 1989, 371: "Catchpole has convincingly argued that Matt. 6:7f. may be a Q piece which Luke has omitted and which may have introduced this Q section on prayer.[15] The Cares tradition in Q (Matt. 6:25ff./Luke 12: 22ff.) is clearly closely related to the section on prayer, whether or not it belonged to precisely the same literary context within Q."

371[15]: "Catchpole [1983; see above], 'Friend at Midnight', 422."

Catchpole 1993, 208-209: "Luke 11:8 made 11:7 reflect adversely on the character of the petitioned person, but it could only do so because the implication of 11:7, and specifically its role in 11:5-7, was misunderstood. It was taken as an actual and a negative response, whereas it was non-actual; it was taken to reflect adversely on the petitioned person, whereas it was intended to point to a positive response by someone who could be presumed to be honourable and sensitive to need. In short, 11:8 has imposed on 11:7 a scheme contributed to by 18:2, 4-5. Correspondingly, κόπος is what brings results in 18:5 whereas it was irrelevant, because ignored, to the outcome in 11:7. That is, the outcome was achieved by means of κόπος in 18:5 but was intended to emerge without being affected by κόπος in 11:7. The natural inference is that LukeR is involved in 11:5-8. This was what changed the focus from the petitioned person to the petitioner, and thus to the manner of petitioning. This was what [209] imported the idea of persistence although it had neither been mentioned explicitly nor suggested implicitly in 11:5-7, itself the *total* description of the relevant data. This was what generated confusion and a twofold interpretation of the parable's meaning. This influence of 18:1-8 on 11:5-8 can, however, be reversed, and the ensuing problems made to melt away, once we remove as LukeR intervention the words εἰ καὶ οὐ δώσει αὐτῷ ἀναστὰς διὰ τὸ εἶναι φίλον αὐτοῦ, διά γε τὴν ἀναίδειαν αὐτοῦ. Then there is left a thoroughly satisfactory parable in which the concluding declaration, now clear and unmuddled, genuinely does express the hearers' implied answer to the question posed in 11:5-7, 'Of course, no one!'"

226: "If ἀναίδειαν belongs to Luke 11:8 by virtue of LukeR, πολυλογία cannot belong to Matt 6:7 by virtue of MattR, and so must stem from Q. Therefore Luke responded editorially to pressure from both Luke 18:1-8 and Matt 6:8. It is entirely unsurprising that he should have omitted Matt 6:7-8, since the inconsistency between it and the point he was making in 11:8 was clear for all to see."

Con

Knox 1957, 25: "Again Matthew has expanded his source, adding at vi. 7 a saying from his anti-Gentile collection, and following it with the Lord's prayer, derived from current liturgical tradition and practice."

Schenk 1981, 61: Reconstruction: no introduction.

International Q Project 1990, 500: Reconstruction: no introduction.

Hagner 1993, 146: "Material closely related to v 8 is found in Q (Matt 6:32; Luke 12:30), but the similarity is probably due to a similar point being made independently rather than Q being the source of, or dependent upon, the present passage."

Mack 1993, 89: Reconstruction: no introduction.

Mell 1994, 158: Reconstruction: no introduction.

158[70]: "Die Zusammenstellung des Vatergebetes in Q mit prophetischen Mahnsprüchen zur Erhörungsgewißheit sowie die kurze formkritische Einleitung daselbst (προσεύχεσθε) dürften auf den Q-Red. zurückgehen."

Evaluations

Carruth 1995: Neither Luke 11:1-2a nor Matt 6:7-8 was in Q {B}, [()][2].

While a few scholars favor something like Luke's introduction to the Prayer as derived from Q (Castor, Marriott, Montefiore), there is otherwise general agreement that the description of Jesus at prayer is certainly Lukan. The Lukan vocabulary and interest along with the evidence for Luke's tendency to formulate introductory settings allow us to exclude this part of Luke's introduction from Q with certainty.

There are, however, a number of scholars who suppose, with varying degrees of conviction regarding the wording, that Luke derived the request of the disciples for instruction in prayer from Q (B. Weiß, Von der Goltz, Holtzmann, Loisy, Dibelius, Bussmann, Klostermann, Dupont, Polag, Gundry, Zeller, Schürmann). If it is agreed that Luke has preserved the Q position of the Prayer, this might be supported by preceding material in Q which implies a distinction between those who follow Jesus and some others (Q 10:21,22, 23,24). But the identity of the others remains ambiguous and those who follow Jesus are not identified as disciples. It can be argued that the interest in distinguishing Jesus from John is Lukan.

The vocabulary and formulation is more easily attributed to Luke than to Q. In Q the address of Jesus as κύριε, meaning teacher, is implied in Q 6:46. The address is also used by the royal official in Q 7:6, and by a would-be disciple in Q 9:59. Such an address may also be implied in Q 13:25. But the designation of Jesus as κύριος is also characteristically Lukan (Hawkins, Carruth) and Luke uses the address to formulate introductions to Q material elsewhere.

Luke, rather than Matthew, may preserve Q's verb διδάσκω in Q 12:12 (the International Q Project 1995, 481, included the verb with a {C} grade) and in Q 13:26 (the International Q Project 1995, 482, included this verb at {C}), but the Q use of the verb is not firmly established and Luke uses the verb as frequently as does Matthew in any case (Cadbury). Whereas Q uses the term μαθητής to refer to the disciples of John in Q 7:19 and to make reference to the character of a disciple in Q 6:40, the use of the term for those who follow Jesus is not doubly attested elsewhere in Q. Matthew probably preserves it from Q in Q 6:20a (International Q Project 1990, 501) and Luke probably preserves it from Q in Q 14:26,27 (International Q Project 1992, 507). Its occurrences in Q material in Matt 8:21; 9:37 and 10:25 are probably Matthean additions (International Q Project 1993, 503; International Q Project 1991, 496; International Q Project 1992, 502). Luke has probably added it in Luke 7:18 (International Q Project 1994, 497) but may have omitted one instance of Q's usage in Luke 14:26 (International Q Project 1992, 507).

The few occurrences of εἶπεν with Jesus as subject in Q are not enough to show that it is typical of Q. Given the frequency of the use of εἶπεν by Luke and the fact that in the introduction to the Prayer it depends on the preceding request, it is most likely that the expression εἶπεν δὲ αὐτοῖς is Lukan and did not occur in Q at this point.

A preface for the Prayer in Q (Easton) is conceivable but, since Luke, as well as Q, is interested in distinguishing Jesus and John, and since the vocabulary and formulation of the disciples' request is not characteristic of Q but can be seen as Lukan, it is not likely that the request stems from Q. An introduction for the prayer using the verb "pray" in some form is sufficient to serve as a transition from the preceding material and to preface the Prayer.

Robinson 1995: Neither Luke 11:1-2a nor Matt 6:7-8 was in Q {B}, [()]².

The Lucanisms indicate that the Lucan text is not derived from Q. But the reference to John is less clearly redactional. Two instigations for the Prayer, one that Jesus was praying, the other that the disciples requested a prayer comparable to that of John's disciples, are not both necessary, and indeed stand somewhat unrelated to each other. For the fact that Jesus was observed praying does not call for the codification of a shared prayer.

The references to John in Q are limited to Q 3 and 7 (with the possible exception of 16:16), so that one would not expect such a reference here in Q 11. Luke has added to the question about the fact that John's disciples fast also that they pray (Luke 5:33). Hence one may ascribe to Luke the resumption of this redactional interest here. Of course if the reference to John were in Q 11:1, Luke 5:33 could be explained as an anticipatory reminiscence.

Matthew's introduction (Matt 6:7-8) concludes with a repetition of the conclusion (Q 12:30) of a Q section (Q 12:21-31) similar to the Prayer. Both contain the invidious reference to Gentiles and the assurance that "your Father" already knows what you need. But, rather than this suggesting that the Matthean introduction was also in Q, such redundancy is better understood as a reminiscence of Q 12:30 moved forward redactionally into Matt 6:7-8.

Had the repudiation of babbling garrulousness (Matt 6:7) been in Q, Luke would hardly have interpolated a parable providing a model for prayer (Luke 11:5-8), i.e. an otherwise appropriate commentary on the Prayer, that ends by advocating shameless persistence (Q 11:8). The reverse logic would be valid only if the argument could be made cogent that Luke 11:8, favoring shameless persistence, is Lucan redaction. For this would explain Luke's omission of Matt 6:7-8, opposing such garrulousness, had he found it in Q (Catchpole).

Neither the Lucan nor the Matthean introduction flows well from the immediately preceding Q context (Q 10:23b-24). Indeed the reference in Q 10:24 to the Q people "hearing" what previously could not be heard stands in some tension to the Matthean introduction's reference to Gentiles trying to force God to "hear." Of course lack of continuity is frequent in Q, but in any case the preceding Q context does not commend either introduction.

If there were some text here, it would be difficult to reconstruct it critically, since there is no overlap between Luke and Matthew, and since both Luke and Matthew have to a considerable extent clearly adapted the material to their contexts.

Q 11:~~1-2a,~~2b³: Luke's ὅταν προσεύχησθε λέγετε, or Matthew's οὕτως οὖν προσεύχεσθε ὑμεῖς.

Luke = Q: [ὅταν]³ προσεύχ[η]³σθε ( )³ [λέγετε]³

Pro

Loisy 1907, 599: "Les deux évangélistes dépendent, en dernière analyse, d'une même version grecque de l'Oraison dominicale, et Luc, qui en a gardé le préambule original, pourrait en avoir aussi mieux gardé le texte."

Schulz 1972, 85: "Mt bietet im übrigen in 6,9a eine Lk 11,2 sachlich entsprechende Einleitung: Mt: προσεύχεσθε—Lk: ὅταν προσεύχησθε, λέγετε. Eine ähnliche kurze Einführung des Vaterunsers könnte also schon in Q gestanden haben. Sicherheit ist hier allerdings nicht zu gewinnen, da Lk möglicherweise auch V 2a formuliert haben könnte."

Polag 1979, 48: Reconstruction. But ὅταν and λέγετε with a lower degree of certainty.

Schenk 1981, 61: Reconstruction.

Mack 1993, 89: Reconstruction.

Schürmann 1994, 177: "Eine Einleitung wie [Luke 11] V 2a ist für Q sicher: Matthäus hat ὅταν προσεύχησθε nach 6,5 vorgezogen und dann 'in 6,9a eine Lk 11,2 sachlich entsprechende Einleitung' gebildet[30]."

177[30]: "So Schulz, Q 85."

Con

Cadbury 1920, 202: Although this example is not cited by Cadbury, he says, "οὕτως is a word that could scarcely have given offence to Luke, yet he seems to avoid it in some cases."

Easton 1926, 175: "Lk understands that the Lord's Prayer should form part of all Christian devotions (ὅταν; 'whenever')."

176: "ὅταν and the subjunctive are of course from Lk; they presuppose Christian liturgical practice."

Schulz 1972, 85: See Q 11:~~1-2a,~~2b³ Luke = Q, Pro.

Kloppenborg 1987, 203: "Redaction by the evangelists has obscured the original Q Introduction, although both Matthew and Luke agree in the use of a form of προσεύχομαι and an imperative (Matt, προσεύχεσθε; Luke, ὅταν προσεύχησθε, λέγετε)."

Nolland 1993, 612: "ὅταν προσεύχησθε, 'whenever you pray,' appears in identical form in Matt 6:5, a little before Matthew's version of the Lord's Prayer, but this is probably fortuitous."

Matt = Q: (Οὕτως οὖν)³ προσεύχ(ε)³σθε (ὑμεῖς)³ [ ]³

Pro

B. Weiß 1908, 31: Reconstruction.
International Q Project 1990, 500: <...> προσεύχεσθε.
Mell 1994, 158: Reconstruction.
158⁷⁰: See Q 11:~~1-2a,~~2b² Matt = Q, Pro.

Con

B. Weiß 1878, 421: See Q 11:~~1-2a,~~2b-4⁰ Luke and Matthew = Q, Pro.
McNeile 1915, 77: "The sentence is probably due to Mt., who inserts the Prayer at this point, the emphatic ὑμεῖς standing in contrast with the ἐθνικοί of v. 7."
Bonnard 1963, 82: "Les premiers mots [Matt 6:9a] sont une formule intro-ductive rédactionnelle reliant la prière à l'instruction précédente. ... Le οὖν matthéen n'annonce pas une conclusion logique."
Schürmann 1968, 119: "Daß Matthäus in der Redequelle auch die Ein-leitung zum Vaterunser Lk 11,2a (ὅταν προσεύχησθε) gelesen hat, kann noch nicht sicher aus der Aufforderung Mt 6,9a ... geschlossen werden, da diese ihre vorliegende Gestalt gewiß im Gegensatz zu Mt 6,7 erhalten hat. Zumindest vermutet werden darf aber, daß ὅταν προσεύχησθε Mt 6,5 eine Reminiszenz an eine Vorlage wie Lk 11,2a ist, denn ursprünglich hat hier—wie Mt 6,2 ὅταν ποιῇς—der Singular gestanden (vgl. V.6 ὅταν προσεύχῃ ...) ὅταν προσ-εύχησθε begegnet dann auch außer an diesen beiden Stellen im NT sonst nie wieder."
Schulz 1972, 84-85: "Mit οὕτως οὖν zieht Mt aus der vorangehenden War-nung vor der Gebetspraxis der Heiden die Folgerung und auch das betont am Schluß stehende ὑμεῖς scheint auf die Antithese zum Gebet der Heiden abzuheben. Beides ist also sek. Der Imperativ [85] προσεύχεσθε wird ebenfalls auf Mt zurückgehen, da er die Imperative in V 7 und V 8 weiterführt."
Gundry 1982, 105: "Two Mattheanisms—οὖν (35,11) and οὕτως (18,5)—replace Luke's ὅταν. The first forges a link with the preceding context; the second emphasizes a manner of prayer that contrasts with wordiness. In this respect the insertion of ὑμεῖς (15,3) emphasizes the contrast between pagans and Jesus' disciples. The tradition did not have such a contrast (cf. Luke). The imperative mood comes over to the verb of praying, and Luke's λέγετε drops out."
Luz 1985, 334⁵: "Οὕτως οὖν προσεύχεσθε ὑμεῖς V9a ist vermutlich von ihm formuliert: Red. sind vorangestelltes οὕτως οὖν und nachgestelltes ὑμεῖς."

46 [ET 1989, 64]: Luz's chart shows that οὕτως occurs 32× in Mt, 10× in Mk, and 21x in Lk. It is used ca 22× redactionally in Mt.

Luz 1985, ET 1989, 370⁵: "Οὕτως οὖν προσεύχεσθε ὑμεῖς v. 9a is probably formulated by him: the οὕτως οὖν in first position and ὑμεῖς at the end are redactional."

Gnilka 1986, 214: "Die Einführung 'So also sollt ihr beten' ist MtR⁷, baut aber auf einer ähnlichen Einführung in Q auf (vgl. Lk 11,2a)."

214⁷: "οὖν ist für Mt typisches Anschlußwort, betont nachgestelltes ὑμεῖς kontrastiert zu den Heiden in V 7."

Schenk 1987, 381: "οὖν ...

     Mt 57: Mk 5: Lk 31 + 62: Joh 194 ...

"οὖν für konsekutive Imp. ...:

     Mt 22 = (Mk 1 + 6) + (Q 1 + 7) + (A-Mt 1)

"3,8 (=Q); 5,48 (+Q); 6,8f (+Q)."

448: "καὶ ὑμεῖς *auch ihr*

     Mt 10: Mk 2: Lk 4

"Damit ist zugleich die häufigste textsyntaktische Verwendungsweise bei Mt als *verstärkende Weiterführung schon angeredeter Adressaten* bezeichnet, die ferner 5,13f (+Q); 6,9 (+Q); 10,20 (=Mk).31 (+Q); 26,31 (+Mk) vorliegt (also insgesamt 16mal)."

Kloppenborg 1987, 203: See Q 11:~~1-2a,~~2b³ Luke = Q, Con.

Davies and Allison 1988, 599: "οὕτως οὖν προσεύχεσθε ὑμεῖς. This is presumably redactional, although οὕτως οὖν appears only here in Matthew."

Catchpole 1993, 29: "The paraenetic introduction (6:7-8) also has a polemical thrust ..., it must be a secondary addition to the prayer itself, since the original purpose of the prayer can hardly have been to serve as a model of a certain simple style of praying—that would be to trivialize it—but rather as instruction on what should be prayer. Indeed, Matthew's introductory 'Pray then like this (οὕτως)' is rather less suitable than Luke's 'When you pray say ...' (Luke 11:2)."

Undecided

Katz 1973, 258-259: "Die Einleitung in Mt 6,9a οὕτως οὖν προσεύχεσθε ὑμεῖς ist durch den Kontext, die Gegenüberstellung mit den Gebetspraktiken der Heiden, veranlaßt. Diese Formulierung gibt keinen Aufschluß über ihre Herkunft. Sie kann von Matthäus formuliert sein als Pendant zu V. 7: προσευχόμενοι δὲ μὴ βατταλογήσητε ὥσπερ οἱ ἐθνικοί; sie könnte auch in Anlehnung an den Wortlaut der Logienquelle formuliert sein, falls dieser in Lk 11,2 vorliegen [259] sollte: εἶπεν δὲ αὐτοῖς· ὅταν προσεύχησθε, λέγετε. Die Entscheidung muß also offen bleiben."

Evaluations

Carruth 1995: Luke = Q {C}, [[ὅταν]³] προσεύχ[[η]³]σθε [()³] [[λέγετε]³].
When one assumes Luke has preserved the position of the prayer in Q, some kind of transition to the Prayer from preceding Q material is reasonable. Since both Matthew and Luke attest a form of the verb προσεύχομαι, we may be sure a form of this verb was in Q here. There is considerable evidence for Matthean redaction from the point of view of vocabulary and formulation (Schulz, Gundry, Luz, Gnilka, Schenk) and the context into which Matthew has inserted the Prayer (Schulz, Gundry, Catchpole). Luke's version is less obviously redactional and, although it may reflect his other changes in the prayer in the direction of emphasizing its dailiness, Luke may also be dependent on Q for his introduction.

Robinson 1995: Luke = Q {C}, [[ὅταν]³] προσεύχ[[η]³]σθε [()³] [[λέγετε]³·].
If Q had no antecedent introductory material on the topic of prayer (such as Luke 11:1-2a or Matt 6:7-8), the Lucan clause in Luke 11:2b ("Whenever you pray") would function less abruptly to lead into the new topic than does the Matthean ("Thus then pray"), which presupposes some antecedent introduction to the topic of prayer, such as is found in Matt 6:5-6,7-8.
There must have been some transition in Q to the Prayer. For in the immediately preceding saying (Q 10:23b-24) Jesus, in the first person singular, is addressing his followers in the second person plural, and could hardly without some transition proceed, in the first person plural, to address the Father in prayer in the second person singular. (The transition would have been more satisfactory from Q 10:21 to Q 11:2b-4, had they originally belonged together. For though Q 10:21 speaks in the first person singular to the Father and Q 11:2b-4 in the first person plural to the Father, this transition could have been mediated by the νηπίοις with which Q 10:21c ends. Indeed Q 10:21d could have been a congregational response, with ναί representing ἀμήν, introducing the communal Prayer of Petitions.)
The prayer of Thanksgiving also has a quotation formula (Q 10:21a), though in this case there is an easier transition from the preceding context that refers explicitly (though in the third person) to God (τὸν ἀποστείλαντά με, Q 10:16).
The Lucan transitional formula has been considered redactional on the grounds that it presupposes the redactional narrative introduction in Luke 11: 1-2a. But, as the Cult Didache in the Matthean context illustrates (Matt 6: 2,5,16), such a syntactical construction does not require a narrative context. Nor does the repetitiveness implicit in the formulation ("Whenever you pray …") require a liturgical setting more advanced than what needs to be

presupposed for the community of Q. Presumably already Jesus himself participated in prayer at meals!

Though the Lucan transitional expression is syntactically similar to opening clauses in the Cult Didache of the Matthean context, it would be somewhat forced to say that the formulation in Matt 6:5, verbally identical with that in Luke 11:2b, is simply the Q phrase carried forward to the item in the Cult Didache having to do with prayer. For the same formulation occurs in all three items of the Cult Didache.

The Cult Didache's fluctuation from singular to plural is hardly a reminiscence in Matt 6:5 of the plural in the Q transitional clause in Luke 11:2b. For the singular, though occurring in the second part of each of the three items of the Cult Didache (Matt 6:3-4,6,17-18), occurs in the opening formulation only in the third item (Matt 6:16). Thus it is the minority usage of the singular in this opening of the third item that, if anything, calls for some explanation or derivation. It may in fact echo the singular used in the second part of each of the three items.

The Matthean transitional expression can be well explained in terms of the Matthean context. Over against two false ways to pray (ostentatiously, Matt 6:5-6; and garrulously, Matt 6:7-8), Matt 6:9a occurs in a context that already has its focus on prayer, and needs only to provide as a consequence (οὖν) an appropriate way (οὕτως) to prayer, standing in contrast to the other two (hence the emphatic last position of ὑμεῖς).

Q 11:~~1-2a,~~2b⁴: Matthew's address with ἡμῶν.

Luke = Q: Πάτερ ( )⁴

Pro

von Harnack 1907, 48: "Eine Urform (die Anrede πάτερ u. die 4.-6. Bitte) muß existiert haben, und nichts spricht dagegen, daß sie in Q stand."

von Harnack 1907, ET 1908, 65: "An original form (πάτερ and the fourth, fifth, and sixth petitions) must have existed."

Loisy 1907, 601-602⁴: "L'emploi du simple *abba* est garanti par saint Paul, et le πάτερ de Luc peut représenter [602] la forme de l'invocation dans le texte primitif de la prière."

Castor 1912, 230: Reconstruction.

McNeile 1915, 76: "As regards the omission of clauses Lk.'s form is probably nearer to the original; he could not have omitted them had the longer form been known to him; and the tendency of liturgical formulas is towards enrichment rather than abbreviation."

Zahn 1920, 443: "Die Anrufung Gottes mit dem schlichten πάτερ ohne ein hinzutretendes ἡμῶν ὁ ἐν τοῖς οὐρανοῖς ist nicht minder jüdisch als diese vollere Form bei Mt 6,9 ... und, was den Mangel des Possessivs anlangt, gerade echt palästinisches Aramäisch. ... Abba (אבא, nicht אבי) sprach Jesus zu seinem Vater (Mr 14,36) und beteten die Christen sowohl im einsamen als im gemeinsamen Gebet. Die Griechen und die griechisch redenden Juden setzten dafür im eigenen Gebet wie als Übersetzer aramäisch gesprochener Gebete πάτερ oder ὁ πατήρ."

443¹⁰: "Rm 8,15 ... Gl 4,6 ... als förmliche Übersetzung seitens des Schriftstellers steht das griech. Wort neben dem aram. nur Mr 14,36. Daher ist Abba vorauszusetzen auch Mt 11,26.27; Lc 10,21; 22,42; 23,34.42; Jo 11,42; 12,27.28; 17,1.5.21.24 (cf. 17,11.25), cf. auch Lc 15,18,21 1Pt 1,17. Nur Mt 26,39.42 πάτερ μου."

Easton 1926, 176: "Lk's simple 'Father' is certainly original."

Schmid 1930, 233: "Die primäre Gestalt bewahrt Lk sicher in V2. Denn die Gottesbezeichnung ὁ πατὴρ ἡμῶν ὁ ἐν τοῖς οὐρανοῖς (oder ὁ οὐράνιος) entspricht dem besonderen Sprachgebrauch des Mt¹ und eine Weglassung der Worte ἡμῶν ὁ ἐν τοῖς οὐρανοῖς ließe sich durch nichts begründen."

233¹: "Einfaches ὁ πατήρ aber findet sich bei allen Synoptikern, ist also nicht spezifisch lukanisch; z.B. Mt 11,25.26; 24,36; Mk 14,36. Viel häufiger ist ὁ πατήρ μου (ὑμῶν)."

Manson 1937, 168: "The originality of Lk. is shown by the recorded prayer of Jesus Himself (Mk. 14:36) and the testimony of Paul (Rom. 8:15; Gal. 4:6)."

266: Reconstruction.

Hirsch 1941, 102: "Luk hat die zugrundeliegende Gestalt [of the Our Father] bis auf zwei Kleinigkeiten, die schon in Lu I geändert sein mögen, bewahrt, Matth aber hat erheblichere Erweiterungen des Vaterunsers vorgenommen." See 11:~~1-2a,~~2b⁴ Matt = Q, Con.

Dupont 1958, 65-66¹: "... [66] ... A noter enfin que l'expression 'Notre Père' ('qui es dans les cieux') correspond à l'usage du judaïsme palestinien, tandis que 'Père', l'invocation courte, se rattache au judaïsme hellénistique (cf. Sap., 14,3; 3 Macc., 6,3.8) et aux usages des chrétientés pauliniennes (cf. Gal., 4,6; Rom., 8,15; Eph., 3,14); on voit d'ailleurs par Luc, 23,34.46 que notre évangéliste conçoit volontiers une prière commençant par πάτερ."

Hahn 1963, 320: "Das bloße πάτερ der Lukas-Fassung geht auf ein ursprüngliches אבא zurück, während πάτερ ἡμῶν mit dem Zusatz ὁ ἐν τοῖς οὐρανοῖς eine sekundäre, der liturgischen Tradition des Judentums folgende Umbildung darstellt."

Jeremias 1966, 158: "So werden wir also in dem gemeinsamen Bestand, d.h. in der Lukasfassung, den ältesten Text zu erblicken haben. Die heidenchristliche Kirche hat ihn uns aufbewahrt."

Jeremias 1967, 12: "die lukanische Kurzform ist in der Matthäus-Fassung vollständig enthalten. Nach allem, was wir über die Gesetzmäßigkeit der Überlieferung liturgischer Texte wissen, hat in einem solchen Fall, in dem die kürzere Fassung in der längeren enthalten ist, die kürzere als die ursprünglichere zu gelten. Wer sollte es gewagt haben, zwei Bitten des Vater-Unsers zu streichen, wenn sie zum ältesten Überlieferungsbestand gehörten? Dagegen ist das Umgekehrte, daß liturgische Texte in der Frühzeit, ehe eine Verfestigung der Formulierung eintritt, ausgestaltet, erweitert, angereichert werden, vielfältig belegt."

12-13: "Schließlich spricht für die [13] Ursprünglichkeit der Lukas-Fassung auch die Wiederkehr der kurzen Anrede 'lieber Vater' (Abba) in den Gebeten der ältesten Christen, wie wir aus Röm. 8,15 und Gal. 4,6 sehen."

Jeremias 1967, ET 1964, 11: "the shorter form of Luke is completely contained in the longer form of Matthew. This makes it very probable that the Matthean form is an expanded one, for according to all that we know about the tendency of liturgical texts to conform to certain laws in their transmission, in a case where the shorter version is contained in the longer one, the shorter text is to be regarded as original. No one would have dared to shorten a sacred text like the Lord's Prayer and to leave out two petitions if they had formed part of the original tradition. On the contrary, the reverse is amply attested, that in the early period, before wordings were fixed, liturgical texts were elaborated, expanded, and enriched."

12: "a final point in favor of the originality of the Lucan version is the reappearance of the brief form of address 'dear Father' (*abba*) in the prayers of the earliest Christians, as we see from Romans 8:15 and Galatians 4:6."

Schwarz 1968-69, 245-246: "Zu beurteilen und zu entscheiden, welche der beiden Fassungen (ob die matthäische Langform oder die lukanische Kurzform) die ursprüngliche ist, kann kaum schwerfallen. Denn:

"1. das merkwürdige Schwanken des Vokativs πάτερ im Text der Synoptiker, 'das sich nur durch ein an allen Stellen zugrunde liegendes aramäisches *'Abba* erklären läßt';

"2. der bei Markus (xiv. 36) erhaltene Gebetsruf Jesu in Gethsemane (ἀββᾶ ὁ πατήρ = *'Abba* mit Übersetzung; Matthäus: πάτερ μου, Lukas: πάτερ);

"3. der Sprachgebrauch der gesamten Urchristenheit, in deren Gebetssprache es in seiner aramäischen Form *'Abba* eingegangen ist (Röm. viii. 15 und Gal. iv. 6), [246] sprechen eindeutig für das πάτερ (= *'Abba*) des Lukas. ... Aus all dem ergibt sich, daß nicht die matthäische Langform, sondern die lukanische Kurzform die ursprüngliche Anrede bietet also: πάτερ (= *'Abba*)."

Schweizer 1973, 92: "Erweiterungen sind also festzustellen bei der Anrede, nach den zwei Du-Bitten und nach der letzten Bitte. Ursprünglich folgten sich demnach die kurze Anrede 'Vater,' zwei kurze parallele Du-Bitten, darauf zwei längere, parallel zueinander verlaufende Wir-Bitten und eine kurze dritte, besonders hervorgehobene Schlußbitte."

Schweizer 1973, ET 1975, 148: "We thus find expansions in the address, after the first two (second person singular) petitions, and after the last petition. This suggests the prayer originally began with the brief address 'Father' followed by two second person singular petitions in parallel and then two longer parallel first person plural petitions, concluding with a third short petition expressed emphatically."

Polag 1977, 59: "Sie [the address to the Father in the Lord's Prayer] findet sich in Q nur Lk 11,2 par Mt 6,9 zu Beginn des Vaterunsers; dort wird die lk Form πάτερ als wörtliche Übersetzung des aramäische אבא allgemein für ursprünglich gehalten."

Polag 1979, 48: Reconstruction.

Schmithals 1980, 130: "Die uns geläufigere Form des 'Vater-Unser' findet sich Mat. 6,9-13; sie wurde gegenüber der Vorlage in der Spruchquelle Q, die Lukas in V.2-4 im wesentlichen festgehalten hat, erst von Matthäus in die vorliegende Form gebracht."

Beare 1981, 170-171: "It will be noticed that here [in the Lukan form] 'Father' is used alone, without the [171] familiar 'our' and 'in heaven'. This at least seems to be the original form, for Jesus himself addresses God simply as 'Father' in his own prayers (Mk.14:36; Mt.11:25f.; etc.), and Paul indicates that the convert at his baptism learned to say 'Abba, Father,' probably along with this Prayer (Gal.4:6; Rom.8:15f.). The Matthaean form looks like a liturgical elaboration; it is also in line with the phrasing of rabbinical prayers."

Schenk 1981, 61: Reconstruction.

Strecker 1982, 14: "Die Urform setzte mit der schlichten Vater-Anrede ein, wie diese sich bei Lukas findet, dessen Fassung im ganzen in die matthäische hineinpaßt."

Gerhardsson 1984, 217-218: "That the brief invocation 'Father' (πάτερ) found in the Lukan version of the Lord's Prayer (Luke 11:2) must be considered original is, I think, inescapable. 'Our Father in heaven' seems to be an expansion which took place within the Matthaean tradition; a liturgical formula already in use in the synagogue has been taken over. The phrase 'the heavenly Father'—in slightly varying forms—is characteristic of the Matthaean tradition, occurring twenty times in Matthew. By way of contrast, there are no exact parallels in Luke (cf., however, [218] 11:13), and only one in Mark (11:25)—and the reading there is disputed."

Schnackenburg 1984, 96: "Die lukanische kurze Anrede 'Vater' ist sicher das Ursprüngliche."

Schnackenburg 1984, ET 1995, 63: "The Lukan brief address 'Father' is certainly the original."

Zeller 1984, 56: Reconstruction.

Fitzmyer 1985, 897: "Matthew appended phrases: to the end of the opening address. ... These elements, which suit indeed the spirit of the prayer, have scarcely been excised by Luke."

902: "the fact that 'abbā' is preserved in Mark 14,36 Gal 4:6 Rom 8:15 argues for this Lucan form of address as more original than Matthew's."

Schneider 1985, 65-66: "Die Gegenprobe kann darin bestehen, daß man nach einer eventuellen Vorliebe des Lukas für einfaches *ho patēr* bzw. für absolutes *pater* als Anrede fragt. Hier läßt sich zwar erkennen, daß der auf Gott bezogene Vokativ *pater* bei Lukas relativ häufig vorkommt.[28] Man kann aber nicht beweisen, daß er dabei Erweiterungen wie [66] 'der in den Himmeln' (hier kämen Lk 6,36; 11,13; 12,20 in Betracht) oder Verbindungen mit Pronomina[29] vermeidet. Die Stellen Lk 6,36; 11,13; 12,30, an deren Parallelen das Mt-Evangelium einen längeren Text bezeugt, reichen nicht hin, um in dieser Hinsicht eine Kürzung der Q-Vorlage von seiten des Lukas zu beweisen."

65[28]: "Absolutes *pater* (Vokativ) steht als Gottesanrede: Lk 10,21b par Mt 11,25; 10,21d (*ho patēr* als Vokativ) par Mt 11,26; 11,2c diff Mt 6,9b; 22,42 diff Mk 14,36 (*abba ho patēr*); 23,34a Sg. diff Mk (15,24); 23,46 Sg. diff Mk (15,37)."

66[29]: "*Ho patēr* wird an folgenden Stellen aus Lk/Apg (z.T. in Verbindung mit Pronomina) auf Gott bezogen: Lk 2,49 *mou* Sg.; 6,36 *hymōn* diff Mt 5,48 (add *ho ouranios*); 9,26 absolut diff Mk 8,38 (add *autou*); 10,21d absolut als Vokativ; siehe oben Anm. 28. 10,22a *mou* par Mt 11,27a; 10,22b absolut par Mt 11,27b; 10,22c absolut par Mt 11,27c; 11,13 absolut diff Mt 7,11 (*hymōn ho en tois ouranois*); 12,20 *hymōn* vorangestellt, diff Mt 6,32 (*ho patēr hymōn ho ouranios*); 12,32 *hymōn* diff Mt 6,34; 22,29 *mou* Sg.; 24,49 *mou* Sg.; Apg 1,4 absolut; 1,7 absolut; 2,33 absolut."

Gnilka 1986, 214: "Die lk Gebetsanrede 'Vater' ist die ältere."

Davies and Allison 1988, 591: Reconstruction.

Taussig 1988, 25: Reconstruction.

30: "The Lukan Πάτερ ('Father') is most probably a translation of the Aramaic אבא ('abba'), and therefore is taken to be the earlier version."

Stritzky 1989, 10-11: "In der Forschung, die sich mit dieser Problematik ausführlich auseinandergesetzt hat und sie mit dem hypothetischen Versuch einer Rückübersetzung in die Ursprache einer Lösung zuführen wollte, hat sich die Meinung durchgesetzt, daß das entscheidende Kriterium für die Ursprünglichkeit darin zu sehen ist, daß die Lukasfassung in der des Matthäus vollständig enthalten ist. Der kürzere Text des Lukas, der mit seinen fünf Gebetsrufen wohl den Inhalt des Gebetes Jesu [11] wiedergibt, dürfte der Urform ihrem Umfang nach nahekommen, während die Mt-Rezension Zusätze bietet."

International Q Project 1990, 500: Πάτερ.

Kloppenborg 1990, 49: Reconstruction.

Catchpole 1993, 29: "We have no evidence from Luke's use of Mark that he preferred short references to God as Father."

30: "We know that in a different but also closely associated saying Luke was content to retain a reference to 'the heavenly Father' (Matt 7:11/Luke 11:13), just as elsewhere he was content to retain a rather formal and extended invocation of the 'Father, Lord of heaven and earth' in prayer (Matt 11:25/ Luke 10:21). So there is no reason to suppose that Luke would have shortened Matt 6:9, had he known it."

Hagner 1993, 145: "Jeremias is almost certainly correct in his conclusion that Luke preserves an earlier form of the prayer (expansions are more likely than omissions)."

Mack 1993, 89: Reconstruction.

Cullmann 1994, 54: "An Stelle der uns aus dem Matthäustext vertrauten Anrede … steht im Lukasevangelium (11,2) nur das Wort 'Vater' (πάτερ). Sehr viele Ausleger sehen hier wohl mit Recht den Lukastext als ursprünglich an. Für ihn spricht die Tatsache, daß Jesus in seinen eigenen Gebeten im griechischen Text nur 'Vater' oder 'mein Vater' sagt (Mk. 14,36 par.,[72] auch Mt. 11,25, Luk. 10,21[73]), besonders aber das aramäische Grundwort 'abba', das in dieser Form im Gethsemanegebet neben der griechischen Übersetzung ὁ πατήρ steht und offenkundig Jesu besondere Gottesanrede war."

54⁷²: "In Mk. 14,36 steht als Übersetzung für 'abba' ὁ πατήρ, also der als *Vokativ* gebrauchte Nominativ, in Mt. 26,39 πάτερ μου, in Luk. 22,42 πάτερ."

54⁷³: "Bei Matthäus und Lukas steht im gleichen Vers das erste Mal πάτερ, das zweite Mal ὁ πατήρ als Vokativ, bei beiden das erste Mal ähnlich wie im Vaterunser (des Matthäus) verbunden mit 'Herr des Himmels und der Erde'."

Cullmann 1994, ET 1995, 41: "Instead of the address 'Our Father in heaven … the Gospel of Luke has only the word 'Father' (*pater*). A great many exegetes, probably rightly, regard the Lukan text as original. In support of this is the fact that in his own prayers, in the Greek text Jesus says only 'Father', or 'my Father' (Mark 14.36 par.;⁷² also Matt. 11.25; Luke 10.21⁷³), and also in particular the underlying Aramaic word 'Abba', which in this form stands in the prayer in Gethsemane alongside the Greek translation *ho patēr*, and was evidently Jesus' special way of addressing God."

156⁷²: "In Mark 14.36 ὁ πατήρ stands as a translation for '*abba*', i.e. the nominative used as a vocative. Matt. 26.39 has πάτερ μου, and Luke 22.42 πάτερ."

156⁷³: "In Matthew and Luke the same verse first has πάτερ and then the second time ὁ πατήρ as a vocative; both of these are first, as in the Our Father (Matthaean version), combined with 'Lord of heaven and earth'."

Mell 1994, 158: Reconstruction.

Con

Wernle 1899, 68: "Die Anrede mag Lc gekürzt haben, da er 'unser Vater' im Himmel durchgehends vermeidet."

B. Weiß 1901, 459: "Daher [daß 'man in einer Zeit, wo der Buchstabe der Herrnworte noch keineswegs als unantastbar galt, um es leichter behaltbar und darum gebräuchlicher zu machen, alles irgend Entbehrliche fortliess', erklärt sich] schon das einfache πάτερ der Gebetsanrede, das ja durch Jesus selbst (10,21) sanktionirt war."

B. Weiß 1907 , 72¹: "Dass all diese Abweichungen von Matthäus auf schriftstellerischer Reflexion beruhen, macht es schlechthin undenkbar, dass Lukas in der Hauptabweichung das Ursprüngliche erhalten haben sollte."

Lagrange 1921, 321: "Luc a pu croire que ces mots [Lagrange considers here in general all material in Matthew's Prayer but not in Luke's] qui n'ajoutaient rien de substantiel étaient moins nécessaires aux gentils. D'autant que dans son text on reconnaît sa main: τὸ καθ' ἡμέραν, αὐτοί, παντί. Son text paraît moins primitif; s'il a donné à son original sa couleur propre, ne pourrait-il pas aussi l'avoir abrégé? C'est ce qui nous paraît le plus probable."

Lagrange 1923, 124: "Sur les différences entre Mt. et Lc., voir le commentaire de Lc., où nous essayons de montrer que c'est lui [Luke] qui a abrégé; le texte de Mt. [in all material additional to that in Luke's Prayer] est donc primitif."

Soiron 1941, 328: "Die feierliche Anrede bei Mt beschränkt er [Luke] auf die kurze: πάτερ—eine Gewohnheit, die er durch sein ganzes Evangelium hindurch beibehält (vgl. Lk 6,36 gegenüber Mt 5,48; Lk 12,30 gegenüber Mt 6,32 ferner Lk 10,21; 22,42; 23,34.46)."

Ott 1965, 122-123: "Wie ein Vergleich des Vaterunsers des Matthäus mit dem Vaterunser-Text der Didache (8,2) zeigt, wird man annehmen dürfen, daß schon zu der Zeit, als Lukas schrieb, das Vaterunser als Gebetsformular seine endgültige Gestalt—die im Matthäusevangelium überlieferte—im wesentlichen angenommen hatte. Wenn der Lukastext nicht eine Überarbeitung dieses Gebetsformulars, sondern eine—ebenfalls verbreitete—kürzere Variante des Vaterunsers wäre, wäre es äußerst unwahrscheinlich, daß die matthäische Form des Vaterunsers die lukanische so schnell und spurlos verdrängt hätte, daß sich in den Handschriften zwar eine große Zahl von Angleichungen des Lukastextes an den Matthäustext finden, die schon sehr früh einsetzen, aber bisher keine Handschrift bekannt ist—in den Apparaten der kritischen Ausgaben ist jedenfalls keine solche verzeichnet—, die den Matthäustext an den ihrem Schreiber vielleicht geläufigeren kürzeren und auch sonst abweichenden Lukastext angleicht. G. Klein, *ZNW* 7 (1906) 35 tritt wohl nicht ohne Recht dafür ein, daß wir die Urgestalt des Vaterunsers bei Matthäus besitzen, 'denn nur in dieser Form entspricht es den Anforderungen, die an ein jüdisches Gebet gestellt wurden', wie er in seinem Aufsatz des weiteren nachweist. Selbst Lohmeyer, der für zwei nebeneinander bestehende Traditionen eintritt, erkennt die 'jüngere Herkunft' der lukanischen Form des Vaterunsers an (VU 210). Lagrange dürfte also recht behalten, wenn er feststellt: 'La forme de Mt. semble être la forme liturgique usitée chez les chrétiens.'... Der Text des Lukas 'paraît moins primitif; s'il a donné à son original sa couleur propre, ne pourrait-il pas aussi l'avoir abrégé? C'est ce qui nous paraît le plus probable' (*Lk-Komm.* 321). Aus all dem ergibt sich mit großer Sicherheit, daß das lukanische Vaterunser eine Überarbeitung und Verkürzung des Vaterunsers in der matthäischen Form darstellt, die weder vor noch neben der matthäischen Gestalt als in den frühchristlichen Gemeinden gebräuchliches Gebetsformular einige Verbreitung gefunden hat. Die lukanische Form des Vaterunsers hat als lukanische Überarbeitung des Gebetsformulars ihren Platz innerhalb der lukanischen Gebetsparänese. Innerhalb dieser lukanischen Gebetsparänese ist es nicht mehr 'nicht vorstellbar, daß Lukas dieses Gebet verkürzt hätte, wenn er es in der Matthäusfassung vorgefunden hätte' (so Schmid *Mt-Komm.* 122), zumal wenn es zutrifft (wie

Schmid selbst anerkennt), daß Lukas den Text nicht als ein Gebetsformular [123] verstanden hat, sondern als 'ein Muster eines inhaltsreichen und echt christlichen Gebets' (*Lk-Komm.* 197)."

Schürmann 1994, 180: "Die schlichte Vokativ-Anrede πάτερ des *Lukas* begegnet als Gebetsanrede Jesu in Q nicht, außer mit erläuterndem zweitem Vokativ noch Lk 10,21a par Mt (10,21b par Mt 11,26 aber ὁ πατήρ!). Dagegen ist sie für Lukas anscheinend charakteristisch; vgl. noch 22,42 diff Mk, in luk R auch wohl 23,46 und vielleicht (v.l.) 23,34.[50] Stammt die gut griechische Anrede also in dieser Form von Lukas? Wahrscheinlich; aber es muß die Möglichkeit offengehalten werden, daß Lukas mit der Anrede πάτερ die in seiner Gemeindetradition übliche (und der Grundform ἀββᾶ noch nähere; s.u.) Form in die Q-Fassung (entsprechend dann vielleicht auch in die anderen vorstehend genannten Stellen) eingetragen hat."

180[50]: "Vgl. dann auch Joh 11,41; 12,27.28; 17,1.5.21.24(v.l.).25(v.l.).")."

Matt = Q: Πάτερ (ἡμῶν)⁴

Pro

B. Weiß 1876, 181-182: "Daß umgekehrt der erste Evangelist, der ohnehin die Quelle vollständiger und treuer zu reproduciren pflegt und das Gebet grade als Muster eines kurzen körnigen Gebets giebt, ihm eine Reihe von 'entbehrlichen' Zusätzen hinzugefügt haben sollte (vgl. besonders Camph.) ist ganz unwahrscheinlich und [182] wird durch die zu Tage liegende secundäre Gestalt der übereinstimmenden Bitten bei Luc. völlig ausgeschlossen."

von der Goltz 1901, 42: "Was Mt. über Lc. hinaus mehr hat, sind durchaus dem Geist des Herrn entsprechende Bitten, ob sie nun formell ursprünglich hierher gehören oder nicht. Die Annahme späterer Hinzufügung ist durchaus möglich, aber von dem Bedenken gedrückt, ob die Bitten, wenn später eingefügt, auch so einfach und wahr, den übrigen in Form und Geist entsprechend aussehen würden. Die Auslassung erklärt sich leichter bei der freien Auffassung der Bedeutung des Gebets, die wir auch zur Zeit der Abfassung des Lukasevangeliums noch voraussetzen können."

B. Weiß 1907, 72: "jedenfalls ist eine Erweiterung des Gebets durch Matthäus, nachdem Jesus eben noch vor den 'vielen Worten' gewarnt hatte, durchaus unwahrscheinlich."

B. Weiß 1908, 31: Reconstruction.

Lagrange 1921, 321: "La forme de Mt. semble être la forme liturgique usitée chez les chrétiens, mais on ne saurait en conclure que ce qu'elle a de plus n'est pas authentique, car la liturgie est très tenace dans ses formules (cf. *Didachè*, viii,2)."

Lagrange 1923, 124: "le texte de Mt. [in all material additional to that in Luke's Prayer] est donc primitif."

127: "Dans la formule de Jésus, *notre* a paru secondaire et ajouté par Mt. Mais c'est précisément l'intermédiaire entre le Père de Luc, plus intelligible aux gentils, et le Dieu père d'Israël."

Dupont 1958, 65-66[1]: "Nous voyons différentes raisons d'attribuer la priorité à l'invocation longue 'Notre Père, qui es dans les cieux': ... le témoignage de Marc, 11,25. Marc n'a pas conservé le texte du Pater, mais en revanche il connaît une recommandation de Jésus qui fait écho à la cinquième demande: 'Quand vous vous tenez en prière, pardonnez ce que vous pourriez avoir [66] contre quelqu'un, afin que votre Père qui est dans les cieux vous pardonne aussi vos offenses'. Ce texte ne semble pas avoir été rédigé sans référence au contenu de la prière chrétienne par excellence; c'est d'ailleurs le seul endroit où Marc emploie l'expression 'le Père qui est dans les cieux'. Marc semble donc connaître le Pater avec son invocation initiale longue, telle qu'on la lit chez Matthieu (cf. V. Taylor, *The Gospel according to St. Mark*, London, 1952, p. 467). ... A noter enfin que l'expression 'Notre Père' ('qui es dans les cieux') correspond à l'usage du judaïsme palestinien."

Berger 1969, 1148: "Die Anrede dürfte bei Mt ursprünglicher erhalten sein als bei Lk (vgl. Lk 6,35 / Mt 5,45; Lk 11,13 / Mt 7,11; sonst bei Mt. 5,45 48; 6, 1 9 2 26). Die Anrede 'unser Vater' ist hier nicht etwa für das Gottesverhältnis Jesu oder der Jünger typisch, sondern findet sich in jüdischen Gebetsformel: Vorbild im AT sind bereits Is 63,16 (LXX: ἡμῶν εἶ πατήρ); 64,7 (πατὴρ ἡμῶν σύ); aufschlußreich ist LXX 1 Chr 29,10: ὁ πατὴρ ἡμῶν (MT: Gott unseres Vaters Israel); im Spätjudentum findet sich die Anrede in Weish 14,3 (πάτερ), im Apokryphon Ezechiel (= 1 Clem 8,3: πάτερ), in 3 Makk 6,3 8 (πάτερ am Ende des Gebetes), in TestIsaak 8,10 (πάτερ), in rabbinischen Gebeten im Schᶜmone Esre (b Rez. 5; p Rez. 4.6: אבינו) und im Neujahrsgebet Abinu Malkenu. Die Anrede 'unser Vater im Himmel' findet sich im Seder Elijahu 7 (33) und in Tama debe Elijahu 21."

Zeller 1981, 123: "In the Lord's Prayer, 'Father' is primarily the way the *disciples* address God, unless this originated with the oldest Jewish-Christian community in Palestine. According to this, the Matthean form 'our Father' is probably more original: It conforms to the plural pronouns of the subsequent petitions."

Lambrecht 1985, 131: "Further, elsewhere in his gospel Luke apparently likes to use 'Father' by itself (see 15:12,21; 22:42; 23:34,46; the vocative without a pronoun is better Greek). It is therefore probably advisable to consider the Matthaean 'Our Father in the heavens' more original than the Lucan 'Father'."

Schürmann 1994, 180: "Es ist nicht sicher auszumachen, ob diese Q-Fassung auch schon das im Gemeinschaftsgebet naheliegende ἡμῶν führte; das ὑμῶν Mk 10,25 (par Mt 6,14f) läßt das aber vermuten⁴⁸."

180⁴⁸: "Auch das ὑμῶν Lk 12,[30] par Mt 6,32 Q—vormals im Kontext von Lk 11,2(-4) stehend—macht das ἡμῶν für Lk 11,2 Q möglich. Lukas kann es aufgrund seiner Gebetstradition hier (wie 11,13) gestrichen haben." See also Q 11:~~1-2a,~~2b⁴ Luke = Q, Con.

Con

Hawkins 1899, 7: A chart shows that πατὴρ ἡμῶν, σου, αὐτῶν occurs 20× in Matthew's gospel: never in chs. 1 and 2, 10× in places peculiar to Matthew and 10x in places common to the synoptics.

Loisy 1907, 600: "l'usage liturgique explique aisément l'amplification de la formule, un peu courte, de Luc."

J. Weiß 1907, 286: "Dieser Gebetsruf ohne jeden Zusatz findet sich auch sonst, namentlich bei Gebeten Jesu, in Gethsemane, und bei den Worten am Kreuz (Lk 23:34,46; Joh. 11:41; 12:27,28;17:1ff.). Im Vergleich damit ist die ausführlichere Anrede bei Matthäus eine liturgische Ausschmückung."

von Dobschütz 1914, 303: "The address is the shortest possible: 'Father.' Much has been said about the 'communicative' value of 'our,' and about the importance of reminding oneself that this father is not an earthly one but is so high that he inspires at once awe and trust—awe for his holiness and trust in his power. That is well; but a later addition interests us less, and we may well fear any interpretation which turns the Lord's Prayer into a sermon on religious and moral topics."

Loisy 1924, 315: "'Notre Père qui es aux cieux', formule chère au premier évangile et qui doit représenter un développement liturgique."

Klostermann 1927, 56: Thinks it is "möglich, daß in der Form des Mt das den Synagogengebeten entsprechende ἡμῶν nachträglich hinzugekommen ist."

Bussmann 1929, 67: "Im allgemeinen wird grade anerkannt, daß Mt eine Erweiterung in der Anrede und die Einfügung der dritten und letzten Bitte hat, während L [Luke] den ursprünglichen Text bietet."

Bacon 1930, 276: In his translation of Matthew, Bacon prints the word "our" in bold-face italics to indicate his view that it is a change of wording by the evangelist (Redactor).

Creed 1930, 155: "The Matthaean version is fuller than the Lucan and probably reflects the influence of liturgical usage upon a simpler form similar to that given in Lk."

156: "Matthew adds ἡμῶν. ..."

Manson 1937, 168: "For 'Our Father which art in heaven' Lk. has simply 'Father.' Mt's phrase is an adaptation of the original 'Father' to conform to Jewish liturgical usage."

Hirsch 1941, 101: "Bei Matth ... sind folgende Änderungen eingetreten: a) Die Anrede ist erweitert."

Kilpatrick 1946, 21: "The first phrase is in the Matthean style, ὁ πατὴρ ὑμῶν ὁ ἐν τοῖς οὐρανοῖς or similar words being common in the Gospel. ... The evidence of style and context seems to be strongly in favour of the view that the elements which do not derive from Q were composed by the evangelist."

Schmid 1956, 122: "'Unser (oder: mein, euer) Vater im Himmel' aber ist für die Ausdrucksweise des Matthäus charakteristisch. Es findet sich bei ihm zwanzigmal, bei Markus (11,25) nur einmal, bei Lukas überhaupt nicht (vgl. Mt 5,48 = Lk 6,36; 6,26.32 = Lk 12,24.30; 10,32f = Lk 12,8f; 12,50 = Mk 3,35)."

Knox 1957, 61: "The prayer no doubt existed in the liturgical use of the Church quite apart from the tract, and Matthew has substituted the version of his own Church for that of the source, the longer Matthean version being presumably an expansion of the original."

Davies 1964, 310: Davies prints the word "our" in italics in the prayer to indicate that he considers it to be a liturgical elaboration.

Jeremias 1966, 158: "So werden wir also in dem gemeinsamen Bestand, d.h. in der Lukas-Fassung, den ältesten Text zu erblicken haben. Die heidenchristliche Kirche hat ihn uns aufbewahrt, während die judenchristliche Kirche, die aus einer Welt reicher liturgischer Schätze und vielfältiger liturgischer Gebetsübung kam, das Vater-Unser ausgestaltete."

Jeremias 1967, 12: "die lukanische Kurzform ist in der Matthäus-Fassung vollständig enthalten. Nach allem, was wir über die Gesetzmäßigkeit der Überlieferung liturgischer Texte wissen, hat in einem solchen Fall, in dem die kürzere Fassung in der längeren enthalten ist, die kürzere als die ursprünglichere zu gelten. ... Dieser Schluß, daß die Matthäusfassung eine Erweiterung darstellt, wird durch weitere Beobachtungen bestätigt. Einmal finden sich die drei Matthäus-Überschüsse am Schluß, nämlich am Schluß der Anrede, am Schluß der Du-Bitten und am Schluß der Wir-Bitten; das entspricht genau dem, was wir auch sonst beim Wachstum liturgischer Texte beobachten: sie lieben den volltönenden Abschluß."

Jeremias 1967, ET 1964, 11: "the shorter form of Luke is completely contained in the longer form of Matthew. This makes it very probable that the Matthean form is an expanded one, for according to all that we know about the tendency of liturgical texts to conform to certain laws in their transmission, in a case where the shorter version is contained in the longer one, the shorter text is to be regarded as original. ... This conclusion, that the

Matthean version represents an expansion, is confirmed by three supplementary observations. First, the three expansions which we find in Matthew, as
compared with Luke, are always found toward the end of a section of the
prayer—the first at the end of the address, the second at the end of the 'Thou-
petitions,' the third at the end of the 'We-petitions.' This again is exactly in
accordance with what we find elsewhere in the growth of liturgical texts."

Grundmann 1968, 199: "Matthäus erweitert die Anrede, die bei Lukas
in dem kurzen 'Vater' = abba, durch Röm. 8,15 und Gal. 4,6 bestätigt,
ursprünglich ist, in der Weise jüdischer Gebetsanreden: Aus abba gewinnt er
das in ihm enthaltene, aber bei Lukas und Paulus nicht ausgesprochene πάτερ
ἡμῶν, durch das das Gebet zum Gebet der Jüngergemeinde wird, bzw. wenn
es der einzelne betet, er es als Glied der Jüngergemeinde tut."

Jeremias 1971, 189-190: "Die entscheidende Beobachtung bezüglich der
Ursprünglichkeit ist, daß die Lukasfassung in der [190] Matthäusfassung
vollständig enthalten ist. Da liturgische Texte die Tendenz haben, sich anzureichern, und der kürzere Wortlaut hier gewöhnlich der ältere ist, dürften die
Überschüsse bei Matthäus Erweiterungen darstellen. ... Daß der kürzere Text
der ältere ist, wird durch weitere Beobachtungen bestätigt. Die drei Überschüsse der Matthäusfassung finden sich jeweils an entsprechender Stelle im
Text: am Ende der (ursprünglich nur aus einem Wort bestehenden) Anrede,
am Ende der Du-Bitten und am Ende der Wir-Bitten. Das entspricht
wiederum dem, was sich andernorts beobachten läßt: liturgische Texte werden
gern volltönend abgeschlossen[79]."

190[79]: "Beispiele: Mt 26,28 verglichen mit den Paralleltexten; Phil 2,11."

Jeremias 1971, ET 1971, 195: "The most decisive feature in favour of originality is that the Lucan version is contained in its entirety within that of
Matthew. As liturgical texts tend to be elaborated, and the shorter wording
is usually the earlier, the additional material in Matthew may amount to
elaborations. It is improbable that anyone should have deleted the third and
seventh petitions, whereas the opposite process is easily imaginable. Further
considerations confirm that the shorter text is the earlier. The three additional
passages in the Matthaean version in each instance come at the same place in
the text: at the end of the address (which originally consisted in only one word),
at the end of the petitions in the second person, and at the end of the petitions
in the first person plural. This also corresponds with what is to be observed elsewhere: there is a tendency to conclude liturgical texts with a full stress.[1]"

195[1]: "Examples: Matt. 26.28 compared with the parallel texts; Phil. 2.11."

Morgenthaler 1971, 191: "Eine Bitte scheint bei Mt erweitert zu sein
(6,9b)."

Schulz 1972, 85: "Die Wendung πατήρ + Pronomen findet sich nur bei
Mt gehäuft."

85[189]: "Allerdings sonst nur als πατὴρ ἡμῶν (σου) red wahrscheinlich auch Mt 5,45; 7,11 außerdem im Sondergut 5,16; 6,1.4.6.8.18; 10,20."

Schweizer 1973, 92: "Während die Anrede bei Lukas nur 'Vater' lautet, ist sie bei Matthäus schon zu der im Judentum gebräuchlichen Form mit der Zufügung von 'unser' und 'im Himmel' entfaltet worden. ... Erweiterungen sind also festzustellen bei der Anrede, nach den zwei Du-Bitten und nach der letzten Bitte. Ursprünglich folgten sich demnach die kurze Anrede 'Vater', zwei kurze parallele Du-Bitten, darauf zwei längere, parallel zueinander verlaufende Wir-Bitten und eine kurze dritte, besonders hervorgehobene Schlußbitte."

Schweizer 1973, ET 1975, 148: "In Luke, God is addressed simply as 'Father'; in Matthew, the term of address is a form current in Judaism, expanded by the addition of 'our' and 'in heaven.'... We thus find expansions in the address, after the first two (second person singular) petitions, and after the last petition. This suggests the prayer originally began with the brief address 'Father' followed by two second person singular petitions in parallel and then two longer parallel first person plural petitions, concluding with a third short petition expressed emphatically."

Edwards 1976, 107: "Recent research has emphasized the eschatological implications in the prayer, as well as the apparent earliness of Luke's version. Matthew's version shows all the signs of Jewish liturgical practice."

Schneider 1977, 256: "Mt fügt: 'unser' [Vater] hinzu." Square brackets are Schneider's.

Marshall 1978, 456: "The longer form [of the address] can well have arisen in Jewish circles under the persistent influence of the Jewish liturgy."

Schmithals 1980, 130: "Die uns geläufigere Form des 'Vater-Unser' findet sich Mat. 6,9-13; sie wurde gegenüber der Vorlage in der Spruchquelle Q, die Lukas in V.2-4 im wesentlichen festgehalten hat, erst von Matthäus in die vorliegende Form gebracht."

Schürmann 1981, 20: "Die Zusätze der erweiterten Fassung des *Matthäus* verschieben das Zueinander der einzelnen Glieder und ändern damit den formalen Aufbau des Ganzen: Die *Anrede* hat feierlich-liturgische Form angenommen und hebt sich nun als selbständiger Vorbau von dem folgenden Gebetswunsch ab."

Gundry 1982, 106: "In anticipation of the later first person plural pronouns, Matthew's addition of 'Our' immediately brings into focus the communal nature of the prayer. The addition of 'who are in heaven' does not merely distinguish God from earthly fathers it points to divine majesty as a complement to divine fatherhood."

Gerhardsson 1984, 210: "With any degree of probability we can attribute only three additions to the Matthaean tradition (at the close of the invocation, at the close of the 'thou-petitions' and at the close of the 'we-petitions')."

Schnackenburg 1984, 96: "Die lukanische kurze Anrede 'Vater' ist sicher das Ursprüngliche. Die Juden haben aus Ehrfurcht vor Gott das Bemühen, Gottes Erhabenheit zu wahren, und diesem ehrfürchtigen Reden von Gott fühlt sich auch Matthäus weiter verpflichtet."

Schnackenburg 1984, ET 1995, 63: "The Lukan brief address 'Father' is certainly the original. Out of respect for God the Jews go to great pains to guard God's grandeur, and Matthew also feels obliged by this reverential speech."

Schneider 1985, 62: "Die Traditionsgeschichte des Herrengebets zeigt, daß wir es mit einem *Anwachsen* des Umfangs zu tun haben, wie es analog z.B. auch in jüdischen Gebeten der Jesuszeit zu beobachten ist.[19] ...

"Dieses traditionsgeschichtliche Anwachsen ging nach der Abfassung der Evangelienschriften weiter. Die *Didache* (8,2) greift die Langform auf, die sich Mt 6,9-13 findet,—möglicherweise unabhängig vom kanonischen Mt-Evangelium; doch sie bietet eine Erweiterung, die wiederum an die traditionelle Fassung 'angehängt' ist: 'Denn dein ist die Kraft und die Herrlichkeit in Ewigkeit.'"

62[19]: "Vgl. die beiden 'Rezensionen' des 18-Bitten-Gebets bei W. Staerk, *Altjüdische liturgische Gebete*, Kleine Texte 58, Berlin, ²1930, 9-19, und die deutsche Übersetzung bei (Strack/) Billerbeck, *Kommentar zum Neuen Testament aus Talmud und Midrasch*, I-IV, München, ²1956, IV, 1, 210-214 (unter anderem die Zufügung der Birkath ha-minim), sowie das Kaddisch (Staerk, a.a.O., 29-32)."

64-65: "Es fällt auf, daß die Rede vom 'Vater, der in den Himmeln (ist)' im Munde Jesu vor allem in Verbindung mit den Pronomina 'mein' und 'euer' bezeugt ist. Es handelt sich um eine Redeweise, die fast ausschließlich Mt bezeugt.[25] Die [65] singuläre Verbindung mit 'unser' Mt 6,9b kann daher als mit 'euer Vater, der in den Himmeln' zusammenhängend bzw. davon abgeleitet gelten, zumal hier Jesus nicht zusammen mit seinen Jüngern Gott anredet, sondern die Jünger beten lehrt.

"Die Rede vom 'Vater, der im Himmel (ist)' war im zeitgenössischen Judentum verbreitet, und es lag nahe, sie mit der einfachen Vateranrede des Herrengebets zu verknüpfen. Aber es kann nicht bewiesen werden, daß dies schon vor Abfassung des Mt-Evangeliums geschah. An den Stellen Mt 5,16; 6,1; 7,11; 18,14 dürfte die Wendung mit 'euer' redaktionell sein; das gleiche gilt für die Verbindung mit 'mein' Mt 7,21; 10,32.33; 12,50; 16,17; 18,10.19."

64-65[25]: "Die Formulierung *ho patēr mou ho en (tois) ouranois* steht im NT an folgenden Stellen (nur im Munde Jesu):

"Mt 7,21 diff Lk 6,46; 10.32 diff Lk 12,8 ('die Engel Gottes'); 10,33 Sg. (vgl. 10,32); 12,50 diff Mk 3,35 (*ho theos*); 16,17 Sg. diff Mk (8,29) [65] 18,10 Sg. diff Lk (15,3); 18,19 Sg.

"*Ho patēr hymōn ho en (tois) ouranois* findet sich im NT gleichfalls nur in Jesusworten:

"Mt 5,16 Sg. diff Lk (8,16); 5,45 diff Lk 6,35 (*hypsistos*); 6,1 Sg.; 7,11 diff Lk 11,13 (*ho patēr*); 18,14diff Lk 15,7 ('Himmel'); Mk 11,25 diff Mt 6,14 (*ho patēr hymōn ho ouranios*)."

Gnilka 1986, 214: "Die lk Gebetsanrede 'Vater' ist die ältere. Die voller tönende des Mt gleicht sich liturgischem Sprachgebrauch an. ... Es ist aber darauf hinzuweisen, daß, von der einzigen Ausnahme in Mk 11,25 abgesehen, die Rede von 'eurem/meinem Vater in den Himmeln' nur Mt kennt (12mal)."

Davies and Allison 1988, 600: "'Our ... who art in the heavens', certainly bears all the hallmarks of being Matthean ...; yet many have wondered whether the evangelist would have had the freedom to alter what was undoubtedly a sacred, liturgical text;[33] and it may also be observed that Matthew has only once introduced into Markan material the phrase, '(My, our, your) Father in (the) heavens' (12.50 = Mk 3.35). Nevertheless, given Matthew's frequent expansions of other words of the Lord and indeed his implied ascription of redactional creations to Jesus himself (as in 6.34), the objections are not so weighty as they at first seem."

600[33]: "On the other hand, one might argue that the words of the Our Father were not absolutely fixed until they were set down in writing."

Taussig 1988, 30: "The ἡμῶν ὁ ἐν τοῖς οὐρανοῖς ('Our ... in heaven') is to be considered then as Matthean."

Stritzky 1989, 10-11: "In der Forschung, die sich mit dieser Problematik ausführlich auseinandergesetzt hat und sie mit dem hypothetischen Versuch einer Rückübersetzung in die Ursprache einer Lösung zuführen wollte, hat sich die Meinung durchgesetzt, daß das entscheidende Kriterium für die Ursprünglichkeit darin zu sehen ist, daß die Lukasfassung in der des Matthäus vollständig enthalten ist. Der kürzere Text des Lukas, der mit seinen fünf Gebetsrufen wohl den Inhalt des Gebetes Jesu [11] wiedergibt, dürfte der Urform ihrem Umfang nach nahekommen, während die Mt-Rezension Zusätze bietet, die in der judenchristlichen Gemeinde formuliert wurden, nämlich die Erweiterung in der Vaterrede, die 3. Du-Bitte (Mt 6,10c), die die Bitte um das Kommen des Reiches unterstreicht, und den 2. Teil der 4. Wir-Bitte (Mt 6,13b)."

Trudinger 1989, 50: "The [Matthean] writer (or editor) would thus have changed the simple invocation 'Abba', which from a Jewish point of view would have been a rather too familiar way in which to address God, to 'Our Father, which art in the heavens', an invocation which gives God seemingly more respect and 'distance'."

Catchpole 1993, 30: "The one Marcan reference to 'your Father who is in heaven' (Mark 11:25) occurs in a saying which Luke does not retain. That saying is transferred by Matthew to his 6:14 as a commentary on the prayer for forgiveness in the Lord's prayer. This makes it easy to see the initial and lengthy invocation of 'our Father who art in heaven' (6:9) as preparation for that same commentary saying. ... So there is ... every reason to suppose that Matthew is responsible for lengthening an earlier short version."

Hagner 1993, 146: "The prayer itself in Matthew begins with (1) a typically Matthean formula as the invocation: 'our Father in heaven' (v. 9b)."

Nolland 1993, 612: "The discussion is finally balanced over which form of address has greater claim to originality, particularly as each form suits its present Gospel setting. (God is Father in heaven in Matt 5:16, 45 [48]; 6:1, [14, 26, 32]; 7:11,21; 10:32, 33; 12:50; 16:17; 18:10, 14, 19 [35]; with the exception of 11:25, 26 and 24:36 an accompanying personal pronoun is uniformly to be found in the forty-five references to God as Father in Matthew; beyond the Lord's Prayer, only in 11:25, 26 is God addressed as 'Father,' and only in the latter verse does this address stand alone as in Luke's form of the prayer. ...)"

Cullmann 1994, 54 [ET 1995, 41]: See Q 11:~~1=2a,~~2b⁴ Luke = Q, Pro.

56: "Die Tatsache, daß dieses [the Word 'abba'] bei Matthäus mit *unser* Vater (πάτερ ἡμῶν) übersetzt ist und daß es in Anlehnung an die jüdischen Gebete durch den Zusatz 'im Himmel' erweitert ist (wie auch ähnlich in Mt. 11,25, Luk. 10,21), steht nicht in Widerspruch zu Jesu Gebetshaltung, auch wenn er wahrscheinlich nur Abba gesagt hat. Denn die im Gebrauch dieses Wortes zum Ausdruck kommende Familiarität geht für Jesus zusammen mit seiner Anbetung der Heiligkeit Gottes, mit der 'Heiligung seines Namens', die Gegenstand der gleich nachfolgenden ersten Bitte ist. Man kann sogar sagen, daß die Hinzufügung der Worte 'im Himmel' gerade *wegen* der Anrede 'Abba' als notwendige Ergänzung im Sinne Jesu erfolgte. Dann ist mit dem Hinweis auf den 'Himmel' weniger der Unterschied zum leiblichen Vater, auch weniger die Befreiung von der Bindung an Zion oder Garizim betont, als vielmehr die Transzendenz Gottes."

Cullmann 1994, ET 1995, 42: "The fact that in Matthew this is translated *our* Father (patēr hēmōn) and that, following Jewish prayers, this is given the addition 'in heaven' (as also similarly in Matt.11.25; Luke 10.21), does not go against Jesus' attitude in prayer, even if probably he only said 'Abba'. For Jesus, the familiarity expressed in the use of this word goes with his adoration of the holiness of God, with the 'hallowing of his name', which is the subject of the first petition that follows immediately. One can even say that the addition of the words 'in heaven' followed as a necessary expansion of Jesus' meaning precisely because of the form of address 'Abba'. In that case the reference to 'heaven' does not so much emphasize the difference from a physical father, far less liberation from the tie to Zion or Gerizim, as the transcendence of God."

Meier 1994, 355: "the expansions in Matthew clearly betray the special style of Matthean tradition and/or redaction. 'Our' and 'who [are] in heaven' are often appended to 'Father' by Matthew or his tradition; see 5:16,45; 6:1; 7:11,21; 10:32-33; 12:50; 16:17; 18:10,14,19. The phrase is never used by Luke. … Not by accident, the three additional Matthean clauses occur at the end of the address, the end of the 'you petitions,' and the end of the 'we petitions'—exactly at the locations where additions could be most easily inserted into a tightly constructed oral unit. While it is clear why Matthew or his tradition would desire to insert these phrases, there is no reason why Luke would have deleted them if they had already stood in the venerable prayer he had inherited."

Meadors 1995, 180-181[156]: See Q 11:1-2a,2b⁰ Luke and Matthew = Q, Pro.

Evaluations

Carruth 1995: Luke = Q {A}, πάτερ ()[4.5].

A Lukan preference for the simple address of God as "Father" is not clearly established (Fitzmyer, Schneider, Catchpole). And the fact that the simple address πάτερ without the possessive occurs in the Q prayer in 10:21 supports the same address in this place. On the other hand, the evidence for Matthew's redactional tendency to add a possessive modifier to the word πατήρ is extensive. Since this is especially so in Matthew's Sermon on the Mount, it is reasonable to suppose that Matthew is responsible for that modifier in the Prayer.

Robinson 1995: Luke = Q {A}, πάτερ()[4.5].

The evidence seems clear from the statistics that Luke prefers simply the vocative "Father," whereas Matthew prefers an additional genitive pronoun. It is generally assumed that it is Matthew who has added rather than Luke who has deleted. Attempts to argue for the reverse process break down on the absence of a genitive pronoun in other instances of the address to God in Paul (Rom 8:15; Gal 4:6), Mark 14:36 and Q 10:21. Indeed here in Mark, where, as in Paul, the vocative ὁ πατήρ is presented as the translation of אבא, Matthew (26:39) has added the possessive pronoun μου lacking in Mark, indicating the direction in which the procedure was moving.

The presence of the possessive pronoun ὑμῶν in the indicative statement of Q 12:30 cannot function as a strong counter-argument with regard to the vocative usage in Q. It is the form of address that is here in question.

Mark 11:25 has the fuller form (the only place it occurs in Mark), and may reflect awareness of the Lord's Prayer, though the Prayer's τὰ ὀφειλήματα has become τὰ παραπτώματα, and the Prayer is not itself fully quoted. This may indicate that the Markan community (like that of the *Didache*) was aware of the Prayer with the Matthean form of address. It is less likely that the Markan language influenced Matthew to introduce secondarily here the fuller language, since it is quite characteristic of Matthew throughout. Indeed in this instance Matthew does not use the form found in the Matthean Prayer and in Mark, but a slightly abbreviated Matthean alternative, ὁ οὐράνιος for ὁ ἐν τοῖς οὐρανοῖς. Mark 11:26 hardly has strong enough manuscript support to be included in the critical text, but rather may be best explained as a textual corruption based on Matt 6:15 (which however lacks ὁ ἐν τοῖς οὐρανοῖς present in Mark).

It has been suggested that Mark 11:25 may not be based on the Matthean form of the Prayer, but rather could go back to Jesus (indeed to Sir 28:2). But such a conjecture that "your Father in heaven" was used by Jesus to refer to God is otherwise unattested, and in any case would not contribute strongly to a discussion of how Jesus and/or the Q community addressed God.

If the reference to temptation in Gethsemane could be taken as an allusion to the Lord's Prayer in Mark 14:38, then one could assume that the reference in Mark 14:36 to what God rather than Jesus wills might be a reminiscence of the Matthean form of the Lord's Prayer, which would confirm Mark's acquaintance with that form of the Prayer. But this reminiscence only becomes clear in the case of Matthew itself (see at ⁶). The Lucan shift from a verbal form to the substantive θέλημα (Luke 22:42) for Jesus' will, and implicitly for God's will, is a stylistic improvement not necessarily reflecting the Matthean form of the Prayer.

The argument that Matthew would not have added the embellishments to the Prayer just after criticizing Gentile prayer for its babbling garrulousness loses its force when one recognizes that the embellishments were more likely those of the Matthean community that came to the Evangelist as already part of the Prayer. It is only in comparison with the much briefer Q form of the Prayer attested by Luke that the Lord's Prayer in Matt 6:9-13 would seem to stand in any tension with Matt 6:7-8. Gentile (and Jewish) prayers were often much longer.

Q 11:~~1-2a,~~2b⁵: Matthew's ὁ ἐν τοῖς οὐρανοῖς.

Luke = Q: Πάτερ ( )⁴ ( )⁵,

Pro

von Harnack 1907, 48 [ET 1908, 65]: See Q 11:~~1-2a,~~2b⁴ Luke = Q, Pro.

Loisy 1907, 599: "Les deux évangélistes dépendent, en dernière analyse, d'une même version grecque de l'Oraison dominicale, et Luc, qui en a gardé le préambule original, pourrait en avoir aussi mieux gardé le texte."

Castor 1912, 230: Reconstruction.

McNeile 1915, 76: See Q 11:~~1-2a,~~2b⁴ Luke = Q, Pro.

Zahn 1920, 443: "Die Anrufung Gottes mit dem schlichten πάτερ ohne ein hinzutretendes ἡμῶν ὁ ἐν τοῖς οὐρανοῖς ist nicht minder jüdisch als diese vollere Form bei Mt 6,9."

Manson 1937, 168: See Q 11:~~1-2a,~~2b⁴ Luke = Q, Pro.
266: Reconstruction.

Hirsch 1941, 102: See Q 11:~~1-2a,~~2b⁴ Luke = Q, Pro.

Jeremias 1966, 158: "So werden wir also in dem gemeinsamen Bestand, d.h. in der Lukasfassung, den ältesten Text zu erblicken haben. Die heiden-christliche Kirche hat ihn uns aufbewahrt."

Jeremias 1967, 12, 12-13 [ET 1964, 11, 12]: See Q 11:~~1-2a,~~2b⁴ Luke = Q, Pro.

Schwarz 1968-69, 246: "Der für Matthäus typische Zusatz zum Vater-namen (ὁ ἐν τοῖς οὐρανοῖς), den er—im Unterschied zu Lukas—auch sonst gebraucht, scheint nicht seine eigene, sondern eine Spracheigentümlichkeit seiner Tradition zu sein, die er nur weiterführt. Aus all dem ergibt sich, daß nicht die matthäische Langform, sondern die lukanische Kurzform die ursprüngliche Anrede bietet; also: πάτερ (= 'Abba)."

Schweizer 1973, 92 [ET 1975, 148]: See Q 11:~~1-2a,~~2b⁴ Luke = Q, Pro.

Polag 1979, 48: Reconstruction.

Schmithals 1980, 130: See Q 11:~~1-2a,~~2b⁴ Luke = Q, Pro.

Beare 1981, 170-171: See Q 11:~~1-2a,~~2b⁴ Luke = Q, Pro.

Schenk 1981, 61: Reconstruction.

Strecker 1982, 14: See Q 11:~~1-2a,~~2b⁴ Luke = Q, Pro.

Zeller 1984, 56: Reconstruction.

Fitzmyer 1985, 897: See Q 11:~~1-2a,~~2b⁴ Luke = Q, Pro.

Schneider 1985, 65-66: See Q 11:~~1-2a,~~2b⁴ Luke = Q, Pro.
70-73: "Hier müssen noch zwei Argumente [against a simple 'Father' in Q] überprüft werden. Sie werden von Mk 11,25 und von Lk 11,13 aus [71]

gegen die Ursprünglichkeit der einfachen Anrede *pater* angeführt, die ... vor allem mit dem Rückgriff auf die typisch-jesuanische Gebetsanrede *'abbā* begründet wird.

"Mk 11,25 bietet die der Langform der Vater-Anrede (im Vaterunser des Mt) entsprechende Wendung 'euer Vater in den Himmeln'. Wir haben schon vermerkt, daß das Vorkommen dieser Wendung für sich noch keinen Anhalt dazu bietet, daß sie dem 'Vaterunser' (des Mt oder einer vor-mt Tradition) entnommen sei. Da es aber Indizien dafür gibt, daß Mk 11,24f. auf das Herrengebet bezogen ist, darf man vielleicht mit einer Beeinflussung der Vaterbezeichnung in Vers 25 durch das Vaterunser rechnen. Anzeichen, die auf das Vaterunser verweisen, sind u.a. folgende: Das einleitende, auf die Jesusjünger bezogene Partizip *proseuchomenoi*, die an die mt Vergebungsbitte erinnernde doppelte (auf die Jünger und auf Gott bezogene) Verwendung von *aphiēmi* und die Tatsache, daß Mt 6,14 (15) das Jesuslogion erläuternd an den Vaterunsertext anschließt. Doch das weisheitliche Wort Mk 11,25 'hat in Sir 28,2 eine genaue Parallele und in Sir 28,3-12 deren konkrete Explikation', und es gibt keinen Grund, 'das Wort Jesus abzusprechen, das mit dem Gesamtduktus seiner Verkündigung vorzüglich harmoniert' (R. Pesch, *Das Markusevangelium* II ... Freiburg, 1977 (²1980), 207). Von daher besteht auch keine Veranlassung, das Logion nicht als jesuanische Sachparallele zur Vergebungsbitte des Vaterunsers anzusehen, die unabhängig vom Vaterunser Jesu formuliert worden ist. Zur Sprechweise Jesu wird 'euer Vater in den Himmeln' durchaus gehört haben; doch ist diese Tatsache von der Frage nach der Vater-*Anrede* Jesu zu unterscheiden. Das traditionsgeschichtlich [72] alte Jesuswort Mk 11:25 kann vielleicht seinerseits die Erweiterung der Vergebungsbitte Mt 6,12b par Lk 11,4b mitbedingt haben. Jene Erweiterung unterliegt im übrigen genauso dem Verdacht, ein judenchristlicher Zusatz zu sein, wie die erweiterte Vater-Anrede.

"Lk 11,13 wird wegen der merkwürdigen (und textkritisch nicht sicher bezeugten) Formulierung *ho patēr (ho) ex ouranou dōsei pneuma hagion* für die Behauptung in Anspruch genommen, Lukas habe hier die für Q vermutete Wendung 'euer Vater, der in den Himmeln' (so Mt 7,11) abgeändert. Das wiederum spreche für ein analoges Abkürzungsverfahren des Lukas bei der Vater-Anrede Lk 11,2 par Mt 6,9. Bei der Erörterung dieser These muß auf den näheren Kontext des Vaterunsers in der Logienquelle eingegangen werden. ... [73] In dieser (Luke = Q 11,2-4.5-9.10.11-13;12,22-31) Gebetsunterweisung Jesu für seine Jünger fällt neben der geradezu rahmenden Funktion der Forderung, vorrangig um die *basileia* zu bitten bzw. diese zu suchen (Lk 11,2; 12,31 par Mt), auch die Verwendung von *patēr* in bezug auf Gott auf. In der näheren Formulierung unterscheiden sich die beiden Synoptiker:

Mt	Lk
6,8 *oiden gar ho patēr hymōn*	
6,9 Unser Vater in den Himmeln!	11:2 Vater!
7,11 euer Vater in den Himmeln	11,13 der Vater (der) vom Himmel
wird geben	wird geben
6,26 euer himmlischer Vater	12,24 *ho theos*
6,30 *ho theos*	12,28 *ho theos*
6,32 *oiden gar ho patēr hymōn ho*	12,[30] *hymōn de ho patēr oiden*
ouranios	

"Die obige Übersicht kann zeigen, daß in der Logienquelle die Gebetsunterweisung Jesu von einer Inklusion mit dem Ausdruck 'euer Vater' (Mt 6,8;
6,32 par Lk 12,[30]) zusammengefaßt wird. Außerdem wird ersichtlich, daß
Mt 6,26.32 im Unterschied von Lk 12,[24.30] statt 'Gott' den Ausdruck
'euer *himmlischer* Vater' einbrachte. So liegt die Schlußfolgerung nahe, daß
die lukanische Verwendung des einfachen *patēr* (Lk 11,2.13[; 12,30]) den Text
der Logienquelle wiedergibt. Die erweiterte Vater-Anrede Mt 6,9 wird man
folglich als 'redaktionell' ansehen dürfen." Square brackets are Schneider's.

Sand 1986, 126: "Die lk. Anrede 'Vater' gibt die ursprüngliche Fassung
wieder, wie ein Vergleich mit Joh 17,1 und Mk 14,36 (die erweiterte Bezeichnung in Mk 11,25 ist Übernahme der jüdischen Trad., wie sie von Mt in 6,14
bezeugt wird) zu erkennen gibt (siehe auch Röm 8,15 und Gal 4,6)."

Davies and Allison 1988, 591: Reconstruction.

Taussig 1988, 25: Reconstruction.

Stritzky 1989, 10-11: See Q 11:~~1-2a,~~2b⁴ Luke = Q, Pro.

Kloppenborg 1990, 49: Reconstruction.

Catchpole 1993, 29, 30: See Q 11:~~1-2a,~~2b⁴ Luke = Q, Pro.

Hagner 1993, 145: See Q 11:~~1-2a,~~2b⁴ Luke = Q, Pro.

Mack 1993, 89: Reconstruction.

Mell 1994, 158: Reconstruction.

Con

Wernle 1899, 68: "Die Anrede mag Lc gekürzt haben, da er 'unser Vater im
Himmel' durchgehends vermeidet."

Lagrange 1921, 321: See Q 11:~~1-2a,~~2b⁴ Luke = Q, Con.

Lagrange 1923, 124: See Q 11:~~1-2a,~~2b⁴ Luke = Q, Con.

Soiron 1941, 328: See Q 11:~~1-2a,~~2b⁴ Luke = Q, Con.

Schrenk 1954, 985-986: "War es einfach Mt, der erweiternd 'Vater in den
Himmeln' gesagt hat, während Jesus sich wahrscheinlich so nicht auszudrücken
pflegte? Die Erforschung der Schicht Q (Redequelle) macht dieses Urteil fragwürdig. Es drängt sich auf, daß Lk einige Male aus dem dort überlieferten

Wortlaut 'Vater in den Himmeln' als jüdische Redeweise ausgemerzt hat. Verdächtig ist Lk 6,35 υἱοὶ ὑψίστου,²⁵³ während Mt 5,45: υἱοὶ τοῦ πατρὸς ὑμῶν τοῦ ἐν οὐρανοῖς hat. Noch stärker gibt Lk 11,13: ὁ πατὴρ ὁ ἐξ οὐρανοῦ δώσει²⁵⁴ (Mt 7,11: ὁ πατὴρ ὑμῶν ὁ ἐν τοῖς οὐρανοῖς δώσει) Anlaß zu vermuten, daß [986] hier Q bei Mt ursprünglicher erhalten ist. Es ist wahrscheinlich, daß Lk Eingriffe vornahm, die seinem Zweck, für die gr Welt zu schreiben, entsprachen. Daß auch Mk das überlieferte 'euer Vater in den Himmeln' wohlbekannt war, zeigt 11,25. Hier blieb die Formel als zähes Traditionsgut stehen. Sonst ist festzustellen, daß Lk, wo er in Q 'Vater' vorfand, es nicht ausgemerzt hat. Nur bei 'Vater in den Himmeln' griff er radikal ein."

985²⁵³: "ὑψίστου ist dem οὐρανοί verwandt (vgl Lk 2,14; 19,38; Mk 11,10; Mt 21,9). Lk liebt auch sonst diese feierliche Bezeichnung für Gott (1,32. 35. 76; Ag 7,48)."

985²⁵⁴: "Auch βασιλεία τῶν οὐρανῶν hat Lk vermieden u sagt (32 mal) βασιλεία τοῦ θεοῦ. An sich scheut er den semitischen Gebrauch von οὐρανός (-οί) nicht."

Schrenk 1954, ET 1957, 985-86: "Was it just Mt. who wrote the longer 'Father in the heavens,' whereas Jesus Himself probably did not normally use this? Research in Q makes this judgment dubious. It is obvious that Lk. sometimes cuts down the longer 'Father in the heavens' as a Jewish expression. Suspect is υἱοὶ ὑψίστου in LK. 6:35,²⁵³ where Mt. 5:45 has: υἱοὶ τοῦ πατρὸς ὑμῶν τοῦ ἐν [986] οὐρανοῖς. Lk. 11:13: ὁ πατὴρ ὁ ἐξ οὐρανοῦ δώσει²⁵⁴ (Mt. 7:11: ὁ πατὴρ ὑμῶν ὁ ἐν τοῖς οὐρανοῖς δώσει) gives us even more reason to suppose that here the original Q is better preserved in Mt. It is probable that Lk. made changes consonant with his purpose of writing for the Gk. world. That the traditional 'your Father in the heavens' was known to Mk. may be seen from 11:25. Here the formula was retained as a stubborn part of the tradition. Elsewhere it may be stated that when Luke found 'Father' in Q he did not cut it out or replace it. He made radical changes only in respect of 'Father in the heavens.'"

985²⁵³: "ὑψίστου is related to οὐρανοί, cf. Lk. 2:14; 19:38; Mk. 11:10; Mt. 21:9. Lk. is also fond of this solemn designation elsewhere, 1:32, 35, 76; Ac. 7:48."

986²⁵⁴: "Lk. also avoided βασιλεία τῶν οὐρανῶν and used (32 times) βασιλεία τοῦ θεοῦ. He was not afraid of the Semitic use of οὐρανός (-οί) as such but saw an active correspondence between heaven and earth."

Dupont 1958, 65-66¹: "... [66] ... Luc manifeste une évidente prévention contre le complément 'qui es dans les cieux'. ... On constate en tout cas que Luc a le souci d'éviter ces expressions, trop juives à son goût. ... Il est manifeste que Luc n'aime pas l'expression 'dans les cieux' ou 'céleste' et qu'il était porté à l'omettre. ... A noter enfin que l'expression 'Notre Père' ('qui es dans les cieux') correspond à l'usage du judaïsme palestinien, tandis que 'Père', l'invocation courte, se rattache au judaïsme hellénistique (cf. Sap., 14,3; 3 Macc., 6,3.8) et aux usages des chrétientés pauliniennes (cf. Gal., 4,6; Rom., 8,15 Eph., 3.14)."

Ott 1965, 122: See Q 11:1̶=̶2̶a̶,2b⁴ Luke = Q, Con.

Trudinger 1989, 51: "The editorializing then would have been the work of Luke, who, writing at the time that the Christian faith was spreading to a Gentile world, would not be nearly as concerned about maintaining the Jewishness of the prayer. For Luke's audience the intimate, almost informal address, 'Abba!' ('Father') would perhaps have had great appeal. God was addressed as being 'at hand' to hear our requests as a generous and loving father would be to his children. All mention of 'heaven' with its sense of distance, thus lessening the intimacy and closeness of God, is eliminated. 'Who art in heaven' and 'Thy will be done on earth *as in heaven*' have been by this interpretation judiciously omitted by Luke for editorial, theological reasons."

Nolland 1993, 612: "The discussion is finally balanced over which form of address has greater claim to originality, particularly as each form suits its present Gospel setting. (... By contrast [to Matthew] Luke never has God as Father in heaven [closest is 11:13, where it is probably the giving that is from heaven, not the Father who is from heaven (cf. Acts 2:33)]; God is addressed as 'Father' in Luke 10:21 [2×]; 11:2; 22:42; 23:34 [?], 46; and in all but one of these texts this address stands alone.)" Square brackets are Nolland's.

Schürmann 1994, 180: See Q 11:1̶=̶2̶a̶,2b⁴ Luke = Q, Con.

Matt = Q: Πάτερ (ἡμῶν)⁴ (ὁ ἐν τοῖς οὐρανοῖς)⁵

Pro

B. Weiß 1876, 181-182: See Q 11:1̶=̶2̶a̶,2b⁴ Matt = Q, Pro.
von der Goltz 1901, 42: See Q 11:1̶=̶2̶a̶,2b⁴ Matt = Q, Pro.
B. Weiß 1907, 72: "jedenfalls ist eine Erweiterung des Gebets durch Matthäus, nachdem Jesus eben noch vor den 'vielen Worten' gewarnt hatte, durchaus unwahrscheinlich."
B. Weiß 1908, 31: Reconstruction.
Lagrange 1921, 321: See Q 11:1̶=̶2̶a̶,2b⁴ Matt = Q, Pro.
Lagrange 1923, 124: See Q 11:1̶=̶2̶a̶,2b⁴ Matt = Q, Pro.
127: "— ὁ ἐν τοῖς οὐρανοῖς (om. par Lc.) est l'araméen דבשמיא. Dans Mc. ix,25; cf. Lc. xi.13, tandis que Mt. emploie cette formule ou une équivalente vingt fois. Dira-t-on qu'il l'a empruntée à l'usage juif, ou n'est-il pas beaucoup plus vraisemblable qu'il a conservé plus textuellement le langage de Jésus? Chrys. et Aug. ont pris soin de montrer que si Dieu n'est pas renfermé

dans le ciel, comme tout Israélite le savait (Jér. xxiii,24), cette expression est utile aux imaginations simples."

Dupont 1958, 65-66[1]: "Nous voyons différentes raisons d'attribuer la priorité à l'invocation longue 'Notre Père, qui es dans les cieux': 1. Nous venons de signaler un indice, fourni par Luc lui-même, dans le procédé d'inclusion où la péricope sur la prière s'achève en parlant du Père céleste. Inclusion analogue chez Matthieu, où la troisième demande se terminant par 'comme dans le ciel, ainsi sur la terre', la mention du ciel (ou des cieux: le mot est pluriel en araméen) dans la finale du premier groupe de demandes (celles qui concernent Dieu, avant de passer aux besoins des hommes on pourrait se souvenir du schéma: 'Dieu est au ciel, toi sur la terre', Eccl. 5,1) appelle d'une certaine manière la même mention au début. ... — 2. Autre indice, plus révélateur encore: le témoignage de Marc, 11,25. Marc n'a pas conservé le texte du Pater, mais en revanche il connaît une recommandation de Jésus qui fait écho à la cinquième demande: 'Quand vous vous tenez en prière, pardonnez ce que vous pourriez avoir [66] contre quelqu'un, afin que *votre Père qui est dans les cieux* vous pardonne aussi vos offenses'. Ce texte ne semble pas avoir été rédigé sans référence au contenu de la prière chrétienne par excellence; c'est d'ailleurs le seul endroit où Marc emploie l'expression 'le Père qui est dans les cieux'. Marc semble donc connaître le Pater avec son invocation initiale longue, telle qu'on la lit chez Matthieu. ... Matthieu parle très volontiers des 'cieux'. Il reflète ainsi le langage juif de l'époque mais ce serait une erreur de conclure qu'il introduit ce langage dans le texte. ... 4. A noter enfin que l'expression 'Notre Père' ('qui es dans les cieux') correspond à l'usage du judaïsme palestinien."

Brown 1965, 225[31]: "there are several other factors to be considered: (1) While Mk does not record the PN, Mk 11:25 is reminiscent of it: 'And whenever you stand praying, forgive ... so that *your* Father *who is in heaven* may also forgive you your trespasses.' This verse in Mk is closer to Mt's form of the PN than to Lk's. (2) The Lucan form of the title, besides having no 'our,' has no 'who are in heaven.' Yet a few verses later, Lk 11:13 seems to recall the latter phrase: '... how much more will the *heavenly* Father give the Holy Spirit to those who ask him.' By a type of inclusion, this verse might be considered an indication that the word 'heavenly' was originally in the title of the PN. (3) In Jewish Aramaic *abba* means both 'father' and 'my father.' Lohmeyer, *op. cit.,* 20, cites a place where it seems to stand for 'our father.' Thus, a case might be made for the idea that Lk and Mt are giving us variant translations of the same Aramaic substratum: however, this is quite unlikely, and Lohmeyer himself rejects the suggestion." Brown himself prefers the solution that Luke has preserved Q. He makes these comments in a footnote to indicate other possibilities. See below Q 11:~~1-2a,~~2b⁵ Matt = Q, Con.

Berger 1969, 1148: "Die Anrede dürfte bei Mt ursprünglicher erhalten sein als bei Lk (vgl. Lk 6,35 / Mt 5,45; Lk 11,13 / Mt 7,11; sonst bei Mt. 5,45 48; 6, 1 9 2 26)."

Guelich 1982, 287: "the statistical difference itself does not justify assigning the phrase in 6:9 to Matthew's redaction. First, Mark's use of the concept in 11:25, par. Matt 6:14, in a context involving prayer, demonstrates the existence of a pre-Matthean traditional usage. Second, Matthew has very rarely introduced the phrase into Marcan tradition (once in 12:50 cf. Mark 3:35). Third, Luke never uses the qualification and apparently reworks it in 11:13, par. Matt. 7:11, which may mean that other Q parallels may be traditional rather than redactional (5:45, cf. Luke 6:35 5:48, cf. Luke 6:36). Fourth, Matthew's own source may also have used the phrase (e.g., 16:17). Therefore, no convincing evidence supports either a traditional or a redactional source for in heaven." Note that the author does not come to a decision.

Lambrecht 1985, 131: "a typically Jewish phrase with heaven/heavens is also present in Mk 11:25 ... and Lk 11:13. ... It is therefore probably advisable to consider the Matthaean 'Our Father in the heavens' more original than the Lucan 'Father'."

Schürmann 1994, 179-180: "πάτερ ist in der Mt-Fassung durch ὁ ἐν τοῖς οὐρανοῖς charakterisiert. Hier dürfte die Q-Fassung bewahrt sein: Mk 11,25 (vgl. Mt 6,14f) beweist wohl, daß schon Markus aus der Gebetstradition (oder aus einer Vorform von Q?) das Gebet ... mit diesem Zusatz kannte; der Anklang steht doch hier recht auffallend, da außerhalb von Mt der 'Vater' synoptisch nirgends im NT als 'himmlischer', 'im Himmel' gekennzeichnet wird. Wenn—in vormals unmittelbarer Folge (s. u. z. St.)—Mt 7,11 par Lk 11,13 (v.l.) irgendwie *der* oder *die* Himmel genannt waren, möchte man auch in diesem Q-Text den Einfluß der Q-Fassung der [180] Vaterunser-Anrede vermuten⁴⁷ (selbst wenn in diesem ursprünglich das Vaterunser interpretierenden 'Kommentarwort' Lk 11,11ff par der 'himmlische' Vater vom 'irdischen' abgehoben werden mußte; s. dort)."

180⁴⁷: "Dann wäre wohl auch die Einfügung Mt 12,50 diff Mk und 5,45 diff Lk durch die in Q überlieferte Vaterunser-Anrede beeinflußt. Ein Nachklang kann auch vorliegen, wo Matthäus den Vater οὐράνιος charakterisiert, vgl. bes. 6,14 (und 18,35) diff Mk, dann wohl auch 5,48; 6,26.32 diff Lk und 15,13; 23,9 S (das nirgends sonst in Q oder im NT begegnet)."

Con

Plummer 1896, 294: "The widespread omission is inexplicable, if the three clauses are genuine; the widespread insertion is quite intelligible, if they are not."

von Harnack 1907, 48: "Was sich darüber [the address πάτερ and the so-called fourth to sixth petitions] hinaus bei Matth. findet, sind Zusätze, die sich die judenchristlichen Urgemeinden gestattet haben, als sie das gemeinschaftliche Gebet in ein solennes Gemeindegebet unter starker Anlehnung an die synagogalen Gebete verwandelten, oder sie stammen von Matth. selbst."

von Harnack 1907, ET 1908, 64: "All the other clauses found in St. Matthew are either accretions which attached themselves to the common prayer during the process of transformation into a solemn congregational prayer in the primitive Jewish Christian communities and under the dominating influence of the prayers of the synagogue, or they were added by St. Matthew himself."

Loisy 1907, 600: "l'usage liturgique explique aisément l'amplification de la formule, un peu courte, de Luc."

J. Weiß 1907, 277: "Die Anrede lautet bei Lukas nur ganz kurz: 'Vater'. Dieser Gebetsruf ohne jeden Zusatz findet sich auch sonst, namentlich bei Gebeten Jesu, in Gethsemane, und bei den Worten am Kreuz (Lk. 23,34.46; Joh. 11,41; 12,27,28; 17,1ff.). Im Vergleich damit ist die ausführlichere Anrede bei Matthäus eine liturgische Ausschmückung; der Zusatz 'im Himmel', den Matthäus so gerne hinzufügt, entspricht der jüdischen Neigung, die Erhabenheit Gottes besonders stark zu betonen."

Haupt 1913, 85: "Bemerke ..., wie die hier gebrauchten Ausdrücke im Sondergut des Mt wiederkehren: ὁ πατήρ ὁ ἐν τοῖς οὐρανοῖς bei Mt 20mal."

von Dobschütz 1914, 303: See Q 11:~~1-2a,~~2b⁴ Matt = Q, Con.

McNeile 1915, 76: "As regards the omission of clauses Lk.'s form is probably nearer to the original; he could not have omitted them had the longer form been known to him; and the tendency of liturgical formulas is towards enrichment rather than abbreviation."

78: "The frequency with which ὁ ἐν [τοῖς] οὐρανοῖς occurs in Mt. may have been due to the influence of the Prayer in the form that he knew it." Square brackets are McNeile's.

Loisy 1924, 315: "'Notre Père qui es aux cieux', formule chère au premier évangile et qui doit représenter un développement liturgique."

Easton 1926, 176: "Mt's 'who art in Heaven' was an easy expansion through the influence of current Jewish formulas."

Bussmann 1929, 67: "Im allgemeinen wird grade anerkannt, daß Mt eine Erweiterung in der Anrede und die Einfügung der dritten und letzten Bitte hat, während L [Luke] den ursprünglichen Text bietet."

Bacon 1930, 276: In his translation of Matthew, Bacon prints the words "in heaven" in bold-face italics to indicate his opinion that the wording is a change by the evangelist (Redactor).

Creed 1930, 155: "The Matthaean version is fuller than the Lucan and probably reflects the influence of liturgical usage upon a simpler form similar to that given in Lk."

156: "Matthew adds ... the characteristic expansion ὁ ἐν τοῖς οὐρανοῖς."

Schmid 1930, 233: See Q 11:~~1-2a,~~2b⁴ Luke = Q, Pro.

Manson 1937, 168: "For 'Our Father which art in heaven' Lk. has simply 'Father.' Mt's phrase is an adaptation of the original 'Father' to conform to Jewish liturgical usage."

Hirsch 1941, 101: See Q 11:~~1-2a,~~2b⁴ Matt = Q, Con.

Kilpatrick 1946, 21: "The first phrase is in the Matthean style, ὁ πατὴρ ὑμῶν ὁ ἐν τοῖς οὐρανοῖς or similar words being common in the Gospel. ... The evidence of style and context seems to be strongly in favour of the view that the elements which do not derive from Q were composed by the evangelist."

Schmid 1956, 122: See Q 11:~~1-2a,~~2b⁴ Matt = Q, Con.

123: "Das bei Matthäus beigefügte 'im Himmel' entspricht der Art, wie die Rabbinen seit dem ersten Jahrhundert n. Chr. von Gott redeten, um jede Verwechslung mit einem menschlichen Vater auszuschließen und zugleich Gottes Erhabenheit zum Ausdruck zu bringen."

Knox 1957, 61: See Q 11:~~1-2a,~~2b⁴ Matt = Q, Con.

Beare 1962, 61: "The comparison between the version of the prayer found in Matthew and that which is given ... by Luke indicates that the Matthaean additions have resulted from liturgical shaping. 'Who art in heaven' is ... one of Matthew's own characteristic phrases."

61[26]: "It does not occur in any other New Testament writer, except for one saying in Mark xi.25."

Robinson 1964, 197: "Unter den vielen Verben, die im AT in Frage kommen, begegnet jetzt nur noch das mittelhebräischen Verb ידה, und zwar nur im Impf. der 1. Person sg. Darauf folgt als Objekt immer Adonai (allerdings אלי 1 QH 11,3.15). Die Begründung wird immer (außer 1 QM 11,15) mit כי (oder כיא) eingeleitet, das vom Hymnus übernommen worden ist. Aus diesen Präzisierungen entsteht die fast unveränderliche Formel אודכה אדני כי."

Brown 1965, 225: "The use of 'Father' for God was, of course, known both to pagan ('Father Zeus') and Jew. However, the contemporary Jewish prayers tended to use the Hebrew term *ab* and to accompany it by a possessive such as 'our'—thus, 'Our Father,' *abînû*. They did not use the Aramaic *abba* without qualification.

"From this we may suspect that in 'Our Father' Mt is giving us an adaptation of the more original Lucan 'Father' to the standard Jewish prayer formula."

Davies 1966, 5: "The difference in setting of this material in the two Gospels makes it clear that a prayer taught by Jesus to the disciples has become a prayer for use by the Church in Matthew, and words in italics are best understood as liturgical formulations designed to make the prayer appropriate for common worship."

4-5: Words in Italics are "Our", "which art in heaven" [5] "Thy will be done, On earth as it is in Heaven."

Jeremias 1966, 158: "Die heidenchristliche Kirche hat ihn [the oldest text of the Prayer] uns aufbewahrt, während die judenchristliche Kirche [Matthew's Church], die aus einer Welt reicher liturgischer Schätze und vielfältiger liturgischer Gebetsübung kam, das Vater-Unser ausgestaltete."

Jeremias 1967, 12 [ET 1964, 11-12]: See Q 11:1̶-̶2̶a̶,2b⁴ Matt = Q, Con.

Grundmann 1968, 199: "Matthäus erweitert die Anrede ferner [beyond ἡμῶν] durch den bei den Rabbinen üblichen Zusatz 'in den Himmeln', der der Unterscheidung des himmlischen Vaters gegenüber dem irdischen Vater dient und zugleich die Distanz zwischen Gott und Mensch wahrt."

Jeremias 1971, 189-190 [ET 1971, 195]: See Q 11:1̶-̶2̶a̶,2b⁴ Matt = Q, Con.

Morgenthaler 1971, 191: "Eine Bitte scheint bei Mt erweitert zu sein (6,9b)."

Schulz 1972, 85: "Die Wendung πατήρ + Pronomen findet sich nur bei Mt gehäuft. Dasselbe gilt von der Prädikation ἐν τοῖς οὐρανοῖς.¹⁹⁰"

85¹⁹⁰: "Sie erscheint bei Mt ca 11mal red; eindeutig trad Belege fehlen!"

Schweizer 1973, 92 [ET 1975, 148]: See Q 11:1̶-̶2̶a̶,2b⁴ Matt = Q, Con.

Frankemölle 1974, 161: "Bei der Wendung ὁ πατήρ μου ὁ ἐν τοῖς οὐρανοῖς liegt ein bewußter Rückgriff auf rabbinische Spracheigentümlichkeiten vor, da οὐρανός im klassischen Griechisch—daher auch meist in der LXX—fast ohne Ausnahme im Singular steht, im hebräischen AT und im rabbinischen Schrifttum dagegen von Jahwes Wohnen im Himmel nur in der pluralischen Form gesprochen wird."

163: "Daß in der Formel ὁ πατὴρ ὑμῶν ὁ ἐν τοῖς οὐρανοῖς mt Redaktion vorliegt, zeigt der synoptische Vergleich von Mt 7,11 mit Lk 11,13 (ὁ πατὴρ ὁ ἐξ οὐρανοῦ), Mt 5,45 mit Lk 6,35 (υἱοὶ ὑψίστου), Mt 5,48 mit Lk 6,36 (ὁ πατὴρ ὑμῶν), Mt 10,32 mit Lk 12,8 (ἔμπροσθεν τῶν ἀγγέλων), Mt 10,33 mit Lk 12,9 (ἐνώπιον τῶν ἀγγέλων τοῦ θεοῦ), Mt 12,50 mit Lk 8,21 und Mk 3,35. Der These, Lk habe die in Q gebräuchliche, semitisch gefärbte längere Formel für seine griechischen Hörer gekürzt und Mt habe die ursprünglichere Lesart der Redequelle bewahrt, stehen vor allem Lk 11,13; 6,35; 12,8 und Mk 3,35 entgegen."

Edwards 1976, 107: See Q 11:1̶-̶2̶a̶,2b⁴ Matt = Q, Con.

Ernst 1977, 359-360: "Mt hat durch den Zusatz 'im Himmel' die Vertraulichkeit der Anrede wieder relativiert, wahrscheinlich aus einer berechtigten Sorge um eine mögliche Verharmlosung und Verniedlichung des Gottesbildes. In der Gebetsfassung des 1. Ev klingt noch deutlich das Staunen und Erschrecken über die Größe des Geschehens nach. Lk hat [360] dagegen naiv und in kindlicher Freude wiedergegeben, was die Jünger angesichts dieser einzigartigen Mitteilung Jesu empfinden mußten."

Schneider 1977, 256: "Mt fügt: 'unser' [Vater] hinzu; ferner: 'der im Himmel (ist)'." Square brackets are Schneider's.

Marshall 1978, 456: "The longer form [of the address] can well have arisen in Jewish circles under the persistent influence of the Jewish liturgy."

Schürmann 1981, 20: See Q 11:~~1-2a,~~2b⁴ Matt = Q, Con.

Gundry 1982, 106: See Q 11:~~1-2a,~~2b⁴ Matt = Q, Con.

Strecker 1982, 15: "Die Erläuterung 'der in den Himmeln ist' gibt typisch (vor)matthäisches Sprachgut wieder."

Gerhardsson 1984, 210: See Q 11:~~1-2a,~~2b⁴ Matt = Q, Con.

Schnackenburg 1984, 96 [ET 1995, 63]: See Q 11:~~1-2a,~~2b⁴ Matt = Q, Con.

Fitzmyer 1985, 897: "Matthew has appended phrases: to the end of the opening address. ... These elements, which suit indeed the spirit of the prayer, have scarcely been excised by Luke."

Luz 1985, 46 [ET 1989, 64]: Luz's chart shows the occurrence of οὐράνιος in the synoptics as follows: 7x in Matthew, not in Mark, 1x in Luke. Seven or perhaps fewer of the Matthean occurrences are judged to be redactional, but all occurrences are with πατήρ μου/ὑμῶν.

48 [ET 1989, 65]: Luz's chart shows the occurrence of πατήρ ὁ ἐν (τοῖς) οὐρανοῖς in the synoptics as follows: 12x in Matthew, 1x in Mark and not in Luke. Of the Matthean occurrences about 11 are redactional.

335: "Hilfreicher ist aber der Hinweis auf spontane Variationen jüdischer Gebete. Sie machen sowohl die zusätzlichen Bitten bei Matthäus als auch mögliche Veränderungen des Wortlauts verständlich. Die Ergänzungen im vormt Unservater sind alle leicht als sekundäre Variationen zu verstehen: Die Anrede wurde nach dem Vorbild der eben damals wichtig werdenden jüdischen Gebetsanrede 'Vater in den Himmeln' erweitert.⁶⁰"

341⁶⁰: "Die ältesten Belege: MekhEx 81a zu 20,25 = Bill. I 283 (Johanan ben Zakkai um 70); Seder Elij R 28,149 = Bill. I 394 (Zadok, nach 70); Sota 9,15 = Bill. I 394 (Eliezer ben Hyrkan, um 90)."

Luz 1985, ET 1989, 370-71: "But the reference to spontaneous variations of Jewish prayers is more helpful. They make understandable both the additional petitions [371] in Matthew and the possible alterations of the wording. The supplements in the pre-Matthean Lord's Prayer are all easily understandable as secondary variations: The address was enlarged, according to the example of the Jewish prayer address 'Father in the heavens,' which was becoming prominent at that time."

377⁶⁰: "The oldest examples [of 'our Father in the heavens', in Jewish liturgical use]: *Mek.Exod.* 81a on 20:25 = Str-B [Strack-Billerbeck] I 283 (Yohanan ben Zakkai, ca. 70); *Seder Elij. R.* 28.149 = Str-B I 394 (Eliezer ben Hyrcanus, ca. 90)."

Schneider 1985, 62, 64-65: See Q 11:~~1-2a~~,2b⁴ Matt = Q, Con.

Schnackenburg 1985, 64: "Die längere Fassung bei Mt dürfte auf den Gebrauch in seiner Gemeinde zurückgehen. Gegenüber Lk sind drei Erweiterungen bemerkenswert: der Zusatz 'im Himmel' bei 'unser Vater', der dritte Gebetswunsch 'dein Wille geschehe …' und der Zusatz zur letzten Bitte 'sondern rette uns vor dem Bösen'. … Das Vaterbild Gottes, das auch mütterliche Züge trägt (Jes 49,15; 66,13), reicht in Israel weit zurück (Hos 11,1-4), und aus ihm schöpft Israel seine Hoffnung (Hos 2,1; Jubiläenbuch 1,24f). In Israels Gebeten mischen sich Vertrauen und Ehrfurcht ('unser Vater, unser König'), die noch den schuldigen Abstand wahren will. Aus judenchristlicher Haltung hat Mt das festgehalten (Zusatz 'in den Himmeln' oder 'himmlischer' 5,16.45.48 u.o.)."

Gnilka 1986, 214: See Q 11:~~1-2a~~,2b⁴ Matt = Q, Con.

Schenk 1987, 382: "οὐρανός

　　　Mt 79 (ohne Mt 16,3f): Mk 17: Lk 34 + 26: Joh 18

　　　=(Mk 17 - 1 + 34) + (Q 6 + 17) + (A-Mt 6) davon 32mal red. …

"ἐν οὐρανοῖς/–ῷ …

　　　Mt 33: Mk 5: Lk 6

　　　=(Mk 5 - 2 + 15) + (Q 2 + 6) + (A-Mt 7)

… 6,10 (+Q Ort der Willensverwirklichung)."

Davies and Allison 1988, 600: See Q 11:~~1-2a~~,2b⁴ Matt = Q, Con.

Taussig 1988, 30: See Q 11:~~1-2a~~,2b⁴ Matt = Q, Con.

Stritzky 1989, 10-11: See Q 11:~~1-2a~~,2b⁴ Matt = Q, Con.

Trudinger 1989, 50: See Q 11:~~1-2a~~,2b⁴ Matt = Q, Con.

Catchpole 1993, 30: See Q 11:~~1-2a~~,2b⁴ Matt = Q, Con.

Hagner 1993, 146: See Q 11:~~1-2a~~,2b⁴ Matt = Q, Con.

Nolland 1993, 612: See Q 11:~~1-2a~~,2b⁴ Matt = Q, Con.

Meier 1994, 355: See Q 11:~~1-2a~~,2b⁴ Matt = Q, Con.

Meadors 1995, 180-181[156]: See Q 11:~~1-2a~~,2b⁰ Luke and Matthew = Q, Pro.

Evaluations

Carruth 1995: Luke = Q {A}, πάτερ ()⁴ ()⁵.

Apart from the view that the Matthean ὁ ἐν τοῖς οὐρανοῖς is an expansion due to the usage of Matthew's church, the evidence in favor of Matthean redaction is convincing (Haupt, Creed, Kilpatrick, Beare, Frankemölle, Ernst, Strecker, Luz, Schenk). In addition, the observation that all three of the additional phrases in Matthew are at the ends of sections and that they can easily be attributed to liturgical usage supports the conclusion that they are expansions of an originally shorter version of the prayer. The fact that Luke keeps Q's κύριε τοῦ οὐρανοῦ καὶ τῆς γῆς in 10:21 shows that he does not avoid a reference to heaven with the address of God. He also includes an expression with the word οὐρανός at 11:13. Thus Luke would not necessarily exclude these elements if he read them in his source. The phrase ὁ ἐν τοῖς οὐρανοῖς is more easily understood as a Matthean expansion than a Lukan omission.

Robinson 1995: Luke = Q {A}, πάτερ ()⁴ ()⁵.
The Evaluation of ⁴ is also relevant here.

The appeal to Q 10:21b as a Q precedent having more than just the vocative "Father," namely κύριε τοῦ οὐρανοῦ καὶ τῆς γῆς, loses its force when one recognizes that κύριε is a standard part of the Hodayot formula shared here with Qumran: אודכה אדני כי. Indeed the secondary element is here πάτερ, a Christianizing of the Hodayot formula. Hence it is no coincidence that this particular formulation accompanying the vocative πάτερ does not recur in the Gospels, where there is no other instance of Jesus using the Hodayot formula. Thus the vocatives πάτερ in Q 10:21b and ὁ πατήρ in Q 10:21d confirm πάτερ as the form of address in Q 11:2.

The Commentary to the Prayer does have a reference to heaven, necessitated by the need to distinguish God from a human father. Here too Matthew (Matt 7:11) presents the familiar Matthean form used in the Prayer (Matt 6:9). In Luke 11:13 it is textually uncertain whether the statement means that the Father who is from (!) heaven will give, or that the Father will give from heaven (Acts 2:33), which in effect seems more obvious. In any case the typically Matthean formulation is not to be regarded as the Q reading simply because Luke 11:13 has an unclear text.

Matthew's preference for "kingdom of *heaven*" may be analogous to the Matthean preference for "Father *who art in heaven*," in that both reflect a concern for the sanctity of God, whose name is to be avoided, or who is not to be confused with human fathers. In neither case can the directionality of the redactional activity be reversed, as e.g. Paul confirms. To assume that Luke, since writing for Gentiles, would delete Judaisms, ignores the elegant Septuagint style that Luke on occasion (e.g. Luke 1-2) can affect, no doubt on the assumption that his readers would appreciate it.

The probability that Q 6:35 has been changed by Luke to υἱοὶ ὑψίστου does not thereby elevate the typically Matthean alternative in Matt 5:45 to the Q reading.

Q 11:1-2a,2b⁶: Matthew's γενηθήτω τὸ θέλημά σου, ὡς ἐν οὐρανῷ καὶ ἐπὶ γῆς.

Luke = Q: ( )⁶

Pro

> **von Harnack** 1907, 48 [ET 1908, 65]: See Q 11:1-2a,2b⁴ Luke = Q, Pro.
> **Loisy** 1907, 599: See Q 11:1-2a,2b³ Luke = Q, Pro.
> **J. Weiß** 1907, 288: "So ist diese Bitte nur eine Ausführung der vorherge-henden. Sie ist für den Gedankenfortschritt entbehrlich. Wir werden daher die Lukas-Form, in der sie fehlt, für ursprünglich halten."
> **Castor** 1912, 230: Reconstruction.
> **McNeile** 1915, 76: See Q 11:1-2a,2b⁴ Luke = Q, Pro.
> **Montefiore** 1927, 99: "The form of the Lord's Prayer in Luke is shorter and perhaps more original. The *seven* petitions in Matthew are characteristic, for that holy number is a favourite with him."
> **Bussmann** 1929, 67: "Im allgemeinen wird grade anerkannt, daß Mt eine Erweiterung in der Anrede und die Einfügung der dritten und letzten Bitte hat, während L [Luke] den ursprünglichen Text bietet. Denn was sollte ihn bewogen haben, die beiden Bitten wegzulassen; die Gründe die dafür ange-führt werden, lohnt es nicht zu widerlegen."
> **Manson** 1937, 266: Reconstruction.
> **Hirsch** 1941, 102: "D.h. Luk hat die zugrundeliegende Gestalt bis auf zwei Kleinigkeiten, die schon in Lu I geändert sein mögen, bewahrt, Matt aber hat erheblichere Erweiterungen des Vaterunsers vorgenommen."
> **Jeremias** 1966, 158: See Q 11:1-2a,2b⁴ Luke = Q, Pro.
> **Jeremias** 1967, 12 [ET 1964, 11]: See Q 11:1-2a,2b⁴ Luke = Q, Pro.
> **Schweizer** 1973, 92 [ET 1975, 148]: See Q 11:1-2a,2b⁴ Luke = Q, Pro.
> **Polag** 1979, 48: Reconstruction.
> **Schmithals** 1980, 130: See Q 11:1-2a,2b⁴ Luke = Q, Pro.
> **Schenk** 1981, 61: Reconstruction.
> **Zeller** 1984, 56: Reconstruction.
> **Fitzmyer** 1985, 897: "In the number of impvs. [imperatives], the Lucan form is undoubtedly closer to that of 'Q' and to the wording of Jesus himself. ... [The additional elements found in Matthew], which suit indeed the spirit of the prayer, have scarcely been excised by Luke."
> **Luz** 1985, 336: "Wir gehen deshalb davon aus, daß die Fünfzahl der Bitten der ältesten erreichbaren Fassung entspricht. Wie die spätere mt Fassung, so ist auch sie formal geschlossen."
> **Luz** 1985, ET 1989, 371: "Therefore we proceed from the assumption that the count of five petitions agrees with the oldest achievable version. Like the later Matthean version, so it also is formally compact."

Gnilka 1986, 214: "Es läßt sich kein plausibler Grund für eine Auslassung angeben."

Davies and Allison 1988 591: Reconstruction.

Taussig 1988, 25: Reconstruction.

Stritzky 1989, 10-11: See Q 11:~~1-2a~~,2b⁴ Luke = Q, Pro.

International Q Project 1990, 500: Reconstruction.

Kloppenborg 1990, 49: Reconstruction.

Catchpole 1993, 30: "Since Luke also adopts with slight verbal adjustments the prayer of Mark 14:36, and shows himself elsewhere to be concerned about 'doing the will of the Lord' (Luke 12:47), it is again difficult to see Luke excising the petition that the Father's will be done. It is not a matter of 'dropping this hint of fatalism'⁶⁷, and even if it were it would be curious that an evangelist with so strong a sense of the divine should find such a hint unattractive. Although Mark 14:36 and also Acts 21:14 contrast sharply submission to the will of God and what is preferable in human terms, this is not the case in Matt 6:10. So it is hard to see Luke dropping this petition and extremely easy to see Matthew introducing it."

30⁶⁷: "Goulder, *Luke II*, 496."

Mack 1993, 89: Reconstruction.

Hagner 1993, 145: See Q 11:~~1-2a~~,2b⁴ Luke = Q, Pro.

Mell 1994, 158: Reconstruction.

Betz 1995, 392: "There is no convincing reason why Luke should have excised the third petition (according to the SM [Sermon on the Mount]) had he read it, which he most likely did not; his church seems to have used the shorter form." Betz does not attribute the Prayer to Q. This comment merely supports the opinion of others who do not imagine the omission of the phrase to be due to Lukan redaction.

Con

B. Weiß 1878, 422: "ὅταν προσεύχησθε, λέγετε) Hienach fasst Luk., abweichend von Matth. 6,9, das Gebet offenbar als eine den Jüngern gegebene Gebetsformel, die er eben darum noch verkürzt hat, um sie leichter behaltbar und daher gebräuchlicher zu machen (vgl. Weiss, Matth. p. 181). Wie das einfache πάτερ die gewöhnliche Gebetsanrede, so lässt Luk. die dritte Bitte fort, weil sie nur enthält, was sich mit der Vollendung des Gottesreichs von selbst verwirklicht."

J. Weiß 1892, 466: "Die Weglassung der sog. 3. Bitte (falls sie nicht ein Zusatz des Mt ist) mag damit zusammenhängen, dass man schon früh die Herrschaft Gottes in der Erfüllung seines Willens bei den Menschen verwirklicht sah. Eine Parallele zu dieser Streichung bietet die Weglassung der δικαιοσύνη in den Makarismen."

Resch 1895, 229-230: "Bezüglich der Quellenkritik ist *dreierlei* fest-zustellen: ... dass Lc. nach seiner Gewohnheit kürzend, den [230] Quellentext nicht ohne wichtige Weglassungen, namentlich—wie häufig bei ihm—am Schlusse, reproduciert hat, während der Urtext von dem ersten Evangelisten in annähernder Vollständigkeit wiedergegeben sein dürfte."

B. Weiß 1901, 459: "Daraus ['dass unsere Evangelien nicht zu historischen, sondern zu erbaulichen Zwecken geschrieben sind'] erklärt sich auch am einfachsten die Verkürzung des Gebets bei Lk; denn dass die Fassung bei ihm die ursprüngliche sein sollte …, ist schon darum höchst unwahrscheinlich, weil, je höher allmählich die Werthschätzung dieses Gebets stieg, man um so weniger daran denken konnte, dasselbe mit eigenen Zusätzen zu erweitern, wird aber dadurch völlig ausgeschlossen, dass alle anderen Abweichungen des Lk durchaus sekundärer Natur sind und sich aus schriftstellerischen Motiven so leicht erklären, dass ihre Zurückführung auf Uebersetzungsfehler (Aufl. 8) ganz entbehrlich ist. Leicht begreiflich ist aber, dass man in einer Zeit, wo der Buchstabe der Herrnworte noch keineswegs als unantastbar galt, um es leichter behaltbar und darum gebräuchlicher zu machen, alles irgend Ent-behrliche fortliess."

Lagrange 1921, 321: See Q 11:~~1-2a~~,2b⁴ Luke = Q, Con.

Lagrange 1923, 124: See Q 11:~~1-2a~~,2b⁴ Luke = Q, Con.

Soiron 1941, 328: "Die dritte Bitte streicht er [Luke], weil sie ihn als Wiederholung der zwei ersten erschien und weil sie nur für die Juden mit ihren nationalpolitischen Ideen vom Reiche Gottes eine Erklärung gab."

Dupont 1958, 65¹: "le texte du Luc, beaucoup moins bien rythmé et balancé que celui de Matthieu, semble écourté."

Ott 1965, 122: "Aus all dem ergibt sich mit großer Sicherheit, daß das lukanische Vaterunser eine Überarbeitung und Verkürzung des Vaterunsers in der matthäischen Form darstellt, die weder vor noch neben der matthäischen Gestalt als in den frühchristlichen Gemeinden gebräuchliches Gebetsformular einige Verbreitung gefunden hat. Die lukanische Form des Vaterunsers hat als lukanische Überarbeitung des Gebetsformulars ihren Platz innerhalb der lukanischen Gebetsparänese. Innerhalb dieser lukanischen Gebetsparänese ist es nicht mehr 'nicht vorstellbar, daß Lukas dieses Gebet verkürzt hätte, wenn er es in der Matthäusfassung vorgefunden hätte' (so Schmid *Mt-Komm.* 122), zumal wenn es zutrifft (wie Schmid selbst anerkennt), daß Lukas den Text nicht als ein Gebetsformular verstanden hat, sondern als 'ein Muster eines inhaltsreichen und echt christlichen Gebets' (*Lk-Komm.* 197)." For the full context of Ott's argument see Q 11:~~1-2a~~,2b⁴ Luke = Q, Con.

Schwarz 1968-69, 244: Schwarz speculates on why Luke might have omit-ted this petition. "Soviel wir sehen, gibt es zwei Möglichkeiten. Entweder: er kannte sie nicht, weil sie in den Gemeinden, in denen er zuhause war, nicht gebetet wurde, oder: er kannte sie zwar,[4] ließ sie aber (an dieser Stelle) absichtlich weg, weil ihr Wortlaut für Theophilus, den Adressaten (an dieser Stelle)[6]—womöglich—politisch anstößig gewesen wäre: falls nämlich Theophilus römischer Staatsbeamter gewesen ist, für den dann selbstverständlich allein des Cäsars Wille (wie—bzw. als—eines Gottes Wille) zu gelten hatte."

244[4]: "Dafür spricht zweifelsfrei seine Fassung der Gethsemane-Bitte (Luk. xxii.42b: πλὴν μὴ τὸ θέλημά μου ἀλλὰ τὸ σὸν γινέσθω), die, vergleicht man sie mit den Fassungen der Seitenreferenten (Mark. xiv.36c: ἀλλ᾿ οὐ τί ἐγὼ θέλω ἀλλὰ τί σύ, Matth. xxvi.39c: πλὴν οὐχ ὡς ἐγὼ θέλω ἀλλ᾿ ὡς σύ), deutlich erkennen läßt, daß er (und zwar: absichtlich!) die verbale Konstruktion der ihm vorliegenden Markus-Fassung fallenläßt und statt dessen zurückgreift auf die ihm (dort!) nicht vorliegende substantivische Fassung, wie sie bei Matthäus in der dritten σου-Bitte des Vater-Unsers begegnet und die ihm also von anderswoher bekannt gewesen sein muß; nämlich—der Schluß ist zwingend—: von seinem eigenen und seiner Gemeinden Vater-Unser her."

244[6]: "Im Zusammenhang mit der zweiten σου-Bitte (ἐλθάτω ἡ βασιλεία σου), die, im Kontext gelesen, zu dem Mißverständnis Anlaß geben könnte, es handle sich bei der βασιλεία um eine politische Herrschaft und bei dem θέλημα um einen politischen Willen."

Feldkämper 1978, 186: "Im Vergleich mit 6,10 'fehlt' bei Lukas die Bitte: γενηθήτω τὸ θέλημά σου. In abgewandelter Form jedoch liegt das Thema in den Rahmentexten 10,25-42 und 11,27f vor. Lukas spricht auch sonst nicht—mit Ausnahme von 22,42 par Mk/Mt—vom Geschehen oder Tun des Willens Gottes. Wo Jesus bei Mattäus zum Tun des Willens seines Vaters im Himmel (7,21; 12,50) auffordert, da ermahnt er bei Lukas zum 'Hören' und 'Tun' seines eigenen bzw. des Wortes Gottes (6,46 red; 6,47-49 par Mt; 8,21). Dasselbe paränetische Anliegen kommt, wie wir gesehen haben, in den Rahmenperikopen 10,25-42 und 11,27f zur Sprache. Man darf deshalb wohl diese Rahmenstücke auch als 'Ersatz' für die 'fehlende' dritte Du-Bitte ansehen." But note 186[16]: "Die Frage nach der Ursprünglichkeit der beiden VU-Fassungen braucht hier nicht behandelt zu werden. Unser Vergleich an dieser Stelle ist ausschließlich synchron."

Trudinger 1989, 51: "God was addressed as being 'at hand' to hear our requests as a generous and loving father would be to his children. All mention of 'heaven' with its sense of distance, thus lessening the intimacy and closeness of God, is eliminated. 'Who art in heaven' and 'Thy will be done on earth *as in heaven*' have been by this interpretation judiciously omitted by Luke for editorial, theological reasons."

Betz 1995, 392: "The omission [of Matt 6:10c] in Luke 11:2 remains unexplained, but it is hardly 'original.'"

Matt = Q: (γενηθήτω τὸ θέλημά σου, ὡς ἐν οὐρανῷ καὶ ἐπὶ γῆς)⁶

Pro

B. Weiß 1876, 181-182: See Q 11:~~1-2a~~,2b⁴ Matt = Q, Pro.
von der Goltz 1901, 42: See Q 11:~~1-2a~~,2b⁴ Matt = Q, Pro.
Klein 1906, 35: "Nach meinem Dafürhalten besitzen wir die Urgestalt des Vaterunsers bei Matthäus; denn nur in dieser Form entspricht es den Anforderungen, die an ein *jüdisches* Gebet gestellt wurden.

"Nach Ps 119,164 wurden sieben Eulogien für den Tag festgesetzt. Daher kannte man vor der Zerstörung des Tempels nur Birkath Scheba, das 'Sieben-Gebet'.—Das Vaterunser mit der Schlußdoxologie besteht aus sieben Bitten.

"Ein Gebet soll aus drei Teilen bestehen. Es beginne mit einem Hymnus, mit einer Verherrlichung Gottes (שבח). Darauf folge das individuelle Gebet (תפלה) und den Schluß bilde eine Doxologie, eine Danksagung (הודיה).
—Diese Ordnung findet sich auch im Vaterunser. —Die ersten drei Bitten enthalten eine Verherrlichung Gottes, denn Gottes Name wird verherrlicht, wenn sein Reich kommt und sein Wille geschieht. Die mittleren drei Bitten enthalten die eigentliche Tefillah, das individuelle Gebet. Und die siebente Bitte enthält die Doxologie."

B. Weiß 1907, 72: See Q 11:~~1-2a~~,2b⁴ Matt = Q, Pro.
B. Weiß 1908, 31: Reconstruction.
Klein 1909, 258: Cites one Jewish source to show that three petitions introduce prayers. "Im Traktate Soferim 14,22 lautet ein Gebet: Erhaben und gepriesen und geheiligt ... werde der Name des Königs aller Könige ... in den Welten, die er geschaffen ... nach seinem Willen und dem Willen seines ganzen Volkes Israel. Möge erscheinen und sich offenbaren sein Reich." He offers still a third reason for the originality of Matthew's form of the prayer: it corresponds to the thought-world (Gedankenwelt) of Jesus evident especially in passages elsewhere in the Sermon on the Mount. "Dasselbe Kapitel in Matthäus, das das Vaterunser enthält, führt uns auch in die Gedankenwelt Jesu ein. Es handelt von den Gaben, die denen zuteil werden sollen, die nach dem Reich Gottes trachten. Und seine Gedanken zusammenfassend, spricht Jesus: Euer himmlischer Vater weiss ja, dass ihr dies alles bedürfet. Trachtet aber zuerst nach seinem Reich und Recht, so wird euch dies alles zugelegt werden. Sorget nun nicht auf den morgenden Tag; der morgende Tag wird für sich selbst sorgen. Diese Worte in unmittelbarer Nähe des Vaterunsers bilden gleichsam eine Erklärung und nähere Begründung der ersten drei resp. vier Bitten. V. 32 'Euer himmlische Vater' entspricht dem 'Unser Vater, der du bist in den Himmeln' V. 33 'Trachtet (ζητεῖτε, gleich dem hebr. בקשו, בקשה =Gebet, Bitte) aber zuerst nach seinem Reich' entspricht dem: 'es komme dein

Reich' 'und Recht' entspricht dem: 'es geschehe dein Wille', denn der Wille Gottes ist identisch mit Recht, mit משפט und צדקה. 'Sorget nicht auf den morgenden Tag' entspricht dem: 'unser nötiges Brot gib uns heute.'"

McNeile 1915, 79: See Q 11:~~1-2a,~~2b⁶ Matt = Q, Con.

Lagrange 1921, 321: See Q 11:~~1-2a,~~2b⁴ Matt = Q, Pro.

Lagrange 1923, 124: See Q 11:~~1-2a,~~2b⁴ Matt = Q, Pro.

129: "Il n'y a aucune raison de penser que Mt. aurait ajouté la troisième demande pour atténuer le caractère eschatologique de la seconde. Elle est de plus nécessaire au parallélisme de 3 + 3. C'est donc Lc. qui l'a retranchée."

Soiron 1941 325-327: Cites Klein favorably and at length.

Dupont 1958, 65[1]: "Chez Matthieu, trois demandes simples, puis trois demandes doubles; la dernière de chaque groupe est un peu plus développée, de manière à marquer la pause. C'est du style oral (cf. les deux séries de trois recommandations parallèles en Luc, 11,9-10 = Mat., 7,7-8); à cet égard, le texte de Matthieu est plus satisfaisant que celui de Luc."

Ott 1965, 122: concurs with Klein "daß wir die Urgestalt des Vaterunsers bei Matthäus besitzen." For full context of the argument see 11:~~1-2a,~~2b⁵ Luke = Q, Con.

Wrege 1968, 103-104: "Daß Mt diese Bitte selbst geschaffen habe, ist durch die Didache ausgeschlossen: das Formular 8,2 weist sie als selbst-verständlichen Bestandteil der Überlieferung aus, wie sie tatsächlich in den Gemeinden gebetet wurde. ... Ebenso wichtig ist die Feststellung, daß sich die 3. Bitte sachlich der jüdischen Gebetssprache einfügt (Vgl. Ps 135,6; 1 Makk 3,60, s. dazu Billerbeck I, S. 419f), und daß sie, wie das die Rückübersetzung Kuhns[7] gezeigt hat, schon der aramäischen Vorform der Mt-Fassung angehört haben wird. [104] Die Anrede 'unser Vater in den Himmeln' und 'dein Wille geschehe wie im Himmel so auch auf der Erde' sind formal und in der Sache aufeinander bezogen. Betont die Erwähnung des Himmels als Lebens- und Machtbereich Gottes in der Anrede seine herrscherliche Majestät, so stellt die 3. Bitte den Beter 'auf Erden' in diesen Machtbereich hinein."

103[7]: "[K.G. Kuhn,] *Achtzehngebet* [*und Vaterunser und der Reim*, WUzNT 1, Tübingen 1950], S. 34f."

Crossan 1983, 98: "I propose (i) that the Lord's Prayer was earlier but secret Q tradition (ii) that it was known to Q in the Jewish-Christian seven-petition form that was accepted in Matt. 6:9-13 but changed to the Gentile-Christian five-petition format by Luke 11:2-4 (see Jeremias, 1967a: 89) and (iii) that it was acceptable to the later Q theology only as commented on by Aphorisms 67-68 [Q 11:9-13]."

Hagner 1993, 146: "As to the petitions in the Lord's Prayer, it is arguable, though it must remain uncertain, that Matthew's third petition is not original but had probably been modeled upon the first two before the evangelist's writing." Hagner does not attribute the Prayer to Q. This statement only records Hagner's suggestion that the petition in question may not be due to Matthew but may derive from pre-Matthean redaction.

Con

Plummer 1896, 294: See Q 11:~~1-2a,~~2b⁵, Matt = Q, Con.

von Harnack 1907, 48 [ET 1908, 64]: See Q 11:~~1-2a,~~2b⁵ Matt = Q, Con.

Loisy 1907, 600: "l'usage liturgique explique aisément l'amplification de la formule, un peu courte, de Luc."

Castor 1912, 53-54: "'Thy will be done on earth as it is in heaven' is only a further definition of 'Thy kingdom come.' So also 'Deliver us from evil' only states in a positive form what 'Lead us not into temptation' expresses negatively. These clauses amplify, but they add no new element of thought; nor do they contain anything distinctively Jewish which Gentiles would have any reason to omit. The very reverse is [54] nearer the truth. Both petitions are to be explained as interpretative additions due to liturgical use, and not as Lukan omissions."

Haupt 1913, 85: "Jedenfalls hat Mt, da der Lc-Text sehr viel kürzer ist, stark erweitert (Anrede 1. 3. und 8. Bitten. Bemerke auch, wie die hier gebrauchten Ausdrücke im Sondergut des Mt wiederkehren: ... θέλημα cf. 7,21 18,14 21,31 26,42 ...)."

McNeile 1915, 78: "The source of the first four words [γενηθήτω τὸ θέλημά σου] was probably the prayer in Gethsemane, as Mt. gives it (xxvi. 42); a prayer used by the Lord might safely be added to the prayer which He taught."

79: "For the correspondence between the earthly and the heavenly cf. [Matt] xvi. 19, xvii. 18. If the clause was not originally part of the Prayer, its origin cannot be determined."

Zahn 1920, 448: "Die bei Lc fehlende 3. Bitte ist nur eine erläuternde Ergänzung der 2."

449: "die spätere Einfügung der 3. und 7. Bitte bei Mt ist wahrscheinlicher, als nachträgliche Tilgung derselben durch Lc oder seine Gewährsmänner."

Loisy 1924, 316: "Ne sont aucunement représentées [in Luke's prayer] la troisième demande de Matthieu: 'que ta volonté se fasse sur la terre comme au ciel', et la dernière: 'mais délivre-nous du mal', qui n'appartenaient probablement ni l'une ni l'autre à la forme primitive de la prière."

Klostermann 1927, 57: "Andererseits erscheint dann allerdings die 3. Bitte neben der 1. und 2. für den Gedankenfortschritt entbehrlich, wie sie ja auch bei Lc fehlt."

Bacon 1930, 276: In his translation of Matthew, Bacon prints the entire petition in bold-face italics to indicate his opinion that the wording represents a change by the evangelist (redactor).

Creed 1930, 155: "The Matthaean version is fuller than the Lucan and probably reflects the influence of liturgical usage upon a simpler form similar to that given in Lk."

Hirsch 1941, 101: "Bei Matth ... sind folgende Änderungen eingetreten: ... b) Die Bitte Jesu aus der Gethsemanegeschichte ist in passender Gestalt als dritte Bitte eingefügt."

102: "D.h. Luk hat die zugrundeliegende Gestalt bis auf zwei Kleinigkeiten, die schon in Lu I geändert sein mögen, bewahrt, Matt aber hat erheblichere Erweiterungen des Vaterunsers vorgenommen."

Kilpatrick 1946, 21: "In the second addition it is to be noticed that while heaven and earth are associated twice in Mark at xiii. 27, 31, once or twice in Q, Matt. v.18 parallel to Luke xvi.17, Matt. xi.25 parallel to Luke x.21, and five times in Luke, in Matthew they are associated thirteen times, Matt. v.34f., vi.19f., xvi.19(2), xviii.18(2), 19, xxx.9, xxiv.35, xxiii.18, the two Q passages and here. ... The evidence of style and context seems to be strongly in favour of the view that the elements which do not derive from Q were composed by the evangelist."

Schmid 1956, 122: "Von den sieben Bitten im Matthäus-Text fehlen bei Lukas die dritte ... und die siebente. ... Es ist nicht vorstellbar, daß Lukas dieses Gebet verkürzt hätte, wenn er es in der Matthäus-Fassung vorgefunden hätte. Andererseits kann man die dritte Bitte als eine sachliche Erläuterung der zweiten und die siebente als eine Ergänzung der negativen sechsten in positiver Form (Zahn) verstehen."

Knox 1957, 61: See Q 11:~~1-2a,~~2b⁴ Matt = Q, Con.

Beare 1962, 61: See Q 11:~~1-2a,~~2b⁵ Matt = Q, Con.

Brown 1965, 220: "It is much more likely that the Matthean tradition represents a prayer to whose original petitions have been joined other sayings of Jesus. This is a well-attested phenomenon in Mt, for Mt's eight beatitudes (as compared to Lk's four) and Mt's long Sermon on the Mount (as compared to Lk's shorter Sermon on the Plain) represent conflations of material."

235: "The petition is not found in Lk; indeed, the vocabulary is distinctively Matthean.[67] The same petition appears again in Mt's version of the Agony in the Garden and forms Christ's prayer when He withdraws from the sleepy disciples a second time (Mt 26:42). Since in the Marcan parallel to this verse (Mk 14:39) we have only the general statement, 'He prayed saying the same words,' we may suspect that Mt is using the petition to fill in the actual words of the prayer. Thus the stray logion 'May your will come about' is employed twice in Mt to fill out sequences."

235[67]: "The aorist passive of *ginesthai* is not found in Jn, and only once in Mk and Lk (and there it is a quotation from the LXX shared by Mt). Mt has seven other occurrences."

Davies 1966, 5: See Q 11:~~1-2a,~~2b⁵ Matt = Q, Con.

Jeremias 1966, 158: See Q 11:~~1-2a,~~2b⁵ Matt = Q, Con.

Jeremias 1967, 12: "die lukanische Kurzform ist in der Matthäus-Fassung vollständig enthalten. Nach allem, was wir über die Gesetzmäßigkeit der Überlieferung liturgischer Texte wissen, hat in einem solchen Fall, in dem die kürzere Fassung in der längeren enthalten ist, die kürzere als die ursprünglichere zu gelten. Wer sollte es gewagt haben, zwei Bitten des Vater-Unsers zu streichen, wenn sie zum ältesten Überlieferungsbestand gehörten? Dagegen ist das Umgekehrte, daß liturgische Texte in der Frühzeit, ehe eine Verfestigung der Formulierung eintritt, ausgestaltet, erweitert, angereichert werden, vielfältig belegt. Dieser Schluß, daß die Matthäusfassung eine Erweiterung darstellt, wird durch weitere Beobachtungen bestätigt. Einmal finden sich die drei Matthäus-Überschüsse am Schluß, nämlich am Schluß der Anrede, am Schluß der Du-Bitten und am Schluß der Wir-Bitten; das entspricht genau dem, was wir auch sonst beim Wachstum liturgischer Texte beobachten: sie lieben den volltönenden Abschluß. Weiter ist bezeichnend, daß bei Matthäus der stilistische Aufbau weiter durchgegliedert ist: den drei Wir-Bitten (die 6. und 7. Matthäus-Bitte hat man als eine Bitte empfunden) entsprechen bei ihm drei Du-Bitten; und die bei Lukas durch ihre Kürze abrupt wirkende dritte Wir-Bitte ist bei Matthäus in der Länge und Zweiteiligkeit den beiden ersten Wir-Bitten angeglichen. ... Dieses Bestreben, den Gleichklang der Glieder (Parallelismus membrorum) herzustellen, ist ein Kennzeichen liturgischer Überlieferung."

Jeremias 1967, ET 1964, 11-12: "the shorter form of Luke is completely contained in the longer form of Matthew. This makes it very probable that the Matthean form is an expanded one, for according to all that we know about the tendency of liturgical texts to conform to certain laws in their transmission, in a case where the shorter version is contained in the longer one, the shorter text is to be regarded as original. No one would have dared to shorten a sacred text like the Lord's Prayer and to leave out two petitions if they had formed part of the original tradition. On the contrary, the reverse is amply attested, that in the early period, before wordings were fixed, liturgical texts were elaborated, expanded, and enriched. This conclusion, that the Matthean version represents an expansion, is confirmed by three supplementary observations. First, the three expansions which we find in Matthew, as compared with Luke, are always found toward the end of a section of the prayer— the first at the end of the address, the second at the end of the 'Thou-petitions,' the third at the end of the 'We-petitions.' This again is exactly in accordance with what we find elsewhere in the growth of liturgical texts.

"Second, it is of further significance that in Matthew the stylistic structure is more consistently carried through. Three 'Thou-petitions' in Matthew correspond to the three 'We-petitions (the sixth and seventh petitions in Matthew were regarded as one petition). The third 'We-petition,' which in Luke seems abrupt because of its brevity, is in Matthew assimilated to the first two 'We-petitions.' ... [12] ...

"This endeavor to produce parallelism in lines (*parallelismus membrorum*) is a characteristic of liturgical tradition."

Grundmann 1968, 200-201: "Das Gebet der Jünger soll 'erst den Vater anreden', zu dem es aufschaut, 'bevor es bittend in die Zukunft zielt, erst das Antlitz des gegenwärtigen Vaters suchen, bevor es Ausschau hält nach dem kommenden Gott'.

"[Matt 6:]10 Das geschieht mit der zweiten Bitte. Die Eschatologie Jesu gründet in seiner [201] Theologie. Auf die Ankündigung des kommenden Königtums Gottes mit dem Ruf zur Umkehr antwortet sie: 'Es komme dein Königtum.' Die so beten, haben Gott als ihren Vater kennengelernt und liefern sich seinem kommenden Königtum aus in einer Welt, die sich Gottes Königtum entzieht und ihn nicht als Vater kennt. Ihr Weiterbestehen aber läßt fragen, was Gottes Wille für den Jünger in der Welt sei. Darum fügt Matthäus—aus Jesu Gethsemane-Gebet? —die dritte Bitte ein. Die Frage nach dem Willen Gottes ist eine der zentralen Fragen des Evangelisten Matthäus (vgl. 7,21; 12,50; 18,14; 21,28-32). So wird die dritte Bitte zur Antwort auf die Verkündigung des Willens Gottes und bekommt gerade in der Bergpredigt ihren klaren Platz. Gottes Wille soll jetzt geschehen durch das Tun der Jünger, und er soll als Heilsverwirklichung geschehen im Kommen des Königtums Gottes."

Berger 1969, 1149: "Inhaltlich bedeutet das Herrschen Gottes nichts anderes als die Durchsetzung seines Willens; eine unbeachtete wörtliche Parallele findet sich in Lib Ant VI 11 (Abraham bittet um den Vollzug eines gerechten Gerichtes: 'Fiat voluntas Dei'). Mt hat auch in 26,42b das Ölberggebet Jesu gegen seine Mk-Vorlage nach dem V. gestaltet, indem er Jesus bitten läßt: γενηθήτω τὸ θέλημά σου."

Jeremias 1971, 189-190: "Die entscheidende Beobachtung bezüglich der Ursprünglichkeit ist, daß die Lukasfassung in der [190] Matthäusfassung vollständig enthalten ist. Da liturgische Texte die Tendenz haben, sich anzureichern, und der kürzere Wortlaut hier gewöhnlich der ältere ist, dürften die Überschüsse bei Matthäus Erweiterungen darstellen. Es ist unwahrscheinlich, daß jemand die dritte und siebte Bitte gestrichen haben sollte, während der umgekehrte Vorgang gut vorstellbar ist. Daß der kürzere Text der ältere ist, wird durch weitere Beobachtungen bestätigt. Die drei Überschüsse der Matthäusfassung finden sich jeweils an entsprechender Stelle im Text: am Ende der (ursprünglich nur aus einem Wort bestehenden) Anrede, am Ende der Du-Bitten und am Ende der Wir-Bitten. Das entspricht wiederum dem, was sich andernorts beobachten läßt: liturgische Texte werden gern volltönend abgeschlossen[79]. Für die Ursprünglichkeit des Lukasumfangs spricht schließlich, daß durch die von Matthäus überlieferten Zusätze der stilistische Aufbau des Vaterunsers ausgeglichen wird. Insbesondere ergänzt die siebte Bitte den Parallelismus membrorum, dessen Fehlen in der lukanischen Schlußbitte sehr auffällig ist."

190[79]: "Beispiele: Mt 26,28 verglichen mit den Paralleltexten; Phil 2,11."

Jeremias 1971, ET 1971, 195: "The most decisive feature in favour of originality is that the Lucan version is contained in its entirety within that of Matthew. As liturgical texts tend to be elaborated, and the shorter wording is usually the earlier, the additional material in Matthew may amount to elaborations. It is improbable that anyone should have deleted the third and seventh petitions, whereas the opposite process is easily imaginable. Further considerations confirm that the shorter text is the earlier. The three additional passages in the Matthaean version in each instance come at the same place in the text: at the end of the address (which originally consisted in only one word), at the end of the petitions in the second person, and at the end of the petitions in the first person plural. This also corresponds with what is to be observed elsewhere: there is a tendency to conclude liturgical texts with a full stress.[1] Finally, the fact that the additions transmitted by Matthew balance the stylistic construction of the Lord's Prayer also suggests that the Lucan version is original. In particular, the seventh petition completes the parallelism, the absence of which is very striking in the closing petition of Luke."

195[1]: "Examples: Matt. 26.28 compared with the parallel texts; Phil. 2.11."

Morgenthaler 1971, 191: "Jedenfalls steht 6:10b und 6:13b als S des Mt da."

Schulz 1972, 86: "*Die Bitten, die sich nur bei Mt finden*: Die Kurzfassung des Lk ist nicht als Kürzung der Mt-Fassung zu erklären, sondern die Mt-Fassung wird, was die Zahl der Bitten anbelangt, gegenüber Lk sek sein. Das Vokabelmaterial der über Lk hinausgehenden Bitten verrät die Hand des Mt.[202]"

86[202]: "Mt 6,10b geht auf den Redaktor zurück: vom θέλημα Gottes spricht Mt ca 3mal red (7,21 18,14 26,42). Die Wendung οὐρανὸς καὶ γῆς wird von Mt bezeugt (Mt 13mal Mk 2mal Lk 5mal)."

Schweizer 1973, 92: "Das auffälligste ist das Fehlen der dritten Bitte in der Lukasfassung. Sie ist also erst später dazugewachsen, vielleicht auf Grund der Bitte Jesu in Gethsemane. Allerdings findet diese sich nur Mt.26,42 wörtlich gleich wie im Unservater, und zwar in einem Vers, den er gegenüber Markus neu formuliert (anders V. 39 = Mk.14,36)."

92 [ET 1975, 148]: See Q 11:1̶ 2̶a̶,2b⁴ Matt = Q, Con.

Schweizer 1973, ET 1975, 147: "The most striking difference is the omission in Luke of the third petition. This petition is therefore a later accretion, probably based on the prayer of Jesus in Gethsemane. Only in Matthew (26:42) is the Gethsemane petition expressed in the same words as in the Lord's Prayer, and that in a verse reformulated by Matthew from Mark (put differently in Matt. 26:39 = Mark 14:36)."

Frankemölle 1974, 276-277: "Aufgrund der Komposition [of Matt 5-7] ist das Wort von der Verwirklichung des θέλημα τοῦ πατρὸς ἐν τοῖς οὐρανοῖς (6,10b) als konkretisierende redaktionelle Interpretation seiner βασιλεία (6,10a) der Ansatz der mt 'Gesetzes'-Auffassung. Dies wird noch durch ein weiteres Moment konkreter und für Mt aufschlußreicher: 6,10b ist die einzige Bitte im Herrengebet, für die es im Gegensatz zu allen anderen Bitten keine jüdische Parallele gibt. Um so dringlicher wird dann die Frage, was Mt mit der Bitte, Gott möge sein θέλημα verwirklichen, hat aussagen wollen.

"Zunächst gibt der nähere Kontext einen Hinweis zur Auslegung. Die Bitte steht ja nicht isoliert, sondern ist formal und sachlich verbunden mit den anderen Bitten, daß Gott seine βασιλεία herbeiführen möge und die Heiligung seines Namens besorgen soll. Alle drei Bitten variieren das eine große Zentralanliegen Jesu nach Mt: Gottes Basileia soll sichtbar und erfahrbar werden, der damit implizierte Wille Gottes soll nicht nur erkannt, sondern auch getan werden, so daß Gottes Name geheiligt wird. Mag in der ursprünglichen Q-Fassung die eschatologische Komponente[16] dominierend [277] gewesen sein, so kennt doch bereits das AT wie das Judentum den Gedanken, daß der Name Gottes durch Israel geheiligt wird, indem es Gottes Willen, d.h. den Geboten der Thora gehorcht. Diese irdische Verwirklichung hat Mt redaktionell betont (vgl. 6,10b): Gottes Herrschaft verwirklicht sich auf Erden dort, wo sie anerkannt und praktiziert wird, was mit der Heiligung seines Namens identisch ist. Wenn dabei für das irdische Erfüllen der himmlische Maßstab ('im Himmel') angegeben ist, so wird damit lediglich die Vollkommenheits-Forderung von 5,48 variiert."

276-277[16]: "Von der endzeitlichen Verherrlichung seines Namens durch Jahwe spricht [277] nicht nur das AT (vgl. Ez 20,41; 28,22-26; 38,16-23) und das Judentum (vgl. K.G. Kuhn, ἅγιος, in: ThW I 99), sondern dies ist auch Grundüberzeugung des NT (dazu O. Procksch, ἁγιάζω, in: ThW I 113)."

Edwards 1976, 107: See Q 11:~~1-2a,~~2b⁴ Matt = Q, Con.

Schlosser 1980, 285-286: "*1) Γενηθήτω τὸ θέλημά σου.*

"Marc et Luc ne parlent que très rarement de la 'volonté de Dieu' d'une façon expresse [Mc 3,35; Lc 22,42.], Matthieu est moins discret en la matière [Matt 6,10; 7,21; 12,50; 18,14; 26,42.]. Notons immédiatement deux faits:

"a) Dans les cinq attestations du vocable chez Mt θέλημα est en relation avec πατήρ [On peut y ajouter l'emploi correspondant dans la parabole des deux fils (Mt 21,31)]. [286]

"b) L'association de θέλημα et de πατήρ est le fait du rédacteur matthéen, certainement en 12,50 (diff. Mc 3,35) et probablement en 7,21[271] et en 26,42." Square brackets, except for [286], are Schlosser's.

317[271]: "De l'avis général de la critique ce verset, à comparer avec Lc 6,46, contient une part importante de rédaction matthéenne."

286-287: "En Mt 6,10 et dans sa reprise secondaire de 26,42, θέλημα est sujet de γενηθήτω. Dans le reste du NT ces deux termes ne sont employés ensemble qu'en Lc 22,42 et Ac 21,14 (γινέσθω dans les deux cas). Que signifie l'expression?

"L'antiquité païenne connaît des formules analogues pour exprimer soit la résignation, soit une sorte d'ajustement de la volonté humaine à celle des dieux. Ce sens pourrait convenir à la rigueur en Ac 21,14, mais il est à exclure sans doute pour la prière de Gethsémani, en toute hypothèse pour la troisième demande du Notre Père.

"La formule rabbinique *yhy rṣwn*, à laquelle on renvoie parfois, n'est pas davantage éclairante: usitée dans les prières juives, elle signifie 'qu'il te plaise de' et suppose un verbe qui la suit.

"L'explication, en fait, est à chercher dans un emploi particulier du verbe γίνομαι. Dans le NT le passif de ποιέω est à peu près inexistant. Comme c'est le cas ailleurs dans la Koinè, le passif inusité y est suppléé par γίνομαι. Un simple regard sur la LXX montre que γίνομαι tient là aussi le rôle du passif, —ce verbe pouvant traduire *ᶜśh* au niphal et *ᶜbd* au hithpᵉel. En Mt 6,10b (et 26,42) aussi, γενηθήτω est à prendre suivant toute vraisemblance comme substitut du passif de ποιέω. Certes, le verbe γίνομαι, qui est attesté 75 fois en Mt, signifie 'arriver, se produire' dans la très grande majorité des cas. Mais les exceptions pourraient bien être moins rares qu'il ne semble à première vue. A Mt 6,10b et 26,42, en effet, il convient d'ajouter au moins Mt 5,18. En outre, parmi les textes où, comme en Mt 6,10b, γίνομαι est à la forme passive de l'aoriste (ἐγενήθν — γενηθήτω),[284] Mt 8,13; 9,29 et 15,28 paraissent employer γίνομαι au sens de 'être fait'. E. Lohmeyer pense même que γίνομαι est mis pour le passif de ποιέω dans tous les textes matthéens où γίνομαι est à la forme passive de l'aoriste. [287]

"En somme et selon toute probabilité, nous avons en Mt 6,10b la forme passive de l'expression 'faire la volonté' de Dieu qu'on lit en 12,50 et en 7,21. [287]

"Les vocables du premier membre de Mt 6,10b sont caractéristiques de Matthieu, pour l'expression comme pour le contenu. Mais il convient de noter de suite que les mêmes motifs—la 'volonté du Père', 'faire la volonté du Père qui est aux cieux'—apparaissent singulièrement proches des formules et des idées rabbiniques, et que l'emploi de γίνομαι comme passif de ποιέω n'est pas propre à Matthieu [Voir par ex. Mc 2,27, Lc 14,22; Jn 1,3; Ac 19,26.]." Square brackets, except for [287], enclose Schlosser's footnotes.

318²⁸⁴: "L'aoriste passif se lit dans la citation du Ps 117(118),22 attestée par la triple tradition (Mc 12,10 par.), mais nulle part ailleurs en Mc et seulement deux fois en Lc (10,12 et 18,23). Chez Mt par contre il se trouve encore 7 fois, 5 fois à l'impératif (6,10; 8,13; 9,29; 15,28; 26,42) et 2 fois à l'indicatif (11,23; 28,4). La comparaison syn. révèle que cette forme est typique du rédacteur matthéen."

318²⁸⁷: "'Faire la volonté du Père' est encore utilisé en 21,31a à propos d'un maître humain. Noter que Mt 21,28-31a est vraisemblablement une création de Matthieu, comme nous verrons."

287: "2) Ὡς ἐν οὐρανῷ καὶ ἐπὶ γῆς.

"L'examen littéraire du second membre de phrase établit les faits suivants:

"a) La corrélation ὡς ... καί n'est attestée qu'ici dans l'évangile de Mt.

"b) En elle-même l'expression ἐν οὐρανῷ est bien matthéenne. Son caractère rédactionnel n'est cependant pas évident. En effet, si en Mt 6,20 diff. Lc 12,33 le changement du pluriel en singulier peut être attribué à Matthieu, dans les autres passages, qui sont dépourvus de parallèles, on ne peut être à ce point affirmatif, d'autant moins que l'auteur du premier évangile ne reprend pas ἐν οὐρανῷ aux deux endroits où il a lu l'expression dans Mc [Matt 19,21 diff. Mc 10,21; Mt 24,36 diff. Mc 13,32.]. Tout au plus peut-on remarquer d'une manière très générale que, tous emplois confondus (pluriel et singulier), Mt est statistiquement plus riche que les deux autres synoptiques.²⁹²

"c) La formule ἐπὶ γῆς ne se lit chez les synoptiques qu'en Mt 6,10 et Lc 2,14. Munie de l'article, l'expression est plus fréquente en Mt qu'en Mc et qu'en Lc.²⁹³

"d) Le binôme 'ciel-terre' enfin est courant dans le premier évangile [Matt 5,18; 5,34-35; 6,10.19; 11,25; 16,19 (2 fois); 18,18 (2 fois); 24,35; 28,18.], plus rare dans Mc [Mc 13,27.31.] et dans Lc [Lc 10,21; 12,56; 16,17; 21,23.].

"Par certains traits la touche matthéenne du vocabulaire apparaît nette; on ne peut affirmer cependant que l'expression soit vraiment caractéristique de la rédaction même du premier évangile." Square brackets are Schlosser's.

319²⁹²: "Voici les indications complémentaires:

"- ἐν οὐρανοῖς: Mt 5,45; 12,50; 18,10.19; 19,21.

"- ἐν τοῖς οὐρανοῖς: Mt 5,12.16; 6,1.9; 7,11.21; 10,32.33; 16,17.19 (2 fois); 18,14.

"Mc 11,25.26; 12,25.

"Lc 10,20; 12,33; 18,22."

319²⁹³: "Compte non tenu des textes où γῆ désigne la terre ferme, le rivage, l'expression se lit 10 fois en Mt (6,19; 9,6; 16,19 (2 fois); 18,18 (2 fois); 18,19; 23,9.35; 28,18), mais seulement 3 fois en Mc (2,10; 4,31; 9,3) et 4 fois en Lc (5,24; 18,18; 21,23.25)."

Beare 1981, 171: "More striking is the fact that the petition, 'Let your will be done' (with the supplementary, 'as in heaven, so upon earth') is not found at all in Luke. This clause too may be secondary, whether Matthaean or pre-Matthaean, designed to make explicit the essential meaning of the petition, 'Let your Kingdom come.'"

Schürmann 1981, 20: "Die Zusätze der erweiterten Fassung des *Matthäus* verschieben das Zueinander der einzelnen Glieder und ändern damit den formalen Aufbau des Ganzen: Die *Anrede* hat feierlich-liturgische Form angenommen und hebt sich nun als selbständiger Vorbau von dem folgenden Gebetswunsch ab. Es folgt eine Strophe mit *drei Gebetswünschen*: um die Heiligung des Namens, das Kommen des Reiches und zusätzlich noch um das Geschehen des Gotteswillens, die unverbunden-lapidar aufeinander folgen, aber doch streng in Reih und Glied gestellt sind durch das allen gemeinsame Stichwort 'dein' und das betont vorangestellte Zeitwort."

70: "Die lukanische Fassung des Gebetes kennt diese Bitte nicht; hier ist der Wunsch nach dem Kommen des Königtums in seiner Einzigartigkeit und Konkurrenzlosigkeit belassen. Ist sie bei Lukas vielleicht darum fortgelassen, weil sie nach dem Urteil dessen, der das Gottesreich als den großen Schatz gefunden und um sein Kommen gebetet hat, im Grunde nichts Neues mehr erfleht? Aber wer sollte es gewagt haben, so eine Bitte nachträglich zu streichen? Tatsächlich faßt der neue Gebetswunsch nur etwas ins Wort, was schon in der vorigen Bitte mitenthalten ist, wenn hier auch etwas in Worte gefaßt ist, was bislang noch nicht ausdrücklich genannt war: der Wille Gottes. Diese ausdrückliche Erwähnung bedeutet schon eine zusätzliche Betonung, wohl auch eine von ganz bestimmtem Interesse geleitete Akzentuierung. Der Mensch ist in seiner Verantwortung dafür, daß Gottes Wille verwirklicht werde, stärker angesprochen (was der Tendenz des Matthäusevangeliums sehr entspricht[107]). Sonst scheint aber die neue Bitte inhaltlich—wie man sie auch deuten mag—in der vorigen enthalten zu sein und diese interpretieren zu sollen. Bei der sonstigen Prägnanz des Gebetes, das kein überflüssiges Wort kennt, ist diese breite Verdoppelung gewiß auffällig."

171[107]: "Wahrscheinlich formuliert hier die Mt-Tradition oder Matthäus selbst. Vom 'Willen des Vaters' ist in den synoptischen Evangelien nur noch Mt 12,50 (Markusredaktion), 7,21 (anders die Lk-Parallele) und 21,31 (Sondergut) die Rede (vgl. ähnlich noch 18,14); 'dein Wille' noch 26,42 (Markusredaktion)."

Giesen 1982, 226-227: "(2) Für [Matthean] Redaktionsarbeit spricht der Imperativ γενηθήτω, zumal Mt 9,29 die Mk-Vorlage (10,52; vgl. Lk 18,42) ausdrücklich ändert; dasselbe geschieht auch in Mt 15,28 gegenüber Mk 7,29. In Mt 26,42 bringt Mt zudem dieselbe Wendung γενηθήτω τὸ θέλημά σου wie in 6,10b, wobei Mt 6,10b eher von 26,42 beeinflußt sein dürfte, als umgekehrt, da der Evangelist diesen Gedanken gut aus dem vorhergehenden V 39d πλὴν οὐχ ὡς ἐγὼ θέλω ἀλλ᾿ ὡς σύ, der eine Parallele in Mk 14,36d hat, entwickeln konnte.

"(3) Schließlich findet sich im Mt auch die Gegenüberstellung von οὐρανός und γῆ häufiger als bei den beiden anderen Synoptikern.

"(4) Nimmt man zu diesen Einzelbeobachtungen die nicht bestrittene paränetische Tendenz unseres Evangelisten hinzu, kann es kaum zweifelhaft sein, daß die dritte Vaterunserbitte aus seiner Feder geflossen ist. Hätte Mt unsere Bitte dennoch aus der Tradition übernommen, hätte er es nur getan, weil sie bestens in sein theologisches Konzept paßt, so daß der Vers auch dann im Sinne der Redaktion zu verstehen wäre.

"(5) Eine weitere Beobachtung vermag diesen Befund zu bestätigen: Mt fügt nämlich die Bitte 'Dein Wille geschehe' an die Bitte 'Dein Reich komme' an, die in Lk 11,2 eine wörtliche Parallele hat. Hier wird eine Denkbewegung deutlich, die wir bereits in Mt 6,33 kennengelernt haben. Wie Mt dort der Vorlage gegenüber dem Suchen nach dem Reich die nach der Gerechtigkeit des Vaters folgen läßt, um so neben dem Ziel auch den Weg dorthin zu weisen, so nennt er hier nach der Bitte um das Kommen des Reiches sogleich jene um das Tun des Vaterwillens. Das Ziel, die Herrschaft des Vaters, kann nur über das Tun seines Willens erreicht werden. Die Aussage nähert sich darin der von 7,21, die das Tun des Vaterwillens zur Voraussetzung für den Eintritt in die Himmelsherrschaft macht. [227]

"Nimmt man alle Gründe zusammen, so kann man m.E. kaum umhin, die dritte Vaterunser-Bitte dem ersten Evangelisten zuzusprechen."

Gundry 1982, 106: "in his additions Matthew is lashing out against antinomians, whose lawless conduct grows out of failure to reverence the Father. ... In order to stress obedience to the law as expounded by Jesus in the Sermon on the Mount, Matthew magnifies the element of realized eschatology. θέλημα is among his favorites (3,1 cf. θέλω-18,8). ... Elsewhere, too, he interpolates the particular form γενηθήτω several times (8:13 9:29 15:28). Thus, in wording typical of his style and interests, he constructs 6:10b and conforms 26:42d to it in order to draw a parallel between Jesus and the disciples in their obedience to the heavenly Father's will."

Guelich 1982, 290: "This petition lacks a parallel in Luke 11:2 and most likely stems from Matthew's redaction on the basis of the following evidence: First, the theme of the will of God occurs once in Mark (3:35, par. Matt 12:50) and once in Luke 22:42 but five times in Matthew, all but one of which are redactional (6:10, cf. Luke 11:2; 7:21, cf. Luke 6:46; 18:14, cf. Luke 15:7; 26:42, cf. Mark 14:39; 12:50, par. Mark 3:25; cf. 21:31). Second, Matthew alone of the synoptists uses the aorist passive of γίνομαι, and he has it five times as an imperative in contrast to his parallels (6:10, cf. Luke 11:2; 8:13, cf. Luke 7:10 (13:29) 9:29, cf. Mark 10:52; 15:28, cf.

Mark 7:29; 26:42, cf. Mark 14:39). Third, the additional phrase as in heaven so on earth also betrays Matthew's concept of heaven as the dynamic sphere of God's rule (cf. 'Kingdom of Heaven,' and 5:34; 16:2; 18:18). ... Matthew shows particular interest in the relationship between the Kingdom and the will of the Father (6:10a,b 7:21; 21:31; 26:42)."

291: "Matthew uses this combined expression (as in heaven so on earth) eight times, twice from Q (5:18, par. Luke 16:17 11:25, par. Luke 10:21) and once from Mark 13:31, par Matt 24:35."

Strecker 1982, 13: "Fragen wir nach dem ursprünglichen Wortlaut, also der ältesten Traditionsschicht, so ist kaum zweifelhaft, daß Lukas dem Urtext nähersteht. Dies gilt zumindest für die Fünfzahl der Bitten, während die Erweiterungen bei Matthäus einer späteren Überlieferungsstufe angehören."

Gerhardsson 1984, 210: See Q 11:1̶-̶2̶a̶,2b⁴ Matt = Q, Con.

Schnackenburg 1984, 96-97: "Die Bitte, daß Gottes Wille geschehe, ist eine [97] Entfaltung des großen Gebetswunsches, daß sein Reich komme. Sie bringt darum gegenüber diesem umfassenden Verlangen nichts grundsätzlich Neues, sondern verdeutlicht es."

Schnackenburg 1984, ET 1995, 64: "The petition that God's will be done is a development of the great prayerful wish that his kingdom come. Thus, it offers nothing fundamentally new vis-à-vis this comprehensive request, but elucidates it."

Fitzmyer 1985, 108: "As a finishing touch Matthew added 'on earth as also (it comes to pass) in heaven' to the first couplet."

897: "Matthew appended phrases: ... to the end of the second-person wishes expressed to God."

Luz 1985, 335: "Hilfreicher ist aber der Hinweis auf spontane Variationen jüdischer Gebete. ... Der unsymmetrisch kurze Anfangsteil der beiden Du-Bitten wurde um eine dritte Bitte erweitert, die den ersten Teil des Gebets geziemend abschloß."

Luz 1985, ET 1989, 370-371: "But the reference to spontaneous variations of Jewish prayers is more helpful. ... [371] ... The asymmetrical brief beginning part of the two you-petitions was enlarged by a third petition which appropriately concluded the first part of the prayer."

Schneider 1985, 62: See Q 11:1̶-̶2̶a̶,2b⁴ Matt = Q, Con.

74: "Die dritte Du-Bitte um den Vollzug des göttlichen Vaterwillens ist aus mehreren Gründen als typisch 'matthäisch' auszumachen. Dabei ist wiederum die Alternative zu berücksichtigen, daß der Evangelienverfasser entweder von sich aus die Erweiterung vornahm oder daß er die Bitte dem Vaterunser seiner Gemeinde entnehmen konnte. Im zweiten Fall müßte man freilich die Schlußfolgerung ziehen, daß diese (traditionelle) Bitte die Theologie des Matthäus in ungewöhnlich starkem Ausmaß geprägt haben muß. Ausschließlich bei Mt sind bezeugt: die Rede vom *thelēma* Gottes als dem Willen des himmlischen Vaters,[57] ferner die Verwendung der Verbform *genēthētō*.[58] Die Bitte um das 'Geschehen' des göttlichen Vater-Willens ist primär auf Gottes eigenes endgültiges Handeln bezogen, hat aber eine auf das gehorsame Tun des göttlichen Willens bezogene Komponente. Echt 'matthäisch' ist endlich auch die Idee einer Entsprechung von himmlischem und irdischem Geschehen (vgl. Mt 16,19; 18,18; 28,18).[60]"

74[57]: "*Thelēma* steht in den synoptischen Evangelien nur bei Mt in engem Bezug zum Willen Gottes als des *Vaters*: Mt 6,10 und 26,42 gleichlautend *genēthētō to thelēma sou*, an weiteren Stellen ist vom *Tun* des Vaterwillens Gottes die Rede: 7,21; 12,50; bezogen auf den Vater des Gleichnisses 21,31; siehe ferner 18,14 (*ouk estin thelēma*)."

74[58]: "Der Imperativ Aorist *genēthētō* kommt neben Röm 11,9 (LXX-Zitat) im NT nur bei Mt vor: Mt 6,10 und 8,13 diff Lk, Mt 9,29; 15,28; 26,42 diff Mk. Die Imperativ-Form geht also auf mt Redaktion zurück. Lukas schreibt hingegen zweimal *to thelēma ... ginesthō* (Lk 22,42; Apg 21,14). Daß *Did* 8,2 *genēthētō* bezeugt, ist ein gutes Argument für (literarische) Abhängigkeit von Mt 6,10. *Mart Polyc* 7,1 hat den Imperativ (*to thelēma tou theou genesthō*), spielt aber vielleicht auf Apg 21,14 an."

74[60]: "Bei Mt lassen folgende Stellen die Doppelung 'im Himmel ... auf Erden' (mit den Präpositionen *en ... epi*) als 'redaktionell' vermuten: Mt 6,10 diff Lk; 6,19f. diff Lk; 16,19b diff Mk; 16,19c diff Mk; 18,18a Sg.; 18,18b Sg.; 18,19 Sg.; 28,18 Sg."

Schnackenburg 1985, 64: See Q 11:~~1-2a,~~2b⁵ Matt = Q, Con.

Gnilka 1986, 214: "Während die 1. und 2. Bitte bei Mt/Lk vollständig übereinstimmen, bietet Lk die 3. nicht. Hat er sie gekannt, wie mit Hinweis auf Lk 22,42 behauptet wird? Es läßt sich kein plausibler Grund für eine Auslassung angeben.[10] Die Bitte fügt sich in das Konzept: Für die Gegenüberstellung von Himmel und Erde ist besonders auf 28,18; 5,18 zu verweisen. Diese Ausweitung ist eine logische Folge der erweiterten Gebetsanrede, wie schon Kuhn erkannte.[11] Die dort betonte Jenseitigkeit Gottes machte eine Erläuterung seines Machtbereiches notwendig. Vor allem gebraucht Mt θέλημα immer vom Willen des Vaters (6mal).[12]"

214[10]: "Schwarz, Matthäus 6,9-13, nennt als Grund die Anstößigkeit der 3. Bitte. Falls Theophilos Staatsbeamter gewesen sei, habe für ihn nur Caesars Wille gegolten (244). Dieses Argument kann nicht überzeugen. Der Änderung im Vergleich von Mk 14,36/Lk 24,42 (verbale/substantivische Formulierung) ist keine große Bedeutung beizumessen. Die Formulierung stimmt auch nicht mit Mt 6,10 überein."

214[11]: "Achtzehngebet [und Vaterunser und der Reim (WUNT 1) Tübingen 1950] 35."

214¹²: "Mk 3,35: Wille Gottes. Bei Lk läßt sich nur 24,42, evtl. 12,47 vergleichen."

Sand 1986, 126: "Die dritte und siebte Bitte bei Mt ist Hinzufügung, wie die mt. Vorzugsworte 'Wille', 'Himmel und Erde' ... deutlich zu erkennen geben."

Schenk 1987, 132: "γενηθήτω ... Mt 5: Mk 0: Lk 0 + 1 (NT nur noch in LXX-Zitaten Apg 1,20 Röm 11,9). Der Imp. Aor. 3. Sing. steht red. rahmend in den beiden Gebetsstellen 6,10 (+Q, wo ὡς als Vergleichspunkt verbunden ist) am Anfang und 26,42 (+Mk) am Schluß mit dem Subj. 'dein Wille'."

284: "θέλημα Mt 6: Mk 1: Lk 3 ... 6,10 (+Q)."

382: "οὐρανός ... γῆ ... Mt 14: Mk 2: Lk 4."

Davies and Allison 1988, 605: "The word statistics are consistent with a redactional origin,[42] as are those for 6.10c; and the evangelist has introduced the exact words 'thy will be done' in the story of Gethsemane (26.42: cf. 12.50). Nevertheless, for the reasons cited when considering the genesis of 9b, many would remain hesitant to assign 10b-c to Matthew (see esp. Schlosser 1, pp. 287, 289-90). Would the evangelist have changed a received liturgical prayer?"

605[42]: "The aorist passive imperative of γίνομαι is redactional in 8.13; 9.29; 15.28; and 26.42. It does not appear in Mark or Luke. θέλημα: Mt 6 (always of the Father's will); Mk: 1; Lk: 4."

606: "Although ὡς ... καί appears only here in the First Gospel, this hardly eliminates the possibility of a redactional origin for the clause in which it is found.[43]"

606[43]: "ὡς: Mt: 40; Mk: 21; Lk: 51. οὐρανός: Mt: 82; Mk: 18; Lk: 34. οὐρανός ... γῆ: Mt: 10; Mk: 2; Lk: 4-5."

Wiefel 1988, 215: "Matthäus bietet das Vaterunser in der Bergpredigt dar, im Rahmen der Auseinandersetzung mit verkehrten Frömmigkeitsformen; es hat eine ausgeführte Anrede und sieben Bitten. Die Kurzfassung des Lukas beruht nicht auf Kürzung, kann vielmehr nach Struktur und Aufbau als die ältere Gestalt gelten. Lukas dürfte sie in Q vorgefunden haben."

Catchpole 1993, 30: "No opportunity is lost by Matthew in stressing that 'doing the will of my Father who is in heaven' is the ultimate test of religious authenticity.[66] Once again there is a single Marcan reference which proved stimulating to the later evangelist: 'Whoever does the will of God ...' (Mark 3:35). And it was a modest Matthaean modification of the prayer of the Marcan Jesus in Gethsemane (Mark 14:36) which produced exactly the same wording as in Matt 6:10, 'thy will be done' (Matt 26:42). ... So it is hard to see Luke dropping this petition and extremely easy to see Matthew introducing it."

30[66]: "Cf. 7:21; 12:50; 18:14; 21.31."

Nolland 1993, 615: "Luke has no equivalent to Matthew's next clause, which is best taken as an expansion of the petition for the coming of the kingdom of God (then God's will *will* be done on earth as it is currently in heaven; the expansion may well owe a debt to the Gethsemane prayer [Matt 26:42; cf. Luke 22:42])."

Ludwig 1994, 96-97: "Das Argument, Mt habe diese Bitte [Matt 6:10b] aus dem Unser-Vater in die Gethsemane-Szene eingefügt (und deshalb sei sie in 6,10 ursprünglich und Lk habe sie gestrichen), ist nicht überzeugend. Eher ist es genau umgekehrt: In 26,39 folgt Mt nämlich seiner Mk-Vorlage, indem er die Aussage mit einem Verb statt mit dem Substantiv formuliert: '...jedoch nicht wie ich will (θέλω), sondern wie du (willst)!' Erst wo Mt frei formuliert, gebraucht er das Substantiv θέλημα. Da also der Wortlaut von V.42b wohl von Mt stammt, ist es gut möglich, daß er eben diesen Wortlaut der Bitte selbst ins Unser-Vater eingefügt hat. Damit wäre die lukanische Form, die diese Bitte nicht überliefert, ursprünglicher. [97]

"Denn daß Lk das Substantiv θέλημα nicht vermeidet, demonstriert er in 22,42, wo er gegen Mk statt des Verbs θέλειν das Substantiv benutzt. Allerdings liegt bei Lk keine besondere Betonung des Terminus vor. In 12,47 benutzt Lk θέλημα (τοῦ κυρίου) αὐτοῦ zwei Mal in einem Zusatz zur Geschichte vom zuverlässigen Verwalter, den Mt nicht bietet. In Lk 23,25 bezieht sich der Ausdruck τῷ θελήματι αὐτῶν darauf, daß Pilatus Jesus (nach) dem Willen des Volkes ausliefert. Hier schwingt wohl die Bedeutung 'Mutwille' mit."

Meier 1994, 355: "the expansions in Matthew clearly betray the special style of Matthean tradition and/or redaction. ... Elsewhere in the Gospels 'thy will be done' occurs only in the Matthean version of Jesus' prayer in Gethsemane before his arrest (Matt 26:42) and obviously comes from Matthew's redactional hand rewriting the Marcan narrative he has inherited. ... Not by accident, the three additional Matthean clauses occur at the end of the address, the end of the 'you petitions,' and the end of the 'we petitions'—exactly at the locations where additions could be most easily inserted into a tightly constructed oral unit. While it is clear why Matthew or his tradition would desire to insert these phrases, there is no reason why Luke would have deleted them if they had already stood in the venerable prayer he had inherited."

Schürmann 1994, 190-191: "Die zusätzliche *Bitte des Mt* (6,10b) γενηθήτω τὸ θέλημά σου wird fast allgemein als nachträgliche Erweiterung des Herrengebets verstanden, die dann weithin auch in den luk Text sekundär eindrang. Als ursprünglich selbständiges 'Stoßgebet' Jesu ist sie nicht zu erhärten, da Mk 14,36c (wie anders auch u. zu Mk 11,25), noch deutlicher Mt 26,42b, bereits von unserer Vaterunser-Bitte abhängig sein wird.[124] Die Bitte verrät Eigentümlichkeiten der matth Gemeindesprache[125] [191] und verundeutlicht die majestätische Einsamkeit ... des einzigen ... Du-Wunsches um das Kommen der Basileia, dem sie inhaltlich auch nichts hinzufügt. Sie kommentiert diesen Basileia-Wunsch nur in einer einseitigen, für die Gemeinde des Matthäus aber charakteristischen Weise: daß Gottes Heilsplan zur Vollendung komme und sich durchsetze. Eine in seinen Gemeinden übliche Gebetsform des Herrengebetes kann freilich den Evangelisten veranlaßt haben, seine Q-Tradition (=Lk) hier zu ergänzen."

190¹²⁴: "τὸ θέλημα γινέσθω Lk 22,42b diff Mk und Apg 21,14 ist offenbar stereotype Ergebenheitskundung und kein Nachklang von Mt 6,10b (gg. Schwarz, a.a.O. 244 Anm. 3 und 4 [See Schwarz 1968-69, 244, Q 11:2b⁶ Luke = Q, Con.]), zumal ihr passiver Sinn nicht mit der Vaterunser-Bitte harmoniert."

190¹²⁵: "Vom 'Willen des Vaters' ist in den syn Evv noch die Rede Mt 12,50 diff Mk; 7,21 diff Lk; 21,31 matth S (vgl. 18,14); 'dein Wille' noch Mt 26,42 diff Mk."

Meadors 1995, 180-181¹⁵⁶: See Q 11:~~1-2a,~~2b⁰ Luke and Matthew = Q, Pro.

Evaluations

Carruth 1995: Luke = Q {A}, ()⁶.

Among the most convincing arguments that the phrase comes from Matthew and not from Q is the fact that doing the will of God is an expressly Matthean interest which he has worked into Q material elsewhere in the Sermon, e.g., Matt 7:21 // Luke 6:46. It is also regularly noted that Matthew includes precisely this phrase in his formulation of Jesus' second prayer in Gethsemane (Matt 26:42). In the Prayer the phrase comes at the end of a section and this position also makes it suspect as a redactional addition.

Ott does not explain why this phrase would not fit Luke's instruction on prayer and Crossan does not explain why its omission would make it a more appropriate Gentile-Christian prayer. With respect to Schwarz's view that Luke would drop the phrase for apologetic reasons, it can be pointed out that at least one commentator reads Luke 2:1-20 as showing Jesus "to be in direct confrontation with the emperor" (Richard A. Horsley, *The Liberation of Christmas: The Infancy Narratives in Social Context* [New York: Crossroad, 1989] 33). If, in his special material, Luke shows Jesus to be in confrontation with the emperor, he would not have reason to omit a phrase from the prayer which might be understood to oppose God's will and the emperor's will. Thus, there is no compelling reason to draw the conclusion that Luke read this petition in his source and chose to omit it. It is best understood as a redactional addition by Matthew.

Robinson 1995: Luke = Q {A}, ()⁶.

This formulation, lacking in Luke, is typically Matthean. It recurs almost verbatim in the redactional variation of and supplement to Q 6:46 (Matt 7:21): οὐ πᾶς ὁ λέγων μοι· κύριε κύριε, εἰσελεύσεται εἰς τὴν βασιλείαν τῶν οὐρανῶν, ἀλλ' ὁ ποιῶν τὸ θέλημα τοῦ πατρός μου τοῦ ἐν τοῖς οὐρανοῖς. In the Gethsemane scene Matthew (26:41-42) adapts the Markan narrative in clear dependence on the Matthean form of the Lord's Prayer, προσεύχεσθε, ἵνα μὴ εἰσέλθητε εἰς πειρασμόν· ... πάτερ μου ... γενηθήτω τὸ θέλημά σου. In Matt 18:14, Q 15:7 is explicated redactionally by reference to θέλημα ἔμπροσθεν τοῦ πατρὸς ὑμῶν τοῦ ἐν οὐρανοῖς. In Matt 12:50 the simple τὸ θέλημα τοῦ θεοῦ (Mark 3:35) is expanded to the full Matthean expression. Here is a consistent Matthean redactional pattern.

Matthew can also interpret the kingdom in terms of righteousness, in substance parallel to its association with God's will in Matt 7:21. For in Matt 6:33 ζητεῖτε δὲ πρῶτον τὴν βασιλείαν τοῦ θεοῦ καὶ τὴν δικαιοσύνην αὐτοῦ provides the Matthean interpretation to Q 12:31 (ζητεῖτε τὴν βασιλείαν αὐτοῦ). Matt 5:20 makes entrance into the kingdom contingent upon outstanding δικαιοσύνη. Also δικαιοσύνη is added redactionally to the Beatitude of Q 6:21a at Matt 5:6, and is again associated with the kingdom in an additional Matthean Beatitude (Matt 5:10).

Both Matthean formulations are present in Matt 21:31-32, where doing τὸ θέλημα τοῦ πατρός provides access into the kingdom, which is associated then with John coming ἐν ὁδῷ δικαιοσύνης.

In general, the vocabulary of the petition, with its association of heaven and earth, the Father's θέλημα, and γενηθήτω, is especially typical of Matthew.

Luke would have no reason to delete such a petition, had it stood in the Q Prayer. In Luke 12:47 a theologically transparent parable makes clear that one should do τὸ θέλημα τοῦ κυρίου.

Q 11:3

Matt 6:11	Q 11:3	Luke 11:3
τὸν ἄρτον ἡμῶν τὸν	τὸν ἄρτον ἡμῶν τὸν	τὸν ἄρτον ἡμῶν τὸν
ἐπιούσιον [ ]¹δ(ὸς)¹	ἐπιούσιον [ ]¹δ(ὸς)¹	ἐπιούσιον [δί]¹δ[ου]¹
ἡμῖν (σ)²ἡμερ(ο)²ν·	ἡμῖν (σ)²ἡμερ(ο)²ν·	ἡμῖν [τὸ καθ']² ἡμέρ[α]²ν·

¹ Luke's δίδου or Matthew's δός.
² Luke's τὸ καθ' ἡμέραν or Matthew's σήμερον.

Q 11:3¹: Luke's δίδου or Matthew's δός.

Luke = Q: τὸν ἄρτον ἡμῶν τὸν ἐπιούσιον [δί]¹δ[ου]¹

Pro

Con

B. Weiß 1876, 186: "Vor Allem aber hat dies die Verwandlung des δός in δίδου nothwendig gemacht, weil es sich nun um ein dauerndes (tägliches) Thun Gottes handelt, während doch die Analogie aller andern Bitten zeigt, daß der Imp. aor. ursprünglich ist."

B. Weiß 1878, 422: "δίδου) statt δός bei Matth. ist gewiss weniger ursprüng-lich, weil gegen die Analogie der übrigen Impp. Aor. Der Imp. Präs. bezeichnet das dauernde (tägliche) Geben Gottes und correspondirt dem ächt lukanischen (19,47. Act. 17,11) τὸ καθ' ἡμέραν: Tag für Tag betreffend, täglich."

J. Weiß 1892, 466: "δίδου) statt des Aor. könnte gewählt sein wegen der in dem lukan. ([9,23]. 19,47. Act 17,11) τὸ καθ' ἡμέραν liegenden Wiederho-lung."

B. Weiß 1901, 460: "δίδου) statt des δός Mt 6,11, war nothwendig geworden durch den Zusatz τὸ καθ' ἡμέραν (wie Act 17,11) statt des σήμερον, da nun an ein immer wiederholtes tägliches Geben gedacht ist."

von Harnack 1907, 45: "Das Δίδου ist griechisch korrekter, da es sich um eine allgemeine Anweisung handelt."

48: "Matthäus bietet das Gebet, wie es täglich gebetet wird; Luk. gibt die Gebetsanweisung; daher das Präsens. Ebendasselbe gilt von der Korrektur τὸ καθ' ἡμέραν für σήμερον, wobei noch zu bemerken ist, daß τὸ καθ' ἡμέραν nur bei Luk. im N.T. vorkommt (s. c. 19,47; Act. 17,11)."

von Harnack 1907, ET 1908, 60: "Δίδου is more correct Greek, seeing that the command is general."

64-65: "With the correction δίδου compare St. Luke's similar correction of St. Matt [5:]42. St. Matthew gives the prayer as it was meant to be, and as indeed it was, used daily; St. Luke gives it as an instruction in prayer, therefore the present tense. This also explains the substitution of τὸ καθ᾽ ἡμέραν for σήμερον, as to which it is to be noted that τὸ καθ᾽ ἡμέραν occurs elsewhere in the New Testament only in St. Luke (xix.47; Acts xvii.11)."

B. Weiß 1907, 72¹: "Daß Lk. 11,3 absichtlich der Imperativ des Aor. in den des Präs. verwandelt ist, zeigt, ganz ähnlich wie 9,23, das τὸ καθ᾽ ἡμέραν (statt σήμερον), das darauf reflektiert, daß das Geben des ἄρτος ἐπιούσ. uns täglich gleich notwendig ist."

McNeile 1915, 79: "Lk. has a generalized request, δίδου ἡμῖν καθ᾽ ἡμέραν, which may have been an early variation due to the account of the manna (τὸ καθ᾽ ἡμέραν εἰς ἡμέραν, Ex. xvi. 5); but the expression, which is class., is confined to Lk. in the N.T. (xix. 47, Ac. xvii. 11), and see his καθ᾽ ἡμέραν which he adds in ix. 23)."

Lagrange 1921, 323: "La formule de Lc. δίδου 'donne constamment' … convient mieux pour une prière à dire une fois."

Easton 1926, 176: "τὸ καθ᾽ ἡμέραν is 'Lukan'. … And Lk's present imperative δίδου … depends on this phrase. Mt is consequently original (J. Weiß)."

Klostermann 1927, 56: "Das momentane δός … σήμερον ist die Form des Gebets 'wie es täglich gebraucht werden soll', das durative δίδου … καθ᾽ ἡμέραν wohl Korrektur des Lc, der mehr erbittet als Mt."

Bussmann 1929, 67: "So wird Mt auch das τὸ καθ᾽ ἡμέραν in σήμερον vereinfacht, L [Luke] aber statt δός auch hier wie schon einmal δίδου geschrieben, auch das παντί [Luke 6:30] zugesetzt haben."

Klostermann 1929, 124: "die Verallgemeinerung des σήμερον in das lukanische τὸ καθ᾽ ἡμέραν (19:47, Act 17:11) brachte auch die Umformung des Tempus des Imperativs mit sich, s. Blaß 337,4."

Creed 1930, 157: "δός harmonises with the other aorists. The present tense in Lk. fits τὸ καθ᾽ ἡμέραν 'day by day.'"

Schmid 1930, 233²: "Τὸ καθ᾽ ἡμέραν ist lukanisch …, δίδου statt δός ist durch καθ᾽ ἡμέραν veranlaßt."

Manson 1937, 266: "The Lucan form of the petition is less original than the Matthaean. The request in Mt. asks for enough to-day to provide for to-morrow. In Lk. this is generalized into the request that every day we may have enough for the next day."

Soiron 1941, 328: "Absichtlich verwandelte sodann Lk den Imperativ des Aorist in den präsentischen bei der Brotbitte (δός in δίδου) und bewußt setzte er τὸ καθ᾽ ἡμέραν statt σήμερον in dem Gedanken, daß das Brot uns an jedem Tage gleich notwendig ist, daß wir seiner fortwährend bedürfen."

Brown 1965, 244: "Both Lk and the *Didache* use a present tense. This is probably the same tendency away from eschatology which we encountered in the Lucan version of the fourth petition." See Q 11:3² Luke = Q, Con.

Jeremias 1967, 13-14: "Das 'heute' ist also [in Luke] auf jeden Tag ausgedehnt; die Bitte ist dadurch erweitert, was zur Folge hat, daß die Antithese 'morgen—heute' fortfiel; außerdem mußte im Griechischen das Wort 'gib' mit dem Imperativ des Präsens ausgedrückt werden, während sonst durchweg im Vater-Unser der Imperativ der Vergangenheit (Aorist) steht. Aus alledem ergibt sich, daß die [14] Matthäus-Fassung der Brotbitte die ältere ist."

Jeremias 1967, ET 1964, 13: "Luke expands 'this day' into 'each day'; the petition is thereby broadened into a generalized saying, with the consequence that the antithesis 'this day—for the morrow' drops out. Moreover, in Luke the Greek word for 'give' now had to be expressed with the present imperative (δίδου, literally 'keep on giving!'), whereas elsewhere throughout the prayer the aorist imperative is used, which denotes a single action. Matthew also has the aorist imperative in this petition: 'give!' From all this it may be concluded that the Matthaean form of the petition for daily bread is the older one."

Wrege 1968, 104: "In der Brotbitte stimmt Lk mit Mt überein, fügt aber ein τὸ καθ' ἡμέραν zu, um auf diese Weise σήμερον zu ersetzen. ... in der Tat mag sich das lk Präsens von τὸ καθ' ἡμέραν her bestimmen."

Jeremias 1971, 190: "Was sodann den *Wortlaut* angeht, so wird die Brotbitte in der lukanischen Fassung generalisiert durch das Präsens δίδου, übrigens das einzige im Vaterunser, und durch die Setzung von τὸ καθ' ἡμέραν statt σήμερον. Das gibt Matthäus den Vorzug."

Jeremias 1971, ET 1971, 195-196: "Next, as far as *wording* is concerned, the petition for bread in the Lucan version is given a general form by the present δίδου, which is in [196] fact the only present in the Lord's Prayer, and by the replacement of σήμερον with καθ' ἡμέραν. This makes Matthew preferable."

Schulz 1972, 85: "Das lk καθ' ἡμέραν mag auch die Umformung des Tempus des Imperativs (δίδου anstelle von δός) mit sich gebracht haben."

Schweizer 1973, 93: "Im einzelnen ersetzt die lukanische Version bei der Bitte um Brot das 'heute' durch 'täglich' und ändert auch die Form des Verbums so, daß an die immer wiederholte Gabe gedacht ist."

Schweizer 1973, ET 1975, 148-149: "Luke's version ... replaces the 'today' of the [149] petition for bread with 'daily,' and also changes the form of the verb so as to suggest repeated giving."

LaVerdière 1983, 113: "When the prayer proved inadequate for a new situation the Matthean community simply added further elements at the end of the section. ... Luke on the other hand preserved an adapted form which had become more suited to his community's view of salvation history and the daily challenge of missionary commitment."

Fitzmyer 1985, 897: "[Luke] has changed the aor. impv. *dos* (of Q) to the pres. *didou*."

Lambrecht 1985, 132: "One may assume that Luke had to choose this tense when he replaced the 'today' by 'each day'. ... Luke sees further than one single day; he de-eschatologizes the text."

Luz 1985, 335-336: "Umgekehrt [to the expansion of the Lord's Prayer by Matthew] sind die Änderungen des Lk am Wortlaut der beiden [336] Wir-Bitten sekundär: Sie spiegeln die Parusieverzögerung (δίδου Imp Praes; τὸ καθ' ἡμέραν)."

Luz 1985, ET 1989, 371: "By contrast [to the expansion of the Lord's Prayer by Matthew], the changes of Luke in the wording of the two we-petitions are secondary; they mirror the delay of the parousia (δίδου, imperative present; τὸ καθ' ἡμέραν)."

Schneider 1985, 66-67: See Q 11:3² Luke = Q, Con.

Gnilka 1986, 214-215: "Brot- und Vergebungsbitte hat Mt in ihrer vor-gegebenen Gestalt bewahrt. Ihre Veränderungen bei Lk lassen sich von den Anliegen des 3. Evangelisten her verständlich machen. Lk korrigiert die Escha-tologie (Tempuswechsel: δίδου—ἀφίομεν), dies tut auch die Didache [215] (ἀφίεμεν)[13]."

215[13]: "Did bietet die klassische, Lk eine volkstümliche Form des Präsens von ἀφίημι. Die Wendung καθ' ἡμέραν in der lk Brotbitte ist typisch lk."

Taussig 1988, 35: "Luke seems to have wanted to prolong the amount of time that the petition for bread would be said by substituting δίδου (a present imperative used in the iterative sense) and τὸ καθ' ἡμέραν ('each day') for the more immediate Q requests."

Wiefel 1988, 215-216: "Der Vergleich der Einzelheiten zeigt ..., daß bei abweichender Formulierung Matthäus eher die ältere Fassung zu bieten scheint, während in der lukanischen Version Spuren aktualisierender Umge-staltung erkennbar sind. ... [215] ... Die Bitte um das Brot ist bei ihm [Luke] durch den iterativen Präsensimperativ δίδου an Stelle des Aorist und durch τὸ καθ' ἡμέραν (=täglich), das dem iterativen Imperativ entspricht, gegenüber Matthäus abweichend. Gegenüber dem harten σήμερον, das nur das Brot für den jeweiligen Tag erbittet, meint das καθ' ἡμέραν das Existenzminimum für alle Tage. Darin wird ein Sicheinrichten in der Welt im Zeichen der Parusieverzögerung erkennbar."

Evans 1990, 482: "in view of the aorist tenses throughout, and the aorist imperative *dos* in this petition in Matthew, Luke's present imperative *didou* looks secondary, as is *to kath' hēmeran* = 'daily' in comparison with Matthew's *sēmeron* = 'today'."

Catchpole 1993, 29: "Some of the distinctive details of Luke 11:2-4 are readily explicable as Luke R. A change from δὸς ... σήμερον to δίδου ... τὸ καθ' ἡμέραν would fit Lucan usage elsewhere.⁶³ Such a change adjusts the prayer to life during an indefinite period of time and removes the urgent tone of Matthew's petition for food."

29⁶³: "Cf. 9:23 diff Mark 8:34; 19:47 diff Mark 11:18."

Nolland 1993, 615: "the verb is a present imperative in Luke and an aorist imperative in Matthew. This is compatible with a second difference, which is that Matthew has 'today,' where Luke has 'day by day,' τὸ καθ' ἡμέραν. Since this last phrase is Lukan, the alterations may be Luke's own (see 19:47 and cf. 9:23; 16:19; 22:53; Acts 2:46,47; 3:2; 17:11)."

Cullmann 1994, 71: "Die Lukasversion hat abstrakter das *immer* nötige Brot im Auge¹³³."

161¹³³: "Dementsprechend setzt Lukas das Präsens δίδου statt des Aorists δός des Matthäus."

Cullmann 1994, ET 1995, 54: "The Lukan version is more abstract, and envisages the bread that we always need.¹³³"

161¹³³: "Accordingly Luke puts the present δίδου instead of Matthew's aorist δός."

Meier 1994, 355: "Luke's modification of the wording is both theological and stylistic. The substitution of the present imperative in the first 'we petition' (*didou*, 'keep giving,' as opposed to Matthew's aorist *dos*) blatantly breaks with the string of punctiliar aorist imperatives that make up the body of the prayer, even in his own version. The durative or iterative present imperative fits the pastoral concerns of Luke, the theologian of salvation history, who knows that the church must settle down for the long haul of life in this present world. This sense of ongoing Christian life in the present age is reinforced by his replacement of 'today' with 'every day'; similarly, he inserts 'every day' into the Synoptic command to take up one's cross (9:23; contrast Mark 8:34 // Matt 16:24)."

Schürmann 1994, 192: "In der Lk-Fassung denkt der Beter nicht nur betend an das Heute (wie par Mt. σήμερον): 'Tag für Tag' (τὸ καθ' ἡμέραν)—vgl. dazu noch die betonte Endstellung!—soll das Brot nicht fehlen, was entsprechend auch der iterative Imperativ Präsens (δίδου) zum Ausdruck bringt. Damit ist ebenfalls an das hiesige Brot gedacht.

"Freilich will Lukas seine Beter auch bescheiden: Gewünscht wird nur das jeweils für den Tag Notwendige, wie das Manna (außer am Vortage des Sabbats) immer nur für den einen Tag gegeben wurde (vgl. Ex 16,4.16. 18.21)¹³⁴."

192¹³⁴: "Auch die matth Fassung (= Q) denkt sich die Parusie nicht am nächsten Tag, so daß Lukas—bei einem übertragenen Verständnis—nicht durch das Iterativum die Zeit hätte dehnen müssen."

Matt = Q: τὸν ἄρτον ἡμῶν τὸν ἐπιούσιον [ ]¹δ(ὸς)¹ ἡμῖν

Pro

B. Weiß 1908, 31: Reconstruction.

von Dobschütz 1914, 314: "The difference between Matthew's 'give us today,' with its aorist tense (δός), and Luke's 'give us day by day,' with its present (δίδου)—it is remarkable how accurately the tenses are used in this popular Greek—may be explained by the purpose of the prayer for use in the evening, just as the translation 'tomorrow' seems to be governed by liturgical motives. Matthew's version is here supported by symmetry as well as by internal evidence."

Lagrange 1921, 323: "L'aor. δός, 'donne une fois', et σήμερον 'aujourd'hui' de Mt. conviennent mieux pour une prière liturgique à dire chaque jour."

Klostermann 1927, 56: "Das momentane δός ... σήμερον ist die Form des Gebets 'wie es täglich gebraucht werden soll', das durative δίδου ... καθ' ἡμέραν wohl Korrektur des Lc, der mehr erbittet als Mt."

Creed 1930, 157: "Mt ... is likely to be more primitive. δός harmonises with the other aorists."

Schmid 1930, 233: "In V11f hat Mt in allem den primären Text."

Schwarz 1968-69, 246: Reconstruction.

Polag 1979, 48: Reconstruction.

Vogler 1982, 58-59: "Wir fragen zunächst nach der älteren der beiden uns überlieferten Textformen der Brot-Bitte. Von der Bezeugung des gesamten Vaterunsertextes her legt sich die Vermutung nahe, daß die Matthäusfassung die jüngere ist. Denn es ist eher anzunehmen, daß diejenige Überlieferung, die in allen Bitten dasselbe Tempus (Aorist) aufweist, auf eine spätere Angleichung zurückgeht, als daß diese Übereinstimmung im Tempus später beeinträchtigt wurde. Tatsächlich wird jedoch—vom Inhalt der Brot-Bitte her (Lukas gegenüber Matthäus: schwebende bzw. verallgemeinernde Aussage, darum sekundär)—weithin das Gegenteil angenommen. Da dieser Anhaltspunkt jedoch kein sicheres Kriterium darstellt, müssen wir, um die hier anstehende Frage entscheiden zu können, nach zuverlässigeren Anhaltspunkten fragen. Dafür bieten sich noch einmal die von uns in Abschnitt II angewandten Kriterien an.

"Hat, wie wir sahen, der Kontext des Vaterunsers stets den jeweiligen ('heutigen') Tag—mit der Zuspitzung des Verbots der Vorsorge für den 'morgigen' Tag—im Blick, so entspricht dem, daß die in der Verkündigung Jesu auf den Hörer bzw. Leser zukommende Gottesherrschaft diesen 'heute' zur Umkehr ruft. Und war, wie wir weiter feststellten, im Frühjudentum die

Vorstellung verbreitet, daß dessen Glaube fragwürdig ist, der sich den Kopf darüber zerbricht, was er 'morgen' essen wird, so ordnet sich dem die Gottes-verkündigung Jesu zu, nach der der Vater denen, die—wie die Jünger—von der Nachfolge Jesu in Anspruch genommen, keine Vorsorge für ihren Lebens-unterhalt treffen können, gibt, was diese 'heute' brauchen. [59]

"Legt sich angesichts dessen der Schluß nahe, daß die matthäische Über-lieferung der 1. Wir-Bitte mit der Herausstellung des 'heute' (in der Tat) älter ist als die des Lukas, die dieses Wort nicht führt, so wird diese Annahme nun noch durch das Vaterunser selbst erhärtet.

"In den drei ersten Bitten dieses Gebets geben die Beter auf ein grund-legendes Anliegen der Verkündigung Jesu Antwort: Durch sie erflehen sie die endzeitliche Offenbarung von Gottes heilschaffendem Tun. Da die Beter (=die Gemeinde) aber bereits ein Stück Verwirklichung dieser endzeitlichen Offenbarung von Gottes heilschaffendem Tun darstellen, haben diese drei Bit-ten eine doppelte Zielrichtung. Durch sie bitten die Beter darum, daß dieses eschatologische Handeln mehr und mehr zur Entfaltung kommt: 'heute' bei ihnen selbst und in baldmöglichster Zukunft bei allen anderen Menschen. Diesem 'heute' der drei Du-Bitten entsprechen die Wir-Bitten des Vater-unsers, die—im Gegensatz zu jenen—die Beter im Blick haben. Durch sie bitten diese darum, daß ihnen das bereits zuteil gewordene göttliche Heil 'heute' nicht verlustig geht; daß dieses ihnen—allem, was sie 'heute' davon abzubringen droht, zum Trotz—erhalten bleibt, ja daß dieses—wie das in den Du-Bitten zum Ausdruck kommt—'heute' in ihrem Leben mehr und mehr Raum gewinnt. Ist damit (auch) das Vaterunser ganz von dem 'heute' bestimmt, das in der matthäischen Fassung der Brot-Bitte expressis verbis genannt wird, so läßt das mit ziemlicher Sicherheit darauf schließen, daß diese Fassung der 1. Wir-Bitte die ältere der beiden griechischen Bezeugungen dieser Bitte ist."

LaVerdière 1983, 113: "In this case Matthew is very likely the one who preserved the oldest form. When the prayer proved inadequate for a new situation, the Matthean community simply added further elements at the end of the section. ... It did not alter wording that was already in place."

Davies and Allison 1988, 591: Reconstruction.

Taussig 1988, 25: Reconstruction.

International Q Project 1990, 500: τὸν ἄρτον ἡμῶν τὸν ἐπιούσιον δὸς ἡμῖν σήμερον.

O'Neill 1993, 13: "I am conjecturing that the original Greek of the prayer was τὸν ἄρτον ἡμῶν τῇ ἐπιούσῃ δὸς ἡμῖν."

Schürmann 1994, 193: "Entsprechend [to σήμερον being original as opposed to τὸ καθ' ἡμέραν] muß der komplexive Aorist δός des Matthäus als ursprünglicher gelten als der iterative Imperativ δίδου."

Con

Gundry 1982, 107: "Luke puts the verb of giving into the iterative present (δίδου) and has τὸ καθ' ἡμέραν. This phraseology indicates a succession of daily provisions. It is often thought that the delay of Jesus' parousia caused Luke (or his source) to substitute an extension of history for waning eschatological hope. But we might expect that in speaking to 'the poor,' Jesus would tell them to pray for daily provisions (see E.M. Yamauchi in *WTJ* 28 [1966] 145-56). Probably Matthew has assimilated the wording to the context into which he has imported the Lord's Prayer. The shifts from the present tense of giving to the aorist (δός), and from 'each day' to 'today' take away emphasis on the repetition of giving. In Matthew's form the petition now agrees with the passage coming in vv 25-34, especially with v 34: 'therefore do not worry about tomorrow, for tomorrow will worry about itself. ...' σήμερον is a Mattheanism (4,3). Just as Matthew has shifted emphasis from the future coming of God's rule to its present coming in the obedience of disciples, so also he shifts emphasis from the future succession of daily provisions to the provisions for this day alone. No room remains for anxiety over tomorrow."

Evaluations

Carruth 1995: Matt = Q {A}, τὸν ἄρτον ἡμῶν τὸν ἐπιούσιον [ ]¹δ(ός)¹.

The scholarly opinion reviewed for this study is virtually unanimous in its preference for the Matthean aorist here as reproducing Q. A decision is frequently based on the assumption of Lukan redaction for τὸ καθ' ἡμέραν which goes together with the present tense of the verb. It is also frequently noted that all the other imperatives of the prayer are aorist and that the aorist imperative is "regularly used in prayers" (BDF 337,4). This is convincing evidence in favor of the aorist imperative here.

The immediacy of the prayer for bread coheres with such a tone elsewhere in Q when basic human needs are in view, such as in Q 6:20b-21 and Q 12: 22-31. Luke may have changed Q in this instance according to his tendency to generalize and in accord with his view of the delay of the parousia.

Robinson 1995: Matt = Q {A}, τὸν ἄρτον ἡμῶν τὸν ἐπιούσιον [ ]¹δ(ός)¹.

The same shift in Q from δός (Matt 5:42) to δίδου (Luke 6:30, underlined by πάντι), with a quite similar meaning, as well as comparable shifts within the Prayer itself at Q 11:3² and Q 11:4⁴, present a consistent picture. In the case of Q 11:3² Lucan parallels indicate that it is Luke who makes the change. The consistent use of the aorist rather than the present in the other petitions also suggests that it is Luke who makes the change here.

Explanations of these Lucan shifts are not made explicit in the texts themselves. Hence interpretations should be cautious about ascribing more meaning than seems inherent in the texts. Originally the petition seems addressed to a specific instance of need at the moment, but then became generalized into a constant repetitive need inherent in a lifestyle. This may reflect a secondary stage in which concrete experiences merge into a pattern for a community.

Kloppenborg 1995: Matt = Q {A}, τὸν ἄρτον ἡμῶν τὸν ἐπιούσιον [ ]¹δ(ός)¹.
The analogy of Q 6:30 (above, Robinson 1995), the consistency of Matthew's aorist with the other aorist imperatives of the prayer, and the fact that the Lukan version is closely related to another likely redactional change (11:3²) combine to support the Matthaean against the Lukan version. The literature is virtually unanimous in support: there is no support for Luke=Q at all. Gundry's argument against Matt=Q also entails regarding σήμερον as Matthaean (see below), and depends on the supposition that Matthew converted the present to the aorist in order to achieve consonance with Matt 6:34 (one could add 6:26, 31). However, Matthew has the present imperative at 6:25 and second plural present verbs at 6:28. In other words, there is no clear pattern visible in Matthew's use of aorist vs. present imperatives to sustain Gundry's objection, whereas there is a consistent usage of aorist imperatives in the prayer itself.

Q 11:3²: Luke's τὸ καθ' ἡμέραν or Matthew's σήμερον.

Luke = Q: [δί]δ[ου]¹ ἡμῖν [τὸ καθ']² ἡμέρ[α]²ν·

Pro

Mack 1993, 89: Reconstruction.

Con

B. Weiß 1876, 185: "Dagegen ist das ohnehin dem Luc. eigenthümliche τὸ καθ' ἡμέραν (19:47. Act 17:11, vgl. noch 8 mal καθ' ἡμέραν) offenbar sekundäre Änderung, obwohl Camp. das σήμερον durch Reflexion auf 6:34 entstanden sein läßt und doch selbst zugeben muß, daß Luc. bereits denselben Sinn ausdrückt, nur ohne die angebliche 'polemische Nebenbeziehung' (S.85)."

B. Weiß 1878, 422: See Q 11:3¹ Luke = Q, Con.

J. Weiß 1892, 466: See Q 11:3¹ Luke = Q, Con.

Plummer 1896, 296: "In N.T. τὸ καθ' ἡμέραν is peculiar to Lk. (xix. 47; Acts xvii. 11). This fact and the insertion of his favourite παντί with ὀφείλοντι, and the substitution of his favourite καὶ αὐτοί for καὶ ἡμεῖς with ἀφίομεν, incline us to believe that some of the differences between this form of the Prayer and that in Mt. are due to Lk. himself."

Hawkins 1899, 19: On a chart Hawkins shows that καθ' ἡμέραν is used by Luke 5x in the gospel: 9:23, 11:3, 16:19, 19:47, 22:53. Matthew and Mark each use the expression once. In addition the expression occurs 6x in Acts.

Holtzmann 1901, 364: "die Reflexion auf etwas Zukünftiges wird ausgeschlossen durch das an Stelle von σήμερον tretende, durchaus lucanische τὸ καθ' ἡμέραν (vgl. 16,19; Act 17,11), welchem übrigens auch die präsentische Imperativform statt δός entspricht."

von Harnack 1907, 48: "Matthäus bietet das Gebet, wie es täglich gebetet wird; Luk. giebt die Gebetsanweisung; daher das Präsens. Ebendasselbe gilt von der Korrektur τὸ καθ' ἡμέραν für σήμερον, wobei noch zu bemerken ist, daß τὸ καθ' ἡμέραν nur bei Luk. im N.T. vorkommt (s. c. 19,47; Act. 17,11)."

von Harnack 1907, ET 1908, 65: "Matthew gives the prayer as it was meant to be, and as indeed it was, used daily; St. Luke gives [the prayer] as an instruction in prayer, therefore the present tense. This also explains the substitution of τὸ καθ' ἡμέραν for σήμερον, as to which it is to be noted that τὸ καθ' ἡμέραν occurs elsewhere in the New Testament only in St. Luke (xix.47; Acts xvii.11)."

B. Weiß 1907, 72¹: "Daß Lk. 11,3 absichtlich der Imperativ des Aor. in den des Präs. verwandelt ist, zeigt, ganz ähnlich wie 9,23, das τὸ καθ' ἡμέρα (statt σήμερον), das darauf reflektiert, daß das Geben des ἄρτος ἐπιούσ. uns täglich gleich notwendig ist."

Castor 1912, 54-55: "On the other hand, the Lukan form of this prayer also shows indications of editorial change. τὸ καθ᾽ ἡμέραν is found only in Luke 19:47; Acts 17:[11] [55] and may be an interpretation of that evangelist."

McNeile 1915, 79: "Lk. has a generalized request, δίδου ἡμῖν καθ᾽ ἡμέραν, which may have been an early variation due to the account of the manna (τὸ καθ᾽ ἡμέραν εἰς ἡμέραν, Ex. xvi. 5); but the expression, which is class., is confined to Lk. in the N.T. (xix. 47, Ac. xvii. 11), and see his καθ᾽ ἡμέραν which he adds in ix. 23)."

Cadbury 1920, 115-118: Cadbury discusses as one of Luke's "changes attributable to literary predilections," his inclination to generalizations. Under this topic he says on p. 117, "The distributive use of κατά c. acc. is a grammatical peculiarity of Luke in temporal phrases; καθ᾽ ἡμέραν occurs in Matt. 26,55 = Mark 14,49 = Luke 22,53, but elsewhere only in Luke 9,23; 11,3; 16,19; 19,47; Acts 2,46.47; 3,2; 16,5; 17,11; 19,9."

Lagrange 1921, 321: "D'autant que dans son texte [Luke's text] on reconnaît sa main: τὸ καθ᾽ ἡμέραν, αὐτοί, παντί. Son texte paraît moins primitif."

323: "καθ᾽ ἡμέραν (propre à Lc., xix, 47 et Act. xvii,11) convient mieux pour une prière à dire une fois."

Easton 1926, 176: "τὸ καθ᾽ ἡμέραν is 'Lukan'."

Klostermann 1927, 56: "das durative δίδου ... καθ᾽ ἡμέραν [ist] wohl Korrektur des Lc, der mehr erbittet als Mt."

Klostermann 1929, 124: "die Verallgemeinerung des σήμερον in das lukanische τὸ καθ᾽ ἡμέραν (19:47, Act 17:11) brachte auch die Umformung des Tempus des Imperativs mit sich, s. Blaß 337,4."

Schmid 1930, 233²: "Τὸ καθ᾽ ἡμέραν ist lukanisch (vgl. 9,23 + 16,19; 19,47; Apg 17,11)."

Manson 1937, 266: See Q 11:3¹ Luke = Q, Con.

Hirsch 1941, 101: "Bei der Bitte ums Brot ist 'heute' durch 'täglich' ersetzt."

Soiron 1941, 328: "bewußt setzte er τὸ καθ᾽ ἡμέραν statt σήμερον in dem Gedanken, daß das Brot uns an jedem Tage gleich notwendig ist, daß wir seiner fortwährend bedürfen."

Schmid 1951, 197: "Daß Lukas den Text so [not as a 'Gebetsformular,' but as a 'Muster eines inhaltsreichen und echt christlichen Gebetes'] verstanden hat und daß zu seiner Zeit das Vaterunser noch nicht zu einem festen Formular geworden war, beweist die nicht unerhebliche Verschiedenheit der Lukas-Fassung von der des Matthäus und beweisen ein paar sprachliche Korrekturen, die er am Text vorgenommen hat. In V. 3 schreibt Lukas 'täglich' (statt 'heute'), und in V. 4 'denn auch wir vergeben jedem' (statt 'wie wir erlassen haben'). Beides beruht auf späterer Reflexion: jeden Tag brauchen wir die lebensnotwendige Nahrung, und die Pflicht der Vergebung gilt immerfort."

Bonnard 1963, 85: "Luc a rendu cet *aujourd'hui* en *jour après jour* ce qui introduit une idée de durée et de répétition probablement étrangère au texte de Mat."

Brown 1965, 239: "Lk's 'daily' (*to kath' hēmeran*) is distributive and non-eschatological.⁸⁵ The best interpretation of the Lucan rendering is that, with the passing of the tension about the Second Coming (or in communities where such tension was not overly prominent), the eschatological interpretation of the PN yielded to the more pressing daily outlook. The Lucan emphasis on the poor of this world as the recipients of the Gospel message is well known ...; and among such, the eschatological aspect of the prayer for bread could soon lose its primacy."

239⁸⁵: "It is a Lucan expression found in Lk 19:47 and Acts 17:11, but not in Mt, Mk, or Jn. A good example of Lk's preference for 'daily' is found in the logion on taking up the cross (Mt 16:24; Mk 8:34; Lk 9:23); only Lk has the expression 'to take up the cross daily (*kath' hēmeran*).'"

Jeremias 1967, 13-14 [ET 1964, 13]: See Q 11:3¹ Luke = Q, Con.

Grundmann 1968, 201-202: "In der vierten Bitte hat Matthäus im Unterschied zu Lukas den Imperativ im Aorist und nicht im Präsens, und er liest σήμερον statt des lukanischen [202] τὸ καθ᾿ ἡμέραν. Unverkennbar gibt Lukas damit der Bitte einen allgemeinen Sinn, der sie für einen längeren Gebrauch zurichtet, während Matthäus den Vorzug der Ursprünglichkeit verdient."

Wrege 1968, 104: "In der Brotbitte stimmt Lk mit Mt überein, fügt aber ein τὸ καθ᾿ ἡμέραν zu³, um auf diese Weise σήμερον zu ersetzen."

104³: "S. auch Lk 9,23/Mk 8,34; Lk 19,47/Mk 11,17f (vgl. Mk 14,49; Mt 26,55; Lk 22,53) AG 2,46f; 3,2; 16,5; 17,11.(17); 19,9. — Lk 16,19."

Berger 1969, 1151: "Die Brotbitte verändert Lk durch den Zusatz τὸ καθ᾿ ἡμέραν."

Jeremias 1971, 190 [ET 1971, 195-196]: See Q 11:3¹ Luke = Q, Con.

Schulz 1972, 85: "Das lk καθ᾿ ἡμέραν mag auch die Umformung des Tempus des Imperativs (δίδου anstelle von δός) mit sich gebracht haben."

Schweizer 1973, 93: "Im einzelnen ersetzt die lukanische Version bei der Bitte um Brot das 'heute' durch 'täglich' und ändert auch die Form des Verbums so, daß an die immer wiederholte Gabe gedacht ist."

Schweizer 1973, ET 1975, 148-149: "Luke's version ... replaces the 'today' of the [149] petition for bread with 'daily,' and also changes the form of the verb so as to suggest repeated giving."

Schneider 1977, 257-258: "Indirekt zeigt die lukanische Retusche 'das Brot für morgen gib uns *täglich*' (diese Formulierung in V 3 ist lukanisch, vgl. 19,47, Apg 17,11), daß nun an [258] Gottes *Vorsehung* gedacht ist."

Marshall 1978, 459: "Since τὸ καθ' ἡμέραν is a Lucan phrase (19:47; Acts 17:11; cf. Ex. 16:4 cf. Lk. 9:23 diff. Mk.), the generalised form may be due to Luke himself."

Schürmann 1981, 175[138]: "Der griechische Wortlaut verrät, daß Lukas selbst das 'Tag für Tag' eingefügt hat; vgl. die Wendung mit Artikel auch 19,47 (gegen Mk); Apg 17,11."

Guelich 1982, 291: "Whereas Matthew has give us today (σήμερον), a completed action, Luke has 'give us continually day after day' (τὸ καθ' ἡμέραν). This change most likely stems from Luke's redaction, since he has introduced the same use of 'day after day' in Mark 8:34, cf. Luke 9:23, and Mark 11:18, cf. Luke 19:47."

Fitzmyer 1985, 897: "[Luke] has altered the adv. *sēmeron*, 'today,' to the distributive phrase *to kath' hēmeran*, 'each day.'"

Lambrecht 1985, 132: "One may assume that Luke had to choose this tense when he replaced the 'today' by 'each day.' ... Luke sees further than one single day; he de-eschatologizes the text."

Luz 1985, 335 [ET 1989, 371]: See Q 11:3¹ Luke = Q, Con.

Schneider 1985, 66-67: "Während bei Mt dieses Brot für 'heute' erbeten wird (wahrscheinlich im Morgengebet), bittet die [67] Lk-Fassung um die (wiederholte[31]) Gewährung des Brotes 'Tag für Tag'. Da *to kath' hēmeran* lukanische Redaktion verrät[32] und die Präsensform *didou* sachlich mit dieser Änderung zusammenhängt, wird man die Mt-Fassung in diesem Punkt für ursprünglich halten dürfen."

67[31]: "*Didou* (Lk) ist als iteratives Präsens zu verstehen, im Unterschied zu dem Aorist *dos* (Mt), der das einmalige Geben (für 'heute') erbittet."

67[32]: "*To kath' hēmeran* steht im NT nur im lukanischen Werk: Lk 11,3 diff Mt; 19,47 diff Mk; Apg 17,11 v.l.—Einfaches *kath' hēmeran* findet sich häufiger, jedoch überwiegend im lukanischen Werk: Mt 26,55 par Mk 14,49 par Lk 22,53; Lk 9,23 diff Mk; Lk 16,19 Sg.; Apg 2,46.47; 3,2; 16,5; 17,11; 19,9; 1 Kor 15,31; 2 Kor 11,28; Hebr 7,27; 10,11."

Gnilka 1986, 215[13]: "Die Wendung καθ' ἡμέραν in der lk Brotbitte ist typisch lk."

Sand 1986, 126: "Bei der Brotbitte spricht Mt vom Brot für 'heute', Lk dagegen vom Brot für 'jeden Tag'; aufgrund des Gebrauchs in Lk 9,23; 11,3 (Text); 16,9; 19,47; 22,53 ist 'jeder Tag' als lk. Änderung anzusehen."

Davies and Allison 1988, 607: "Luke has ... instead of σήμερον (Mt: 8; Mk: 1; Lk: 11), τὸ καθ' ἡμέραν (cf. Exod 16.5). This last is surely Lukan (κατά + ἡμέρα: Mt: 1; Mk: 1; Lk: 5)."

Taussig 1988, 35: See Q 11:3¹ Luke = Q, Con.

Wiefel 1988, 215-216: See Q 11:3¹ Luke = Q, Con.

Evans 1990, 482: "in view of the aorist tenses throughout, and the aorist imperative *dos* in this petition in Matthew, Luke's present imperative *didou* looks secondary, as is *to kath' hēmeran* = 'daily' in comparison with Matthew's *sēmeron* = 'today'."

Catchpole 1993, 29: See Q 11:3¹ Luke = Q, Con.

Ernst 1993, 269: "Lk hat den ursprünglichen Text der Logienquelle im Vergleich mit Mt 6,9-13 besser erhalten, aber kaum in der Originalfassung, wie an einigen red Überarbeitungen und Zusätzen (V. 3: täglich; …) zu erkennen ist."

Nolland 1993, 615: "the verb is a present imperative in Luke and an aorist imperative in Matthew. This is compatible with a second difference, which is that Matthew has 'today,' where Luke has 'day by day,' τὸ καθ' ἡμέραν. Since this last phrase is Lukan, the alterations may be Luke's own (see 19:47 and cf. 9:23; 16:19; 22:53; Acts 2:46,47; 3:2; 17:11)."

Cullmann 1994, 71: "Das Wort 'heute' ist hier ganz angebracht. Es ist, weil konkret, dem 'für jeden Tag', das wir statt dessen bei Lukas (11,3) lesen, vorzuziehen. Die Lukasversion hat abstrakter das *immer* nötige Brot im Auge."

Cullmann 1994, ET 1995, 54: "The word 'today' is quite appropriate here. It is to be preferred to 'for every day', which we read instead in Luke (11.3). The Lukan version is more abstract, and envisages the bread that we always need."

Schürmann 1994, 193: "Der hier die Vorlage der Redenquelle geändert hat, war Lukas selbst; dabei ist es weniger wahrscheinlich, daß eine vorlukanische Gebetspraxis Lukas dazu veranlaßt haben soll, weil seine eigene Sprache hier zu deutlich erkennbar wird: Lukas hätte σήμερον hier nicht stehen lassen müssen, weil das für ihn charakteristische akzentuierte 'Heute' hier nicht vorliegt[135]. Dagegen ist τὸ καθ' ἡμέραν wahrscheinlich lukanisch[136] (ebenso wie καθ' ἡμέραν[137])."

193[135]: "Freilich kann Lukas σήμερον auch theologisch unbefrachtet verwenden: so Lk 12,28 par Mt; 22,34.61 par Mk und 9mal in Apg."

193[136]: "Die Wendung begegnet mit Art. im NT nur hier und Lk 19,47 (diff Mk). Apg 17,11 v.l., auch Lk 22,53 v.l. kann, muß sie aber nicht von der luk Vaterunserfassung her eingedrungen sein."

193[137]: "Wie Mk 14,49 par und Lk 16,19 S; 22,53 par Mk; Apg 2,46.47; 3,2; 16,5; 17,11; 19,9."

Matt = Q: [ ]¹δ(ὸς)¹ ἡμῖν (σ)²ἡμερ(ο)²ν·

Pro

Klein 1906, 36-38: "In dem Berichte vom Manna heißt es Ex 16,4: 'Und Jahve sprach zu Mose: Siehe, ich werde euch regnen lassen Brot vom Himmel, und [37] das Volk soll hinausgehen und sammeln den täglichen Bedarf an seinem Tage, damit ich es prüfe, ob es wandeln wird nach meiner Unterweisung, oder nicht.'

"In der Mechilta z. St. finden sich zwei Deutungen dieses Verses. R. Eleasar aus Modiim findet hier das Verbot, von einem Tag auf den andern Manna zu lesen. Die Worte: דבר יום ביומו deutet er: den Bedarf des Tages *für diesen Tag; denn wer den Tag schuf, der schuf auch seine Nahrung.* Aus dieser Stelle folgert R. Eleasar: wer für heute zu essen hat und fragt: was werde ich morgen essen? der gehört zu den Kleingläubigen, denn es heißt: damit ich es prüfe. (Nur der bewährt sich in der Prüfung, ob er Gottesvertrauen hat, der für den andern Tag nicht sorgt.)…

"Wie aber hat Jesus gebetet? Darauf antwortet das Evangelium mit klaren Worten. Nach Mt 6,34 lehrte Jesus: 'Sorget nicht für den morgenden Tag, der morgende wird für sich selbst sorgen.' Das entspricht ganz der angeführten Lehre R. Eleasars. Jesus fährt fort: 'Jeder Tag hat genug an seiner Plage'. … [38]

"Jesus wird demnach gebetet haben: unser nötiges Brot gib uns *heute.*

"Lehrreich ist, daß Lukas in der Parallelstelle 12,29 Jesu Spruch Mt 6,34 gar nicht hat. Nach unserer Darstellung des Sachverhalts ist das kein Zufall, sondern der Spruch wurde mit Absicht fortgelassen."

B. Weiß 1908, 31: Reconstruction.

Castor 1912, 230: Reconstruction.

Lagrange 1921, 323: "L'aor. δός, 'donne une fois', et σήμερον 'aujourd'hui' de Mt. conviennent mieux pour une prière liturgique à dire chaque jour."

Easton 1926, 176: "τὸ καθ' ἡμέραν is 'Lukan'. … Mt is consequently original (J. Weiß)."

Klostermann 1927, 58: "das durative δίδου … καθ' ἡμέραν [ist] wohl Korrektur des Lc, der mehr erbittet als Mt."

Schneider 1977, 257: "Die Brotbitte richtet sich in der ursprünglichen Fassung des Gebets auf das Brot, das Gott 'heute' geben möge (Mt)."

Polag 1979, 48: Reconstruction.

Schenk 1981, 61: Reconstruction.

Zeller 1984, 56: Reconstruction.

Davies and Allison 1988, 591: Reconstruction.

Taussig 1988, 25: Reconstruction.

International Q Project 1990, 500: τὸν ἄρτον ἡμῶν τὸν ἐπιούσιον δὸς ἡμῖν σήμερον.

Kloppenborg 1990, 49: Reconstruction.

Hagner 1993, 145: "Matthew's language at a number of points is the more original (e.g., … σήμερον, 'today,' for Luke's τὸ καθ' ἡμέραν, 'the daily')."

Mell 1994, 158: Reconstruction.

Con

Bussmann 1929, 67: "So wird Mt auch das τὸ καθ' ἡμέραν in σήμερον vereinfacht … haben."

Gundry 1982, 107: "Probably Matthew has assimilated the wording to the context into which he has imported the Lord's Prayer. The shifts from the present tense of giving to the aorist (δός), and from 'each day' to 'today' take away emphasis on the repetition of giving. In Matthew's form the petition now agrees with the passage coming in vv 25-34, especially with v 34: 'therefore do not worry about tomorrow, for tomorrow will worry about itself. …' σήμερον is a Mattheanism (4,3)." See Q 11:3¹ Matt = Q, Con.

Meier 1994, 355: See Q 11:3¹ Matt = Q, Con.

Undecided

Schnackenburg 1984, 98: "Schwierig ist die Frage zu beantworten, wie die Brot-Bitte ursprünglich gelautet hat. Weder das matthäische '… gib uns heute' noch das lukanische 'täglich' kann eindeutig einen Vorrang beanspruchen. Das hängt mit dem schwierigen Beiwort bei 'Brot' zusammen. … Der Sinn wird durch diese Unsicherheit schwerlich verändert; auf die Absicht Jesu können wir durchblicken."

Schnackenburg 1984, ET 1995, 64-65: "It is difficult to answer the question how the bread petition originally read. Neither the Matthean 'give us this day' nor the Lukan 'daily' can unequivocally claim precedence. That is because of the difficult adjective accompanying 'bread.' … [65] The meaning is hardly altered by this uncertainty; we are still able to see Jesus' intent."

Evaluations

Carruth 1995: Matt = Q {A}, [ ]¹δ(ὸς)¹ ἡμῖν (σ)²ἡμερ(ο)²ν·

With the exception of Mack, Bussmann and Gundry, scholarly opinion is on the side of Matthew as representing the Q reading in this case. It is surely correct to see the verb tense and the temporal expression as forming a pair, as was noted in the scholarly opinion for this as well as for the preceding variation unit. In addition there appears to be sufficient evidence that the expression τὸ καθ' ἡμέραν is typical of Luke. It may be another aspect of his generalizing tendency which Cadbury notes. The expression can be attributed to Luke here, and one can with reasonable certainty accept σήμερον as the reading of Q.

Robinson 1995: Matt = Q {A}, [ ]¹δ(ὸς)¹ ἡμῖν (σ)²ἡμερ(ο)²ν·

The idiom τὸ καθ' ἡμέραν occurs in the NT only at Luke 19:47 (not at Acts 17:11, according to the current critical edition, in distinction from older editions presupposed in much of the earlier scholarly literature). This is too meagre evidence to provide a statistical basis for an inference of a Lukan preference of this idiom. But καθ' ἡμέραν (without τό) is rather frequent in Luke-Acts but only once in Mark // Matthew. Even without τό the idiom performs for Luke much the same function when added to the saying on taking up one's cross (not in the Q position, Q 14:27, but at the Markan position, Luke 9:23). The changes at Q 11:3¹ and Q 11:4⁴ are consistent with this Lucan change at Q 11:3².

Kloppenborg 1995: Matt = Q {A}, [ ]¹δ(ὸς)¹ ἡμῖν (σ)²ἡμερ(ο)²ν·

In addition to the evidence against the Lukan formulation, it should be observed that σήμερον is attested once in minimal Q (12:28), whereas the parallel Lukan expression (τὸ καθ' ἡμέραν, καθ' ἡμέραν) is not.

Q 11:4

Matt 6:12-13		Luke 11:4
καὶ ἄφες ἡμῖν	καὶ ἄφες ἡμῖν	καὶ ἄφες ἡμῖν
τὰ (ὀφειλήματα)[1] ἡμῶν,	τὰ (ὀφειλήματα)[1] ἡμῶν,	τὰ[ς ἁμαρτίας][1] ἡμῶν,
(ὡς)[2] καὶ	(ὡς)[2] καὶ	καὶ [γὰρ][2]
(ἡμεῖς)[3]	(ἡμεῖς)[3]	[αὐτοὶ][3]
ἀφ(ήκα)[4]μεν	ἀφ(ήκα)[4]μεν	ἀφ[ίο][4]μεν
(τοῖς)[5]	(τοῖς)[5]	[παντὶ][5]
ὀφειλ(έταις)[5.6] ἡμ(ῶ)[6]ν·	ὀφειλ(έταις)[5.6] ἡμ(ῶ)[6]ν·	ὀφείλ[οντι][5.6] ἡμ[ῖ][6]ν·
6:13 καὶ μὴ εἰσενέγκῃς	καὶ μὴ εἰσενέγκῃς	καὶ μὴ εἰσενέγκῃς
ἡμᾶς εἰς πειρασμόν,	ἡμᾶς εἰς πειρασμόν	ἡμᾶς εἰς πειρασμόν
(ἀλλὰ ῥῦσαι ἡμᾶς ἀπὸ	()[7].	( )[7].
τοῦ πονηροῦ)[7].		
˪Matt 6:9[1]	˪Q 11:1[1]	˪Luke 11:1[1]
\Matt 6:9[0]	\Q 11:1[0]	\Luke 11:1[0]

[1] Luke's τὰς ἁμαρτίας or Matthew's τὰ ὀφειλήματα.
[2] Luke's conjunction γάρ or Matthew's ὡς
[3] Luke's pronoun αὐτοί or Matthew's ἡμεῖς.
[4] Luke's ἀφίομεν or Matthew's ἀφήκαμεν.
[5] Luke's παντί or Matthew's τοῖς.
[6] Luke's ὀφείλοντι ἡμῖν or Matthew's ὀφειλέταις ἡμῶν.
[7] Matthew's phrase ἀλλὰ ῥῦσαι ἡμᾶς ἀπὸ τοῦ πονηροῦ.

Q 11:4[1]: Luke's τὰς ἁμαρτίας or Matthew's τὰ ὀφειλήματα.

Luke = Q: τὰ[ς ἁμαρτίας][1] ἡμῶν

Pro

Bussmann 1929, 67:"Ob ὀφειλήματα oder ἁμαρτίας ursprünglich, wird schwer auszumachen sein; man weist darauf hin, daß das ὀφείλοντι noch für ὀφειλήματα zeuge, aber kann nicht grade Mt dadurch veranlaßt es anstatt ἁμαρτίας gesetzt haben?"

Wrege 1968, 104: "Bei der Vergebungsbitte zeigt das lk παντὶ ὀφείλοντι, daß der Stamm ὀφειλ- auch im Vorsatz (11:4a) ursprünglich war. Aber Lk repräsentiert auch so geprägten Sprachgebrauch[7], so daß sein jetziger Bestand nicht notwendig erst auf ihn selbst zurückgehen muß."

104[7]: "Alle 11 Belege für ἁμαρτία im Lk-Ev sind mit ἀφιέναι verbunden, von den 8 AG-Belegen nur 3,19; 7,60; 22,16 nicht. Vgl. auch Mk 1,4; 2,5.7.9.10; Kol 1,14; Mt 26,28."

Ernst 1977, 363 (= 1993, 270-271): "Während Mt von den Schulden spricht (ὀφειλήματα) und ein mehr geschäftlich-juridisches Verständnis nahelegt, verwendet Lk den im Zusammenhang von Vergebungsaussagen (Mk 1,4 = Lk 3,3; Mk 2,10 = Mt 9,6 = Lk 5,24; Mk 2,5 = Mt 9,2 = Lk 5,20; ferner Lk 7,47; 24,47; Apg 2,38; 5,31; 10,43; 13,38; 26,18) geläufigen Ausdruck 'Sünden'. Wegen des formelhaften Sprachgebrauchs darf man annehmen, daß die Fassung des Lk ursprünglicher ist (... Die Tatsache, daß der Gebrauch [of the verbal connection ὀφειλήματα ἀφιέναι] für die ntl. Zeit unsicher ist und erst in der rabbinischen Literatur 'wächst und blüht', spricht nicht gerade für die Mt-Priorität). Vielleicht ist hier das in dem Begriff 'Nachlassen' (ἀφιέναι) noch erkennbare profane Bild (Nachlassen einer materiellen Schuld Mt 18,27.32) mit der Sachaussage (Gott verzeiht die Sünden) ineinander geflossen. Das Wort 'Schuldner' kann kaum als Argument für die Ursprünglichkeit der Mt-Fassung in Anspruch genommen werden."

Con

B. Weiß 1876, 188: "Dagegen ist in der 5. [petition] das τὰς ἁμαρτίας offenbar Erklärung des bildlichen τὰ ὀφειλήματα; denn daß nicht Mtth. in beiden Sätzen den gleichförmigen Ausdruck hergestellt ..., sondern Luc. in dem bildlichen Ausdruck des zweiten Gliedes ein Zeugniss für das Ursprüngliche erhalten, zeigt das steigernde παντὶ ὀφείλοντι ἡμῖν."

Plummer 1896, 297: "Anyone accustomed to LXX would be likely to prefer the familiar ἄφες τὰς ἁμαρτίας (Ps. xxiv. 18; comp. Num. xiv. 19; Ex. xxxii. 32; Gen. l. 17), even if less literal. Moreover, ὀφειλήματα would be more likely to be misunderstood by Gentile readers."

Wernle 1899, 68: "Für ὀφειλήματα hat Lc ἁμαρτίαι eingesetzt trotz der Fortsetzung, die er wieder individualisiert hat (παντί)."

B. Weiß 1901, 460: "τ. ἁμαρτ.) ersetzt durch den gewöhnlichen Ausdruck ([Luke] 5,20. 7,47) das bildliche ὀφειλ. aus Mt 6,12, dessen Ursprünglichkeit schon daraus erhellt, dass im Begründungssatz das Bild beibehalten und nur durch παντὶ ὀφ. ἡμ. noch gesteigert wird."

von Harnack 1907, 48: "Ὀφείλημα ist dem Luk. wohl als vulgäres Wort anstößig gewesen; daß es das ursprüngliche ist, ist zweifellos."

von Harnack 1907, ET 1908, 65: "Ὀφείλημα was most probably distasteful to St. Luke because it belonged to the vulgar idiom—there is no doubt that it is the original word."

B. Weiß 1907, 72¹: "Daß das bildliche ὀφειλήματα Lk. 11,4 durch ἁμαρτίας erläutert ist, erhellt unwiderleglich daraus, daß das bildliche ὀφείλοντι schließlich doch beibehalten wird."

von Dobschütz 1914, 315: "In this petition, likewise, the wording of Matthew seems to come nearer to the original than that of Luke; 'remit debts' is a familiar figure with Jesus for the forgiveness of sins (compare Matt. 18,23). Luke likes to explain, and therefore says 'sins' instead of 'debts,' keeping, however, 'debtors' in the second part of the petition."

Cadbury 1920, 85: Cadbury gives four examples of places where Luke has changed Mark by substituting a synonym for a repeated word. Mk 10,47f. = Lk 18,38f.; Mk 12,42 = Lk 21,2; Mk 14,37 = Lk 22,45; Mk 15,37.39 = Lk 23,46.

Lagrange 1921, 323: "τὰς ἁμαρτίας est un terme plus précis de l'homme à Dieu (v,20; vii,47) que les dettes ὀφειλήματα de Mt., et Lc. confesse son changement en lisant ὀφείλοντι."

von Harnack 1923, 26¹: "Das Wort, welches sich bei Matthäus hier findet, hat Lukas als vulgär vermieden."

Lagrange 1923, 130: "La formule de Mt. 'nos dettes' garde l'image transcrite par Lc. en 'nos péchés'. De même 'nos débiteurs' est moins élégant que παντὶ ὀφείλοντι ἡμῖν. Si l'on reconnaît ses retouches de Lc., pourquoi ne pas reconnaître aussi ses retranchements?"

Abrahams 1924, 95: "The wording [of Matt 6:12/Luke 11:4], it is true, differs, and that not merely or chiefly in Luke's use of ἁμαρτίας (sins) for Matthew's ὀφειλήματα (debts). This difference is not very significant, and more seems to have been made of it than is justifiable. Matthew no doubt points to a more accurate reproduction of an Aramaic original. But as Luke, in the second clause, actually introduces the verb (παντὶ ὀφείλοντι ἡμῖν), his use of ἁμαρτίας may be no more than an elegance of style."

Loisy 1924, 316: "Les 'péchés' (ἁμαρτίας) sont interprétation des 'dettes' (ὀφειλήματα)."

Klostermann 1927, 58: "[Matt 6,] 12 τὰ ὀφειλήματα: ursprünglich vgl. Did. 8,2 τὴν ὀφειλήν. Lc hat es durch das gewöhnte τὰς ἁμαρτίας ersetzt, obwohl er selbst nachher παντὶ ὀφείλοντι sagt."

Klostermann 1929, 125: "Das geläufigere τὰς ἁμαρτίας ersetzt bei Lc den ursprünglichen Ausdruck τὰ ὀφειλήματα, das doch durch das folgende παντὶ (Luc) ὀφείλοντι bestätigt wird."

Creed 1930, 157: "ἁμαρτίας is a stylistic improvement for ὀφειλήματα, which, however, somewhat obscures the parallelism between the clauses."

Schmid 1930, 233: "In V11f hat Mt in allem den primären Text.²"

233²: "Τὰς ἁμαρτίας ist gewöhnlicher als τὰ ὀφειλήματα."

Hirsch 1941, 101: "Bei der Bitte um Vergebung ist ὀφειλήματα durch ἁμαρτίας ersetzt."

Soiron 1941, 328: "Ἁμαρτίαι ist eine Erläuterung des bei den Juden wirk-sameren bildlichen ὀφειλήματα, aber das Bild wird mit ὀφείλοντι von Lk doch aufgenommen, nachdem es durch ἁμαρτίαι vorbereitet ist."

Grundmann 1961, 233: "Die Bitte um die Vergebung ist ebenfalls gegen-über Matthäus verändert; an Stelle des Ausdruckes ὀφειλήματα im Vordersatz, den Lukas durch seinen Nachsatz auch voraussetzt, ist das allgemeinere ἁμαρτίαι getreten."

Brown 1965, 244: "Lk's 'sins' might be an adaptation to a Gentile audi-ence.¹⁰³"

244¹⁰³: "Yet Lk uses the word 'debtor' in the second clause of the petition (thus favoring the originality of 'debts' in the first clause) and also in 7:41."

Jeremias 1967, 14: "Nun muß man wissen, daß es eine Eigenart der Mut-tersprache Jesu, des Aramäischen, ist, daß man für Sünde das Wort 'ḥoba' gebrauchte, das eigentlich die Geldschuld bezeichnet. Matthäus übersetzt das Wort ganz wörtlich mit 'Schulden' und läßt auf diese Weise erkennen, daß das Vater-Unser auf einen aramäischen Wortlaut zurückgeht."

Jeremias 1967, ET 1964, 13: "It was a peculiarity of Jesus' mother tongue, Aramaic, that the word ḥobha was used for 'sin,' though it probably meant a debt, 'money owed.' Matthew translates the word quite literally with 'debts,' ὀφειλήματα, a word which is not usual in Greek for 'sin.' This enables one to see that the Lord's Prayer goes back to an Aramaic wording."

Jeremias 1971, 190: "In der fünften Bitte hat Matthäus τὰ ὀφειλήματα, Lukas τὰς ἁμαρτίας. Der auffällige Ausdruck des Matthäus ist ein Aramais-mus; denn das aramäische Wort für Sünde, ḥoba, heißt eigentlich '(Geld)-schuld'. Τὰ ὀφειλήματα (Matthäus) ist also wörtliche Übersetzung, τὰς ἁμαρ-τίας (Lukas) Gräzisierung. Daß auch die Lukasfassung auf eine Formulierung mit ὀφειλήματα zurückgeht, zeigt das folgende τῷ ὀφείλοντι."

Jeremias 1971, ET 1971, 196: "In the fifth petition, Matthew has τὰ ὀφειλήματα and Luke τὰς ἁμαρτίας. Matthew's striking expression is an Ara-maism. As the Aramaic word for sin ḥoba, really means 'debt (of money)', τὰ ὀφειλήματα (Matthew) is a literal translation and τάς ἁμαρτίας (Luke) its replacement by colloquial Greek. The τῷ ὀφειλοντι that follows in Luke shows that the Lucan version, too, goes back to a formulation with ὀφειλήματα."

Schulz 1972, 85: "Lk hat das im NT seltene ὀφείλημα durch das ihm geläu-figere ἁμαρτία ersetzt."

Dupont 1973, 624¹: "Noter aussi au v. 4a la substitution de 'péchés' à 'dettes'."

Schweizer 1973, 93: "Auf Umgestaltung in der lukanischen Gemeinde deutet ferner das üblichere Wort für 'Sünden' in der Bitte um Vergebung."

Schweizer 1973, ET 1975, 149: "There are also other suggestions of reworking in Luke: he uses a more common term for 'sins' in the petition for forgiveness."

Schneider 1977, 258: "Lukas bezeichnet die Schulden vor Gott verdeut-lichend mit dem eindeutigen Begriff 'Sünden.'"

Schürmann 1981, 93: "Die griechische Vokabel (*ta opheilēmata*) steht nur hier im Neuen Testament und in der Septuaginta in übertragener Bedeutung für das religiös-sittliche Versagen des Menschen. Lukas hat diese seinen Lesern ungewohnte Verwendung beseitigt und die gebräuch-lichere Vokabel 'Sünde' dafür eingesetzt. Da aber auch er im Nachsatz das Bild von der 'Schuld' beibehält, wird Matthäus wohl den ursprünglichen griechischen Wortlaut bewahrt haben, der so sehr der Gleichnissprache Jesu entspricht."

Strecker 1982, 15¹²: "Auf Lukas geht sicher zurück der Ausdruck τὰς ἁμαρτίας (Lk 11,4) für τὰ ὀφειλήματα (Mt 6,12a)."

Taeger 1982, 31-32: "In der [32] (bei ihm) vierten Bitte des Vaterunsers ersetzt Lukas den im Neuen Testament seltenen Begriff ὀφείλημα (Mt 6,12; sonst nur noch Röm 4,4) durch den geläufigeren ἁμαρτία."

Schnackenburg 1984, 98: "Nur die verdeutlichende Formulierung 'Vergib uns unsere Sünden' (statt 'Schulden') dürfte auf Lukas oder seine Vorlage zurückgehen. Wenn in der Fortsetzung von 'jedem Schuldner' die Rede ist, dem auch wir vergeben wollen, verrät sich darin noch der ursprüngliche Wortlaut vom Nachlaß der 'Schulden'."

Schnackenburg 1984, ET 1995, 64: "Only the clarifying formulation 'For-give us our sins' (instead of 'debts') might go back to Luke or his prototype. If we consider the continuation of 'every debtor,' whom we also are to forgive, the original wording is betrayed, that of the forgiveness of 'debts.'"

Fitzmyer 1985, 897: "[Luke] has disturbed the parallelism in *opheilēmata* 'debts' and *opheiletais*, 'debtors' (which Matthew has from 'Q' ...), changing the first to *hamartias*, 'sins.'"

Schneider 1985, 67: "Während Mt 6,12a bildhaft von den 'Schulden' des Menschen gegenüber Gott spricht, löst Lk 11,4a das Bild auf, setzt dafür die 'theologische' Begrifflichkeit ein und spricht von unseren 'Sünden'. Dabei mag der Begriff der 'Sündenvergebung' eingewirkt haben, vielleicht schon in der Tradition des Herrengebets der lukanischen Gemeinde."

Gnilka 1986, 215: "Die Abschwächung des Bildes vom Schuldner, das aber im 2. Teil der lk Vergebungsbitte erhalten blieb, kann man als Gräzisierung bezeichnen: vergib uns unsere Sünden (statt Schulden)."

Davies and Allison 1988, 611: "it is preferable to think that Luke chose for his non-Jewish readers the easier word—a proposal supported by the retention of ὀφείλοντι in Lk 11.4b."

Taussig 1988, 35: "Q recalls the Aramaic by translating the word for sins, חובא literally as ὀφειλήματα or 'debts.' Matthew has preserved Q, while Luke has generalized Q to some degree."

Wiefel 1988, 215-217: "Der Vergleich der Einzelheiten zeigt …, daß bei abweichender Formulierung Matthäus eher die ältere Fassung zu bieten scheint, während in der lukanischen Version Spuren aktualisierender Umgestaltung erkennbar sind. … [216] … Die Bitte um die Vergebung ist ebenfalls gegenüber Matthäus verändert; an Stelle des Ausdrucks ὀφειλήματα (Schulden) im Vordersatz, den Lukas durch seinen [217] Nachsatz auch voraussetzt, ist das allgemeinere, im Griechischen eindeutigere ἁμαρτία getreten."

Evans 1990, 483: "Here again Luke appears secondary. (I) Matthew has debts (*opheilēmata*), and the verb (*aphienai* = 'to let go') has one of its possible meanings, 'to cancel', 'to remit.'… The religious use of 'debt' for 'sin' is rare in the OT, but is common in later Judaism, and in the teaching of Jesus (7,41ff; Matt. 18,23ff.; 6,14 — in Aramaic the same word serves for both). But it was foreign to Greek thought, and alteration to the more conventional 'sins' was natural. That it was an alteration is evident from the second half of the sentence, where the idea of debt is retained. This is awkward as *who is indebted to us* (in Greek the participle followed by the dative) is not a complete equivalent for 'who sins against us', which is required by the first half of the sentence; and the verb now becomes a hybrid, mixing cancellation of debts with forgiveness of sins."

Catchpole 1993, 29: "Similarly the prayer for forgiveness prefers the present form ἀφίομεν and relinquishes the symmetry of the two references to debts for the sake of clarifying at the outset that sins are in mind. That which Matthew achieved by adding 'trespasses' to the Marcan saying about forgiveness Luke achieves by internal editing of the prayer itself."

Ernst 1993, 269: "Lk hat den ursprünglichen Text der Logienquelle im Vergleich mit Mt 6,9-13 besser erhalten, aber kaum in der Originalfassung, wie an einigen red Überarbeitungen und Zusätzen (… V. 4: Sünden; präsentisches 'erlassen' statt 'erließen') zu erkennen ist." But see 1977, 363 (= 1993, 270-271): Q 11:4¹ Lk = Q, Pro.

Hagner 1993, 150: "Here probably Luke has avoided the more archaic ὀφειλήματα which may not have been as easily understood by his gentile readers (but he has kept the root in the participial form at the end of v 4)."

Nolland 1993, 617: "The change is likely to be Luke's, since he retains in the following clause a form cognate to Matthew's term here. Fitzmyer is surely right to explain the motivation for the Lukan form by noting that Matthew's term is not attested in classical or Hellenistic Greek in a religious sense."

Sung 1993, 252: "Lukas hat statt des etwas schwerfälligen ὀφειλήματα die geläufige Wendung ἁμαρτίας gesetzt."

Meier 1994, 355: "Luke's modification of the wording is both theological and stylistic. … Luke apparently felt that the 'debts/debtors' metaphor (Matthew's *opheilēmata* and *opheiletais*) for sins and sinners would not be immediately intelligible to his Greek-speaking audience, which would not ordinarily use 'debt' in Greek as a metaphor for sin. Here Luke compromises with his tradition. He substitutes 'sins' (*hamartias*) for 'debts' in the first half of his petition, while allowing 'debtor' (*opheilonti*, a participial form) to remain in the second half. Presumably Luke thought that the straightforward theological word 'sin' in the first half would make the metaphor in the second half intelligible."

Schürmann 1994, 197: "Matthäus wird das Ursprüngliche bewahrt haben, wenn er an 'Erlaß' der 'Schulden'[168] denken läßt, obgleich τὰ ὀφειλήματα in LXX und im NT nur hier übertragen für das religiös-sittliche Versagen stehen—wohl der Grund, warum die luk Tradition[169] oder Lukas selbst den ungewöhnlichen Sprachgebrauch präzisiert hat. Die luk Fassung hat im Nachsatz das Bild (παντὶ ὀφείλοντι) beibehalten, also auch wohl im Vordersatz ursprünglich geführt. Zudem begegnet es in der Gleichnissprache Jesu in immer neu abgewandelten Formen charakteristisch häufig in unterschiedlichen Traditionsschichten. Jesus stellt den Menschen als 'Schuldner' hin, weil er ihn als 'Knecht', mehr noch: als 'Sohn' Gottes unendlich zurückgeblieben weiß hinter den Forderungen, welche der Vaterliebe Gottes entsprechen würden. Darum machen die Unterlassungen gravierend schuldig."

197[168]: "Der auffällige Ausdruck des Matthäus ist Aramäismus, denn das häufig für Sünde gebrauchte aramäische Wort *hoba* heißt eigentlich '(Geld)-schuld'. Es wurde wortwörtlich ins Griechische übersetzt."

197[169]: "In Q begegnet das Bild Lk 12,57ff par; im luk S 7,41ff; 16,1-8 und Mt 18,23-34 matth S; vgl. auch das Gleichnis von den Talenten oder Minen Lk 19,12-27 bzw. Mt 25,14-30 (in Q oder S?)."

Matt = Q: τὰ (ὀφειλήματα)[1] ἡμῶν

Pro

B. Weiß 1876, 188: "Dagegen ist in der 5. [petition] das τὰς ἁμαρτίας offenbar Erklärung des bildlichen τὰ ὀφειλήματα; denn daß nicht Mtth. in beiden Sätzen den gleichförmigen Ausdruck hergestellt (Camph), sondern Luc. in dem bildlichen Ausdruck des zweiten Gliedes ein Zeugniss für das Ursprüngliche erhalten, zeigt das steigernde παντὶ ὀφείλοντι ἡμῖν."

Plummer 1896, 297: "Mt. has τὰ ὀφειλήματα ἡμῶν, and there is reason for believing that Mt. is closer to the Aramaic original. The ὀφείλοντι of Lk. points to this, and so does τὴν ὀφειλὴν ἡμῶν in the Didache (viii.2)."

B. Weiß 1907, 72[1]: "Daß das bildliche ὀφειλήματα Lk. 11,4 durch ἁμαρτίας erläutert ist, erhellt unwiderleglich daraus, daß das bildliche ὀφείλοντι schließlich doch beibehalten wird."

B. Weiß 1908, 31: Reconstruction.

Castor 1912, 230: Reconstruction.

Easton 1926, 176-177: "'Sin' is the form taken by 'debt' on [177] Gentile soil, and the originality of the latter word is shown by the following 'debtor'."

Klostermann 1927, 58: "τὰ ὀφειλήματα ist ursprünglich vgl. Did 8,2 τὴν ὀφειλήν."

Klostermann, 1929, 125 = 486: "Das geläufigere τὰς ἁμαρτίας ersetzt bei Lc den ursprünglichen Ausdruck τὰ ὀφειλήματα, das doch durch das folgende παντὶ (luk.) ὀφείλοντι bestätigt wird."

Jeremias 1967, 14: "In der lukanischen Fassung ist das Wort 'Schulden', das im Griechischen zur Bezeichnung der Sünde unbekannt war, durch das geläufige griechische Wort für Sünde ersetzt; sie läßt aber im ('denn auch wir vergeben einem jeden, der uns etwas schuldig ist') erkennen, daß es auch im Vordersatz ursprünglich 'Schulden' hieß."

Jeremias 1967, ET 1964, 13: "In the Lucan version, the word 'debts' is represented by the usual Greek word for 'sins,' ἁμαρτίαι, but the wording in the next clause ('for we ourselves forgive everyone who is *indebted to us*') makes it evident that in the initial clause 'debts' had originally appeared."

Grundmann 1968, 202: "Wiederum verdient Matthäus vor Lukas den Vorzug; er sagt statt des allgemeinen lukanischen 'Sünden' das bildhafte ὀφειλήματα, das auch bei Lukas durch die Fortsetzung ὀφείλοντι gefordert wird. Es entspricht der Verkündigung Jesu, vor allem in seinen Gleichnissen, in denen der Mensch als einer gesehen wird, dem ein Vermögen anvertraut wird, dessen Mißbrauch oder Veruntreuung den Belohnten zum Schuldner macht (vgl. 18,25-34; 25,14-30; Luk. 7,41-43; 15,11-32; 16,1-7). Zwar ist dem, der Gott mit Vater anreden darf, seine Schuld erlassen, aber er kann täglich neue Schuld auf sich laden, und die Endabrechnung ist noch nicht erfolgt."

Wrege 1968, 104: See Q 11:4¹ Luke = Q, Pro.

Schwarz 1968-69, 246: Reconstruction.

Polag 1977, 60: "Wenn man fragt, welcher Zug der Basileia-Vorstellung wohl mit dem Gottesbild in Verbindung stehen könnte, auf das die Vateranrede im Gebet zurückzuführen ist, dann wird man wohl am ehesten die Tatsache nennen, daß das eschatologische Handeln Gottes ausgerechnet mit dem Zuspruch eines *Schuldennachlasses*, einer Freudenbotschaft an die 'Armen' beginnt, also mit einer Tat der Barmherzigkeit Gottes."

Schneider 1977, 258: "Das Wort von den 'Schulden', die Gott vergeben möge, wurde ursprünglich im übertragenen Sinn den 'Schulden' unter Menschen gegenübergestellt (Mt/Q)."

Polag 1979, 48: Reconstruction.

Schenk 1981, 61: Reconstruction.

Zeller 1984, 56: Reconstruction.

Fitzmyer 1985, 897: "[Luke] has disturbed the parallelism in *opheilēmata* 'debts' and *opheiletais*, 'debtors' (which Matthew has [from 'Q']…)." Square brackets around "from 'Q'" are Fitzmyer's.

Sand 1986, 126: "In der Bitte um Vergebung dürfte der Terminus 'Schulden' bei Mt ursprünglicher sein als der Begriff 'Sünden' bei Lk, der hier möglicherweise schon an die einzelnen Tatsünden dachte."

Lambrecht 1985, 132: "The use in Lk 11:4b of the verb 'to be indebted to' is an indication that most probably this metaphor was also original in the first half of the verse."

Davies and Allison 1988, 611: "Matthew could retain 'debt' because he could assume his readers' knowledge of the equation, 'sin' = 'debt'."

Taussig 1988, 25: Reconstruction.

Stritzky 1989, 11: "Dem Wortlaut nach scheint Mt 6,12a τὰ ὀφειλήματα dem Original nähergeblieben zu sein, während die für eine in griechischer Tradition wurzelnde Gemeinde verständlichere Formulierung τὰς ἁμαρτίας (Lk 11,4a) wohl auf Lukas selbst oder auf seine Vorlage zurückgeht."

International Q Project 1990, 500: καὶ ἄφες ἡμῖν τὰ ὀφειλήματα ἡμῶν.

Kloppenborg 1990, 49: Reconstruction.

Hagner 1993, 145: "Matthew's language at a number of points is the more original (e.g., ὀφειλήματα, for 'debts,' for Luke's ἁμαρτίας, 'sins'; σήμερον, 'today,' for Luke's τὸ καθ' ἡμέραν, 'the daily')."

Mack 1993, 89: Reconstruction.

O'Neill 1993, 20: Reconstruction.

Cullmann 1994, 73: "Bei Matthäus heißt es Schuld und Schuldner, bei Lukas 'Sünden' (nachher auch Schuldner). Dem Sinne nach besteht hier kein Unterschied, und die beiden griechischen Wörter gehen auf das gleiche aramäische Wort zurück[140]. Die konkretere Übersetzung des Matthäus ist hier wohl als die ursprünglichere anzusehen, zumal Jesus in Gleichnissen gern zur Illustration die Situation des Geldschuldens herangezogen hat."

73[140]: "*hoba*."

Cullmann 1994, ET 1995, 55: "Matthew has 'debt' and 'debtors', Luke 'sins' (and then also debtors). There is no difference in meaning here, and the two Greek terms go back to the same Aramaic word.[140] Matthew's more concrete translation here is probably to be seen as the more original, especially as Jesus was fond of using the situation of financial indebtedness as an illustration."

162[140]: "*hoba*."

Mell 1994, 158: Reconstruction.

Con

Gundry 1982, 108: "Luke gives the figurative meaning first and then reverts to the literal in 'everyone who is in debt,' just as Jesus, in his wordplay, referred first to divine forgiveness of sins and then to human forgiveness of financial debts (see Deut 15:1-2). If Luke represents the Greek tradition used by Matthew (as usually seems to be so), Matthew changes sins to debts in order to match the debtors in the last part of the petition. The change would exemplify his striving for close parallelism."

Evaluations

Carruth 1995: Matt = Q {A}, τὰ (ὀφειλήματα)[1] ἡμῶν.

There is, again, virtual unanimity among scholars in favor of Matthew's ὀφειλήματα as derived from Q. The following καὶ γάρ or ὡς καί shows that the sense of the petition as a whole rests on parallelism. This would tend to favor Matthew's ὀφειλήματα since, as noted by many scholars, the stem ὀφειλ- is attested for Q by both evangelists in the second part of the petition. As many have noted, Luke may have changed because of a generalizing tendency and to make it clear that the metaphor referred to sins. In Luke's special material at 13:2,4 there is a sequence ἁμαρτωλοί-ὀφειλέται in parallel examples of persons who are to be considered neither sinners nor guilty. This, along with Cadbury's evidence showing that in some cases Luke changed Mark by substituting a synonym for a repeated word, is support for the claim that here, too, it is Luke who uses words he may consider synonymous in parallel units.

Robinson 1995: Matt = Q {A}, τὰ (ὀφειλήματα)[1] ἡμῶν.

The forgiving of "sins" is so common for Luke (and for usage in general, including the LXX) that Luke (or his community) could readily have introduced this clarification. "Debts" is more metaphorical, a motif from Jesus' parables (see the similar reciprocity in Matt 18:23-35), "sins" more theological. Luke also avoids repetitious vocabulary.

Mark 11:25 also theologizes with παραπτώματα, which Matt 6:15 uses to exegete God forgiving ὀφειλήματα.

Not asking back what is lent in Q 6:30b, following directly the injunction to give (δός) to the one who begs (Q 6:30a), is a striking parallel to the Prayer's petitions for God to give (δός, Q 11:3[1]) and forgive, as humans forgive debts (Q here). One asks God to act toward oneself as one acts toward others. The practice of the Q community of forgiving debts thus stands in a relation of reciprocity with God's action toward the Q community. This comes to expression most clearly if the statements both of the humans' and of God's action use the same term for what is forgiven: debts.

Debt is a central dimension of the plight of the poor. Aramaic used it as a metaphor for sin. Thus the more unusual Matthean formulation (a *hapax legomenon* in LXX and NT in the meaning "sins"!) fits best the distinctive ethos of the Q community. Like the other changes in the Lucan Prayer, this original nuance faded out, leaving the general petition for the forgiveness of sins.

Did. 8,2, though in details not identical with Matthew, and hence providing somewhat independent attestation, supports Matthew (rather than Luke) as original by reading ἄφες ἡμῖν τὴν ὀφειλήν.

Kloppenborg 1995: Matt = Q {A}, τὰ (ὀφειλήματα)¹ ἡμῶν.

The agreement between Matthew and Luke in the use of ὀφειλέταις/ὀφείλοντι indicates clearly that the metaphor of debt-forgiveness was in use in the prayer. Luke is certainly aware of the use of "debt" as a metaphor for sin (13:2-4; 7:41-50), but it is equally true that this is not the usual metaphorical valence for ὀφείλημα in Hellenistic Greek. Luke uses (i.e., preserves) the metaphor *only in instances where he has already made its metaphorical valence clear*: at 7:41-50 the exemplum of the two debtors is delivered in a context in which forgiveness of sins is plain; and at 13:4 it is clear that sins are at stake, since he has used ἁμαρτωλοί in the parallel formulation in v. 2. Luke 11:4 offers an exact parallel to this procedure: Luke uses ὀφείλοντι in v. 4b only once he has made it clear that he means sins rather than debts. This necessitated the shift from debt to sin in v. 4a.

Q 11:4²: Luke's conjunction γάρ or Matthew's ὡς.

Luke = Q: καὶ [γάρ]²

Pro

Easton 1926, 177: "W [Wellhausen, 1904b] notes that Lk's καὶ γάρ gives a looser and more Semitic construction than Mt's ὡς δέ; Lk would scarcely have changed his favorite ὡς into καί."

Jeremias 1980, 145: "Steigerndes καὶ γάρ wird Lk 7,8 durch die Mt-Parallele (8,9) und Lk 11,4 durch den Kontext (Vaterunser) der Tradition zugewiesen; bei den Belegen für satzverbindendes καὶ γάρ dagegen ist das Bild uneinheitlich: Apg 19,40 wird durch die Apg als lukanisch, Lk 22,59 durch par. Mk 14,70 Mt 26,73 als traditionell kenntlich."

Davies and Allison 1988, 591: Reconstruction.

Mack 1993, 89: Reconstruction.

Con

B. Weiß 1876, 188: "Da nun die echt lucanische Wendung καὶ γάρ αὐτοί (Vgl. zu καὶ γάρ: 6,32.33 7,8 22,37.59 Act. 19,40 und das καί … αὐτοί, das sich etwa 50mal bei Luc. findet) auch nach Camph. das Motiv directer und stärker ausdrückt, zugleich einem durch ὡς nicht ausgeschlossenen Mißverständnisse vorbeugend, so muß sie nach allen kritischen Grundsätzen als nachbessernde Erläuterung gelten."

B. Weiß 1901, 460: "Ganz klar ist auch [as in the replacement of ὀφειλήματα by ἁμαρτίαι] die schriftstellerische Reflexion, wenn das unbestimmte ὡς in καὶ γάρ verwandelt wird."

von Harnack 1907, 46: "καὶ γάρ ist lukanisch (s. die 5. Bitte bei Luk. und dagegen das ὡς καί bei Matth.; bei Matth. findet sich καὶ γάρ 2mal, bei Luk. im Ev. 9mal)."

von Harnack 1907, ET 1908, 62: "καὶ γάρ is Lukan (*vide* the fifth petition of the Lord's Prayer in St. Luke, where St. Matthew has ὡς καί, in St. Matthew καὶ γάρ occurs twice, in St. Luke's gospel nine times.)"

B. Weiß 1907, 72: "jedenfalls ist eine Erweiterung des Gebets durch Matthäus, nachdem Jesus eben noch vor den 'vielen Worten' gewarnt hatte, durchaus unwahrscheinlich[1]."

72[1]: "Das wird aufs klarste dadurch bestätigt, daß auch in den bei beiden Evangelisten erhaltenen Bitten Lukas überall eine sekundäre Form zeigt. … Daß das ὡς καὶ ἡμεῖς ἀφήκαμεν Mt. 6,12 durch das καὶ γάρ αὐτοὶ ἀφίομεν im Sinne von Mt. 18,35 dahin gedeutet ist, daß der Beter sich bewußt sein muß, durch sein ständiges Verhalten der Erfüllung seiner Bitte nicht unwürdig zu sein, zeigt das παντὶ vor ὀφείλοντι."

Cadbury 1920, 145: "[καὶ γάρ] occurs twice in passages peculiar to Luke (1,66; 22,37) ... and besides these only in passages parallel to Matthew, where it is more likely that Luke has introduced it into his sources than taken it over from them."

Lagrange 1921, 323-324: "—καὶ γὰρ αὐτοί est de Lc. (cf. Act. xxiv,15; xxvii,36), moins naturel que ὡς καὶ [324] ὑμεῖς, est peut-être plus expressif, par le γάρ."

Lagrange 1923, 130: "En rendant ὡς καὶ ὑμεῖς par καὶ γὰρ αὐτοί, Lc. exprime la même pensée [that Jesus requires complete pardon] avec nuance: si nous-mêmes pardonnons, combien plus Dieu pardonnera!"

Loisy 1924, 316: "'Car nous-mêmes (καὶ γὰρ αὐτοί) remettons' paraît être une retouche littéraire de: 'comme nous-mêmes (ὡς καὶ ἡμεῖς) remettons'."

Creed 1930, 157: "Lk.'s version is more general: 'Forgive us our sins, for we forgive every one who is indebted to us.' In this and in other respects Lk. appears to be less primitive."

Schmid 1930, 233²: "καὶ γάρ (statt ὡς) ist ... lukanisch, desgleichen παντὶ ὀφείλοντι ἡμῖν statt τοῖς ὀφειλέταις ἡμῶν."

Schmid 1951, 197: "In V. 3 schreibt Lukas 'täglich' (statt 'heute'), und in V. 4 'denn auch wir vergeben jedem' (statt 'wie wir erlassen haben'). Beides beruht auf späterer Reflexion: jeden Tag brauchen wir die lebensnotwendige Nahrung, und die Pflicht der Vergebung gilt immerfort."

Schulz 1972, 85: "καὶ γάρ ist bei Lk häufig (9mal), wird also auch hier gegenüber dem mt ὡς καί sek sein."

Dupont 1973, 624¹: "La version de Luc semble modifiée au niveau de la rédaction."

Schweizer 1973, 93: "Auf Umgestaltung in der lukanischen Gemeinde deutet ... die Formulierung des Nachsatzes: 'denn auch wir vergeben jedem, der uns schuldig wird'."

Schweizer 1973, ET 1975, 149: "There are also other suggestions of reworking in Luke: he uses ... different wording in the apodosis—'for we, too, forgive whoever wrongs us.'"

Taeger 1982, 32: "Die Beziehung zwischen menschlicher und göttlicher Vergebung wird bei Lukas durch 'denn auch' (καὶ γάρ; Mt 6,12: ὡς καί; vgl. dann aber sachlich V. 14) ausgedrückt. Diese möglicherweise redaktionelle Änderung könnte die Abhängigkeit der göttlichen Sündenvergebung von zwischenmenschlichem Schulderlaß unterstreichen."

Schneider 1985, 68³⁶: "*Kai gar* begegnet bei Lukas an folgenden Stellen: Lk 1,66; 6,32b.33a (33b v. l. 34b v. l.); 7,8; 11,4; 22,37.59; Apg 19,40. Da Matthäus *kai gar* in Abhängigkeit von Vorlagen und von sich aus (redaktionell) schreibt (Mt 8,9 par Lk; 15,27 diff Mk; 26,73 par Mk), wird man kaum annehmen, daß er es im Vaterunser getilgt hätte, falls es ihm in Q vorlag. Immerhin kann auch beobachtet werden, daß Matthäus *kai gar* in Mk 10,45 zu *hōsper* abgeändert hat (Mt 20,28).

"Das Mt 6,12 stehende *hōs kai*, das noch zweimal bei Mt vorkommt (18,33 Sg.; 20,14 Sg.), fehlt im dritten Evangelium ganz (abgesehen von Lk 9,54 v. l.). Es findet sich indessen an 6 Stellen der Apg und wird somit von Lukas nicht grundsätzlich gemieden. Die Abänderung von *hōs kai* zu *kai gar* im Vaterunser hängt wohl damit zusammen, daß Lukas an die ständige Vergebungsbereitschaft der Betenden denkt (vgl. Lk 17,4 par Mt 18,21f.). Schließlich ist zu erwägen, ob nicht in Q ein einfaches *kai* den Nachsatz parataktisch einleitete (was auf eine semitische Vorlage hinweisen könnte). Dann hätten Matthäus und Lukas auf je verschiedene Weise die Parataxe aufgelöst und den Nachsatz eindeutig subordiniert: Matthäus mit begründend-vergleichendem *hōs kai* …, Lukas mit begründendem *kai gar*."

Evans 1990, 483: "This ['to establish exact similarity' or 'an appeal for imitation'] could be the force of Luke's probably secondary *for we ourselves* (*kai gar autoi* = 'for also we')."

Nolland 1993, 617: "This could be a translation variant from Aramaic כדי, *kedî* (Grelot [RB91 (1984) 547], but is as well explained as a clarification of the ambiguity of Matthew's text, which could be read as an attempt to strike a bargain with God."

Matt = Q: (ὡς)² καὶ

Pro

B. Weiß 1908, 31: Reconstruction.
Castor 1912, 230: Reconstruction.
Manson 1937, 266: Reconstruction.
Polag 1979, 48: Reconstruction.
Schenk 1981, 61: Reconstruction.
Zeller 1984, 56: Reconstruction.
Taussig 1988, 25: Reconstruction.
International Q Project 1990, 500: ὡς καὶ ἡμεῖς ἀφήκαμεν.
Kloppenborg 1990, 49: Reconstruction.

Con

Bussmann 1929, 67: "ὡς καὶ ἡμεῖς bei Mt erscheint vereinfacht aus καὶ γὰρ αὐτοὶ ἀφίομεν."

Gundry 1982, 108: "As a finishing touch Matthew added 'on earth as also [it comes to pass] in heaven' to the first couplet. He also thinks of Jesus' reference to forgiveness of debtors as a finishing touch to the second couplet of petitions and therefore changes 'for' to 'as' in correspondence with v 10b and his general liking of ὡς (23,8). Stylistically, this change produces the combination 'as also,' which appears three times in the first gospel (6:12; 18:33; 20:14), but never in the other synoptics—a confirmation of his editing." Square brackets are Gundry's.

Davies and Allison 1988, 611: "Matthew's ὡς could be redactional (ὡς καί: Mt: 3; Mk: 0; Lk: 0)."

Schürmann 1994, 198-199: "Aufdringlicher als bei Mt (ὡς καί korrelativ) ist im luk Text die eigene Vergebung—als bereits erfüllte Bedingung der Vergebung Gottes (καὶ γάρ[178])—durch [199] αὐτοί verstärkt herausgestellt. Hier bitten aber Beter, denen schon vergeben ist, erneut um die (ja doch immer nur bedingte …) Vergebung. Hintergrund sind Aufforderungen Jesu, in denen das eigene Vergeben nicht nur Bedingung der göttlichen Vergebung, sondern auch Frucht derselben ist."

198[178]: "καὶ γάρ (sonst. NT ca. 26mal) kennen Mk 10,45; 14,70 parr und QMt 8,9 par 7,8; es muß hier wie auch Lk 6,32.33(34 v.l.); 11,4(v.l.) diff Mt und 1,66; 22,37 S nicht unbedingt—wie Apg 19,40—luk Ursprung sein. …—Die Verwandtschaft der Mt-Fassung mit der von Mt 18,33 καὶ … ὡς κἀγώ (in beiden Gliedern des Vergleichs!) ist recht auffällig." Note his hesitation.

Evaluations

Carruth 1995: Matt = Q {B}, (ὡς)².

Although the evidence is not extensive, Luke seems to have some preference for the connecting expression καὶ γάρ. It is difficult to establish a Matthean preference for ὡς καί on the basis of three occurrences. Luke may have conceivably changed Q's ὡς καί to clarify the meaning of the petition so that one would not understand that God's forgiving is to be preceded by or conditioned by human forgiving.

Robinson 1995: Matt = Q {B}, (ὡς)².

Although the tendency throughout the Prayer for Luke to make the changes in the petitions shared with Matthew predisposes one here too to prefer Matthew, the evidence is in this case much more balanced than in the others.

ὡς in the secondary Matthean petition about doing God's will ὡς in heaven (Q 11:2) not only introduces ὡς redactionally, which could have influenced

Matthew to repeat the term (Q 11:4). For here Matthew also uses it in a comparable comparison between God and humans. In Matt 20:28 ὥσπερ replaces καὶ γάρ (Mark 10:45) in a comparison between the Son of man and humans. ὡς is quite frequent in Matthew. ὡς καί is in Matt 6:12; 18:33; 20:14, never in Mark or Luke (but in Acts 6x). Hence ὡς καί could be due to Matthew here.

Though καὶ γάρ is more common in Luke than in Matthew, and hence could have been inserted by Luke, its usage in Matthew is sufficient to make it hard to assume he would have deleted it. καὶ ... αὐτός is typically Lucan.

καὶ γάρ does occur in Q, at 7:8.

Both γάρ and ὡς could be secondary.

These considerations, taken together, make the vote less certain here.

Kloppenborg 1995: Matt = Q {B}, (ὡς)².

The decision is related to 11:4¹: Luke is aware of the fact that in Koine Greek, ὀφείλημα does not ordinarily mean "sin" but assumes this meaning only when the context supplies that meaning. This means that he cannot assume that there is a logical equivalence or symmetrical relationship between human debt/sin-forgiveness and divine sin-forgiveness in the way that Matthew and presumably Q can, both of whom live in an environment where חובא has the dual valence. The only reason for downgrading what ordinarily should be a {A} to a {B} is the appearance of the redactional phrase ὡς ἐν οὐρανῷ καὶ ἐπὶ γῆς in Matthew.

Q 11:4³: Luke's pronoun αὐτοί or Matthew's ἡμεῖς.

Luke = Q: καὶ [γὰρ]² [αὐτοί]³

Pro

J. **Weiß** 1892, 467: "Das in LQ oft (2,50. [9,36]. 11,46. 14,1.12. 16,28. 17,13. [18,34]. 22,23. 24,14.35.52) vorkommende καὶ αὐτοί bedeutet hier: denn auch wir unsererseits." Note that he is talking about Q^Luke.

Davies and Allison 1988, 591: Reconstruction.

Mack 1993, 89: Reconstruction.

Schürmann 1994, 199-200: "Das präsentische ἀφίομεν muß man mit dem verstärkenden καὶ γὰρ αὐτοί zusammenlesen. Wenn wir auch bei beiden Differenzen—wie auch in der [200] Partizipialform; s.o.—die Q-Fassung vor uns haben können ..., kann Matthäus doch in allen diesen drei Lukas-Differenzen (mit ὡς καὶ ἡμεῖς ἀφήκαμεν τοῖς ὀφειλέταις) eine ältere Fassung aus der Gebetstradition seiner Gemeinde bewahrt und in seine Q-Fassung eingetragen haben."

Con

Plummer 1896, 296: "In N.T. τὸ καθ' ἡμέραν is peculiar to Lk. (xix. 47; Acts xvii. 11). This fact and the insertion of his favourite παντί with ὀφείλοντι, and the substitution of his favourite καὶ αὐτοί for καὶ ἡμεῖς with ἀφίομεν, incline us to believe that some of the differences between this form of the Prayer and that in Mt. are due to Lk. himself."

B. **Weiß** 1901, 460: "Zu dem lukan. καὶ αὐτοί (*auch wir unsrerseits*) vgl. Act 24,15. 27,36."

von Harnack 1907, 48: "ἡμεῖς hat er [Luke] durch αὐτοί ersetzt, um die dreifache Wiederholung desselben Wortes zu vermeiden (auch läßt er gerne das Subjekt-Pronomen vor dem Verbum weg, s. z. Matth. 5,44.48 und sonst)."

von Harnack 1907, ET 1908, 65: "ἡμεῖς is replaced by αὐτοί in order to avoid the threefold pattern of repetition of the same word. (St. Luke is also fond of omitting the pronominal subject before the verb.)" Harnack noted the same kind of change by Luke at Matt 5:44 = Luke 6:27 (p. 61) and Matt 5:48 = Luke 6:36 (p. 63).

Lagrange 1921, 323-324: "—καὶ γὰρ αὐτοί est de Lc. (cf. Act. xxiv,15; xxvii,36), moins naturel que ὡς καὶ [324] ὑμεῖς, est peut-être plus expressif, par le γὰρ."

Lagrange 1923, 130: "En rendant ὡς καὶ ὑμεῖς par καὶ γὰρ αὐτοί, Lc. exprime la même pensée [that Jesus requires complete pardon] avec nuance: si nous-mêmes pardonnons, combien plus Dieu pardonnera!"

Loisy 1924, 316: "'Car nous-mêmes (καὶ γὰρ αὐτοί) remettons' paraît être une retouche littéraire de: 'comme nous-mêmes (ὡς καὶ ἡμεῖς) remettons'."

Easton 1926, 177: "αὐτοί is a refinement."

Schmid 1930, 233²: "Das Personalpronomen ἐγώ läßt Lk gerne weg; vgl. z.B. Mt 5,44<, 5,48<."

Schulz 1972, 85: "ἡμεῖς (Mt) könnte gegenüber αὐτοί bei Lk primär sein, da Lk auch sonst das Subjekt-Pronomen vor dem Verbum wegläßt und eine dreifache Wiederholung desselben Wortes möglicherweise aus stilistischen Gründen vermeiden wollte."

Lambrecht 1985, 132: "The Lucan generalization 'everyone' and the emphasis created by the addition of 'ourselves' betray … a more reflexive character than the Matthean parallel and witnesses to a later stage."

Evans 1990, 483: "This ['to establish exact similarity' or 'an appeal for imitation'] could be the force of Luke's probably secondary *for we ourselves* (*kai gar autoi* = 'for also we')."

Nolland 1993, 617: "The change is probably Luke's since his Gospel has most of the NT occurrences of καὶ αὐτοί."

Matt = Q: (ὡς)² καὶ (ἡμεῖς)³

Pro

B. Weiß 1908, 31: Reconstruction.
Castor 1912, 230: Reconstruction.
Polag 1979, 48: Reconstruction.
Schenk 1981, 61: Reconstruction.
Taussig 1988, 25: Reconstruction.
International Q Project 1990, 500: ὡς καὶ ἡμεῖς ἀφήκαμεν.
Kloppenborg 1990, 49: Reconstruction.

Con

Bussmann 1929, 67: "ὡς καὶ ἡμεῖς bei Mt erscheint vereinfacht aus καὶ γὰρ αὐτοὶ ἀφίομεν."

Gundry 1982, 108: "Even the change from αὐτοί to ἡμεῖς represents conformity to ἡμῖν in the first part of the petition."

Evaluations

Carruth 1995: Matt = Q {B}, καὶ (ἡμεῖς)³.

The evidence for Luke's preference for omitting a subject pronoun is not overwhelming. However, the αὐτοί seems to represent a secondary emphasis and disrupts the flow created by the recurrence of the first person plural pronoun in the rest of the section. For this reason, it can probably be concluded that Matthew's ἡμεῖς represents Q.

Robinson 1995: Matt = Q {B}, καὶ (ἡμεῖς)³.

Luke avoids an expressed subject pronoun before the verb and avoids repetitions such as the first person plural pronoun in the Prayer. Since the Q Prayer is characterized by repetitions (aorist imperatives; forgive; debts), the repetition of the pronoun is probably in Q. Καὶ αὐτοί occurs in Acts 24:15; 27:36. It is usually Luke who changes wording in the Prayer.

Kloppenborg 1995: Matt = Q {B}, καὶ (ἡμεῖς)³.

It may be a matter of Luke's tendency to avoid an expressed subject, but the use of αὐτοί is emphatic and thus replaces the function of an expressed subject. Presumably the use of the emphatic ("we ourselves") is required because of the conscious shift in vocabulary (see above) from sin/forgiveness to debt/remission. The use of the emphatic underscores that an *argument* is being made to the effect that human debt-remission should be treated as analogous to, and an invitation for God's forgiveness of sins. This transformation is related to the above two.

Q 11:4⁴: Luke's ἀφίομεν or Matthew's ἀφήκαμεν.

Luke = Q: καὶ [γὰρ]² [αὐτοὶ]³ ἀφ[ίο]⁴μεν

Pro

Plummer 1896, 297: "The Old Syriac has the future in both Mt. and Lk., and in Lk. it has what may be the original form of the petition: 'Remit to us, and we also will remit.' Tertullian seems to have had the future in his mind when he wrote *Debitoribus denique dimissuros nos in oratione profitemur* (*De Pudic*. ii). If this is correct, ἀφίομεν is closer to the original than ἀφήκαμεν is."

Mack 1993, 89: Reconstruction.

Schürmann 1994, 199: "Wenn Mk 11,25 ein früher Nachklang des Herrengebetes ist[187], bestätigt ἀφίετε sich die präsentische Form des Lk (diff Mt) vielleicht als Lukas vorgegebene alte—wenn auch nicht ursprüngliche ...— Tradition der Redenquelle."

199[187]: "Wenn außerhalb des EvMt nur Mk 11,25 ὁ πατὴρ ὑμῶν ὁ ἐν τοῖς οὐρανοῖς begegnet, ist speziell Abhängigkeit von Q (= Lk 6,4b) sehr wahrscheinlich."

Con

B. Weiß 1901, 460: "Ganz klar ist auch [as in the replacement of ὀφειλήματα by ἁμαρτίαι] die schriftstellerische Reflexion, wenn das unbestimmte ὡς in καὶ γάρ verwandelt wird und das ἀφήκ. in das ständige Verhalten bezeichnende ἀφίομεν (vgl. Apk 11,9)."

Lagrange 1923, 130: "Lc. emploie le présent qui convient bien à καὶ γὰρ αὐτοί, puisque ceux qui prient comparent ce qu'ils font en ce moment à ce qu'ils demandent de Dieu."

Schmid 1930, 233²: "Auch das Perfekt (ἀφήκαμεν) ersetzt Lk bei Mk oft durch den Aorist. Hier ist das Präsens durch τὸ καθ' ἡμέραν veranlaßt."

Creed 1930, 157: "Lk.'s version is more general: 'Forgive us our sins, for we forgive every one who is indebted to us.' In this and in other respects Lk. appears to be less primitive."

Manson 1937, 266: "In Mt. the prayer says 'we have forgiven' and the thought is that definite known cases of offense have been disposed of in this way. Cf. Mt. 5:23f. ... In Lk it is rather a regular practice that is stated in general terms—and statements in general terms are dangerous in prayer. Mt's form is to be preferred."

Soiron 1941, 328: "Zugleich deutet das markantere παντὶ ὀφείλοντι statt τοῖς ὀφειλέταις im Zusammenhang mit dem Präsens ἀφίομεν gegenüber ἀφήκαμεν bei Mt sowie das Präsens in der vierten Bitte darauf hin, daß wir durch die dauernde Übung und Gewohnheit des Vergebens uns der Vergebung vonseiten Gottes wert machen."

Schmid 1951, 197: "In V. 3 schreibt Lukas 'täglich' (statt 'heute'), in V. 4 'denn auch wir vergeben jedem' (statt 'wie wir erlassen haben'). Beides beruht auf späterer Reflexion: jeden Tag brauchen wir die lebensnotwendige Nahrung, und die Pflicht der Vergebung gilt immerfort."

Jeremias 1967, 14-15: "Matthäus [bietet] die schwierigere Fassung ..., denn sein Wortlaut ('wie wir vergeben haben') könnte den irrigen Anschein erwecken, als ob unser Vergeben nicht nur dem Vergeben Gottes vorausgehen müsse, sondern als ob es geradezu das Vorbild darstelle für Gottes Vergebung: vergib uns so, wie wir vergeben haben. In Wahrheit liegt jedoch der Vergangenheitsform des Matthäus im Aramäischen ein sogenanntes Perfectum praesens zugrunde, das eine hier und jetzt eintretende Handlung bezeichnet. Die richtige Übersetzung der Matthäus-Fassung hat also zu lauten: 'wie auch wir hiermit denen vergeben, die uns etwas schuldig sind'. Die lukanische Fassung hat durch die Wahl des Präsens bei den griechisch sprechenden Christen ein Mißverständnis ausschließen wollen, indem sie (sachlich richtig) sagt: 'denn [15] auch wir vergeben einem jeden, der uns etwas schuldig ist'."

Jeremias 1967, ET 1964, 14: "it is readily seen that Matthew has the more difficult form, and in such cases the more difficult form is to be regarded as the more original. Matthew's is the more difficult form, because his wording ('as we have forgiven') could lead to the mistaken impression that our forgiving must not only precede forgiveness on God's part, but also that it provides the standard for God's forgiving us: 'forgive us thus, as we have forgiven.' In actuality, however, there lies behind Matthew's past tense form what is called in Semitic grammar a *perfectum praesens*, a present perfect which refers to an action occurring here and now. The correct translation of the Matthaean form would therefore run, 'as we also herewith forgive our debtors.' By its choice of the present tense form, Luke's version was intended to exclude a misunderstanding among Greek-speaking Christians, since it says (and this catches the sense): 'for we also ourselves forgive everyone who is indebted to us.'"

Wrege 1968, 105: "Das lk Präsens kann—zusammen mit dem der Brotbitte—durch den Evangelisten selbst veranlaßt oder einfach Übersetzungsvariante sein."

Schulz 1972, 85: "Das Präsens ἀφίομεν geht ebenfalls auf Konto des Lk, der bereits in V 3 präsentisch formuliert."

Dupont 1973, 624¹: "Noter aussi ... au v. 4b, l'addition de παντί, qui va de pair avec l'emploi d'un présent au lieu de l'aoriste (retouche analogue au v. 3 ...)."

Schweizer 1973, 93: "Auf Umgestaltung in der lukanischen Gemeinde deutet ... die Formulierung des Nachsatzes: 'denn auch wir vergeben jedem, der uns schuldig wird'."

Schweizer 1973, ET 1975, 149: "There are also other suggestions of reworking in Luke: he uses ... different wording in the apodosis—'for we, too, forgive whoever wrongs us.'"

Schneider 1977, 258: "Unsicher bleibt, ob erst der Evangelist dem begründenden Teil von V 4a die präsentische Form eines Versprechens vor Gott gegeben hat. Das Gleichnis vom unbarmherzigen Knecht (Mt 18,21-35 vgl. 5,23f.) läßt zwar vermuten ..., daß Matthäus an dieser Stelle die gegenseitige menschliche Vergebung als 'Vorleistung' bzw. Voraussetzung der erbetenen Vergebung durch Gott gekennzeichnet hat (Mt 6,12). Der Charakter der Selbstverpflichtung wird bei Lukas durch die Einschaltung von 'jedem' unterstrichen. Da Lukas schon in V 3 präsentisch formuliert, kann es sein, daß er das gleiche auch in V 4a von sich aus tat."

Fitzmyer 1985, 897: "[Luke] has further altered the perf. *aphēkamen*, 'we have forgiven', to a more general pres. *aphiomen*, 'we forgive,' and made 'debtors' more universal 'everyone who does wrong to us.'"

Lambrecht 1985, 132: "Lucan redaction also seems the more probable for 'we forgive' than the position that both verb forms, the aorist in Mt. 6:12b and the present in Lk 11:4b, would ultimately go back to the same Aramaic basic form."

Schneider 1985, 68: "Mt 6,12b setzt mit *aphēkamen* voraus, daß die Beter ihrerseits schon ihren Schuldnern vergeben haben, wenn sie Gott um Vergebung bitten. ... Der Aorist spricht von einem bereits vollzogenen zwischenmenschlichen Vergeben, wie—wenigstens für das matthäische Verständnis—Mt 6,14f. und 18,35 anzeigen. Der zwischenmenschliche Vergebungsakt ist Voraussetzung für ein ehrliches Gebet um die Vergebung Gottes.

"Die lukanische präsentische Fassung Lk 11,4b läßt den Beter hingegen ein Versprechen für die Gegenwart und für alle Zukunft machen. Er erklärt seine Bereitschaft, *immer* und *jedem* zu vergeben. Der lukanisch-redaktionelle Charakter dieser Verschärfung der ethischen Komponente in dem Zusatz zur Vergebungsbitte geht im übrigen aus der Verwendung von *kai gar* sowie von *pas* mit Partizip hervor."

Sand 1986, 126: "Bei Lk ist es [what corresponds to Matt 6:12] die einzige Bitte, die durch die Angabe eines Motivs erweitert ist. Man wird sagen können, daß die Motivangabe vorred. ist, die sprachliche Fassung aber der letzten red. Bearbeitung zuzuschreiben ist."

Gnilka 1986, 214-215: "Brot- und Vergebungsbitte hat Mt in ihrer vorgegebenen Gestalt bewahrt. Ihre Veränderungen bei Lk lassen sich von den Anliegen des 3. Evangelisten her verständlich machen. Lk korrigiert die

Eschatologie (Tempuswechsel: δίδου—ἀφίομεν), dies tut auch die Didache [215] (ἀφίεμεν)."

Ernst 1993, 269: "Lk hat den ursprünglichen Text der Logienquelle im Vergleich mit Mt 6,9-13 besser erhalten, aber kaum in der Originalfassung, wie an einigen red Überarbeitungen und Zusätzen (... V. 4: Sünden; präsentisches 'erlassen' statt 'erließen') zu erkennen ist."

Catchpole 1993, 29: "Similarly the prayer for forgiveness prefers the present form ἀφίομεν and relinquishes the symmetry of the two references to debts for the sake of clarifying at the outset that sins are in mind. That which Matthew achieved by adding 'trespasses' to the Marcan saying about forgiveness Luke achieves by internal editing of the prayer itself."

Nolland 1993, 617: "Also likely to be Lukan is the present tense for the verb (so: 'practice forgiveness'), where Matthew has the perfect; this fits with the 'day by day' of Luke' where Matthew has 'today.'"

Meier 1994, 355: "Luke's modification of the wording is both theological and stylistic. ... Luke, the theologian of universal salvation and personal forgiveness, both universalizes and personalizes the second half of the petition by specifying 'everyone who is indebted to us.' The present-tense form of the verb 'forgive' in the second half (*aphiomen*) may be Luke's clarification of the difficult aorist tense (*aphēkamen*) seen in Matthew's version, although it might instead be an independent attempt to render an Aramaic perfect tense having a present meaning. In any event, the present tense certainly fits Luke's focus on Christian existence continuing to be lived out in this present world."

Matt = Q: (ὡς)² καὶ (ἡμεῖς)³ ἀφ(ήκα)⁴μεν

Pro

Klein 1906, 38: "Unmittelbar an das Vaterunser knüpft Matthäus den Ausspruch Jesu an, unter welchen Bedingungen die Sündenvergebung erfolgt. (Mt 6,14[.15]) ...—In der Parallelstelle Mc 11,25 heißt es, gleichsam bezugnehmend auf das Vaterunser: ...

"Demselben Gedanken gibt Jesus auch folgenden Ausdruck: (Mt 5,23ff.). ...

"Ganz so lehren auch die Rabbinen:[1] Sünden gegen seinen Nebenmenschen werden am Versöhnungstag erst dann vergeben, wenn er seinen Nächsten um Versöhnung gebeten hat. Ohne diese erlangte Versöhnung würde man Jemandem gleichen, der das Reinigungsbad nimmt und gleichzeitig ein verunreinigendes Reptil in seiner Hand hält.[2]

"In Übereinstimmung damit betet Jesus: 'Und vergib uns unsere Schulden, wie auch wir *vergeben haben* unsern Schuldnern.' Die Kluft, die dich von deinen Nebenmenschen trennt, muß bereits überbrückt sein, der Akt der

Aussöhnung muß bereits hinter dir liegen, wenn du Vergebung für deine Sünden erflehen willst.

"In der Parallelstelle Lc 12,58 fehlt Mt 5,23.24, auch das ist kein Zufall."

38[1]: "Mischnah Joma VIII, 9."

38[2]: "Taan. 16a."

von Harnack 1907, 48: "Das Perfekt ἀφήκαμεν ist gewiß ebenso ursprünglich wie das ὡς (s. Matth. 5,23); Luk. hat den wichtigen Gedanken abgeschwächt."

von Harnack 1907, ET 1908, 65: "The perfect ἀφήκαμεν is certainly as original as the ὡς (*vide* St. Matt. v.23); St. Luke has here attenuated the full and important significance of the petition."

B. Weiß 1908, 31: Reconstruction.

Castor 1912, 230: Reconstruction.

Lagrange 1923, 130: "Mt. a l'aor. ἀφήκαμεν pour bien marquer que le pardon doit être acquis."

Manson 1937, 266: Reconstruction.

Jeremias 1967, 14 [ET 1964, 14]: See Q 11:4⁴ Luke = Q, Con.

Wrege 1968, 105: "In Mt 6,12b wird man den Aorist für ursprünglich halten."

Jeremias 1971, 190: "Wenn weiter in der zweiten Hälfte der Vergebungsbitte Matthäus den Aorist ἀφήκαμεν, Lukas das Präsens ἀφίομεν bietet, so darf auch hier der schwierigere Text des Matthäus höheres Alter beanspruchen."

Jeremias 1971, ET 1971, 196: "Furthermore, the fact that in the second half of the petition for forgiveness Matthew offers the aorist ἀφήκαμεν and Luke the present ἀφίομεν suggests that here, too, the more difficult text of Matthew may lay claim to being the earlier."

Polag 1979, 48: Reconstruction.

Schenk 1981, 61: Reconstruction.

Zeller 1984, 56: Reconstruction.

Davies and Allison 1988, 591: Reconstruction.

Taussig 1988, 25: Reconstruction.

International Q Project 1990, 500: ὡς καὶ ἡμεῖς ἀφήκαμεν.

Kloppenborg 1990, 49: Reconstruction.

Sung 1993, 252: "Im Blick auf ἀφήκαμεν (Aor, bzw. aram. Perf. Präs.) bei Mt und ἀφίομεν (Präs.) bei Lk ist die eher etwas mißverständliche schwierige Fassung bei Mt ursprünglich."

Con

Bussmann 1929, 67: "Vielleicht aber erklärt sich der Unterschied hier … daraus, daß Mt das Herrngebet nicht nur in R [Redenquelle], sondern auch in seiner Sonderquelle, wo es ausführlicher war, vor sich gehabt hat. Daher dann auch das Perfekt ἀφήκαμεν."

Gundry 1982, 108: "Yet again for the sake of a more exact parallelism, he shifts from the present tense ἀφίομεν to the aorist tense ἀφήκαμεν (cf. the corresponding aorist tense ἄφες). In these ways he not only satisfies his taste for parallelism, but also takes away the iterative emphasis apparent in Luke ('we repeatedly forgive every time anyone goes in debt to us'). Just as the succession of days for bread giving reduces to the present day in Matthew, so the succession of forgivenesses reduces to the particular forgiveness of others that immediately precedes a request for forgiveness from God. 'Each day has enough trouble of its own' (v 34c, peculiar to this gospel). Matthew conforms the two clauses in this petition to each other in a wholesale fashion. Such conformation makes it unnecessary to suppose translational variants of an Aramaic perfectum praesens in Matthew's ἀφήκαμεν and Luke's ἀφίομεν. Matthew has simply assimilated the verb to its aorist tense in the first clause. At most, the Aramaic perfectum praesens is a happy coincidence."

Davies and Allison 1988, 611: "one might argue that Matthew conformed 12b to 12a (both have the aorist tense, both end in ἡμῶν, and τοῖς ὀφειλέταις better parallels τὰ ὀφειλήματα than does Luke's παντὶ ὀφείλοντι). Moreover, while with ἀφίημι Matthew generally has either ἁμαρτία (9.2,5,6; 12.31) or παραπτώματα (6.14,15), τὴν ὀφειλὴν ... ἀφῆκά σοι does occur in 18.32, which belongs to M material. So the case for redactional activity in Mt 6.12b is, on the whole, strong."

Evaluations

Carruth 1995: Matt = Q {A}, (ὡς)² καὶ (ἡμεῖς)³ ἀφ(ήκα)⁴μεν.

Although it is not unanimous, scholarly opinion is largely in favor of the Matthean reading as representing Q. While Gundry argues that Matthew's tense is redactional to correspond to the tense of ἄφες, the general confidence in a Lukan change to correspond to his other changes, namely, δίδου for δός and τὸ καθ' ἡμέραν for σήμερον (Schmid, Schulz, Noland), is a more convincing basis for thinking that Luke is responsible for a change here as well.

Robinson 1995: Matt = Q {A}, (ὡς)² καὶ (ἡμεῖς)³ ἀφ(ήκα)⁴μεν.

The present tense in Mark 11:25 ἀφίετε // Matt 6:14-15 ἀφῆτε and *Did.* 8:2 (ἀφίεμεν) agrees with Luke, but all this may be the later generalized Christian policy of forgiving debts or sins whenever the occasion arises. Even if Mark 11:25 echoes Matthew's secondary form of the Prayer in ὁ πατὴρ ὑμῶν ὁ ἐν τοῖς οὐρανοῖς (the only occurrence outside of Matthew), he could have altered Matthew's tense within the Prayer to bring the Prayer up to date, and hence cannot be easily used as documentation for the present tense having been in Q. Matthew, following Mark 11:25-26, made the same shift to the present in his commentary to the Prayer in Matt 6:14-15.

The aorist in Matthew may be older and original, reflecting the renunciation of all worldly security at the time of conversion. This decision fits the general position of preferring the aorist (Q 11:3^1) and the specific (Q 11:3^2) throughout the Prayer and ascribing the changes in wording to Luke.

Kloppenborg 1995: Matt = Q {A}, (ὡς)^2 καὶ (ἡμεῖς)^3 ἀφ(ήκα)^{4}μεν.
Agreed: this change is consistent with those introduced by Luke in 11:3.

Q 11:4⁵: Luke's παντί or Matthew's τοῖς.

Luke = Q: [παντὶ]⁵ ὀφείλ[οντι]⁵·⁶

Pro

Wrege 1968, 104: "Zumindest unwahrscheinlich ist es schließlich, daß Lk παντὶ ὀφείλοντι ohne Artikel geschrieben haben sollte: er wird hier wie in 6,30 vielmehr seiner Vorlage folgen."

Jeremias 1980, 144: "Substantiviertes Partizip nach πᾶς ('jeder') schreibt Lukas mit Vorliebe, wie die folgenden Zahlen erkennen lassen: Matt 17, Mark 2, Doppelwerk 51 (27/24), Joh 13. Vgl. noch zur Vorliebe des Lukas für πᾶς, cf. 1,10 Red und zu seiner Vorliebe für Partizipien, cf. 4,5 Red. Ganz anders liegt es bei der Wendung πᾶς + Partizip *ohne* Artikel. Sie findet sich bei Lukas nur ganz vereinzelt, nämlich an unserer Stelle [Luke 6:30] παντὶ αἰτοῦντί σε δίδου und 11,4 ἀφίομεν παντὶ ὀφείλοντι ἡμῖν. Die Seltenheit der Belege zeigt, daß wir es mit nicht-lukanischem Sprachgebrauch zu tun haben; der zweite Beleg stammt ja auch aus dem sicher vorlukanischen Vaterunser."

195: "Substantiviertes Partizip mit πᾶς ohne Artikel ist vorlukanisch."

Mack 1993, 89: Reconstruction.

Schürmann 1994, 199¹⁸⁸: "πᾶς mit Partizip ohne Artikel in Lk/Apg nur noch Lk 6,30, also wohl vorluk."

Con

Plummer 1896, 296: See Q 11:4³ Luke = Q, Con.

297: "The introduction of παντί is in harmony with Luk.'s usage: see on vi. 30; vii. 35; ix. 43."

Wernle 1899, 68: "Für ὀφειλήματα hat Lc ἁμαρτίαι eingesetzt trotz der Fortsetzung, die er wieder individualisiert hat (παντί)."

von Harnack 1907, 48: "Endlich ist die Einschiebung von παντί (mit Partiz. statt Subst.) auch lukanisch, s. z. Matth. 5,42."

45: "Der Zusatz παντί des Luk. in [Matt 5] v. 42, findet sich auch in der 5. Bitte des VU. bei Luk. und sonst."

von Harnack 1907, ET 1908, 65: "the interpolation of παντί (with participle instead of substantive) is also Lukan."

20: "The Lukan insertion of παντί in St. Matthew verse [5:]42, is also found in the Lukan version of the fifth petition of the Lord's Prayer and elsewhere in St. Luke."

B. Weiß 1907, 72¹: "Daß das ὡς καὶ ἡμεῖς ἀφήκαμεν Mt. 6,12 durch das καὶ γὰρ αὐτοὶ ἀφίομεν im Sinne von Mt. 18,35 dahin gedeutet ist, daß der

Beter sich bewußt sein muß, durch sein ständiges Verhalten der Erfüllung seiner Bitte nicht unwürdig zu sein, zeigt das παντὶ vor ὀφείλοντι."

Cadbury 1920, 115: "The prevailing faithfulness of Luke's reproduction of his source is the more impressive when we observe that in details he inclines to generalization, ἅπας, πᾶς, ἕκαστος are favorite words of his, and are sometimes added to his sources." Cadbury then lists places where Luke has added ἅπας or πᾶς to his source. Mk 1,34-Lk 4,40; Mk 3,5-Lk 6,10; Mk 3,7-Lk 6,17; Mt 5,42-Lk 6,30 (Q); Mt 11,19-Lk 7,35(Q); Mk 6,7-Lk 9,1; Mk 6,14-Lk 9,7; Mt 6,12-Lk 11,4(Q); Mk 10,21-Lk 18,22; Mt 7,23-Lk 13,27(Q). Further Luke uses these words to add a general term to those already specific: Mt 23,23-Lk 11,42(Q); Mt 8,11-Lk 13,28(Q); Mk 13,28-Lk 21,29; Mk 15,39-Lk 23,48; Mk 15,40-Lk 23,49. Finally, Luke also uses πᾶς to express generalizations where the word is not used in the parallels: Lk 3,16-Mt 3,11, Mk 1,7(Q); Lk 7,18-Mt 11,2(Q); Lk 8,40-Mk 5,21; Lk 9,43-Mk 9,27.30; Lk 18,43-Mk 10,52; Lk 19,37-Mk 11,9; Lk 24,9-Mk 16,8.

Lagrange 1921, 324: "—παντί, style de Lc. vi,30; vii,35; ix,43."

Creed 1930, 157: "παντὶ ὀφείλοντι is Lucan, cf. vi.30,40; xiv.11 xviii.14."

Schmid 1930, 161²: "Lk liebt πᾶς und ἅπας mehr als die anderen ntl Autoren."

Bussmann 1929, 67: "[Lukas wird] auch das παντί zugesetzt haben."

Soiron 1941, 328: See Q 11:4⁴ Luke = Q, Con.

Jeremias 1967, 15: "Außerdem [the shift from perfect to present] ist in der von Lukas gebotenen Fassung die Vergebungsbitte um den Zusatz 'einem jeden' erweitert, der eine Verschärfung darstellt, indem er betont, daß es keine Ausnahme geben dürfe bei unserem Vergeben."

Jeremias 1967, ET 1964, 14: "in the Lucan form, the petition on forgiveness is broadened by the addition of the word 'everyone,' which represents a sharpening of the meaning, in that it permits no exceptions in our forgiving."

Schulz 1972, 85: "Endlich wird auch die Einschiebung von παντί vor dem Partizip ὀφείλοντι auf Lk zurückgehen."

85²⁰⁰: "Dieselbe Korrektur findet sich in Lk 6,30."

Dupont 1973, 624¹: "Noter aussi ... au v. 4b, l'addition de παντί, qui va de pair avec l'emploi d'un présent au lieu de l'aoriste (retouche analogue au v. 3 ...)."

Schweizer 1973, 93: "Auf Umgestaltung in der lukanischen Gemeinde deutet ... die Formulierung des Nachsatzes: 'denn auch wir vergeben jedem, der uns schuldig wird'."

Schweizer 1973, ET 1975, 149: "There are also other suggestions of reworking in Luke: he uses ... different wording in the apodosis—'for we, too, forgive whoever wrongs us.'"

Schneider 1977, 258: "Der Charakter der Selbstverpflichtung wird bei Lukas durch die Einschaltung von 'jedem' unterstrichen."

Marshall 1978, 461: "The insertion of παντί may be Lucan."

Fitzmyer 1985, 897: "[Luke] has further altered the perf. *aphēkamen*, 'we have forgiven', to a more general pres. *aphiomen*, 'we forgive,' and made 'debtors' more universal 'everyone who does wrong to us.'"

Lambrecht 1985, 132: "The Lucan generalization 'everyone' and the emphasis created by the addition of 'ourselves' betray ... a more reflexive character than the Matthean parallel and witnesses to a later stage."

Luz 1985, 335-336: "Umgekehrt [to the expansion of the Lord's Prayer by Matthew] sind die Änderungen des Lk am Wortlaut der beiden [336] Wir-Bitten sekundär: Sie spiegeln die Parusieverzögerung (δίδου Imp Praes τὸ καθ' ἡμέραν) und den paränetischen Gebrauch (παντὶ ὀφείλοντι)."

Luz 1985, ET 1989, 371: "By contrast [to the expansion of the Lord's Prayer by Matthew], the changes of Luke in the wording of the two we-petitions are secondary; they mirror the delay of the parousia (δίδου, imperative present; τὸ καθ' ἡμέραν)."

Schneider 1985, 68³⁷: "*Pas* mit folgendem substantiviertem Partizip (ohne Artikel) steht im NT selten. Blaß/Debrunner, *Grammatik*, §413, 2, nennen als Beispiele nur Mt 13,19 (diff Mk 4,15); Lk 6,30 (diff Mt 5,42 ...); Lk 11,4b (diff Mt 6,12b); Apk 22,15. Beide Evangelisten verwenden die Konstruktion offensichtlich redaktionell. Nur an den beiden Lk-Stellen folgt auf die besagte Konstruktion ein personal-pronominales Objekt."

Nolland 1993, 617: "Since Luke seems to have been the one who has intervened in this sentence, the singular participle, with its qualifying 'everyone' in place of Matthew's plural noun for the object, is best attributed to Luke's pen as well."

618: "The Lukan change to παντί, 'everyone,' with the singular adds emphasis but does not change the meaning of the Matthean form. Though he has changed from the noun form to the participial form, Luke retains here the use of the imagery of the debt in connection with sin, which he has excluded from the previous clause."

Matt = Q: (τοῖς)⁵ ὀφειλ(έταις)⁵·⁶

Pro

B. Weiß 1908, 31: Reconstruction.
Castor 1912, 230: Reconstruction.
Polag 1979, 48: Reconstruction.
Schenk 1981, 61: Reconstruction.

Zeller 1984, 56: Reconstruction.
Davies and Allison 1988, 591: Reconstruction.
Taussig 1988, 25: Reconstruction.
International Q Project 1990, 500: τοῖς ὀφειλέταις ἡμῶν.
Kloppenborg 1990, 49: Reconstruction.

Con

Gundry 1982, 108: "Also for the sake of parallelism, Matthew changes Luke's participle ὀφείλοντι to the noun ὀφειλέταις (cf. the corresponding noun ὀφειλήματα). For the same reason he switches from the singular of debtor to the plural and drops 'everyone.'"

Evaluations

Carruth 1995: Matt = Q {A}, (τοῖς)⁵ ὀφειλ(έταις)⁵·⁶.
In spite of the observation of Jeremias and Schürmann that πᾶς + a participle without an article is not Lukan, Luke's incontestable preference for adding a generalizing expression such as πᾶς and his generalizing intervention elsewhere in the Prayer makes it likely that it was added by him here. It can also be seen as a secondary emphasis.

Robinson 1995: Matt = Q {B}, (τοῖς)⁵ ὀφειλ(έταις)⁵·⁶.
Luke has replaced the article with παντί both here and at Q 6:30. Since he also made the same change in both sayings from δός to δίδου, he obviously identified the two passages and made in both cases the same generalizing interpretation. Thus in both cases παντί is Lucan redaction.
The shift from Matthew's plural, if in Q, to Luke's singular may have been caused by Luke introducing the singular παντί, which in effect embraces a plurality.

Kloppenborg: 1995: Matt = Q {B}, (τοῖς)⁵ ὀφειλ(έταις)⁵·⁶.
Luke's generalizing tendency, especially in matters that pertain to abandonment of wealth, is well attested and justifies viewing πᾶς as redactional. Once this is done, the choice is almost inevitably in favour of Matthew.

Q 11:4[6]: Luke's ὀφείλοντι ἡμῖν or Matthew's ὀφειλέταις ἡμῶν.

Luke = Q: ὀφείλ[οντι][5.6] ἡμ[ῖ][6]ν·

Pro

Davies and Allison 1988, 591: Reconstruction.

Mack 1993, 89: Reconstruction.

Schürmann 1994, 199: "Daß die Partizipialform ὀφείλοντι die Q-Fassung sein kann, zeigt Lk 6,30 par Mt 5,42—ein Logion, das in der Lk-Fassung diff Mt auch sonst unter dem Einfluß der geläufigen stereotypen Fassung des Gebetes Lk 11,3-4 gestanden haben kann[188]."

199[188]: "Vgl. παντί ... δίδου. Eine solche Annahme hat wohl mehr Wahrscheinlichkeit als die einer unabhängigen—zweimaligen gleichlautenden—Änderung des Lukas, die meist ... angenommen wird."

Con

Cadbury 1920, 133-137: Cadbury discusses the various ways in which Luke alters Mark by substituting a participle for another construction. On p. 136 he notes Luke 11:4 in comparison with Matt 6:12 in connection with the examples of Luke's substitution of a participle for a relative clause. On pp. 135-136 he lists 10 other instances in Q contexts where Matthew has a relative clause and Luke has a participle. They are Matt 5:39//Luke 6:29; Matt 7:24//Luke 6:47; Matt 7:24//Luke 6:48; Matt 7:26//Luke 6:49; Matt 23:35//Luke 11:51; Matt 10:33//Luke 12:9; Matt 12:32//Luke 12:10; Matt 23:12//Luke 14:11; 18:14; Matt 5:32//Luke 16:18.

Lagrange 1923, 130: "La formule de Mt. 'nos dettes' garde l'image transcrite par Lc. en 'nos péchés'. De même 'nos débiteurs' est moins élégant que παντὶ ὀφείλοντι ἡμῖν. Si l'on reconnaît ses retouches de Lc., pourquoi ne pas reconnaître aussi ses retranchements?"

Abrahams 1924, 95: See Q 11:4[1] Luke = Q, Con.

Schmid 1930, 134[5]: "Das substantivierte Partizip ist für Lk charakteristisch."

Soiron 1941, 328: See Q 11:4[4] Luke = Q, Con.

Schweizer 1973, 93: "Auf Umgestaltung in der lukanischen Gemeinde deutet ... die Formulierung des Nachsatzes: 'denn auch wir vergeben jedem, der uns schuldig wird'."

Schweizer 1973, ET 1975, 149: "There are also other suggestions of reworking in Luke: he uses ... different wording in the apodosis—'for we, too, forgive whoever wrongs us.'"

Luz 1985, 335-336 [ET 371]: See Q 11:4[5] Luke = Q, Con.

Sand 1986, 126: See Q 11:4⁴ Luke = Q, Con.

Nolland 1993, 617: "Since Luke seems to have been the one who has intervened in this sentence, the singular participle, with its qualifying 'everyone' in place of Matthew's plural noun for the object, is best attributed to Luke's pen as well."

618: "The Lukan change to παντί, 'everyone,' with the singular adds emphasis but does not change the meaning of the Matthean form. Though he has changed from the noun form to the participial form, Luke retains here the use of the imagery of the debt in connection with sin, which he has excluded from the previous clause."

Meier 1994, 355: See Q 11:4¹ Luke = Q, Con.

Matt = Q: ὀφειλ(έταις)⁵·⁶ ἡμ(ῶ)⁶ν·

Pro

B. Weiß 1908, 31: Reconstruction.
Castor 1912, 230: Reconstruction.
Polag 1979, 48: Reconstruction.
Taussig 1988, 25: Reconstruction.
International Q Project 1990, 500: ὀφειλέταις ἡμῶν.
Kloppenborg 1990, 49: Reconstruction.

Con

Gundry 1982, 108: See Q 11:4⁵ Matt = Q, Con.

Schneider 1985, 69: "Mt 6,12b erwähnt der Beter, daß er zuvor seinen 'Schuldnern' vergeben hat. Da in der Wir-Form gesprochen ist, kann das heißen: Jeder für sich hat seinem Schuldner vergeben. Lk 11,4b ist in seinen Abweichungen von Mt 6,12b im ganzen sekundär [See Q 11:4¹·²·⁴·⁵ Luke = Q, Con]. Die Verschärfung bezieht sich auf die *immerwährende* sowie *alle* Schuldner betreffende Vergebungsbereitschaft."

Davies and Allison 1988, 611: See Q 11:4⁴ Matt = Q, Con.

Evaluations

Carruth 1995: Matt = Q {A}, ὀφειλ(έταις)⁵·⁶ ἡμ(ῶ)⁶ν.

Cadbury gives extensive evidence for instances in which Luke has substituted a participle for various constructions in Mark. He also shows instances of Q sayings where Luke has a participle and Matthew has another construction. Since it can clearly be seen that the differences between Mark and Luke are the result of Luke's preference for the use of participles, it is reasonable to conclude that Luke alters Q in the same way here.

Davies and Allison suggest that Matthew has made the change because τοῖς ὀφειλέταις makes a better parallel with τὰ ὀφειλήματα than Luke's participle, but it is not clear that Matthew has otherwise intervened in the wording of the Prayer for the sake of parallelism. Thus, the best solution is that Matthew represents the Q wording at this point.

Robinson 1995: Matt = Q {B}, ὀφειλ(έταις)⁵·⁶ ἡμ(ῶ)⁶ν.

The use of the singular participle in Q 6:30 may have influenced Luke to assimilate here, since Luke clearly has Q 6:30 in view (as Lukan shifts in both sayings to παντί and δίδου indicate). If he changed both sayings twice to create new agreements, he could have changed here again to create still another agreement, adjusting Q 11:4 to fit the way Q 6:30 in this case already read.

It is not clear that Luke's preference for ὀφείλων is motivated by a desire to shift from debts to sins, since ὀφειλέτης also has both nuances.

Kloppenborg: 1995: Matt = Q {A}, ὀφειλ(έταις)⁵·⁶ ἡμ(ῶ)⁶ν.

The Lukan version is consistent with Luke's preference for participial construction, and his interest in stressing the extent of debt-forgiveness with πᾶς. There is no substantial reason to doubt Matthew's formulation.

Q 11:4⁷: Matthew's phrase ἀλλὰ ῥῦσαι ἡμᾶς ἀπὸ τοῦ πονηροῦ.

Luke = Q: ( )⁷

Pro

von Harnack 1907, 48: "Eine Urform (die Anrede πάτερ u. die 4.-6. Bitte) muß existiert haben, und nichts spricht dagegen, daß sie in Q stand."

von Harnack 1907, ET 1908, 65: "An original form ('πάτερ' and the fourth, fifth, and sixth petitions) must have existed, and there is nothing to say against it having stood in Q."

Loisy 1907, 599: "Les deux évangélistes dépendent, en dernière analyse, d'une même version grecque de l'Oraison dominicale, et Luc, qui en a gardé le préambule original, pourrait en avoir aussi mieux gardé le texte."

J. Weiß 1907, 290: "Um so unwahrscheinlicher ist, daß Lukas oder einer seiner Vorgänger sie absichtlich oder aus Versehen sollte ausgelaßen haben. Vielmehr muß geurteilt werden, daß er auch hiermit die ursprüngliche Form des Gebetes erhalten hat, und daß die siebente Bitte, ebenso wie die dritte ein Zusatz ist."

Castor 1912, 230: Reconstruction.

McNeile 1915, 76: "As regards the omission of clauses Lk.'s form is probably nearer to the original; he could not have omitted them had the longer form been known to him; and the tendency of liturgical formulas is towards enrichment rather than abbreviation."

Montefiore 1927, 99: "The form of the Lord's Prayer in Luke is shorter and perhaps more original. The *seven* petitions in Matthew are characteristic, for that holy number is a favourite with him."

Bussmann 1929, 67: "Im allgemeinen wird grade anerkannt, daß Mt eine Erweiterung in der Anrede und die Einfügung der dritten und letzten Bitte hat, während L [Luke] den ursprünglichen Text bietet. Denn was sollte ihn bewogen haben, die beiden Bitten wegzulassen; die Gründe, die dafür angeführt werden, lohnt es nicht zu widerlegen."

Manson 1937, 266: Reconstruction.

Hirsch 1941, 102: "Luk hat die zugrundeliegende Gestalt [of the Lord's Prayer] bis auf zwei Kleinigkeiten, die schon in Lu I geändert sein mögen, bewahrt, Matth aber hat erheblichere Erweiterungen des Vaterunsers vorgenommen."

Jeremias 1966, 158: See Q 11:4⁷ Matt = Q, Con.

Polag 1979, 48: Reconstruction.

Schenk 1981, 61: Reconstruction.

Schmithals 1980, 130: "Die uns geläufigere Form des 'Vater-Unser' findet sich Mat. 6,9-13; sie wurde gegenüber der Vorlage in der Spruchquelle Q, die

Lukas in V.2-4 im wesentlichen festgehalten hat, erst von Matthäus in die vorliegende Form gebracht."

Zeller 1984, 56: Reconstruction.

Fitzmyer 1985, 897: "In the number of impvs. [imperatives], the Lucan
form is undoubtedly closer to that of 'Q' and to the wording of Jesus himself.
... [The elements in Matthew's Prayer which are not in the Lukan Prayer],
which suit indeed the spirit of the prayer, have scarcely been excised by Luke."

Taussig 1988, 25: Reconstruction.

Stritzky 1989, 10-11: "In der Forschung, die sich mit dieser Problematik ausführlich auseinandergesetzt hat und sie mit dem hypothetischen Versuch einer
Rückübersetzung in die Ursprache einer Lösung zuführen wollte, hat sich die
Meinung durchgesetzt, daß das entscheidende Kriterium für die Ursprünglichkeit darin zu sehen ist, daß die Lukasfassung in der des Matthäus vollständig
enthalten ist. Der kürzere Text des Lukas, der mit seinen fünf Gebetsrufen wohl
den Inhalt des Gebetes Jesu [11] wiedergibt, dürfte der Urform ihrem Umfang
nach nahekommen, während die Mt-Rezension Zusätze bietet."

International Q Project 1990, 500: Reconstruction.

Kloppenborg 1990, 49: Reconstruction.

Jacobson 1992, 159: "But the idea that the father might not give good
things may relate instead to the Lord's Prayer (Q 11:2-4) which concludes
with the request to the father that the utterer not be led into temptation."

Catchpole 1993, 31: "But the same concern for deliverance is clear in
Luke's approach, for Jesus brings freedom for the prisoners (4:18; 13:16), that
is, deliverance from supernatural evil.⁶⁹ The petition in Matt 6:13b would
have been very congenial to him."

31⁶⁹: "Luke 7:21; 8:2; 11:26; Acts 19:11-12."

Mack 1993, 89: Reconstruction.

Hagner 1993, 145: "Jeremias is almost certainly correct in his conclusion
that Luke preserves an earlier form of the prayer (expansions are more likely
than omissions)."

Mell 1994, 158: Reconstruction.

Con

B. Weiß 1876, 188: "Wie Luc. durch Weglassung der dritten Bitte das
schöne Ebenmaß der zwei Gebetsdreiheiten aufgehoben hat, so hat er auch
die Harmonie der beiden doppelgliedrigen Bitten am Schlusse durch Weglassung des Gegensatzes in der letzten gestört."

B. Weiß 1878, 422: "Die zweite Hälfte von Matth. 6,13 lässt Luk. fort,
weil er in der Bewahrung vor der Versuchung bereits die Errettung vom Bösen
sah."

Resch 1895, 229-230: "Bezüglich der Quellenkritik ist *dreierlei* fest-zustellen: … dass Lc. nach seiner Gewohnheit kürzend, den [230] Quellentext nicht ohne wichtige Weglassungen, namentlich—wie häufig bei ihm—am Schlusse, reproduciert hat, während der Urtext von dem ersten Evangelisten in annähernder Vollständigkeit wiedergegeben sein dürfte."

B. Weiß 1901, 459: "Daraus ['dass unsere Evangelien nicht zu historischen, sondern zu erbaulichen Zwecken geschrieben sind'] erklärt sich auch am ein-fachsten die Verkürzung des Gebets bei Lk; denn dass die Fassung bei ihm die ursprüngliche sein sollte …, ist schon darum höchst unwahrscheinlich, weil, je höher allmählich die Werthschätzung dieses Gebets stieg, man um so weniger daran denken konnte, dasselbe mit eigenen Zusätzen zu erweitern, wird aber dadurch völlig ausgeschlossen, dass alle anderen Abweichungen des Lk durchaus sekundärer Natur sind und sich aus schriftstellerischen Motiven so leicht erklären, dass ihre Zurückführung auf Uebersetzungsfehler (Aufl. 8) ganz entbehrlich ist. Leicht begreiflich ist aber, dass man in einer Zeit, wo der Buchstabe der Herrnworte noch keineswegs als unantastbar galt, um es leichter behaltbar und darum gebräuchlicher zu machen, alles irgend Ent-behrliche fortliess."

B. Weiß 1907, 72¹: "Dass all diese Abweichungen von Matthäus auf schriftstellerischer Reflexion beruhen, macht es schlechthin undenkbar, dass Lukas in der Hauptabweichung das Ursprüngliche erhalten haben sollte."

Lagrange 1921, 321: "Luc a pu croire que ces mots [that are in Matthew but not in Luke] qui n'ajoutaient rien de substantiel étaient moins nécessaires aux gentils. D'autant que dans son text on reconnaît sa main: τὸ καθ᾽ ἡμέραν, αὐτοί, παντί. Son text paraît moins primitif; s'il a donné à son original sa couleur propre, ne pourrait-il pas aussi l'avoir abrégé? C'est ce qui nous paraît le plus probable."

Lagrange 1923, 124: "Sur les différences entre Mt. et Lc., voir le commen-taire de Lc., où nous essayons de montrer que c'est lui [Luke] qui a abrégé; le texte de Mt. [in all material additional to that in Luke's Prayer] est donc primitif."

Soiron 1941, 328: "Die siebte Bitte ist für Lk nur die Verdeutlichung der sechsten, die Abwendung der Versuchung verbürgt eben schon die Erlösung vom Übel. Deshalb wird sie von ihm unterdrückt."

Dupont 1958, 65¹: "le texte du Luc, beaucoup moins bien rythmé et balancé que celui de Matthieu, semble écourté."

Feldkämper 1978, 186: "Der 'fehlenden' 7. Bitte (Mt 6,13b) ῥῦσαι ἡμᾶς ἀπὸ τοῦ πονηροῦ, die vielfach als eine andere Form der Reichsbitte verstanden wird, entspricht der Inhalt des Zusammenhanges [Luke] 11,14-26 von der Überwindung der dämonischen Mächte durch Jesus. Hier läge also ebenfalls ein 'Ersatz' für die 'fehlende' Bitte vor." But note 186¹⁶: "Die Frage nach der

Ursprünglichkeit der beiden VU-Fassungen braucht hier nicht behandelt zu werden. Unser Vergleich an dieser Stelle ist ausschließlich synchron."

Trudinger 1989, 51: Including this petition with other material in the Prayer Luke omitted for editorial or theological reasons, Trudinger says, "Also eliminated is any mention of the Evil One, who may not have been such a significant factor among those to whom Luke's Gospel was addressed. There is, be it noted, little reference comparatively speaking, to 'the Devil' in the book of the Acts of the Apostles."

Matt = Q: (ἀλλὰ ῥῦσαι ἡμᾶς ἀπὸ τοῦ πονηροῦ)[7]

Pro

B. Weiß 1876, 181-182: "Daß umgekehrt der erste Evangelist, der ohnehin die Quelle vollständiger und treuer zu reproduciren pflegt und das Gebet grade als Muster eines kurzen körnigen Gebets giebt, ihm eine Reihe von 'entbehrlichen' Zusätzen hinzugefügt haben sollte (vgl. besonders Camph.) ist ganz unwahrscheinlich und [182] wird durch die zu Tage liegende secundäre Gestalt der übereinstimmenden Bitten bei Luc. völlig ausgeschlossen."

von der Goltz 1901, 42: "Was Mt. über Lc. hinaus mehr hat, sind durchaus dem Geist des Herrn entsprechende Bitten, ob sie nun formell ursprünglich hierher gehören oder nicht. Die Annahme späterer Hinzufügung ist durchaus möglich, aber von dem Bedenken gedrückt, ob die Bitten, wenn später eingefügt, auch so einfach und wahr, den übrigen in Form und Geist entsprechend aussehen würden. Die Auslassung erklärt sich leichter bei der freien Auffassung der Bedeutung des Gebets, die wir auch zur Zeit der Abfassung des Lukasevangeliums noch voraussetzen können."

Klein 1906, 35: "Nach meinem Dafürhalten besitzen wir die Urgestalt des Vaterunsers bei Matthäus; denn nur in dieser Form entspricht es den Anforderungen, die an ein *jüdisches* Gebet gestellt wurden.

"Nach Ps 119,164 wurden sieben Eulogien für den Tag festgesetzt. Daher kannte man vor der Zerstörung des Tempels nur Birkath Scheba, das 'Sieben-Gebet'.—Das Vaterunser mit der Schlußdoxologie besteht aus sieben Bitten.

"Ein Gebet soll aus drei Teilen bestehen. Es beginnt mit einem Hymnus, mit einer Verherrlichung Gottes (שבח). Darauf folge das individuelle Gebet (תפלה) und den Schluß bilde eine Doxologie, eine Danksagung (הודיה). — Diese Ordnung findet sich auch im Vaterunser. —Die ersten drei Bitten enthalten eine Verherrlichung Gottes, denn Gottes Name wird verherrlicht, wenn sein Reich kommt und sein Wille geschieht. Die mittleren drei Bitten enthalten die eigentliche Tefillah, das individuelle Gebet. Und die siebente Bitte enthält die Doxologie."

39-40: "Für die *siebente* und letzte Bitte endlich findet sich zwar keine Parallele, aber ich halte es nicht für unmöglich, daß sie von Jesus selbst herrührt. Zunächst konnte Jesus nicht mit 'Bösem' schließen. Nach jüdischem Denken und Fühlen mußte man בדבר טוב mit etwas Gutem [40] schließen.[1] Das geht schon bis auf die prophetische Zeit zurück. Daraus erklären sich manche Zusätze zu den Propheten. Dasselbe Verfahren findet sich auch in der Mischna."

40[1]: "Jer. Meg. 5,7. Soferim 12. Maimonides M. Th. Hilch. Tefilla 13."

B. Weiß 1907, 72: "jedenfalls ist eine Erweiterung des Gebets durch Matthäus, nachdem Jesus eben noch vor den 'vielen Worten' gewarnt hatte, durchaus unwahrscheinlich."

B. Weiß 1908, 31: Reconstruction.

Lagrange 1923, 124: "le texte de Mt. [in all material additional to that in Luke's Prayer] est donc primitif."

132: "Aucune raison de penser que Jésus lui-même n'a pas enseigné ainsi la dernière demande. C'est plutôt Luc qui a abrégé à son habitude."

Dupont 1958, 65[1]: "Chez Matthieu, trois demandes simples, puis trois demandes doubles; la dernière de chaque groupe est un peu plus développée, de manière à marquer la pause. C'est du style oral (cf. les deux séries de trois recommandations parallèles en Luc, 11,9-10 = Mat., 7,7-8) à cet égard, le texte de Matthieu est plus satisfaisant que celui de Luc."

Ott 1965, 122-123: "Wie ein Vergleich des Vaterunsers des Matthäus mit dem Vaterunser-Text der Didache (8,2) zeigt, wird man annehmen dürften, daß schon zu der Zeit, als Lukas schrieb, das Vaterunser als Gebetsformular seine endgültige Gestalt—die im Matthäusevangelium überlieferte—im wesentlichen angenommen hatte. Wenn der Lukastext nicht eine Überarbeitung dieses Gebetsformulars, sondern eine—ebenfalls verbreitete—kürzere Variante des Vaterunsers wäre, wäre es äußerst unwahrscheinlich, daß die matthäische Form des Vaterunsers die lukanische so schnell und spurlos verdrängt hätte, daß sich in den Handschriften zwar eine große Zahl von Angleichungen des Lukastextes an den Matthäustext finden, die schon sehr früh einsetzen, aber bisher keine Handschrift bekannt ist—in den Apparaten der kritischen Ausgaben ist jedenfalls keine solche verzeichnet—, die den Matthäustext an den ihrem Schreiber vielleicht geläufigeren kürzeren und auch sonst abweichenden Lukastext angleicht. G. Klein, *ZNW* 7 (1906) 35 tritt wohl nicht ohne Recht dafür ein, daß wir die Urgestalt des Vaterunsers bei Matthäus besitzen, 'denn nur in dieser Form entspricht es den Anforderungen, die an ein jüdisches Gebet gestellt wurden', wie er in seinem Aufsatz des weiteren nachweist. Selbst Lohmeyer, der für zwei nebeneinander bestehende Traditionen eintritt, erkennt die 'jüngere Herkunft' der lukanischen Form des Vaterunsers an (VU 210). Lagrange dürfte also recht behalten, wenn er feststellt: 'La forme de Mt. semble être la forme liturgique usitée chez les chrétiens.'... Der Text des Lukas 'paraît moins primitif s'il a donné à son original sa couleur propre, ne pourrait-il pas aussi l'avoir abrégé? C'est ce qui nous paraît le plus probable' (*Lk-Komm.* 321). Aus all dem ergibt sich mit großer Sicherheit, daß das lukanische Vaterunser eine Überarbeitung und Verkürzung des Vaterunsers in der matthäischen Form darstellt, die weder vor noch neben der matthäischen Gestalt als in den frühchristlichen Gemeinden gebräuchliches Gebetsformular einige Verbreitung gefunden hat. Die lukanische Form des Vaterunsers hat als lukanische Überarbeitung des Gebetsformulars ihren Platz innerhalb der lukanischen Gebetsparänese. Innerhalb dieser lukanischen Gebetsparänese ist es nicht mehr 'nicht vorstellbar, daß Lukas dieses Gebet verkürzt hätte, wenn er es in der Matthäusfassung vorgefunden hätte' (so Schmid *Mt-Komm.* 122), zumal wenn es zutrifft (wie Schmid selbst anerkennt), daß Lukas den Text nicht als ein Gebetsformular [123] verstanden hat, sondern als 'ein Muster eines inhaltsreichen und echt christlichen Gebets' (*Lk-Komm.* 197)."

Crossan 1983, 98: "I propose (i) that the Lord's Prayer was earlier but secret Q tradition (ii) that it was known to Q in the Jewish-Christian seven-petition form that was accepted in Matt. 6:9-13 but changed to the Gentile-Christian five-petition format by Luke 11:2-4 (see Jeremias, 1967a: 89) and (iii) that it was acceptable to the later Q theology only as commented on by Aphorisms 67-68 [Q 11:9-13]."

Con

Plummer 1896, 294: "The widespread omission is inexplicable, if the three clauses are genuine; the widespread insertion is quite intelligible, if they are not."

von Harnack 1907, 48: "Was sich darüber hinaus [the address πάτερ and the so-called fourth through sixth petitions] bei Matth. findet, sind Zusätze, die sich die judenchristlichen Urgemeinden gestattet haben, als sie das gemeinschaftliche Gebet in ein solennes Gemeindegebet unter starker Anlehnung an die synagogalen Gebete verwandelten, oder sie stammen von Matth. selbst."

von Harnack 1907, ET 1908, 64: "All the other clauses found in St. Matthew [the address πάτερ and the so-called fourth through sixth petitions] are either accretions which attached themselves to the common prayer during the process of transformation into a solemn congregational prayer in the primitive Jewish Christian communities and under the dominating influence of the prayers of the synagogue, or they were added by St. Matthew himself."

Loisy 1907, 600: "l'usage liturgique explique aisément l'amplification de la formule, un peu courte, de Luc."

Castor 1912, 53-54: "'Thy will be done on earth as it is in heaven' is only a further definition of 'Thy kingdom come.' So also 'Deliver us from evil' only states in a positive form what 'Lead us not into temptation' expresses negatively. These clauses amplify, but they add no new element of thought; nor do they contain anything distinctively Jewish which Gentiles would have any reason to omit. The very reverse is [54] nearer the truth. Both petitions are to be explained as interpretative additions due to liturgical use, and not as Lukan omissions."

Haupt 1913, 85: "Bemerke ..., wie die hier gebrauchten Ausdrücke im Sondergut des Mt wiederkehren: ... ὁ (τὸ?) πονηρός cf. 5,37,39; 13,19,38."

von Dobschütz 1914, 317: "It is therefore unfit for his prayer and evidently again a later addition when Matthew adds here, 'but deliver us from the evil one.'"

Cadbury 1920, 85: "Matthew is fond of formulas, and may have been scrupulous in rounding out the parallel members of comparisons."

88: Cadbury lists eight places in Q where "one of two parallel or antithetical clauses is absent from Luke ...": Matt. 5,43-Luke 6,29; Matt. 10,24-Luke 6,40; Matt. 7,12-Luke 6,43; Matt. 13,16-Luke 10,23; Matt. 6,13-Luke 11,4; Matt. 6,19-Luke 12,33; Matt. 7,13-Luke 13,24; Matt. 10,37-Luke 14,26.

Zahn 1920, 448: "Die ... bei Lc fehlende 7. Bitte [ist] eine Erweiterung der negativen 6. Bitte in positiver Form."

449: "die spätere Einfügung der 3. und 7. Bitte bei Mt ist wahrscheinlicher, als nachträgliche Tilgung derselben durch Lc oder seine Gewährsmänner."

Abrahams 1924, 100-101: "The phrase 'Thy will be done' [Matt 6:10b] by itself [101] might be original (cf. Matt. xxvi. 42, Luke xxii. 42) but hardly in this context. Then, too, it is difficult to resist the suggestion that the final petition (ἀλλὰ ῥῦσαι ἡμᾶς ἀπὸ τοῦ πονηροῦ) has a reference to the Jewish doctrine of the evil yeser. Luke's omission of it (in certain MSS) confirms the suggestion that the phrase is redactionary in Matthew."

Loisy 1924, 316: "Ne sont aucunement représentées [in Luke's prayer] la troisième demande de Matthieu ... et la dernière: 'mais délivre-nous du mal', qui n'appartenaient probablement ni l'une ni l'autre à la forme primitive de la prière."

Easton 1926, 177: "The final clause of Mt v.13 contains a theological reference of evil to Satan, which is certainly a gloss (J. Weiß)."

Klostermann 1927, 59: "Sie [the seventh petition] fehlt bei Lc und mag mit ihrem Anklang an synagogale Gebete um endliche Erlösung Israels späterer Zuwachs sein."

Bacon 1930, 276: The petition is printed in bold-face italics to indicate Bacon's opinion that it is a supplementation by the evangelist.

Creed 1930, 155: "The Matthaean version is fuller than the Lucan and probably reflects the influence of liturgical usage upon a simpler form similar to that given in Lk."

Hirsch 1941, 101-102: "Bei Matth ... sind folgende Änderungen einge-treten: ... d) Der Bitte gegen die Versuchung ist als letzte Bitte die gegen den Versucher [102] den Bösen hinzugefügt."

Kilpatrick 1946, 21: "The last clause, ἀλλὰ ῥῦσαι ἡμᾶς ἀπὸ τοῦ πονηροῦ, is unique in the Gospels. ῥύεσθαι is not a common word, occurring again at xxvii. 43, a quotation in a Marcan context from Ps. xxii. 8, and at Luke i. 74 in the Benedictus and elsewhere only in the Epistles. Πονηρός is a Matthean word. Twice in Mark, it occurs eight times in Q, eleven times in Luke, and twenty-four times in Matthew. It is due to the evangelist at ix. 4, xii. 34, and pos-sibly at xii. 45, xiii. 19,28,49, xxii. 10. ... The evidence of style and context seems to be strongly in favour of the view that the elements which do not derive from Q were composed by the evangelist."

Schmid 1956, 122: "Von den sieben Bitten im Matthäus-Text fehlen bei Lukas die dritte ... und die siebente. ... Es ist nicht vorstellbar, daß Lukas dieses Gebet verkürzt hätte, wenn er es in der Matthäus-Fassung vorgefunden hätte. Andererseits kann man die dritte Bitte als eine sachliche Erläuterung der zweiten und die siebente als eine Ergänzung der negativen sechsten in positiver Form (Zahn) verstehen."

Knox 1957, 61: "The prayer no doubt existed in the liturgical use of the Church quite apart from the tract, and Matthew has substituted the version of his own Church for that of the source, the longer Matthean version being presumably an expansion of the original."

Beare 1962, 61: "The comparison between the version of the prayer found in Matthew and that which is given by Luke indicates that the Matthaean additions have resulted from liturgical shaping."

Brown 1965, 220: "It is much more likely that the Matthean tradition represents a prayer to whose original petitions have been joined other say-ings of Jesus. This is a well-attested phenomenon in Mt, for Mt's eight beat-itudes (as compared to Lk's four) and Mt's long Sermon on the Mount (as compared to Lk's shorter Sermon on the Plain) represent conflations of material."

Jeremias 1966, 158: "So werden wir also in dem gemeinsamen Bestand, d.h. in der Lukas-Fassung, den ältesten Text zu erblicken haben. Die heiden-christliche Kirche hat ihn uns aufbewahrt, während die judenchristliche Kirche, die aus einer Welt reicher liturgischer Schätze und vielfältiger liturgi-scher Gebetsübung kam, das Vater-Unser ausgestaltete."

Davies 1966, 4: "'But deliver us from evil' is best understood as a liturgical formulation."

Jeremias 1967, 12: "die lukanische Kurzform ist in der Matthäus-Fassung vollständig enthalten. Nach allem, was wir über die Gesetzmäßigkeit der Überlieferung liturgischer Texte wissen, hat in einem solchen Fall, in dem die kürzere Fassung in der längeren enthalten ist, die kürzere als die ursprünglichere zu gelten. Wer sollte es gewagt haben, zwei Bitten des Vater-Unsers zu streichen, wenn sie zum ältesten Überlieferungsbestand gehörten? Dagegen ist das Umgekehrte, daß liturgische Texte in der Frühzeit, ehe eine Verfestigung der Formulierung eintrat, ausgestaltet, erweitert, angereichert werden, vielfältig belegt. Dieser Schluß, daß die Matthäusfassung eine Erweiterung darstellt, wird durch weitere Beobachtungen bestätigt. Einmal finden sich die drei Matthäus-Überschüsse am Schluß, nämlich am Schluß der Anrede, am Schluß der Du-Bitten und am Schluß der Wir-Bitten; das entspricht genau dem, was wir auch sonst beim Wachstum liturgischer Texte beobachten: sie lieben den volltönenden Abschluß. Weiter ist bezeichnend, daß bei Matthäus der stilistische Aufbau weiter durchgegliedert ist: den drei Wir-Bitten (die 6. und 7. Matthäus-Bitte hat man als eine Bitte empfunden) entsprechen bei ihm drei Du-Bitten; und die bei Lukas durch ihre Kürze abrupt wirkende dritte Wir-Bitte ist bei Matthäus in der Länge und Zweiteiligkeit den beiden ersten Wir-Bitten angeglichen. ... Dieses Bestreben, den Gleichklang der Glieder (Parallelismus membrorum) herzustellen, ist ein Kennzeichen liturgischer Überlieferung."

Jeremias 1967, ET 1964, 11-12: "the shorter form of Luke is completely contained in the longer form of Matthew. This makes it very probable that the Matthean form is an expanded one, for according to all that we know about the tendency of liturgical texts to conform to certain laws in their transmission, in a case where the shorter version is contained in the longer one, the shorter text is to be regarded as original. No one would have dared to shorten a sacred text like the Lord's Prayer and to leave out two petitions if they had formed part of the original tradition. On the contrary, the reverse is amply attested, that in the early period, before wordings were fixed, liturgical texts were elaborated, expanded, and enriched. This conclusion, that the Matthean version represents an expansion, is confirmed by three supplementary observations. First, the three expansions which we find in Matthew, as compared with Luke, are always found toward the end of a section of the prayer—the first at the end of the address, the second at the end of the 'Thou-petitions,' the third at the end of the 'We-petitions.' This again is exactly in accordance with what we find elsewhere in the growth of liturgical texts.

"Second, it is of further significance that in Matthew the stylistic structure is more consistently carried through. Three 'Thou-petitions' in Matthew correspond to the three 'We-petitions (the sixth and seventh petitions in Matthew were regarded as one petition). The third 'We-petition,' which in

Luke seems abrupt because of its brevity, is in Matthew assimilated to the first two 'We-petitions.' ... [12] ...
"This endeavor to produce parallelism in lines (*parallelismus membrorum*) is a characteristic of liturgical tradition."

Grundmann 1968, 203: "Matthäus hat dieser Bitte, die wie ein Notschrei das Gebet beendet, hinzugefügt: 'sondern reiße uns von dem Bösen weg'. Die beiden Hälften der letzten Bitte haben die Form eines antithetischen Parallelismus. Der Abfall lauert als Gefahr, er rührt von der Macht des Bösen her."

Wrege 1968, 104: "Für die 7. Bitte der Mt-Fassung gilt ähnliches: sie kehrt die zum gemeinsamen Mt/Lk-Bestand gehörende 6. Bitte um und ist diesem dadurch fest verbunden. Die zahlreichen Parallelen aus jüdischen Gebeten scheinen aber dafür zu sprechen, daß diese Umkehrung—wie bei den lk Seligpreisungen—erst sekundär in judenchristlichem Milieu zugewachsen ist. So würde sich das Fehlen der 7. Bitte bei Lk, aber auch ihre Überlieferung in einigen Lk-Handschriften und in der Didache erklären: der judenchristliche, vor-mt Zusatz hat sich in der Liturgie immer weiterer Gemeinden durchgesetzt."

Berger 1969, 1147: "Im ganzen dürfte das V. bei Mt ursprünglicher bewahrt sein (bis auf die Schlußbitte bei Mt)."

1150: "Die Schlußbitte, die bei Lk fehlt, dürfte matthäischen Ursprungs sein: Mt bezeichnet mit dem Stamm πονηρός alles, was als widergöttlicher Gegenpart der christlichen Gemeinde in der Endzeit gegenübersteht (vgl. Mt 13,19 mit Mk 4,15; Mt 5,37 39; 13,38)."

Schwarz 1968-69, 236: Schwarz attempts to discover the earliest form of the Prayer by relying heavily on an analysis of its structure and rhythm and says, "die letzte Bitte des Vater-Unsers, abgesehen von der matthäischen Erweiterung (ἀλλὰ ῥῦσαι ἡμᾶς ἀπὸ τοῦ πονηροῦ)—in beiden Fassungen Wort für Wort übereinstimmt."

Jeremias 1971, 189-190: "Die entscheidende Beobachtung bezüglich der Ursprünglichkeit ist, daß die Lukasfassung in der [190] Matthäusfassung vollständig enthalten ist. Da liturgische Texte die Tendenz haben, sich anzureichern, und der kürzere Wortlaut hier gewöhnlich der ältere ist, dürften die Überschüsse bei Matthäus Erweiterungen darstellen. Es ist unwahrscheinlich, daß jemand die dritte und siebte Bitte gestrichen haben sollte, während der umgekehrte Vorgang gut vorstellbar ist. Daß der kürzere Text der ältere ist, wird durch weitere Beobachtungen bestätigt. Die drei Überschüsse der Matthäusfassung finden sich jeweils an entsprechender Stelle im Text: am Ende der (ursprünglich nur aus einem Wort bestehenden) Anrede, am Ende der Du-Bitten und am Ende der Wir-Bitten. Das entspricht wiederum dem, was sich andernorts beobachten läßt: liturgische Texte werden gern volltönend abgeschlossen[79]. Für die Ursprünglichkeit des Lukasumfangs spricht schließlich, daß durch die von Matthäus überlieferten Zusätze der stilistische

Aufbau des Vaterunsers ausgeglichen wird. Insbesondere ergänzt die siebte Bitte den Parallelismus membrorum, dessen Fehlen in der lukanischen Schlußbitte sehr auffällig ist."

1907[9]: "Beispiele: Mt 26,28 verglichen mit den Paralleltexten; Phil 2,11."

Jeremias 1971, ET 1971, 195: "The most decisive feature in favour of originality is that the Lucan version is contained in its entirety within that of Matthew. As liturgical texts tend to be elaborated, and the shorter wording is usually the earlier, the additional material in Matthew may amount to elaborations. It is improbable that anyone should have deleted the third and seventh petitions, whereas the opposite process is easily imaginable. Further considerations confirm that the shorter text is the earlier. The three additional passages in the Matthaean version in each instance come at the same place in the text: at the end of the address (which originally consisted in only one word), at the end of the petitions in the second person, and at the end of the petitions in the first person plural. This also corresponds with what is to be observed elsewhere: there is a tendency to conclude liturgical texts with a full stress.[1] Finally, the fact that the additions transmitted by Matthew balance the stylistic construction of the Lord's Prayer also suggests that the Lucan version is original. In particular, the seventh petition completes the parallelism, the absence of which is very striking in the closing petition of Luke."

195[1]: "Examples: Matt. 26.28 compared with the parallel texts; Phil. 2.11."

Morgenthaler 1971, 191: "Jedenfalls steht 6:10b und 6:13b als S des Mt da."

Schulz 1972, 86: "*Die Bitten die sich nur bei Mt finden*: Die Kurzfassung des Lk ist nicht als Kürzung der Mt-Fassung zu erklären, sondern die Mt-Fassung wird, was die Zahl der Bitten anbelangt, gegenüber Lk sek sein. Das Vokabelmaterial des über Lk hinausgehenden Bitten verrät die Hand des Mt.[202]"

86[202]: "Ebenso [like Matt 6:10b] ist Mt 6,13b red: absolutes ὁ bzw τὸ πονηρός (όν) findet sich bei Mt ca 4mal red (5,37.39; 13,19.38?) allgemein ist πονηρός gut mt (ca 11mal red). ῥύεσθαι läßt allerdings einen sprachlichen Rückschluß nicht zu, da es nur noch einmal in einem AT-Zitat (27,43) vorkommt."

Schweizer 1973, 92: "Ein weiterer Zusatz ist bei Matthäus bei der letzten Bitte zugewachsen ('sondern erlöse uns von dem Bösen')."

Schweizer 1973, ET 1975, 148: "A further addition has been made by Matthew to the last petition ('but deliver us from evil')."

Edwards 1976, 107: "Recent research has emphasized the eschatological implications in the prayer, as well as the apparent earliness of Luke's version. Matthew's version shows all the signs of Jewish liturgical practice."

Schmithals 1980, 130: "Die uns geläufigere Form des 'Vater-Unser' findet sich Mat. 6,9-13; sie wurde gegenüber der Vorlage in der Spruchquelle Q, die

Lukas in V.2-4 im wesentlichen festgehalten hat, erst von Matthäus in die vorliegende Form gebracht."

Schürmann 1981, 20: "Die letzte Bitte ist [in Matthew] zu einem antithetischen Parallelismus ausgewachsen, der, das Gebet abrundend, den abrupten
Schluß der Lukas-Fassung etwas mildert."

112: "Die letzte Bitte gleicht bei Lukas einem kurzen Hilferuf. Die uns
gewohnte matthäische Fassung bindet diesen in einen Parallelismus ein. Es ist
schwer verständlich zu machen, daß Lukas die Bitte gestrichen haben soll.
Eher könnte die Überlieferung des Matthäus in Anlehnung an gewohnte
Gebete ergänzt und eine Siebenzahl von Bitten angestrebt haben, zugleich den
harten Abschluß 'liturgisch' ausformend."

Fitzmyer 1985, 897: "Matthew appended phrases: to the end of the opening address, to the end of the second-person wishes expressed to God, and to
the end of the first-pl. petitions asked of God."

Gundry 1982, 109: "But just as Matthew shifted the emphasis from future
to present in the coming of the kingdom and in the giving of bread, so here
his addition 'but deliver us from the evil one' shifts the reference of the temptation from the coming great tribulation to the current plight of Jesus' disciples. ... he adds the petition for deliverance from the evil one and not only
gains a couplet, but also ties the prayer to its new context, which deals with
the present evil age. πονηρός is a Mattheanism (10,4)."

Strecker 1982, 13: "Fragen wir nach dem ursprünglichen Wortlaut, also
der ältesten Traditionsschicht, so ist kaum zweifelhaft, daß Lukas dem Urtext
näher steht. Dies gilt zumindest für die Fünfzahl der Bitten, während die
Erweiterungen bei Matthäus einer späteren Überlieferungsstufe angehören."

Gerhardsson 1984, 210: "With any degree of probability we can attribute
only three additions to the Matthaean tradition (at the close of the invocation,
at the close of the 'thou-petitions' and at the close of the 'we-petitions')."

Schnackenburg 1984, 97: "Wenn Gott uns von dem Bösen erlösen soll,
gehört das eng als Erläuterung zu dem voranstehenden Satz ('sondern'). Die
'Versuchung', in die uns Gott nicht ... geraten lassen soll, ist eine solche, hinter der die Macht des Bösen steht. ... Wie für die matthäische Gemeinde ist
diese Bitte auch für uns hilfreich, um die 'Versuchung' zu verstehen; aber sie
dürfte noch nicht zum Urbestand des Vaterunsers gehören. Wenn die beiden
überschüssigen Gebetswünsche oder Bitten Lukas schon bekannt gewesen
wären, hätte er sie schwerlich weggelassen."

Schnackenburg 1984, ET 1995, 64: "If God is to deliver us from evil, that
is tied closely to the preceding clause as an elucidation ('but'). The 'temptation' into which God is not to have us slip is one behind which the power of
evil stands. If a person is exposed to such a salvation-threatening danger, that
person is too weak to withstand it on his or her own: the appendix which

forms a new petition is intended to express this. As it was for the Matthean
community, this petition is also to help us understand 'temptation'; however,
it may not belong to the original body of the Lord's Prayer. If the two remain-
ing prayer wishes or petitions had been known to Luke, he would hardly have
omitted them.'"

Luz 1985, 335: "Hilfreicher ist aber der Hinweis auf spontane Variationen
jüdischer Gebete. Sie machen sowohl die zusätzlichen Bitten bei Matthäus als
auch mögliche Veränderungen des Wortlauts verständlich. Die Ergänzungen
im vormt Unservater sind alle leicht als sekundäre Variationen zu verstehen:
… An die letzte Wir-Bitte wurde ein positiv formulierter Parallelsatz angefügt,
wodurch die Nähe zu den anderen Wir-Bitten und die Symmetrie des Ganzen
größer wurden."

Luz 1985, ET 1989, 370-371: "But the reference to spontaneous variations
of Jewish prayers is more helpful. They make understandable both the additional petitions [371] in Matthew and the possible alterations of the wording.
The supplements in the pre-Matthean Lord's Prayer are all easily understandable
as secondary variations: … A positively formulated parallel sentence was added
to the last we-petition whereby the closeness to the other we-petitions and the
symmetry of the whole became greater."

Schneider 1985, 62: "Die Traditionsgeschichte des Herrengebets zeigt, daß
wir es mit einem *Anwachsen* des Umfangs zu tun haben, wie es analog z.B.
auch in jüdischen Gebeten der Jesuszeit zu beobachten ist[19]. …

"Dieses traditionsgeschichtliche Anwachsen ging nach der Abfassung der
Evangelienschriften weiter. Die *Didache* (8,2) greift die Langform auf, die sich
Mt 6,9-13 findet,—möglicherweise unabhängig vom kanonischen Mt-Evangelium; doch sie bietet eine Erweiterung, die wiederum an die traditionelle Fassung 'angehängt' ist: 'Denn dein ist die Kraft und die Herrlichkeit in Ewigkeit.'"

62[19]: "Vgl. die beiden 'Rezensionen' des 18-Bitten-Gebets bei W. Staerk,
Altjüdische liturgische Gebete, Kleine Texte 58, Berlin, ²1930, 9-19, und die
deutsche Übersetzung bei (Strack/) Billerbeck, *Kommentar zum Neuen Testament aus Talmud und Midrasch*, I-IV, München, ²1956, IV, 1, 210-214 (unter
anderem die Zufügung der Birkath ha-minim), sowie das Kaddisch (Staerk,
a.a.O., 29-32)."

76-77: "Mt 6,13b ist sekundär an die dritte Wir-Bitte der Q-Fassung
angeschlossen. Damit bietet der neue Schluß des Vaterunsers eine positive
Bitte, wenngleich man Vers 13b im Sinne des Matthäus nicht als eigen-
ständige (siebente) Bitte bezeichnen sollte. Der sechsten Bitte geht es um
Bewahrung vor Versuchung. Da ihre positiv formulierte Ergänzung dem
'Hineinführen *in* Versuchung' gegenläufig das 'Erretten *von* dem Bösen'
anfügt—die Präpositionen *eis* und *apo* drücken gegensätzliche Richtungen aus
—, darf man annehmen, daß eher an *das* Böse als an *den* Bösen gedacht ist[71].

Die substantivierte [77] Verwendung von *poneros* wird im Neuen Testament bevorzugt von Mt bezeugt[72]. ... Von den insgesamt 15 gezählten Vorkommen des substantivierten *poneros* mit Artikel gehören immerhin vier dem Mt-Evangelium an, was hinsichtlich der Substantivierung an matthäische Redaktion denken läßt[74]."

76[71]: "Siehe den Parallelismus *hēmas eis peirasmon—hēmas apo tou ponērou*."

77[72]: "Greift man die ntl. Stellen heraus, an denen das Adjektiv substantiviert und mit Artikel vorkommt, ergibt sich der folgende Befund (bei dem auf böse Menschen bezogenes *ho ponēros/hoi ponēroi* ausgeklammert bleibt):

"An 8 Stellen (besonders 1 Jo) ist eindeutig *ho ponēros* (*der* Böse) gemeint: Mt 13,19 diff Mk; Joh 17,15; Eph 6,16; 1 Joh 2,13.14; 3,12; 5,18.19.

"Neutrischer Gebrauch (*das* Böse) liegt an 3 Stellen vor: Mk 7,23 (*ta ponēra*); Lk 6,45 diff Mt; Röm 12,9.

"Ob maskulinischer oder neutrischer Gebrauch vorliegt, bleibt an 4 Stellen unentschieden; von diesen finden sich drei in Mt: Mt 5,37 Sg. (*ek tou p.*); Mt 6,13 diff Lk (*apo tou p.*); Mt 13,38 Sg. (*tou p.*); 2 Thess 3,3 (*apo tou p.*)."

77[74]: "Abgesehen von den Stellen im Sondergut (Mt 5,37; 13,38) sind Mt 6,13b diff Lk und Mt 13,19 diff Mk 'redaktionell'."

Gnilka 1986, 215: "Ist die Bitte um Bewahrung vor der Versuchung bei Mt/Lk wieder gleich gefaßt, so liest man bei Mt noch eine 7. Bitte. Auch sie ist wieder mt geprägt. Die Rede vom Bösen in absoluter Verwendung ist kennzeichnend für unser Evangelium (entfernt vergleichbar nur Lk 6,45), ῥύομαι findet sich innerhalb der Evangelien nur noch Mt 27,43."

Sand 1986, 126: "Die dritte und siebte Bitte bei Mt ist Hinzufügung, wie die mt. Vorzugsworte ... 'das Böse' deutlich zu erkennen geben (zu 'retten' vgl. noch 27,43)."

Schenk 1987, 162: "Kennzeichnend für Mt ist weiter der subst. Gebrauch [of πονηρός] (... davon 6mal mit Art.):

"Mt 10: Mk 1 (7,23 Plur.Neutr.): Lk 1 (=Q 6,45 Plur.Mask.)

"6,13 (+Q Sing. + Art.);"

438: "ῥύομαι 6,13 (+Q vom Bösen) 27,43 (+Mk Spott LXX-Ps 21,9) retten Subj. Gott Mt 2 (red.): Mk 0: Lk 1 (1,74) + 0: Joh."

Davies and Allison 1988, 612: "If, as seems most likely, 6.10b-c and 6.13b are secondary expansions (of either Matthew or the tradition before him), the Our Father must originally have ended on a jarring note. Following the address, the two parallel 'Thou' petitions, and the two 'we' petitions, there was appended an unpaired, terse conclusion, a petition formulated unlike the others, in the negative."

614: "Because 'the evil one' is a favourite expression of Matthew, he may either have added the entire line, thus giving a new couplet increasing the parallelism of the Lord's Prayer, or he may have changed the last word."

Taussig 1988, 37-38: "There are three clear reasons to consider this sentence [Matt 6:13b] as a Matthean addition to the Q text: (1) Its addition makes for a more consistent parallelism in the prayer. As we saw earlier, the sentence 'And do not lead us to the test' lacks some of the parallel structure that the rest of the Q prayer has. The addition of 'But deliver us from (the) evil (one)' [38] provides a strong parallel both in terms of content and form. (2) If, as we posited above, the 'test' to be avoided was a specific one—either in the life of Jesus or Q—it is apparent that the composer of 'But deliver us …' does not know about it. This second sentence serves to generalize and mythologize the test. In other words, Matthew has explicated the previous prayer sentence which for him no longer has a referent, by generalizing and mythologizing the test. (3) This prayer sentence can be strongly tied to Matthew's redactional interest in the Exodus."

Wiefel 1988, 215: "Matthäus bietet das Vaterunser in der Bergpredigt dar, im Rahmen der Auseinandersetzung mit verkehrten Frömmigkeitsformen; es hat eine ausgeführte Anrede und sieben Bitten. Die Kurzfassung des Lukas beruht nicht auf Kürzung, kann vielmehr nach Struktur und Aufbau als die ältere Gestalt gelten. Lukas dürfte sie in Q vorgefunden haben."

Stritzky 1989, 10-11: "In der Forschung, die sich mit dieser Problematik ausführlich auseinandergesetzt hat und sie mit dem hypothetischen Versuch einer Rückübersetzung in die Ursprache einer Lösung zuführen wollte, hat sich die Meinung durchgesetzt, daß das entscheidende Kriterium für die Ursprünglichkeit darin zu sehen ist, daß die Lukasfassung in der des Matthäus vollständig enthalten ist. Der kürzere Text des Lukas, der mit seinen fünf Gebetsrufen wohl den Inhalt des Gebetes Jesu [11] wiedergibt, dürfte der Urform ihrem Umfang nach nahekommen, während die Mt-Rezension Zusätze bietet, die in der judenchristlichen Gemeinde formuliert wurden, nämlich die Erweiterung in der Vateranrede, die 3. Du-Bitte (Mt 6,10c), die die Bitte um das Kommen des Reiches unterstreicht, und den 2. Teil der 4. Wir-Bitte (Mt 6,13b)."

Catchpole 1993, 31: "References to evil come easily from Matthew. He is well aware of the opposition of 'the evil one' (Matt 13:19 diff Mark 4:15) and of the constant battle with evil in a variety of forms which is waged in the experience of Jesus and his followers.[68] Here is a threat from outside, yes, and a danger within the community (7:17; 22:10). It is more than credible that the petition 'deliver us from evil' derives from the evangelist."

31[68]: "Matt 5:45; 9:4; 12:39; 13:38; 16:4."

Nolland 1993, 617: "Once again, the additional petition at the end of the Matthean prayer is best taken as an expansion."

Meier 1994, 355: "'But deliver us from the evil one' helps round off and give balance to the prayer's ending. The abrupt, almost harsh 'and lead us not into temptation' is the only negative petition in the Our Father; its dark tone called forth, by way of compensation, not only the Matthean addition but also later on the famous doxology ('for thine is the power and the glory forever'), first seen in the *Didache's* text (8:2). Not by accident, the three additional Matthean clauses occur at the end of the address, the end of the 'you petitions,' and the end of the 'we petitions'—exactly at the locations where additions could be most easily inserted into a tightly constructed oral unit. While it is clear why Matthew or his tradition would desire to insert these phrases, there is no reason why Luke would have deleted them if they had already stood in the venerable prayer he had inherited."

Schürmann 1994, 202-203: "Bei Mt hat die letzte Bitte die Form eines antithetischen Parallelismus. Hier verlagert sich—wie in solchen Fällen üblich—der Akzent auf die zweite Hälfte: Der πειρασμός steht nicht nur gefährlich bevor; das (und der) Böse steht schon als Gefahr gegenwärtig an— in der dritten Generation der matth Gemeinde irgendwie in aktueller Weise wird man deuten dürfen: Es würde der ethischen Tendenz der matth Gemeinde entsprechen, wenn πονηρός hier den πειρασμός sittlich interpretieren würde: auf das sittlich Böse hin, wobei besonders an die 'Gesetzlosigkeit' der Irrlehre gedacht sein könnte (vgl. 7,23; 13,41; 23,28; 24,12), wobei *der* Böse hintergründig mitgedacht wäre. Möglicherweise ist diese formal glättende [203] 'Abrundung' des Gebetes schon im Gebetsbrauch der matth Gemeinde üblich gewesen und von Matthäus der Q-Fassung eingefügt worden, die Lukas noch richtiger wiedergibt. Auch schon als die asymmetrische, formal als die 'schwerere' und auch als die 'kürzere Lesart' hat die Lk-Fassung die Präsumtion der Ursprünglichkeit für sich."

Meadors 1995, 180-181[156]: "... [181] ... If we seek a common source, Matthean priority falters on the fact that there are no Mattheanisms in Luke's prayer. In fact the petitions most characteristic of Matthew are absent from Luke. The expansion of the Lord's Prayer seems more likely than its reduction in light of known tendencies in later transmissions of Greek texts. Do we concede the prayer's background to Q? We hesitate. U. Luz has detected reminiscences of Matthew's version in Mk. 11:25 and 2 Ti. 4:18 and with less certainty Mk. 14:36, 38; Jn. 12:28; 17:15 (*Matthäus* I, 335). This evidence suggests that Matthew's greater length does not require redaction on the on the part of the first Evangelist, but rather the language may attest to the prayer as it existed at a very early stage."

Evaluations

Carruth 1995: Luke = Q {A}, ()[7].

As already noted with regard to the additional petition at the conclusion of the you-petitions, Ott does not offer a reason why Luke would leave this out because of his parenetic intention. Neither does Crossan explain why its omission would make it a more appropriate Gentile-Christian prayer. Editorial or theological reasons for Luke to omit the clause are not strong.

Cadbury's suggestion that Matthew is fond of formulas provides a reason for attributing this parallelism to him (also Zahn, Schmid, Grundmann, Schürmann, Taussig). Since the phrase also occurs at the end of the section of we-petitions and is, thus, formally analogous to the petition at the end of the you-petitions, it seems likely that this one as well is a secondary addition. As noted by many, the vocabulary also betrays itself as Matthean.

Robinson 1995: Luke = Q {A}, ()[7].
Luke would have no reason to omit the petition, if it were in Q.
πονηρός is common in Matthew (but also in Q).
Matthew here, as at Q 11:2b[6], rounds out the second set of petitions with an exegetical antithetical parallel, accenting the positive formulation of God freeing from evil rather than leading into temptation.
The phrase is in *Did* 8,2, which however implies no more than that the *Didache* stands, with regard to the Prayer, in the same tradition as Matthew.

Kloppenborg: 1995: Luke = Q {A}, ()[7].
No convincing reason for Luke's omitting the phrase has been supplied in the database, and the fact that πονηρός is attested in Q is hardly probative, since this is too common a word.

Bibliography

Abbreviations used in the bibliography are those specified in the *Journal of Biblical Literature* instructions for contributors found in the Society of Biblical Literature *Membership Directory and Handbook* or the *Journal of Biblical Literature* 107 (1988) 579-596. If the *JBL* does not specify an abbreviation, then Sigfried M. Schwertner, *Internationales Abkürzungsverzeichnis für Theologie und Grenzgebiete* (Berlin and New York: de Gruyter, 1992) is used.

When more than one edition or printing is given for a work, the one listed at the beginning of the entry is the one cited unless stated otherwise in the bibliographical entry.

Abrahams, I., 1924, *Studies in Pharisaism and the Gospels.* Second Series. Cambridge, MA: University Press. Reprinted, Library of Biblical Studies. Ed. H.M. Orlinsky. New York: Ktav, 1967.

Bacon, B.W., 1930, *Studies in Matthew.* London: Henry Holt & Company.

Beare, F.W., 1962, *The Earliest Records of Jesus.* New York: Abingdon.

—, 1981, *The Gospel according to Matthew.* Oxford: Basil Blackwell.

Berger, K., 1969, "Vaterunser." *Sacramentum Mundi* 4.1147-51.

Betz, H.D., 1995, *The Sermon on the Mount, Including the Sermon on the Plain (Matthew 5:3-7:27 and Luke 6:20-49).* Hermeneia. Minneapolis: Fortress Press.

Blass, F., 1897, *Evangelium secundum Lucam sive Lucae ad Theophilum liber prior secundum formam quae videtur Romanam.* Leipzig: Teubner.

Blass, F. and A. Debrunner, 1961, *A Greek Grammar of the New Testament and Other Early Christian Literature.* Rev. and ed. R.W. Funk. Chicago: University of Chicago Press.

Bonnard, P., 1963, *L'Évangile selon Saint Matthieu.* CNT 1. Neuchâtel: Delachaux & Niestlé. 2ᵐᵉ éd. revue et augmentée, 1970.

Brown, R.E., 1965, *New Testament Essays.* Milwaukee: Bruce Publishing Company.

Bultmann, R., 1931, *Die Geschichte der synoptischen Tradition.* FRLANT 29. 2nd rev. ed. Göttingen: Vandenhoeck & Ruprecht. ET: *The History of the Synoptic Tradition.* Rev. ed. Oxford: Blackwell; New York and Evanston: Harper, 1968.

Bussmann, W., 1929, *Synoptische Studien.* Vol. 2, *Zur Redenquelle.* Halle: Waisenhaus.

Cadbury, H.J., 1920, *The Style and Literary Method of Luke.* HTS 6. Cambridge, MA: Harvard University Press.

Carruth, S., 1987, "Q 11:2-4 Database and Evaluations." Unpublished manuscript.

Castor, G.D., 1912, *Matthew's Sayings of Jesus: The Non-Marcan Common Source of Matthew and Luke.* Chicago: University of Chicago Press, 1918. [This book, which is based upon the author's Ph.D. dissertation at the University of Chicago (1907), was published under the auspices of S.J. Case exactly as left by the author in 1912. Therefore, we quote it with the year 1912.]

Catchpole, D.R., 1983, "Q and 'The friend at Midnight' (Luke xi. 5-8/9)." *JTS* n.s. 34:407-424.

—, 1989, "Q, Prayer, and the Kingdom: A Rejoinder." *JTS* n.s. 40:377-388.

—, 1993, *The Quest for Q.* Edinburgh: T&T Clark.

Creed, J.M., 1930, *The Gospel According to St. Luke: The Greek Text with Introduction, Notes and Indices.* London: Macmillan.

Crossan, J.D., 1983, *In Fragments: The Aphorisms of Jesus.* San Francisco: Harper & Row.

—, 1988, "Aphorism in Discourse and Narrative." *Semeia* (Atlanta: Scholars Press) 43:121-140.

Crum, J.M.C., 1927, *The Original Jerusalem Gospel: Being Essays on the Document Q.* London: Constable & Co. Ltd.

Cullmann, O., 1994, *Das Gebet im Neuen Testament: Zugleich Versuch einer vom Neuen Testament zu erteilenden Antwort auf heutige Fragen.* Tübingen: J.C.B. Mohr (Paul Siebeck). ET: *Prayer in the New Testament.* Minneapolis: Fortress, 1995.

Danker, F.W., 1972, *Jesus and the New Age According to St. Luke: A Commentary on the Third Gospel.* St. Louis: Clayton Publishing House.

Davies, W.D., 1964, *The Setting of the Sermon on the Mount.* Cambridge: University Press.

—, 1966, *The Sermon on the Mount.* Cambridge: University Press.

Davies, W.D. and D.C. Allison, 1988, *A Critical and Exegetical Commentary on the Gospel According to Saint Matthew.* Vol. 1, *Introduction and Commentary on Matthew I-VII.* ICC. Edinburgh: T&T Clark.

Delobel, J., 1989, "The Lord's Prayer in the Textual Tradition: A Critique of Recent Theories and Their View on Marcion's Role." *The New Testament in Early Christianity.* Ed. J.-M. Sevrin. Leuven: University Press/Peeters.

Dibelius, M., 1911, *Die urchristliche Überlieferung von Johannes dem Täufer.* Göttingen: Vandenhoeck & Ruprecht.

Dobschütz, E. von, 1914, "The Lord's Prayer." *HTR* 7:293-321.

Dupont, J., 1958, *Les Béatitudes.* Vol. 1, *Le problème littéraire.* Études bibliques. Bruges: Abbaye de Saint-André; Louvain: Nauwelaerts.

—, 1973, *Les Béatitudes.* Vol. 3, *Les Évangélistes.* Études bibliques. Paris: Gabalda.

Easton, B.S., 1926, *The Gospel According to St. Luke: A Critical and Exegetical Commentary*. Edinburgh: T&T Clark; New York: Charles Scribner's Sons.

Edwards, R.A., 1975, *A Concordance to Q*. Missoula: Scholars Press.

—, 1976, *A Theology of Q: Eschatology, Prophecy and Wisdom*. Philadelphia: Fortress.

Ellis, E.E., 1966, *The Gospel of Luke*, The Century Bible, New Edition. London: Nelson.

Ernst, J., 1977, *Das Evangelium nach Lukas*. RNT 3. 5., völlig neu bearbeitete Auflage. Regensburg: Pustet.

—, 1993, *Das Evangelium nach Lukas*. RNT 3. 6th rev. ed. Regensburg: Pustet.

Evans, C.F., 1963, *The Lord's Prayer*. London: S.P.C.K.

—, 1990, *Saint Luke*. TPI New Testament Commentaries. London: SCM; Philadelphia: Trinity Press International.

Feldkämper, L., 1978, *Der betende Jesus als Heilsmittler nach Lukas*. St. Augustin: Steyler.

Fitzmyer, J.A., 1981, *The Gospel According to Luke, I-IX: Introduction, Translation and Notes*. AB 28. Garden City, NY: Doubleday.

—, 1985, *The Gospel According to Luke, X-XXIV: Introduction, Translation and Notes*. AB 28A. Garden City, NY: Doubleday.

Frankemölle, H., 1974, *Jahwebund und Kirche Christi: Studien zur Form- und Traditionsgeschichte des 'Evangeliums' nach Matthäus*. NTAbh 10. Münster: Aschendorff.

Freudenberger, R., 1968-69, "Zum Text der zweiten Vaterunserbitte." *NTS* 15:419-432.

Gerhardsson, B., 1984, "The Matthaean Version of the Lord's Prayer (Matt 6: 9b-13): Some Observations." *The New Testament Age: Essays in Honor of Bo Reicke*. Ed. W.C. Weinrich. Macon, GA: Mercer University Press. 207-220.

Giesen, H., 1982, *Christliches Handeln: Eine redaktionskritische Untersuchung zum δικαιοσύνη-Begriff im Matthäus-Evangelium*. Frankfurt am Main, Bern: Peter Lang.

Gnilka, J., 1986, *Das Matthäusevangelium*. Erster Teil, *Kommentar zu Kap. 1,1-13,58*. HTKNT 1/1. Freiburg, Basel, and Wien: Herder.

Goltz, E. von der, 1901, *Das Gebet in der ältesten Christenheit: Eine geschichtliche Untersuchung*. Leipzig: J.C.H. Hinrichs'sche Buchhandlung.

Gräßer, E., 1957, *Das Problem der Parusieverzögerung in den synoptischen Evangelien und in der Apostelgeschichte*. BZNW 22. Berlin: de Gruyter. 3., durch eine ausführliche Einleitung und ein Literaturverzeichnis ergänzte Auflage, 1977.

Greeven, H., 1931, *Gebet und Eschatologie im Neuen Testament*. NTF 3/1. Gütersloh: Bertelsmann.

Grundmann, W., 1961, *Das Evangelium nach Lukas.* THKNT 3/2. Berlin: Evangelische Verlagsanstalt.

—, 1968, *Das Evangelium nach Matthäus.* THKNT 1/1. Berlin: Evangelische Verlagsanstalt.

Guelich, R.A., 1982, *The Sermon on the Mount: A Foundation for Understanding.* Waco, TX: Word Books.

Gundry, R. H., 1982, *Matthew: A Commentary on his Literary and Theological Art.* Grand Rapids, MI: Eerdmans.

Hagner, D.A., 1993, *Matthew 1-13.* WBC 33a. Dallas: Word.

Hahn, F., 1963, *Christologische Hoheitstitel.* Göttingen: Vandenhoeck & Ruprecht.

Harnack, A. von, 1904, "Über einige Worte Jesu, die nicht in den kanonischen Evangelien stehen, nebst einem Anhang über die ursprüngliche Gestalt des Vater-Unsers." SPAW. 170-208. Also in *Kleine Schriften zur Alten Kirche. Berliner Akademieschriften 1890-1907.* Leipzig: Nationales Druckhaus, 1980. 663-701.

—, 1907, *Sprüche und Reden Jesu: Die zweite Quelle des Matthäus und Lukas.* Beiträge zur Einleitung in das Neue Testament 2. Leipzig: Hinrichs'sche Buchhandlung. ET: *The Sayings of Jesus.* New York: Putnam & London: Williams & Norgate, 1908.

—, 1923, "Der ursprüngliche Text des Vater-Unsers und seine älteste Gestalt." *Erforschtes und Erlebtes: Reden und Aufsätze,* Neue Folge 4. Gießen: Töpelmann. 24-35.

Hauck, F., 1934, *Das Evangelium des Lukas (Synoptiker II).* THKNT 3/1. Leipzig: Deichertsche Verlagsbuchhandlung.

Haupt, W., 1913, *Worte Jesu und Gemeindeüberlieferung: Eine Untersuchung zur Quellengeschichte der Synopse.* UNT 3. Leipzig: J.C.H. Hinrichs'sche Buchhandlung.

Hawkins, J.C., 1899, *Horae Synopticae: Contributions to the Study of the Synoptic Problem.* Oxford: Clarendon. 2nd ed., rev. and supplemented, 1909. [Page citations are to the 2nd edition.]

Heininger, B., 1991, *Metaphorik, Erzählstruktur und szenisch-dramatische Gestaltung in den Sondergleichnissen bei Lukas.* NTAbh 24. Münster: Aschendorff.

Hirsch, E., 1941, *Frühgeschichte des Evangeliums.* Vol. 2, *Die Vorlagen des Lukas und das Sondergut des Matthäus.* Tübingen: J.C.B. Mohr (Paul Siebeck).

Hoffmann, P., 1972, *Studien zur Theologie der Logienquelle.* NTAbh 8. Münster: Aschendorff. 2., durchgesehene und verbesserte Auflage 1975; 3. durchgesehene Auflage 1982, mit einem bibliographischen Nachtrag über die Literatur von 1970 bis 1981.

Holtzmann, H.J., 1863, *Die synoptischen Evangelien, ihr Ursprung und geschicht-licher Charakter.* Leipzig: W. Engelmann.

—, 1901, *Die Synoptiker.* HKNT I/1. 3., gänzlich umgearbeitete Auflage. Tübingen, Leipzig: J.C.B. Mohr (Paul Siebeck).

Hunter, A.M., 1950, *The Work and Words of Jesus.* London: SCM Press.

International Q Project, 1990, "The International Q Project Work Session 17 November 1989." By J.M. Robinson. *JBL* 109:499-501.

—, 1991, "The International Q Project Work Session 16 November 1990." By J.M. Robinson. *JBL* 110:494-498.

—, 1992, "The International Q Project Work Sessions 12-14 July, 22 November 1991." By J.M. Asgeirsson and J.M. Robinson. *JBL* 111:500-508.

—, 1993, "The International Q Project Work Sessions 31 July-2 August, 20 November 1992." By M.C. Moreland and J. M. Robinson. *JBL* 112: 500-506.

—, 1994, "The International Q Project Work Sessions 6-8 August, 18-19 November 1993." By M.C. Moreland and J.M. Robinson. *JBL* 113:495-499.

—, 1995, "The International Q Project Work Sessions 23-27 May, 22-26 August, 17-18 November 1994." By M.C. Moreland and J.M. Robinson. *JBL* 114:475-485.

Jacobson, A.D., 1978, "Wisdom Christology in Q." Ph.D. diss., Claremont Graduate School. Claremont, CA.

—, 1992, *The First Gospel: An Introduction to Q.* FFNT. Sonoma, CA: Pole-bridge.

Jeremias, J., 1966, *Abba: Studien zur neutestamentlichen Theologie und Zeit-geschichte.* Göttingen: Vandenhoeck & Ruprecht.

—, 1967, *Das Vater-Unser: Im Lichte der neueren Forschung.* Calwer Hefte 50. 4., revidierte Auflage. Stuttgart: Calwer Verlag. ET: *The Lord's Prayer.* Philadelphia: Fortress, 1964. [The 1964 English translation is based on the first German edition of 1962. However the English translation corres-ponded to the 1967 German version in every instance cited in this volume, with the exception that one citation from the English translation does not appear in any German version.]

—, 1971, *Neutestamentliche Theologie.* Erster Teil, *Die Verkündigung Jesu.* Güters-loh: Gütersloher Verlagshaus Gerd Mohn. ET: *New Testament Theology: The Proclamation of Jesus.* New York: Charles Scribner's Sons, 1971.

—, 1980, *Die Sprache des Lukasevangeliums: Redaktion und Tradition im Nicht-Markusstoff des dritten Evangeliums.* MeyerK Sonderband. Göttingen: Vandenhoeck & Ruprecht.

Katz, F., 1973, "Lk 9,52-11,36: Beobachtungen zur Logienquelle und ihrer hellenistisch-judenchristlichen Redaktion." Diss. Mainz.

Kilpatrick, G.D., 1946, *The Origins of the Gospel According to St. Matthew.* Oxford: Clarendon.

Klein, G., 1906, "Die ursprüngliche Gestalt des Vaterunsers." *ZNW* 7:34-50.

—, 1909, *Der älteste christliche Katechismus und die jüdische Propaganda-Literatur.* Berlin: Georg Reimer.

Kloppenborg, J.S., 1987, *The Formation of Q: Trajectories in Ancient Wisdom Collections.* Studies in Antiquity and Christianity. Philadelphia: Fortress.

—, 1990, "The Sayings Gospel Q: Translation and Notes." *Q Thomas Reader* by J.S. Kloppenborg, et al. Sonoma, CA: Polebridge. 35-74.

Klostermann, E., 1927, *Das Matthäusevangelium.* HNT 4. 2., völlig neubearbeitete Auflage. Tübingen: J.C.B. Mohr (Paul Siebeck).

—, 1929, *Das Lukasevangelium.* HNT 5. 5., völlig neubearbeitete Auflage. Tübingen: J.C.B. Mohr (Paul Siebeck).

Knox, W.L., 1957, *The Sources of the Synoptic Gospels.* Vol. 2, *St. Luke and St. Matthew.* Cambridge: Cambridge University Press.

Koester, H., 1990, *Ancient Christian Gospels: Their History and Development.* Philadelphia: Trinity Press International; London: SCM.

Lagrange, M.J., 1921, *Évangile selon Saint Luc.* Études bibliques. Paris: Libraire Lecoffre. [The 8th ed., 1948, is the same as the 1921 edition.]

—, 1923, *Évangile selon Saint Matthieu.* Études bibliques. Paris: Libraire Lecoffre. [The 3rd ed., 1927, is the same as the 1923 edition.]

Lambrecht, J., 1985, *The Sermon on the Mount.* Good News Studies 14. Wilmington: Michael Glazier.

Lampe, G.W.H., 1955, "The Holy Spirit in the Writings of St. Luke." *Studies in the Gospels: Essays in Memory of R.H. Lightfoot.* Ed. D.E. Nineham. Oxford: Basil Blackwell. 159-200.

LaVerdière, E., 1983, *When We Pray ...: Meditations on the Lord's Prayer.* Notre Dame: Ave Maria Press.

Leaney, A.R.C., 1956, "The Lucan Text of the Lord's Prayer (Lk xi 2-4)." *NovT* 1:103-111.

—, 1958, *A Commentary on the Gospel according to St. Luke.* London: Adam & Charles Black. (Second edition 1966, repr. 1971)

Lohmeyer, E., 1952, *Das Vaterunser.* Göttingen: Vandenhoeck & Ruprecht.

Loisy, A., 1907, *Les Évangiles synoptiques.* 1. Ceffonds: Chez l'auteur.

—, 1908, *Les Évangiles synoptiques.* 2. Ceffonds: Chez l'auteur.

—, 1924, *L'Évangile selon Luc.* Paris: Emile Nourry.

Ludwig, M., 1994, *Wort als Gesetz. Eine Untersuchung zum Verständnis von "Wort" und "Gesetz" in israelitisch-frühjüdischen und neutestamentlichen Schriften. Gleichzeitig ein Beitrag zur Theologie des Jakobusbriefes.* EHS.T 502. Frankfurt am Main: Peter Lang.

Luz, U., 1985, *Das Evangelium nach Matthäus*. Vol. 1, *Mt 1-7*. EKKNT 1/1. Zürich: Benziger; Neukirchen-Vluyn: Neukirchener Verlag. ET: *Matthew 1-7: A Commentary*. Minneapolis: Augsburg, 1989.

Mack, B.L., 1993, *The Lost Gospel: The Book of Q and Christian Origins*. San Francisco: Harper.

Magne, J., 1988a, "La Réception de la variante 'Vienne ton esprit saint sur nous et qu'il nous purifie' (Lc 11,2) et l'origine des épiclèses, du baptême et du 'Notre Père.'" *EL* 102:81-106.

—, 1988b, "La Variante du pater de Lc 11,2." *LTP* 44(3):369-374.

Manson, T.W., 1937, *The Sayings of Jesus: As recorded in the Gospels according to St. Matthew and St. Luke arranged with Introduction and Commentary*. London: SCM. Originally published as *The Mission and Message of Jesus*. Book II, *The Sayings of Jesus*. New York: E.P. Dutton. 301-639 [Q: 331-440]. Re-issued as a separate volume 1949, reprinted 1957, 1964, 1977.

—, 1956, "The Lord's Prayer." *BJRL* 38:99-113.

Marriott, H., 1925, *The Sermon on the Mount*. London: SPCK; New York and Toronto: Macmillan.

Marshall, I.H., 1978, *The Gospel of Luke: A Commentary on the Greek Text*. NIGTC. Exeter: Paternoster; Grand Rapids, MI: Eerdmans.

McNeile, A.H., 1915, *The Gospel according to St. Matthew*. London: Macmillan.

Meadors, E.P., 1995, *Jesus the Messianic Herald of Salvation*. WUNT II 72. Tübingen: J.C.B. Mohr (Paul Siebeck).

Meier, John P., 1994, *A Marginal Jew. Rethinking the Historical Jesus*, Vol. 2. *Mentor, Message, and Miracles*. The Anchor Bible Reference Library. New York: Doubleday.

Mell, U., 1994, "Gehört das Vater-Unser zur authentischen Jesus-Tradition? (Mt 6,9-13; Lk 11,2-4)." *BTZ* 2:148-180.

Metzger, B.M., 1971, *A Textual Commentary on the Greek New Testament*, London: United Bible Societies. 2nd ed. Stuttgart: Deutsche Bibelgesellschaft, 1994.

—, 1991, "The Lord's Prayer: Text of the Prayer." *New 20th Century Encyclopedia of Religious Knowledge*. 2nd ed. Grand Rapids, MI: Baker, 520.

Meyer, E., 1921, *Ursprung und Anfänge des Christentums*. Erster Band, *Die Evangelien*. Stuttgart, Berlin: Cotta.

Montefiore, C.G., 1927, *The Synoptic Gospels*. Vol. 2. 2nd ed., revised and partly rewritten. London: Macmillan.

Morgenthaler, R., 1971, *Statistische Synopse*. Zürich and Stuttgart: Gotthelf Keller.

Müller, G.H., 1908, *Zur Synopse: Untersuchung über die Arbeitsweise des Lk und Mt und ihrer Quellen, namentlich die Spruchquelle, im Anschluss an eine Synopse Mk-Lk-Mt.* FRLANT 11. Göttingen: Vandenhoeck & Ruprecht.

Nolland, J., 1993, *Luke 9:21-18:34.* WBC 35B. Dallas: Word.

O'Neill, J.C., 1993, "The Lord's Prayer." *JSNT* 51:3-25.

Ott, W., 1965, *Gebet und Heil: Die Bedeutung der Gebetsparänese in der lukanischen Theologie.* SANT 12. München: Kösel-Verlag.

Patterson, S.J., 1993, *The Gospel of Thomas and Jesus.* FFNT. Sonoma, CA: Polebridge.

Patton, C.S., 1915, *Sources of the Synoptic Gospels.* New York and London: Macmillan.

Perrin, N., 1963, *The Kingdom of God in the Teaching of Jesus.* Philadelphia: Westminster.

Philonenko, M., 1995, "'Que Ton Esprit-Saint vienne sur nous et qu'il nous purifie' (Luc 11,2); l'arrière-plan qoumrânien d'une variante lucanienne du 'Notre Père.'" *RHPR* 75:61-66.

Plummer, A., 1896, *A Critical and Exegetical Commentary on the Gospel According to St. Luke.* ICC. Edinburgh: T&T Clark. 5th edition, 1922. [Page citations are to the 5th edition.]

Polag, A., 1977, *Die Christologie der Logienquelle.* WMANT 45. Neukirchen-Vluyn: Neukirchener Verlag.

—, 1979, *Fragmenta Q: Textheft zur Logienquelle.* Neukirchen-Vluyn: Neukirchener Verlag.

Rengstorf, K.H., 1936, *Das Evangelium nach Lukas.* NTD 3. Göttingen: Vandenhoeck & Ruprecht.

Resch, A., 1895, *Aussercanonische Paralleltexte zu den Evangelien.* Zweiter Theil, *Paralleltexte zu Lucas.* Leipzig: J.C.H. Hinrichs'sche Buchhandlung.

Robinson, J.M., 1964, "Die Hodajot-Formel in Gebet und Hymnus des Frühchristentums." *Apophoreta: Festschrift für Ernst Haenchen.* Ed. W. Eltester. *BZNW* 30. Berlin: Alfred Töpelmann. 194-235.

Sand, A., 1986, *Das Evangelium nach Matthäus.* RNT 1. Regensburg: Pustet.

Sato, M., 1988, *Q und Prophetie: Studien zur Gattungs- und Traditionsgeschichte der Quelle Q.* WUNT II 29. Tübingen: J.C.B. Mohr (Paul Siebeck). ET [of excerpts] "The Shape of the Q-Source." *The Shape of Q: Signal Essays on the Sayings Gospel.* Ed. and trans. J.S. Kloppenborg. Minneapolis, MN: Fortress, 1994. 156-179.

Schenk, W., 1981, *Synopse zur Redenquelle der Evangelisten: Q-Synopse und Rekonstruktion in deutscher Übersetzung mit kürzen Erläuterungen.* Düsseldorf: Patmos.

—, 1987, *Die Sprache des Matthäus: Die Text-Konstituenten in ihren makro- und mikrostrukturellen Relationen.* Göttingen: Vandenhoeck & Ruprecht.

Schlosser, J., 1980, *Le règne de Dieu dans les dits de Jésus.* Paris: Gabalda.

Schmid, J., 1930, *Matthäus und Lukas: Eine Untersuchung des Verhältnisses ihrer Evangelien.* BibS(F) 23. Freiburg: Herder.

—, 1951, *Das Evangelium nach Lukas: Übersetzt und erklärt.* RNT 3. 2., erweiterte Neuauflage. Regensburg: Pustet. Reprinted 1955 and 1965.

—, 1956, *Das Evangelium nach Matthäus: Übersetzt und erklärt.* RNT 1. 3., von neuem umgearbeitete Auflage. Regensburg: Pustet. Durchgesehene Auflagen 1959 und 1965.

Schmithals, W., 1980, *Das Evangelium nach Lukas.* ZBK.NT 3. Zürich: Theologischer Verlag.

—, 1985, *Einleitung in die drei ersten Evangelien.* Berlin and New York: de Gruyter.

Schnackenburg, R., 1984, *Alles kann, wer glaubt: Bergpredigt und Vaterunser in der Absicht Jesu.* Freiburg, Basel, Wien: Herder. ET: *All Things Are Possible to Believers: Reflections on the Lord's Prayer and the Sermon on the Mount.* Louisville: Westminster John Knox, 1995.

—, 1985, *Matthäusevangelium 1,1-16,20.* Die Neue Echter Bibel 1/1. Würzburg: Echter Verlag.

—, 1987, *Matthäusevangelium 16,21-28,20.* Die Neue Echter Bibel 1/2. Würzburg: Echter Verlag.

Schneider, G., 1977, *Das Evangelium nach Lukas.* ÖTBK 3. 2 vols. Gütersloh: Gerd Mohn; Würzburg: Echter Verlag.

—, 1985, "Das Vaterunser des Matthäus." *À cause de l'Évangile: Études sur les Synoptiques et les Actes offertes au P. Jacques Dupont à l'occasion de son 70ᵉ anniversaire.* Lectio Divina 123. Paris: Cerf. 57-90. Also in *Jesusüberlieferung und Christologie: Neutestamentliche Aufsätze 1970-1990.* NT.S 67. Leiden, New York, København, Köln: E.J. Brill, 1992. 52-85.

—, 1986, "Die Bitte um das Kommen des Geistes im lukanischen Vaterunser (Lk 11,2 v.l.)." *Studien zum Text und zur Ethik des Neuen Testaments.* Ed. W. Schrage. Berlin: de Gruyter. Also in *Jesusüberlieferung und Christologie: Neutestamentliche Aufsätze 1970-1990.* NT.S 67. Leiden, New York, København, Köln: E.J. Brill, 1992. 86-115.

Schrenk, G. and G. Quell, 1954, "πατήρ, πατρῷος, πατριά, ἀπάτωρ, πατρικός." *TWNT* 5.946-1016. ET: "πατήρ, πατρῷος, πατριά, ἀπάτωρ, πατρικός." *TDNT* 5.945-1022, 1967. [Schrenk contributed the portion of the article that is cited in the database.]

Schulz, S., 1972, *Q: Spruchquelle der Evangelisten.* Zürich: Theologischer Verlag.

Schürmann, H., 1968, *Traditionsgeschichtliche Untersuchungen zu den synoptischen Evangelien.* KBANT. Düsseldorf: Patmos.

—, 1981, *Das Gebet des Herrn als Schlüssel zum Verstehen Jesu.* 4., verbesserte und erweiterte Auflage. Freiburg, Basel, Wien: Herder.

—, 1994, *Das Lukasevangelium.* Zweiter Teil, Erste Folge, *Kommentar zu Kap. 9,51-11,54.* HTKNT 3/2a. Freiburg, Basel, and Wien: Herder.

Schwarz, G., 1968-69, "Matthäus VI. 9-13/Lukas XI. 2-4: Emendation und Rückübersetzung." *NTS* 15:233-247.

Schweizer, E., 1973, *Das Evangelium nach Matthäus.* NTD 2. 13. Auflage, 1. Auflage dieser neuen Fassung. Göttingen: Vandenhoeck & Ruprecht. ET: *The Good News According to Matthew.* Atlanta: John Knox, 1975.

—, 1982, *Das Evangelium nach Lukas.* NTD 3. 18. Auflage, 1. Auflage dieser neuen Fassung. Göttingen: Vandenhoeck & Ruprecht. ET: *The Good News According to Luke.* Atlanta: John Knox, 1984.

Shelton, J. B., 1982, "'Filled with the Holy Spirit': A Redactional Motif in Luke's Gospel." Diss. University of Stirling.

Soiron, T., 1916, *Die Logia Jesu: Eine literarkritische und literargeschichtliche Untersuchung zum synoptischen Problem.* NTAbh 6/4. Münster: Aschendorff.

—, 1941, *Die Bergpredigt Jesu: Formgeschichtliche, exegetische und theologische Erklärung.* Freiburg: Herder.

Stanton, V. H., 1909, *The Gospels as Historical Documents.* Vol. 2, *The Synoptic Gospels.* Cambridge: Cambridge University Press.

Strecker, G., 1982, "Vaterunser und Glaube." *Glaube im Neuen Testament: Studien zu Ehren von Hermann Binder.* Ed. F. Hahn and H. Klein. Neukirchen-Vluyn: Neukirchener Verlag. 11-28.

Streeter, B.H., 1924, *The Four Gospels: A Study of Origins.* London: Macmillan.

Stritzky, M.B. von, 1989, *Studien zur Überlieferung und Interpretation des Vaterunsers in der frühchristlichen Literatur.* Münster: Aschendorff.

Sung, C.-H., 1993, *Vergebung der Sünden: Jesu Praxis der Sündenvergebung nach den Synoptikern und ihre Voraussetzungen im Alten Testament und frühen Judentum,* WUNT II 57. Tübingen: J.C.B. Mohr (Paul Siebeck).

Taeger, J.-W., 1982, *Der Mensch und sein Heil: Studien zum Bild des Menschen und zur Sicht der Bekehrung bei Lukas.* SNT 14. Gütersloh: Gütersloher Verlagshaus Gerd Mohn.

Talbert, C.H., 1974, *Literary Patterns, Theological Themes, and the Genre of Luke-Acts.* SBLMS 20. Missoula, Montana: Scholars Press.

Tannehill, R. C., 1988, "Aphorism and Narrative: A Response to John Dominic Crossan." *Semeia* (Atlanta: Scholars Press) 43:141-144.

Taussig, H., 1988, "The Lord's Prayer." *Foundations & Facets Forum* 4/4:25-41.

Trudinger, P., 1989, "The 'Our Father' in Matthew as Apocalyptic Eschatology." *Downside Review* 107:49-54.

Tuckett, C.M., 1989, "Q, Prayer, and the Kingdom." *JTS* n.s. 40:367-376.

Vassiliadis, P., 1978, "The Nature and Extent of the Q Document." *NovT* 20:49-73.

—, 1995, "The Understanding of Eucharist in the Primitive Church (Q on Eucharist)." Unpublished lecture at Lund University. Typescript. 18 pp.

Vogler, Werner, 1982, "Gib uns, was wir heute zum Leben brauchen: Zur Auslegung der vierten Bitte des Vaterunsers." *Das Lebendige Wort: Beiträge zur kirchlichen Verkündigung: Festgabe für Gottfried Voigt zum 65. Geburtstag.* Ed. H. Seidel and K.-H. Bieritz. Berlin: Evangelische Verlagsanstalt. 52-63.

Weiß, B., 1876, *Das Matthäusevangelium und seine Lucas-Parallelen.* Halle: Waisenhaus.

—, 1878, *Die Evangelien des Markus und Lukas.* MeyerK 1/2. 6th rev. ed. Göttingen: Vandenhoeck & Ruprecht.

—, 1898, *Das Matthäus-Evangelium.* MeyerK 1/1. 9th ed. Göttingen: Vandenhoeck & Ruprecht.

—, 1901, *Die Evangelien des Markus und Lukas.* MeyerK 1/2. 9th ed. Göttingen: Vandenhoeck & Ruprecht.

—, 1907, *Die Quellen des Lukasevangeliums.* Stuttgart and Berlin: J.G. Cotta.

—, 1908, *Die Quellen der synoptischen Überlieferung.* TU 32.3. Leipzig: J.C. Hinrichs'sche Buchhandlung.

Weiß, J., 1892, "Evangelium des Lukas." *Die Evangelien des Markus und Lukas.* B. Weiß and J. Weiß: MeyerK I/2. 8th ed. Göttingen: Vandenhoeck & Ruprecht. 271-666.

—, 1907, *Die drei älteren Evangelien.* Die Schriften des NT 1. 2., verbesserte und vermehrte Auflage. Göttingen: Vandenhoeck & Ruprecht.

Wellhausen, J., 1904a, *Das Evangelium Matthaei übersetzt und erklärt.* Berlin: Georg Reimer. Reprinted *Evangelienkommentare*, Berlin and New York: de Gruyter, 1987.

—, 1904b, *Das Evangelium Lucae übersetzt und erklärt.* Berlin: Georg Reimer. Reprinted *Evangelienkommentare*, Berlin and New York: de Gruyter, 1987.

—, 1905, *Einleitung in die drei ersten Evangelien.* Berlin: Georg Reimer.

—, 1911, *Einleitung in die drei ersten Evangelien.* 2nd ed. Berlin: Georg Reimer 1914. Reprinted *Evangelienkommentare*, Berlin and New York: de Gruyter, 1987.

Wernle, P., 1899, *Die synoptische Frage.* Freiburg: J.C.B. Mohr (Paul Siebeck).

Wiefel, W., 1988, *Das Evangelium des Lukas.* THKNT 3. Berlin: Evangelische Verlagsanstalt.

Wrege, H.-T., 1968, *Die Überlieferungsgeschichte der Bergpredigt.* WUNT 9; Tübingen: J.C.B. Mohr (Paul Siebeck).

Zahn, T., 1920, *Das Evangelium des Lucas.* 3. und 4. durchgesehene Aufl. Leipzig: A. Deichert.

Zeller, D., 1977, *Die weisheitlichen Mahnsprüche bei den Synoptikern.* FB 17. Würzburg: Echter Verlag.

—, 1981, "God as Father in the Proclamation and in the Prayer of Jesus." *Standing before God: Studies on Prayer in Scriptures and in Tradition with Essays In Honor of John M. Oesterreicher.* Ed. A. Finkel and L. Frizzell. New York: Ktav Publishing House. 117-129.

—, 1984, *Kommentar zur Logienquelle.* SKK.NT 21. Stuttgart: Katholisches Bibelwerk.